A SHORT VIEW
OF ELIZABETHAN DRAMA

A SHORT VIEW

of

ELIZABETHAN

DRAMA

TOGETHER WITH

Some account of its principal playwrights

and the conditions under which it was produced

---

by THOMAS MARC PARROTT

and ROBERT HAMILTON BALL

NEW YORK

Charles Scribner's Sons

PREFACE

THIS *Short View* is a brief presentation of the rise, development, and decline of Elizabethan drama from its beginning in the liturgy of the Church to its sudden end with the closing of the theatres in 1642. The main emphasis is on the major playwrights and their best and most significant plays; the focus is the personality of the dramatist, his characteristics and special merits. The treatment of playwright and play has been set against a background, historical, social, and, more especially theatrical, both because a work of art springs in part from its environment, and because a work of dramatic art which is divorced from the stage tends to become merely a collection of words on a library shelf. The aim of the book is to deepen the understanding and appreciation of one of the most fascinating fields in English humanities.

Collaboration in the *Short View* has been as close and complete as possible. Each chapter as first composed was read, reread, checked, and corrected by both authors, and each author holds himself responsible for opinions expressed as well as for faults of omission and commission.

The original edition of 1943 was based upon a fresh examination of the whole field of Elizabethan drama. By design, minor writers, however interesting, and plays of lesser importance were excluded, and the omission of a chapter on the greatest of Elizabethan dramatists, difficult in any case because of such brief compass, was justified by referring the reader to Parrott's *William Shakespeare—A Handbook*. This handbook has now been republished in a revised edition of 1955.

A Short View has been for some time out of print. This new edition is published in answer to requests for a less expensive book. The two texts are identical and therefore a few minor errors remain and the findings of scholarship since 1943 are not embodied; for example, *Dr. Faustus* would now be assigned to the last year of Marlowe's career. The bibliography, however, has been enlarged and brought up-to-date. The authors again wish to express their gratitude to John Cranford Adams, now President of Hofstra College, for drawing, especially for this book, floor plans of the Globe Playhouse.

T. M. P.
R. H. B.

Princeton University
Queens College of the City of New York

CONTENTS

Chapter One   THE MEDIEVAL BACKGROUND: CYCLES, MORALS, AND INTERLUDES   1

Chapter Two   THE DRAMA IN TRANSITION: NATIVE, CLASSICAL, AND ROMANTIC   27

Chapter Three   ACTORS AND THEATRES   45

Chapter Four   THE FORERUNNERS: LYLY, PEELE, GREENE, KYD, MARLOWE   63

Chapter Five   THE HENSLOWE GROUP: CHAPMAN, DEKKER, HEYWOOD   93

Chapter Six   BEN JONSON   126

Chapter Seven   LATER COMEDY, SATIRIC AND REALISTIC: MARSTON, MIDDLETON, BROME   152

Chapter Eight   BEAUMONT AND FLETCHER   182

Chapter Nine   JACOBEAN TRAGEDY: MARSTON, TOURNEUR, WEBSTER, MIDDLETON, FORD   210

Chapter Ten   THE CURTAIN FALLS: MASSINGER, SHIRLEY, DAVENANT; COURT MASQUES, SUMMARY   253

BIBLIOGRAPHY   295

INDEX   305

CHAPTER ONE

THE MEDIEVAL BACKGROUND:
CYCLES, MORALS, AND INTERLUDES

FROM the earliest days of the Christian era the fathers of the Church bitterly denounced all dramatic entertainments; none the less English drama, like the drama of Western Europe in general, began as a part of the liturgy, the regular prescribed order of worship in the then universal Catholic Church. To understand at once the opposition of the Church to the drama and the rebirth of drama within the Church we must turn back to the Dark Ages, to the Europe of the ninth century.

The classic drama of ancient Greece had its beginning in religious ritual: comedy in the worship of Dionysus, god of wine and merry-making; tragedy in the graver ceremonies about the tomb of some hero-god. To the end dramatic performances in Greece partook of a civil religious festival; an altar was a permanent part of the stage in the Greek theatre. During the Empire Greek theatres were rebuilt to afford opportunity for the more popular entertainments of wild-beast fights and naval combats. To compete with these the acted drama became more and more spectacular and sensationally realistic. At a performance of *Clytemnestra* in Rome a long procession of mules, elephants, and giraffes, along with chariots bearing the treasures of fallen Troy, passed for hours over the stage. Gorgeous ballets representing the Judgment of Paris were danced by lovely, near-naked actresses. Extraordinary tales are told of a savage realism in the theatre: at a performance of *Incendium* the stage-house was set on fire; in a play of Orpheus, the protagonist, a slave no doubt, was torn by wild beasts; in another a condemned criminal was actually crucified upon the stage. But even such exhibitions lacked the drawing power of the characteristic Roman entertainment, the gladiatorial combat. So popular was this that a good and great Emperor, Trajan, exhibited games lasting over four months in which thousands of fighters took part; and baser rulers actually descended into the arena and took part in the fights to win the plaudits of the mob. Prohibited by the first Christian Emperors these games were none the less revived from time to time. Denounced by the Church but attended by many professing Christians, they lasted till a day in 404 A.D. when the monk, Telemachus, sprang into the arena to separate a pair of gladiators and was stoned to death by the infuriated spectators. This outrage put a definite end to such entertainments in the Roman Empire.

It was not against the old Greek drama, performances of which had long since come to an end, but against licentious and bloody shows of the later Empire that the Christian Church directed its attack, and when Christianity became the official religion of the Empire, the Church succeeded in abolishing all forms of dramatic entertainment in Western Europe. The northern barbarians who overran and broke up the Empire had no drama of their own to take the place of what the Church had suppressed. Their folk-games, ritual and mimetic dances, bore indeed a certain likeness to play-acting, but were neither the source of, nor could indeed make important contributions to, a new form of drama.

Little by little even a reading knowledge of classic drama disappeared in Western Europe. A few manuscripts, little read and hardly understood, were buried in cloistered libraries; Terence, indeed, was still taught in some monastic schools, but rather as a model of polite conversation in the universal language of scholars than as a master of comedy or a mirror of manners. In the world outside monastic walls the *mimi*, or actors, of the Roman world had sunk to the low estate of wandering minstrels, jugglers, and acrobats, whose performances, even if by chance they contained some faint element of drama in dialogue or action, were more of the nature of what we call vaudeville than of drama proper.

The dramatic instinct, the natural human desire to take part in or to witness the public representation by words and gesture of some interesting action, lay dormant for centuries after classic drama was dead and forgotten. It finally came to life once more in that institution which in medieval times was the center of all social life, the Catholic Church, and in its public service of worship. This service was, of course, in the sacred language, Latin, less and less intelligible as time went on to the majority of the congregation. To overcome this obstacle art was called on by the clergy to bring home Bible story and Christian doctrine to the illiterate laity. Sculpture and painting, crucifixes, images, frescoes and pictured windows served not merely for decoration of the sacred building, but also for the edification of the people. Finally mimetic and dramatic art entered into the regular service of worship.

The services for the various festivals of the Christian year afforded rich material for dramatic representation. At Christmas the Gospel stories of the shepherds, the Magi, and the Slaughter of the Innocents; at Eastertide the Palm Sunday entrance of Christ into Jerusalem, the Passion itself, and the Resurrection are essentially dramatic: they became more evidently so by the practice of rendering the Gospel lessons for these feasts in the form of antiphonal singing. Minor festivals, Ascension and Pentecost, had their appropriate service, and the calendar of the Church closed with All Saints' Day, November 1, at once a memorial of the martyrs of the past and a vision of their vindication at the Last Judgment. Towards the close of the ninth century we begin to find directions in church service-books for mimetic representation of significant parts of the service, directions which soon developed into liturgical drama, i.e., dramatic performances inserted into, and regarded as an essential part of, the established order of worship for some special festival of the Church. We have first of all dramatic action without speech; such as the Deposition of the Cross on Good Friday, the removal of the Crucifix from its place above the altar, and its burial in a Sepulchre prepared for the occasion, later often a permanent structure within the church. Here it was watched for two nights by monks or priests, sometimes clad in armor to represent the soldiers set by Pilate to guard the grave, a characteristic bit of mimetic representation. Then we get the Easter trope, a chanted paraphrase or expansion of the appropriate Gospel or Psalm for the day. Finally there appears the first specimen of drama acted and vocal in the famous *Quem Quaeritis* of the Easter service. Full directions for this bit of dramatic action and dialogue are found in the *Regularis Concordia* of Ethelwold, Bishop of Winchester, in the third quarter of the tenth century. It runs as follows: [1]

While the third lesson is being chanted, let four brethren vest themselves. Let one of these vested in an alb [a white linen robe] enter as if to take part in the service, and let him approach the sepulchre and sit there quietly with a palm in his hand. Let the other three follow, vested in copes [mantles worn over the alb] bearing in their hands censers with incense, and slowly, as if seeking something, let them come to the place of the sepulchre. These things are done in imitation of the angel seated in the tomb and the women coming with spices to anoint the body of Jesus. When he who sits there beholds the three approach him like folk seeking something, let him begin in a dulcet voice to sing *Quem quaeritis in sepulchro, O Christicolae?* [Whom seek ye in the tomb, O followers of Christ?] When he has sung this to the end, let the three respond in unison *Ihesum Nazarenum, crucifixum, o caelicola* [Jesus of Nazareth, the crucified, O dweller in heaven]. To whom he: *Non est hic; surrexit, sicut praedixerat. Ite, nuntiate quia surrexit a mortuis* [He is not here; he has risen, even as he foretold. Go, announce that he has risen from the dead]. At this bidding let those three turn to the choir saying: *Alleluia! resurrexit Dominus* [Alleluia! the Lord has risen]. This said let the former seating himself, as if recalling them, sing the anthem: *Venite et videte locum* [Come and see the place]. Saying this let him rise and lift the veil and show them the place bare of the cross, but only the cloths in which the cross was wrapped. Seeing this let them set down the censers and take the cloth and spread it out before the clergy and, as if making known to them that the Lord has risen, let them sing this anthem: *Surrexit Dominus de sepulchro* [The Lord has risen from the tomb], and lay the cloth upon the altar. The anthem being ended let the Prior, sharing in their gladness at the triumph of our King, begin the hymn: *Te Deum laudamus* [We praise thee, O God]. And this begun, all the bells chime out together.

Here is the beginning of religious drama in England; its purpose plainly is edification rather than entertainment. Char-

[1] The translation of the original is slightly condensed and altered from that of Adams, *Chief Pre-Shakespearean Dramas.*

acters, action, and speech, even though the simple dialogue is in Latin, all combine to represent and bring home the story of the empty tomb and the risen Lord to the ignorant but reverent audience.

That the little play was a welcome addition to the regular service is seen from the fact that as time went on it was enlarged by the addition of new scenes and characters. The apostles, Peter and John, also visit the Sepulchre; Christ appears to Mary Magdalene in the garden, and reveals himself to the wayfarers at Emmaus. Earlier scenes are prefixed to the primitive play: the *planctus* (lament) of the Marys for the crucified Lord, their purchase of ointment from the *unguentarius* (spice-seller), a character unknown to Scripture, the Passion itself, and the raising of Lazarus. Finally about the time of the Norman Conquest, 1066, we get a complete Passion Play still in Latin and still acted as part of the liturgy.

Naturally enough the other great festival of the church year, Christmas, was not far behind Easter in developing its own dramatic addition to the regular service. This begins in the eleventh century with a *Quem quaeritis in praesepe, Pastores?* (Whom seek ye in the manger, shepherds?) sung alternately by choir boys and deacons as the angels and the shepherds of the Nativity. Like the Easter play this Christmas trope contained the germ of development, and before long we find increments in the form of the Star of Bethlehem and the Magi, King Herod, later a favorite character in Miracle plays, the Slaughter of the Innocents, and the Flight into Egypt. More important still was the introduction into the Christmas service of a Procession of Prophets including Balaam on his ass, testifying in turn to the future birth of Christ. From this Procession there sprang in time a whole series of little plays dealing with the lives of Old Testament characters until we get back to the Creation and earlier yet to the Rebellion in Heaven and the Fall of Satan.

The Ascension festival also began to develop its trope into a playlet and this in turn developed a series of scenes looking forward to the Second Coming, and the Day of Judgment.

A brief summary may serve to show the gradual development of liturgical drama. We have first the lesson and the Psalms of the day read or chanted responsively in Latin; then a ritual procession, symbolic, as in the Deposition of the Cross, rather than representational; then the trope acted with dialogue and with characters representing the sacred figures; finally, as scene was added to scene, the liturgical drama proper, still, of course, in Latin and still regarded as a part of the regular service.

The next step was an amalgamation of the Easter, the Christmas, and the Ascension plays, into a cycle of cosmic range from the Fall of Satan to the Day of Judgment. The performance of so long a series within the limits of the regular service must indeed have been difficult and we find directions pointing to the performance on two successive days, and to the transference of the scene of action outside the church to the church porch, the surrounding graveyard, and even to the market-place. This is naturally the first step in the secularization of the drama.

It must not be supposed, however, that when performances of sacred plays were given in the market-place, the liturgical drama came to an end. On the contrary it lingered, especially on the Continent, down to almost modern times. In England, however, the interesting development of the drama from liturgical to secular took place out of doors.

Several causes led to the transference of sacred drama from the interior of the church to the church porch and the market-place. One of these was the excessive length of the developed play; another was the elaborate setting required for some of these performances. An idea of this can be gained by a sketch preserved of the setting of a sixteenth-century play at Donaueschingen in Germany.[1] Evidently such a setting must have crowded the audience into the narrow aisles to the increase of chances for scandalous disorder. Irreverence on the part of the audience was apparently one of the prime causes for the removal of the drama from the sacred edifice. Little by little elements of comedy had crept into these performances. It began harmlessly enough with the introduction of the *unguentarius* selling spices to the Marys. The ranting Herod of the Nativity plays, the howling devils of the Day of Judgment, most of all perhaps, the figure of Balaam on his ass riding solemnly down the nave were

[1] Chambers, *Medieval Stage*, Vol. 2, p. 84, and elsewhere.

only too likely to provoke irreverent laughter. An elaborate direction for the performance of an Ascension play in Germany forbids the casting down of an image of Satan which was then attacked and beaten with rods by boys in the audience, an action which, we are told, led to mocking laughter and even to *seditionem, i.e.*, rioting. Naturally, the graver members of the clergy protested against such excesses, and medieval records are full of prohibitions against them and against the participation of members of the clergy in performances which were only too likely to provoke them. Once outside the walls of the church, however, the people might laugh and riot to their hearts' content.

In England, by the beginning of the fourteenth century, drama had definitely passed not only out of the church, but out of the control of the clergy. The new drama had come into the hands of laymen who arranged the presentation and acted the parts in the open streets. The primary purpose of the liturgical play, edification, had yielded to entertainment; *officia* (ceremonious rites), as has been said, gave place to *spectacula* (shows).

Liturgical drama had begun in connection with the great festivals of the Church, Easter and Christmas; but as the drama moved out from the shelter of the church walls, weather conditions tended to alter these dates. Easter Day and Christmas are only too likely in England to be inclement seasons, cold and wet, most unpropitious for out-of-door performances. A great new festival, that of Corpus Christi, late in May or early in June, soon became the day of days for the new drama. This festival in honor of the dogma of transubstantiation was ordained by Pope Urban IV in 1264 and confirmed by Clement V in 1316. Its special feature was a solemn procession in which the Host, followed by the clergy, official bodies, and town guilds, was borne in triumph through the streets. The liturgical drama was transferred to Corpus Christi day, and became at once the most popularly interesting part of this procession. The long cycle was broken up into separate scenes, each of which became the property of one of the trade guilds of the town, a society made responsible for its preservation and performance.

These guilds, it must be remembered, were the dominant

bodies in the social and economic life of a medieval town. Originally associations for mutual assistance in time of sickness, poverty, or death, they had grown to be great organizations completely controlling economic and political conditions within the walls. Every free-born citizen was expected to enroll in one of their number, to declare himself a butcher, a carpenter, a goldsmith, or what you will. As they grew in wealth and power, even royalty did not disdain to become at least a nominal member of a guild. Like all medieval associations the guilds were bound to the Church by the closest ties; each had its patron saint, its special church, and its masses for the souls of deceased brethren. The guilds were the normal, even the necessary, bodies for the presentation of the drama when it ceased to be part of the regular service within the church.

Two very important phenomena in the development of the drama appear in this secularization of the old plays. The first is the transition from the sacred Latin of the liturgy, chanted rather than spoken, to the vernacular, French or German on the Continent, English in the British Isles. This transition had already begun in the Church drama; but so long as the main intent of the performance was worship, the sacred language naturally prevailed. When, however, the drama broke away from the liturgy and sought primarily to entertain its audience, the vernacular became essential in spoken dialogue. In the English Miracle plays that have come down to us the dialogue is, save for quotations from Holy Writ, all in English; only the stage-directions in some of the older plays are still in Latin. With this escape from liturgical bondage the drama was free to develop along original lines in a form that appealed directly to its audience, and we get genuine plays, such as the Brome *Abraham and Isaac,* not merely mimetic representations of Bible scenes at their appropriate festivals.

Another equally important factor in the development of the drama was the increasing realism of the plays. As the motive of edification waned and that of entertainment increased, every effort was made to present the sacred stories in forms familiar to the people. Characters pass from the pages of the Bible into the life of contemporary England: the shepherds of the Nativity play become English shepherds on a Yorkshire moor, grousing in true English fashion about the weather, their wives, and their landlords; Mrs. Noah, a character barely mentioned in the Bible, appears again and again in the Miracle plays as a typical English shrew; the Caiaphas of the Wakefield *Buffeting*, who can hardly keep his hands off Jesus, is the fighting prelate familiar enough to such northern cathedral towns as York and Durham. Along with this realism of characterization goes a realism of speech which gets far away from the mere paraphrases of scripture in the early plays. Biblical characters indulge in such coarse, obscene, and even blasphemous language as to shock modern editors, who from time to time delete lines with the comment: "The language is too offensive to be reproduced." Such language was, of course, meant to entertain, to provoke ribald laughter; the very comic elements which had excited the protests of the clergy within the church increased and multiplied in the market-place. Stock characters appearing again and again, Cain's boy, Mrs. Noah, King Herod are given a conscious comic tinge. People then believed so implicitly in the Bible story that they were ready to allow themselves the frankest familiarity with Bible characters. With the completed secularization of the drama in the early fourteenth century, play-writing and performance shook off the shackles of the liturgy and, while still closely connected with religion in the choice of subject matter, became an independent, realistic, and thoroughly national art.

The characteristic English form of this art is the Cycle, a series, usually of some length, of separate plays dealing successively with events of sacred history from the Fall of Satan to the Judgment Day, a series meant for presentation at one fixed time, each play a part of one great whole. Some of these cycles were so long that a full performance extended over three days or even a week.

Four such English cycles have come down to us. They represent the full development and the approaching decay of this form in England. We have evidence that many such have perished, for there is reason to believe that at one time or another every great cathedral, university, or market town of England had its own peculiar cycle.

The remaining four are:

I. The York cycle: 48 plays and a fragment. The manuscript is dated *ca.* 1430–40, but the plays are much older; the cycle is known to have been in existence before 1378.

II. The Towneley, a name derived from a former owner of the fifteenth-century manuscript, more properly the Wakefield cycle: 32 plays. Of later origin than the York cycle, from which in some cases it is plainly derived, it was performed by the guilds of Wakefield at an annual fair, apparently on fixed stages rather than on the usual moving cars.

III. The Chester cycle: 25 plays. This is preserved in a group of manuscripts dating from the very close of the sixteenth and the beginning of the seventeenth century, a fact that shows a living interest in these old plays as late as Shakespeare's day. The cycle is, of course, far older, dating back perhaps to the early fourteenth century. It is the soberest of all the remaining cycles, the most didactic in tone, nearer to the edifying motive of the liturgical plays than are its livelier cousins of Wakefield and of York.

IV. The so-called *Ludus Coventriae:* 42 plays preserved in a manuscript dating 1468. This title is an error due to the fact that these plays were early and wrongly identified with the famous cycle known to have been played at Coventry as late as the time of Shakespeare. Scholars have tried to substitute another name for the misleading *Ludus Coventriae* and have called this cycle the *Hegge Plays* after a former owner of the manuscript, or the *N. Town Plays* after a phrase in the prologue which states that this cycle will be acted next Sunday at N. Town (N. for *nomen, i.e.,* any name may be substituted here). In its present form this cycle seems to have been acted, not by the craftsmen of a certain town, but by strolling players on fixed stages in various towns on their circuit. It is later than the other cycles, less naïve, more pedantically theological, and in its repeated introductions of abstract characters, Contemplation, Truth, Pity, and so on, it shows the influence of the popular Moral plays of the fifteenth century. It is distinguished also from the earlier cycles by the number of plays dealing with extra-biblical legends of the Virgin Mary, a type of play certain to provoke the wrath of Protestant reformers.

Each of these cycles falls naturally into five groups more or less fully developed in each. These are:

I. Plays dealing with the Creation, the Fall of Man, and various incidents in Old Testament history. This group has developed from the early *Processus Prophetarum.*

II. Plays centering around the birth of Christ, developed from the early Christmas play.

III. Plays presenting incidents in the life of Christ, surprisingly few in number.

IV. Passion Plays, developed from the early *Quem Quaeritis.*

V. Ascension Plays, including some on the later history of the Church and the saints down to the Day of Judgment.

All four cycles have plays on the Creation and the Fall, Noah's Flood, Abraham and Isaac, the Shepherds, the Crucifixion, the Resurrection, and Doomsday. There is much variation in other topics presented.

The authors of these cycles, or of the individual plays contained in them, are quite unknown. The cycles are composite works by many hands, written, re-written, added to and revised through at least two centuries, even as the medieval cathedrals were built, rebuilt, enlarged, and altered. Something they owe, no doubt, to the great French cycles, a knowledge of which came to England through Norman French clerks. It is possible, perhaps, here and there to distinguish the work of individual hands, especially in the Towneley cycle, where a group of five plays: *Noah*, the *First* and the *Second Shepherds Play*, the *Magi*, and the *Buffeting of Christ* shows, in rhythm, diction, and vigorous realistic humor, evident traces of the work of one man, the so-called "Wakefield Master," probably a witty clerk of the age of Chaucer.

Let us imagine ourselves present at a typical performance of one of these cycles, at York, for instance, in Chaucer's day. Preparations have been made well in advance of the festival of Corpus Christi. The various plays of the cycle have been allotted by the magistrates to various guilds for presentation on their "pageants."[1] These were movable scaffolds on wheels, something like our modern "floats," but two stories high. The lower story

[1] The name "pageant" came to be attached to each play as well as to the car on which it was acted.

was concealed by curtains where the actors dressed and from which they emerged as their cues came; the upper was an open stage on which the action, visible from all sides, proceeded. In some plays where it was needed, *Doomsday* for instance, this stage was equipped at the corner with a huge dragon's head, open-mouthed and belching flame, from which devils issued and into which sinners were hurled. There are some curious analogies between the subject matter of the play and the producing guild; the Shipwrights took over *The Building of the Ark*, the Fishers and Mariners *Noah and the Flood*, the Goldsmiths *The Magi*, and the Butchers *The Crucifixion*. Naturally, of course, such analogies do not always hold; there seems no special reason for allotting *The Ascension* to the Tailors.

Each guild was bound under penalty to produce its play "well and duly." In the golden age of the cycles the guilds were proud of their task, and ready to spend time and money on a fine performance. Old account-books preserve quaint items of guild money spent on the play: a man who played God the Father received 3s. 4d.; a man who hanged Judas got only 4d., but 4d. more for crowing like a cock when Peter denied his Lord. Some curious lists of properties have also come down to us: five sheep-skins for God's coat (presumably gilded), a tail for the Serpent, a "red rib" for the creation of Eve, and a barrel for the earthquake at Doomsday. The actors in each play were, in the main at least, members of the guild to which the play was assigned. They might be helped out at times, of course, by "clerks"—one recalls Chaucer's Absolon who played the important part of Herod "on a scaffold high"—travelling scholars or minstrels; but production and performance were in the hands of the laity, no longer of the Church.

The great procession starts at 4:30 in the summer morning; the first pageant, *Creation and the Fall of Lucifer*, moves from the general rendezvous to the first "station," or fixed playing-place, presumably some open spot near the city gate, gives its performance there, and moves on to the second station, where it repeats. As it leaves the first station, pageant number two, *The Creation to the Fifth Day*, arrives, performs, and moves on. And so until the whole cycle has been played, not once but over and over—there were twelve stations at York.

The audience stood in the streets about the halted pageant, sat in convenient windows, or perhaps on temporary stands. A great concourse of all sorts and conditions witnessed the performance, nobles, clergy, merchants, craftsmen, and peasants from the countryside. All alike took interest in this community play, for it contained something for all tastes: the familiar sacred story in its most dramatic moments, religious and moral sentiments, lively action, tragic pathos, comic relief, and gross buffoonery. A stage-direction in the *Ludus* reads: "Here Herod rages on the pageant and in the street also." Imagine the laughter of the crowd when the roaring King of Jewry sprang down, flourishing his wooden sword and using it on some unlucky urchin whom he had seized. But as well as laughter there were tears for the agony of Christ and for the sorrows of the Virgin.

And so the great procession passes amid laughter, tears, and at times awed silence, until, as the shadows lengthen, the last pageant leaves the final station, and the whole story of God's dealing with mankind has been publicly performed. The audience breaks up and departs, entertained to the full, but more than merely entertained, confirmed in the belief that all these sacred tales were true and had happened in the past, even as they had just been played. A preaching friar once told his congregation in speaking of Christ's resurrection: 'If you believe not me, go to Coventry, where you may see it acted every year." Could there be better warrant of the truth of the Bible story?

The great age of the cyclical plays extended over two centuries, the fourteenth and the fifteenth. From the beginning of the sixteenth they fell into steadily increasing decay. Performances, to be sure, still took place. The last recorded performance at York was in 1579; the Coventry plays lasted till 1580, and there is record of a single performance at Beverly as late as 1604. Yet many causes combined to bring about the gradual cessation of the cyclical plays. Most important, perhaps, was the loss of the simple faith of the Middle Ages. With the schism of the Reformation, Catholics and Protestants fought furiously over points of doctrine; a communal acceptance of the Catholic faith was lost forever. Protestants objected to plays in honor of the Virgin and the Saints; stricter reformers protested against all religious plays as treating sacred subjects too lightly. Economic causes, also, hastened the decay of the cyclical drama. With the increasing decadence of the medieval guilds these bodies began to object to the expense which the performances entailed; we find them petitioning to be excused from the obligation and actually paying fines for non-performance. It is a typical example of this changing attitude of the guilds towards the plays which had once been their pride that in 1570 the splendid pageant of the Grocers of Norwich was broken up and sold for junk. New interests, moreover, were clamoring for dramatic expression and demanding other than the old traditional forms. The Humanism of the Renaissance introduced classic models of comedy and tragedy, first to the schools and then to the general public. The spirit of nationalism that sprang up under the Tudors demanded historic and patriotic rather than sacred plays. Finally at the close of the century when Shakespeare was at work in London the last recorded performance of a cycle took place at Chester.

The influence upon the English people of such performances over a period of nearly three centuries was deep and lasting. They begot and fostered a taste for acted drama, taught a simple technique of dramatic art, especially in converting narrative into represented action. In more ways than one they laid the foundations of Elizabethan drama; even such masterpieces of that age as *Dr. Faustus* and Shakespeare's Histories show plainly remaining traces of the old Miracle plays.

Certain outstanding characteristics of these plays may be briefly mentioned. The most marked, perhaps, is a strong and simple realism. This shows itself in action: in tragedy the grim brutality of the executioners in the Crucifixion plays who exult in the suffering of their victim; in comedy the domestic squabble of Mak and his wife in that best of early farces, the *Secunda Pastorum*; Mrs. Noah; especially perhaps the Cain of the Wakefield play, a surly, stingy, foul-mouthed North of England peasant. There is no attempt at historic accuracy: Old Testament characters swear alternately by the Trinity or by Mahoun. As in much of medieval art the playwright's effort was to revive the past in terms of the present, to present an old story as if it happened only yesterday.

Other merits of these plays are often obscured to the modern reader by the queer spelling, the unfamiliar diction, and the doggerel meter. Yet there is some, though not very much, fine poetry, a great deal of lively dialogue, and a real sense of dramatic values, as in the prolonged suspense in the Brome *Abraham and Isaac*. The chief merit, after all, however, is a genuine sincerity, rising from the mind and heart of the unknown authors, informing their treatment of their themes, and carrying over their conviction to the audience. When in Elizabethan days drama turned from sacred to profane history, something at least of this sincerity and conviction remained. It was not without reason that Shakespeare's company advertised their great spectacular play on Henry VIII by the title: *All is True*. Truth, rather than fiction, was what the popular audience of Shakespeare's day demanded on the stage.

It was during the golden age of the great cycles that a new form of drama made its appearance in England destined to run beside them, and in its development to point the way to native English comedy. This was the Morality, better called the Moral Play, or simply the Moral. It has been defined as "a play enforcing a moral truth or lesson by means of the speech and action of characters who are personified abstractions, figures representing vices and virtues, qualities of the human mind, or abstract conceptions in general." To put it more briefly, the Moral is dramatized allegory with didactic intent.

Like the liturgical plays the Moral derives from the Church. As the Church liturgy gave rise to the earliest drama, so the Church sermon with its insistence on good life, practical morality, and preparation for the hour of death, a sermon often lightened by interesting anecdote and heightened by dramatic dialogue, furnished the field from which the Moral sprang. This, however, is true only for the didactic purposes of the Moral; its method of teaching by personified abstractions derives from another source, the literary allegory. Allegory had been known as a literary form since the time at least of Plato. It entered into Christian literature with the *Psychomachia* of Prudentius, *ca.* 400 A.D., an epic poem narrating the battle between the Virtues and their corresponding Vices. The Middle Ages with their love of abstract thought fastened eagerly upon the allegory and employed it in various fields, painting, sculpture, and poetry. Drama, however, seems to have been late in adopting this form. It is not until such works as the *Roman de la Rose,* and the widely read *Piers Plowman* had, so to speak, popularized allegory in the fourteenth century that it began to affect the drama.

The first mention we have of the Moral is by Wyclif, in or about the year 1378; it is of a *Pater Noster* "in the English tongue as men see in the play of York," for whose performance a special guild, that of the *Oratio Domini* (the Lord's Prayer) was founded. We know nothing of this play except that one of its sections was known as *Ludus Accidiae,* the Play of Sloth; but an account of another *Pater Noster* play at Beverly is, no doubt, applicable to that of York. Here there were eight pageants, the first that of Vicious (Sinful Man), the other seven those of the Seven Deadly Sins. According to medieval theology each clause of the Lord's Prayer constituted a special protection against one of the deadly Seven. It would seem that the *Pater Noster* play, whether at York or at Beverly, was a dramatic presentation of the conflict for the soul of man between the Vices and the Grace of God personified in characters drawn from the Lord's Prayer.

It is highly probable that the first Morals were cyclic in form, presented like the Miracles in a series of scenes on moving pageants. None such have come down to us; we have only single plays. All of these, so long as the Moral remains true to its original ethical purpose, deal in one fashion or another with but three themes. These are:

I. The Coming of Death, a theme based on the churchly teaching of preparation for man's last hour, the *ars moriendi* (art of dying) of the medieval Church, popularized by the treatment in painting and poetry in the late Middle Ages of the grim motif of the Dance of Death.

II. The Debate of the Heavenly Virtues, Mercy and Peace against Justice and Truth, for the soul of man after death. This particular debate goes back finally to the eighty-fifth Psalm: "Mercy and Truth are met together: Righteousness and Peace have kissed each other," a verse that as early as the twelfth century was developed in dramatic form in French.

III. Most important and most often recurrent, because most

essentially dramatic, is the Conflict of Vices and Virtues for the soul of man. From the time of St. Paul, who bade his converts put on the whole armor of God, down to Bunyan's *Holy War,* the Christian life has been imagined as a warfare against the hosts of Sin, and the *Psychomachia* gave force and form to such a representation.

The longest and probably the oldest extant Moral, *The Castle of Perseverance, ca.* 1450, includes all three of these themes. It might, perhaps, be regarded as a sort of condensation of an older cyclical Moral for performance not by a guild but by a troupe of travelling players at one time and in one place, evidently some town or village green. A rough sketch in the manuscript shows the *mise-en-scène:* a structure like a castle built up on the green, surrounded by water in a moat if possible, if not by a barrier, to keep spectators off the place of action; beneath the castle a bed under which lay, till his cue came, the actor who played Humanum Genus, *i.e.,* Mankind. On the green itself were erected five scaffolds, like the pageants of the cycles, for the World, the Flesh, the Devil, Covetousness, and the throne of God. The manuscript begins with a prologue spoken by banner-bearers announcing the performance a seven-night hence "at N. [*i.e.,* any name might be substituted here] on the green" at nine in the morning. Evidently this play was carried from place to place, and an audience was drummed up beforehand.

The play proper opens with the appearance of the World, the Flesh, and the Devil, each on his scaffold, boasting, like Herod in the Miracles, of his mighty power. Then Humanum Genus appears from beneath his bed, a new-born soul. Angels good and bad contest for him, but he listens to the Bad Angel and mounts the scaffold of the World where he falls a prey to various vices. Rescued from them by the Good Angel, backed by Confession, Shrift, and Penitence—the powers of the Church—Man is led to the Castle of Perseverance. Here he is attacked by all the hosts of sin, led by Satan spitting fire from gunpowder in his hands, his ears, and his hinder parts, a spectacle that must have delighted the rustic spectators. The enemy is beaten back by the defending Virtues with showers of roses, symbols of the saving blood of Christ. Yet even so Man is not safe, for an enemy within betrays him, and Covetousness lures him out of the castle to enjoy worldly wealth. Now the play draws to a close: Death appears to strike Man down; he is borne to the throne of God, the fifth scaffold, where a formal trial is held. Justice prosecutes, Mercy defends him, and at the end God admits the saved soul to heaven. Here in a sense we have a cyclic play, not indeed of the history of the race, but of the whole life of the individual man from his birth through his sinful life to his redemption by the grace of God.

Such an outline of the oldest Moral gives, perhaps, too favorable an impression of the work as drama. It is very long, almost 4,000 lines, and deadly dull reading. Only an audience trained in the tradition of the day-long Miracles would have had the patience to stand and see the show to the end. Its chief characteristic is its serious didactic note. This it shares with the best of the old Morals that has been preserved, *Everyman,* or more properly *The Summoning of Everyman,* late fifteenth century. This little play, about one-quarter of the length of the *Castle,* is as serious as its predecessor, but gains a power and dramatic effect, demonstrated by frequent performances on the modern stage, by unity of theme, the Coming of Death, and by concentration on the central figure, Everyman, his alarm when Death summons him, his vain appeals to friends and worldly goods, and his final departure from this life fortified by Confession and attended to the grave by his Good Deeds.

Makers and actors of Morals, however, soon came to realize that if they were to hold an audience, still more if they were to pass the hat for contributions, they must entertain as well as edify. This is admirably illustrated in the play *Mankind,* contemporary, or almost so, with *Everyman.* On a stage set in the court-yard of an inn the hero, Mankind, a simple peasant, is counselled by Mercy clad as a preacher, and assailed by such quaint vices as Newgyse, Nowadays, and Nought. At first he beats them off with his spade, but on the entrance of the comic devil Titivillus, he falls from grace, and departs to make merry at the tavern. The entrance of the Devil is the high point of the play. He bawls from behind a curtain: "I come with my legs under me"; but before he appears, the play is stopped and a collection taken up. "We intend to gather money," says one of the actors, "else there shall no man him see."

> He loveth no groats, nor pence, nor twopence,
> Give us red royals if ye will see his abominable presence.

A "royal," a coin of about ten shillings in value, was a high price even to see the abominable presence of the Devil, and an actor promptly adds: "Ye that may not pay the one, pay the other," *i.e.*, groats, pennies, or twopence. Mankind is, of course, led back to grace at the end, but the whole moral purpose of the play is overshadowed with the foul speech and buffooneries of Titivillus and his companion vices.

With the dawn of the Renaissance in England in the early years of the sixteenth century new types of the Moral begin to appear. The didactic purpose still remains, but the theme changes and the old ethical exhortation gives place to a humanistic interest in study or to political and theological propaganda. An example of the first class appears in Rastell's *The Nature of the Four Elements, ca.* 1519. Here stress is laid upon the desirability of studying Nature as a first step to the knowledge of God, and such characters as Nature and Experience discourse at interminable length to the hero, Humanity, on the four elements, the shape of the earth, and America, the new world discovered beyond the Atlantic. It is very learned, but quite dull, a fact the author himself seems to realize since he remarks in a little preface: "Ye may leave out much of the sad [*i.e.*, serious] matter and then it [the playing time] will not be past three-quarters of an hour." The action, such as it is, runs along established lines: Humanity is led astray by Sensual Appetite and carried to a tavern to eat, drink, and make merry with little Nell and bouncing Bess. Here at least are real names of real girls, and a further touch of realism is added by the introduction of the Taverner who cracks dirty jokes with Humanity and his boon companion. Humanity returns, indeed, to listen to a lecture by Experience, but this is interrupted by the intrusion of a group of players to entertain the audience with song and dance. We are a long way here from the moral earnestness of *The Castle of Perseverance* or the agony of *Everyman.*

The Reformation entered England in the reign of Henry VIII, and in the religious war that followed the drama in the form of the Moral took an active part. Plays for and against the new movement were produced, applauded, silenced, and prosecuted as the tide of reform flowed, ebbed, and flowed again at Court. Naturally the men of the new religion were the more aggressive; we have but one remaining play, *Respublica, ca.* 1553, which supports the other side. On the other hand John Bale, Bishop of Ossory, a violent reformer, boasts of having written some forty plays more or less. Perhaps the best example of the Moral used as a vehicle of Protestant propaganda is *Lusty Juventus, ca.* 1550, by R. Wever, a disciple of the fighting Bishop. Here the new wine of Puritanism is poured into the old framework of the Moral. Juventus, *i.e.,* Youth, is reclaimed from his natural pursuit of pleasure by Good Counsel and Knowledge, who give him a copy of the New Testament to be his guide. No sooner has he left the stage than a comic devil rises to lament the departure of the younger generation from the good old ways; he summons his child Hypocrisy, who appears and recites a satiric catalogue of the old superstitions that have deceived mankind:

> Holy cardinals, holy popes,
> Holy vestments, holy copes
>
> .   .   .   .   .   .
>
> And a hundred trim-trams mo.

It does not take long for Hypocrisy, masquerading as Friendship, to seduce Juventus and bring him into company with Fellowship and little Bess, a wanton serving-maid, stigmatized in the play as Abominable Living. Juventus, however, is reclaimed; a terrific sermon by Good Counsel brings him to despair, from which he is rescued by a character called God's Merciful Promises, and the play ends with a prayer for "our noble and virtuous king," the young Protestant Edward VI. There is less of the element of realistic comedy in this play than in most of the later Morals; yet, probably because of its anti-Roman polemic, it seems to have been distinctly popular. It was printed twice and is mentioned as part of the repertory of the actors who appear in the play of *Sir Thomas More* in the last decade of the sixteenth century.

Perhaps the most interesting, because the most forward-looking, of these polemic plays is Bale's *King John,* written apparently some time before 1548, and revised in the reign of Elizabeth. Bale abandons the no-man's land in which the action of the Moral is usually laid and tries to dramatize a definite period in English history. It was enough for Bale that King John had striven against the Pope to qualify him as a righteous monarch, "a faithful Moses who withstood proud Pharaoh." In the play John appears as the champion of the poor widow England against her oppressor, the Church of Rome. Allegorical figures, Sedition, Dissimulation, Private Wealth, and Usurped Power, conspire against him and seduce his subjects, Nobility, Clergy, Civil Order, and Commonalty, the poor blind personification of the common people. As the action proceeds, the allegorical figures turn into historic characters; Usurped Power appears as Pope Innocent III, Sedition as Stephen Langton, Archbishop of Canterbury, and Private Wealth as Cardinal Pandulf. John is excommunicated with bell, book, and candle, forced to resign his crown and receive it back as the Pope's vassal. Yet his enemies still pursue him, and Dissimulation, disguised as a monk, poisons him in a wassail bowl. After the King's death Verity enters to tell the truth about the maligned ruler, and Imperial Majesty—plainly a personification of Henry VIII—takes charge of the realm, recalls his subjects to obedience, and sends Sedition to the gallows.

This strange play, whether publicly performed or not, is a striking sign of the shift of interest in the developing drama from the old Moral to the future chronicle play. In spite of its unwieldy length, its obsolescent allegorical machinery, and its violent polemic, *King John* has certain dramatic values: lively dialogue, definite action, above all a strong sense of the reality of the history represented, such as the old Miracles had carried over from the Bible stories.

The Moral, a late medieval and early Renaissance art form, flourished from the fourteenth well into the sixteenth century. It employed dramatic allegory to drive home a lesson, ethical, humanistic, or controversially theological. In a sense it bridges the gap between the earlier Miracles and the later drama. It freed the playwright, to be sure, from his dependence upon the Bible story, a source too sacred to be freely altered; on the other hand it laid down a rather rigid pattern to be followed and imposed a heavy burden of didacticism not to be shaken off till the high tide of Elizabethan drama. Some of its characters: the Good and the Bad Angels, the Seven Deadly Sins, and personifications like Revenge and Justice, carry on into later plays. We recognize them in the work of Kyd and Marlowe. The later Morals, indeed, introduced somewhat shyly characters from real life: the taverner of *The Four Elements,* the serving-maid of *Juventus.* Here, perhaps, we may find the most definite contribution of the Moral to the development of English drama. As it turns from the visionary field of abstractions to deal with real life, it paves the way for the arrival of realistic Elizabethan comedy.

Two characters in particular, comic and realistic, appear again and again in the Morals and pass over into later Elizabethan drama. These are the Devil and the Vice. The Devil, of course, comes from the Miracle plays, but there he is, with perhaps a single exception, the Tutivillus of the Wakefield *Judgment,* a terrible and awe-inspiring figure, the great enemy of man. In the Morals he becomes a serio-comic character, a boaster, a blusterer, a foiled and baffled plotter. His almost constant attendant, the Vice, is a new figure. His ancestor may, perhaps, be found among the Devil's attendants, the Seven Deadly Sins, but he soon assumes the form of an embodied Evil, Sensuality, Hypocrisy, or Sedition, quick to contribute with his coarse jesting and buffoonery some comic relief to the tedious moralizing. Little by little he sloughs off traces of his devilish origin and becomes a jolly, witty mischief-maker, Haphazard or Subtle Shift, thus preparing the way for the Court Fool and the roguish servant of later comedy. As late as Shakespeare's day the Vice in Court Fool's dress, armed with a dagger of lath, swaggered across the stage, to be carried off at times to Hell upon the Devil's back like Miles, the Vice of Greene's *Friar Bacon.*

With the change in the older form of the Moral in the early years of the sixteenth century a new form of drama, the Interlude, begins to appear. There is considerable doubt as to the derivation and exact meaning of this term. Originally applied to almost every form of stage-play, it will be restricted here to short plays, dealing mainly with characters from real life and aiming primarily at entertainment rather than edification. The later Morals had tended to introduce such characters and to emphasize the comic episodes; the distinction of the interlude is that it sloughed off entirely the allegoric abstractions, and discarded, except incidentally and as an after-thought, the didactic aim.

The earliest example of the Interlude, the longlost and lately recovered, *Fulgens and Lucres* (*i.e.*, Fulgentius and Lucrece), *ca.* 1497, is the work of Henry Medwall, chaplain to John Morton, Archbishop of Canterbury under Henry VII, a patron of the new learning. Based upon a Latin treatise, *De vera nobilitate*, very popular in the fifteenth century, this Interlude dramatizes the story of Fulgens, a Roman Senator, and his daughter, Lucres. She has two suitors: Cornelius, an idle patrician, and Flaminius, a wise and virtuous plebeian. Medwall lightens and diversifies the set debates of his original by introducing two comic serving-men, professional actors brought in for the occasion. Rivals for the love of the lady's maid, these clowns seek to win her by mock contests in song, wrestling, and tilting. Evidently performed at a banquet in Morton's palace, the play stops in the middle of the action till the audience can finish dinner, and the usher is ordered to serve them with good wine.

The second part opens with a speech by one of the actors, speaking for Medwall, who reminds the audience of the theme, Of True Nobility, but remarks:

> Divers toyes mingled in the same there was,
> To stir folk to mirth and game.

Some care only for such trifles, he says; some desire only "matter of sadness." He wishes to content every one, and so after a couple of comic scenes and a masked dance the formal debate between the suitors is introduced, and Lucres decides in favor of the plebeian. This appropriate close is Medwall's invention; in his source the rivalry between the suitors is left undecided.

It is hard to overstress the originality of this early Interlude. At a time when the Moral was in full flower Medwall wrote a play about ancient Romans and, with a happy disregard of chronology, modern serving-men. The moral purpose, if any, is lost to sight in the antics of the comedians whose parody of the main action anticipates a common device of later drama. It seems likely that Medwall's early death, *ca.* 1501, was a real loss to the slowly evolving English drama.

The great master of the Interlude is John Heywood (1497?– *ca.* 1578), an early example of the actor-playwright; he was one of Henry VIII's "singing-men," getting a wage of 8d. a day— not bad pay at that time. Heywood was something more than a mere entertainer; he was connected by marriage with More and Rastell, and shared More's attitude to the new movement in intellectual and religious life. One of the early English human- ists, he was ready to recognize and attack abuses in the Church, but not to revolt from the old faith. In the end, when the Reformation triumphed, he abandoned his country and died in exile.

Heywood is the first English writer of plays who has left us a substantial body of work. He is certainly the author of *The Play of Love, Witty and Witless, The Play of the Weather,* and the famous *Four P's,* very probably of *The Pardoner and the Friar* and of *John John, Tib, and Sir John.* Of these the first two can hardly be called plays: they are merely dramatized debates. *The Play of the Weather* approaches real dramatic form since here a group of real people, a gentleman, a lady, a laundress, a little boy, and others, are brought before the throne of Jupiter by Merry Report, the jesting Vice, to beg for such weather as would best suit their manner of life. Naturally each wants something that would not suit the others, and at the end Jupiter tells the assembled suitors that the weather shall remain even as it was.

The Four P's is still more realistic; here is no Jupiter, nor type characters, but four figures from contemporary life, a Palmer, a Pardoner, a Poticary (apothecary or quack doctor), and a Pedlar, engaged in a trial of wit. The Palmer begins by boasting of his many pilgrimages and of the sanctity acquired thereby; the Pardoner retorts that this was labor lost since he, the Par- doner, could sell salvation much cheaper.

> Give me but a penny or twopence,
> And as soon as the soul departeth hence,
> In half an hour or three quarters at most,
> The soul is in heaven with the Holy Ghost.

The Poticary claims that he deserves more credit than either of his fellows, since he has dispatched even more souls to heaven by his drugs:

> Whom have ye known die honestly
> Without the help of the poticary.

The Pedlar suggests a lying match to settle which of the three is the best man. The Pardoner displays his relics: a jaw-bone of All-Hallows, the great toe of the Trinity, some of the drink served at the wedding of Adam and Eve whose special merit is that it makes a man thirst for more,

> After which drinking you shall be as meet
> To stand on your head as on your feet.

The exhibition of the relics runs to an accompaniment of foul-mouthed mockery by the others, and the Poticary takes up the tale: he has a drug which will insure a man against hanging (a quick poison) and another equally good for men and mangy dogs. When challenged to produce his greatest lie he says: the Palmer is an honest man. This starts more controversy, which the Pedlar stops by suggesting that each tell a tale; the teller of the greatest marvel shall be crowned the greatest liar. The Poticary narrates a wondrous cure he wrought on a young woman, unfortunately of such a nature that it cannot be retold. The Pardoner can tell a better; he has done greater ghostly than his rival's bodily cures. An old friend of his, Margery Corson, died suddenly without the help of the sacraments. He sought her in Purgatory without success and went to Hell to find her. The porter at Hell gate, a former acquaintance who used to play the Devil in the Coventry Miracles, secures a passport for him. Satan graciously grants the Pardoner his desire to free the woman; he finds her in the kitchen and leads her out amid the cheers of the devils:

> All the chains in hell did ring
> And all the souls therein did sing

for joy at her departure, for she had such a bitter tongue and temper that she made Hell hotter, even in the Devil's kitchen.

That's a strange tale, says the Palmer, and the strangest part of it is that women make so much trouble in Hell when they are so gentle on earth. For his part he has known 500,000 women and has never seen one lose her temper. His three hearers agree that this is the greatest and most incredible of lies, and the Pedlar awards the prize to the Palmer.

No brief analysis can do justice to *The Four P's*. There is, of course, no plot to be entangled and finally solved; it is more like modern vaudeville than drama. Yet it is not without indications of action on the stage, and shows some grasp of characterization. Its chief merit is its complete abandonment of allegory and its frank aim at entertainment:

> To pass the time in this without offence
> Was the cause why the maker did make it.

The merry play of *John John, Tib, and Sir John,* if it be Heywood's as seems probable, is an interesting example of his versatility. Adapting and improving a little French farce, *Pernet qui va au vin,* he presents the first example in English of the eternal triangle: here a henpecked husband, a shrewish wife, and her lover, the parish priest. It is a genuine little drama, full of action, packed with comic situation, lively dialogue, and recurrent appeals to the audience. It opens with John's threat to beat his wife and ends after a fist-fight between the three with his resolve to pursue her to the priest's house. There is no faint hint of any moral purpose; Heywood has freed comedy as completely from didacticism as from allegory. Yet after all the little play is hardly more than a dramatized anecdote; Heywood carried English comedy as far as it could go until it turned to classic models to learn the technique of complicated plot and varied characterization. With him we are come to the very threshold of Elizabethan drama

CHAPTER TWO

THE DRAMA IN TRANSITION:
NATIVE, CLASSICAL, AND ROMANTIC

ELIZABETH came to the throne in 1558, but it was long before the new drama appeared in its full splendor upon the public stage. In fact the first quarter of a century or so after the Queen's accession might be described as a period of transition in which certain new influences profoundly modified the old native drama, transformed it indeed into what may be called the Elizabethan drama proper. It is well, however, to recall the fact that the old dramatic forms, Miracle, Moral, and Interlude, lingered on throughout the century. Trained in a long dramatic tradition the Elizabethan audience was by no means ready or willing to abandon it for new courtly or academic forms. Elizabethan drama is a popular drama appealing to and finding its main support in a popular audience; and, as a result, many characteristics of the old native drama reappear in the work of the great Elizabethan playwrights.

Chief among these characteristics is the old realism, the attempt to tell in dramatic form a story, sacred or profane, in such a way as to bring its truth home to the audience. Titles like the "True History," the "True Tragedy," abound in Elizabethan drama; the flagrant anachronisms so frequent in Elizabethan plays, like Shakespeare's Romans talking of watches and pistols, are due to the playwright's unconscious and instinctive effort to bring the action up-to-date and thus impose a sense of truth upon the audience. The same cause may account for the often uncritical adherence of the Elizabethan playwright to his source. Here was, he felt, a true tale; it was his business to present it in dramatic form, not to reconstruct it in obedience to the demands of some ideal theory of dramatic art.

Along with this realism goes the insistence of the audience upon lively action on the stage. The Morals and Interludes of the sixteenth century tended more and more to discard long

expository and didactic speeches and to substitute entertaining
dialogue and action. And since a popular audience is more
easily entertained by comic than by serious matter, the result is
that serious Elizabethan drama, in sharp contrast to the classic,
is characterized by an almost constant insertion of comic scenes.
Elizabethan scholar-critics, disciples of the gospel of Aristotle,
screamed with rage at such breaches of decorum and demanded
'a clean-cut separation of tragedy from comedy. But the audience
was the master; it paid the fiddler and called the tune; and as
a result we have such scenes as those of the drunken Porter in
Macbeth and the quibbling Gravedigger in *Hamlet*. Had the
new drama been altogether new, as it was essentially in Italy
and France, these scenes would never have been written; but
Elizabethan drama, it cannot be too often repeated, is an out-
growth and continuance, however greatly modified, of the native
· and popular drama of the late Middle Ages.

The influence of the old tradition was, perhaps, more powerful upon comedy than on tragedy. Here following the technique
of the Interlude it tended to produce a series of lively humorous
scenes rather than complete and well-made plays. Until the
influence of the classic dramatists makes itself felt, the interest
of complicated plot is almost entirely lacking in early popular
comedy. The characters in these scenes are drawn almost exclusively from the lower classes, peasants, half-wits, common
soldiers, and old women. To these we must add, of course, the
comic characters of the Devil and the Vice. As late as 1625 Ben
Jonson recalls a conservative theatre-goer who lamented the
disappearance of these beloved figures from the popular stage:
"the Devil for my money," said Timothy Tattle; "I would fain
see the Devil." The fun consists in showing these characters in
absurd situations as when the Vice in *Cambises*, disguised as
a warrior with a pot for a helmet and a rake for a spear, is chased
off the stage by Meretrix, a common camp-follower. The humor
of early popular comedy was essentially physical, the humor of
fist-fights, kicks, pots of water, and worse, on unsuspecting heads.
The lasting appeal of this form of humor is shown by its appearance in later Elizabethan drama, even in the work of Shakespeare.

The language of this popular comedy in the period of the transition was, naturally, plain everyday English. There is a marked absence of the witty dialogue, the smart repartee, and the gay word-play so frequent in later Elizabethan comedy. On the contrary there is an over-plus of profanity and a "humor of filth," sinking at times to gross obscenity. The dialogue is for the most part composed in doggerel rhymed verse, as in the Miracles and Morals, and apart from the occasional and often charming songs there is nothing of the heightening effects of poetry. The note of romance, more especially of what we call the "love-interest," is notably absent.

Popular tragedy in this period of transition presents a curious blend of boisterous farce and serious action. So far as the audience took an interest in tragic themes, it demanded a realistic treatment. The few specimens of early popular tragedy that have come down to us might rather be called histories than tragedies proper. They fall into two classes: histories of private and of public life. Two plays of the late seventies, whose names alone are preserved: *Murderous Michael* and *The Cruelty of a Step-Mother*, probably represent a fairly numerous class, the dramatization of some startling incident, murder for choice, in contemporary life. Such plays were the direct ancestors of the Elizabethan Domestic Tragedy, of *Arden of Feversham, A Warning for Fair Women,* and *A Woman Killed with Kindness.*

The histories of public life strike the same note of realism. There is no immediate successor to Bale's *King John*; the English chronicle play seems hardly to have appeared on the boards before the middle eighties; it sprang into sudden life on the wave of patriotic enthusiasm that marked the years just before and after the Spanish Armada, 1588. But before this time there were popular plays dealing with legend and history very much in the style of the old Miracles and Morals. A group of plays, *Horestes*, 1567, *Cambises*, 1569, and *Appius and Virginia*, 1575,[1] show the drama turning from sacred to profane history for source material. The first of these is an almost incredible vulgarization of the most tragic theme of Greek drama, the matricide of Orestes. Not only is the serious action repeatedly interrupted by

[1] The dates are those of the first printed editions.

lively fisticuffs, but a couple of peasants are introduced talking vulgar dialect, and Clytemnestra and Egistheus sing an amorous duet. The whole story is presented in lively action: Orestes storms the walls of Mycenae—"make your battle lively," says a stage-direction, "and let it be long ere you can win the city"— defeats his father's murderer, and, quite properly from the English point of view, hangs him from one of the ladders used in the escalade—"fling him off the ladder and let Clytemnestra look where Egistheus hangeth." The Vice, masquerading as Courage and Revenge, plays a main part in both serious and comic scenes, and at the end Orestes is declared free from guilt and crowned King by Truth and Duty. Pikeryng, the author, knew his classic sources, but treated them exactly as the old writers of the Miracles did the Bible stories; he modernized them to make them real and intelligible to a popular audience.

A better known play of the same type is *Cambises*, "a lamentable tragedie, mixed full of pleasant mirth," which held the stage long enough for Shakespeare to see it and laugh at it through the mouth of Falstaff. Here the story of the wicked King of Persia is told in a series of scenes without the slightest dramatic connection. Cambises punishes a corrupt judge, shoots a child through the heart to prove his steady hand when accused of drunkenness, executes his brother on a false charge, murders his queen, and finally meets his own death by accident. This is the "lamentable tragedie"; the "pleasant mirth" consists of the usual scuffles on the stage and the pranks of the Vice, Ambidexter, who plays the role of mischief-maker. The striving after realism is shown in some amusing stage directions: "smite him in the neck with a sword to signify his death," "flay him with a false skin," "a little bladder of vinegar prickt" to represent the blood of a murdered man; and finally "enter the King without a gown, a sword thrust up into his side, bleeding" and after his last words "here let him quake and stir," *i.e.*, writhe in agony. Surely the audience must have gone home assured that they had seen a true presentation of an exciting old story.

Appius and Virginia is in a sense a forerunner of the later Domestic Tragedy. Virginius seems to be an English gentleman with a farm in the country and a pew in the parish church.

Domestic happiness is more strongly emphasized than the guilty passion of Appius, and the serious action is constantly interrupted by songs and scuffles between the very modern servants of this gentle family. The Vice, Haphazard, darts in and out to take part in comic scenes and to prompt Appius in his lustful pursuit of Virginia. At the end two allegorical figures, Justice and Reward, appear to punish the wicked ruler, who kills himself in prison. Characteristically realistic action is shown by the stage-direction when Virginius kills his daughter: "Here tie a hankercher about her eyes and then strike off her head." Since Virginius a little later presents the head to Appius, it would seem that the company which performed this play had a "property" head, such as belonged to Shakespeare's company and was exhibited by them on every possible occasion, notably at the close of *Macbeth*.

Enough has been said to show how strong was the influence of the old native tradition upon popular drama, comedy and tragedy alike, in this period of transition; the realism, the didacticism, the allegorical characters, the Vice, and the intermingling of "lamentable tragedie" and "pleasant mirth" are all inherited from native medieval drama.

At the very opposite pole to the popular drama there appeared in this time of transition another dramatic type closely modelled upon classic patterns. This drama, written for academic and courtly audiences, was a product of the New Learning. Renaissance Humanism was not merely a revival of classical studies; it involved the acceptance of classic characters and classic authors as models of life and literature. A Roman cardinal renounced the reading of the Latin Bible, the Vulgate, lest its barbarisms should mar his Ciceronian style. Henry of Navarre congratulated his young wife on her discovery of Plutarch; "to love him is to love me . . . he has been as my conscience and has whispered to me many maxims for my conduct." The New Learning took firm root in English schools and colleges; the plays of Plautus and Terence became a regular part of the curriculum and were often performed by schoolboys. From that it was but a step to the composition and performance by teachers and students of English plays in imitation of the classics. The first "regular" English comedy, *i.e.*, a play composed according to the accepted classic rules, is *Ralph Roister Doister* written by a schoolmaster, Nicholas Udall, apparently about 1553–54 for performance by his students. Here is a real play, far removed from the simple farce interlude of Heywood, with complicated plot and a satisfactory solution. It is divided according to classical precept into the regulation five acts and is written in smoothly flowing rhymed couplets, remarkably free from the obscenity which marks and mars so many of the popular plays. The central figure, Ralph Roister Doister, is an English version of the Latin *miles gloriosus*; his companion, Matthew Merrygreek, is a combination of the classic parasite and the mischief-making Vice of popular tradition. The pattern is classic, but the setting and sentiment are wholly English; the courtesan of Latin comedy is replaced by a virtuous English widow, mistress of a household of lively English maids, and her accepted suitor is a London merchant, master of a trading ship.

Another English comedy, *Gammer Gurton's Needle*, probably written by William Stevenson, a Cambridge scholar, about 1559–60, for performance at Christ's College, is an even more striking example of the combination of the classic pattern and the native setting. The scene is laid in an English village; the characters are village types: two scolding women; Hodge, a stupid, cowardly boor; the parish curate, Dr. Rat; Diccon, the Bedlam, a wandering beggar discharged from Bethlehem Hospital for the insane,—*cf.* Edgar's assumed role in *King Lear*— and the village Bailiff. The theme is the loss of Gammer Gurton's one and highly valued needle and the trouble in which this loss involves the community—an interesting picture of an age when needles were not to be procured at the next five-and-dime store. The dialogue, much of it in conventional rustic dialect, is more realistic, often much coarser than that of *Roister Doister*. On the other hand the author has followed the classic pattern quite as closely as Udall. He divides the play into five acts and starts a new scene with every fresh entrance of a character upon the stage. More important still, he devises a skilfully planned and well-tangled plot—it is amazing and amusing to see how much he has made of the simple loss of a needle—and he has created a character, Diccon, whose sheer love of mischief is the prime cause of all the complications. Diccon himself is a descendant of the Vice of the Morals, but he has thrown off all the allegorical features of the Vice and has become a real and recognizable English character. His function in the play resembles that of the intriguing slave of Latin comedy. He starts the complications and provides the solution when his blow on Hodge's buttocks discloses the whereabouts of the long-lost needle. There has been nothing like this in English before, and it could never have been written except by an admiring student, though no slavish imitator, of classical comedy.

Even such academic comedies as these retain much of the native tradition of realistic action, contemporary setting, and lively fun. Perhaps the most important gift of classic comedy to English drama is a sense of the significance of the plot. Aided as this was by the five-act convention it enabled the playwright to plan and carry out a definite action with beginning, middle, and end, with complication and solution. One has only to compare the rambling incoherent structure of most of the Morals, or even the plotless nature of such a farce as *The Four P's*, with the work of Udall and Stevenson, to see English comedy working upward to the heights it later attained in the plays of Shakespeare and Ben Jonson.

As English comedy advances, moreover, a fresh gift of the classics becomes apparent. This is the addition to the drama of a number of stock figures drawn from Latin comedy: the worldly-wise and anxious father, the roistering son, the wily servant, the braggart, and the pedant. Commonplace as these may seem to us, they were a real enrichment of English drama, where the Devil and the Vice, plus a pair or two of rustics, had long been almost the sole representatives of the comic spirit.

To the imitation of the classics we may attribute also that sense of style in speech which marks the advance of English comedy. Little by little it replaces the doggerel meters of the native drama with flowing couplets and, somewhat later, polished prose. Gross obscenity gives place to sparkling word-play and witty repartee. Terence, a master of refined dialogue, taught his admiring students that a laugh could be gained otherwise than by a foul jest. Not that the new comedy ever became mealy-mouthed—Shakespeare himself did not disdain a broad joke—but the foul odor which emanates even from Heywood's work is happily absent in the best Elizabethan comedies. That this was a slow process is due to the fact that such adaptations of Latin comedy as those of Udall and Stevenson were written for academic audiences. It was not until the time of Lyly and his followers in the eighties that the new comedy came upon the public stage; it took the best part of this period of transition for the influence of Latin comedy to transform so completely as in the end it did this feature of the old native tradition.

In tragedy the effect of the New Learning upon English drama was at first rather different. In comedy the native tradition was strong enough to assimilate for its own good the influence of the classics. In tragedy, on the other hand, there was little or nothing of such a tradition. A wide gulf, moreover, separated popular practice from the classical theory of tragedy. The first presented action as realistically as possible; the second pushed action to a great extent off the stage and reported in the long narrations of the Nuntius what could not easily be represented. Popular practice enlivened a tragic theme with interpolations of "comical mirth"; classical theory rigidly excluded comic scenes and characters from the tragic stage. Popular tragedy presented homely English scenes as in the murder plays, or brought distant scenes and characters home to the audience by giving them a familiar English dress. Classical tragedy, on the contrary, chose its themes by preference from the remote legendary or mythological past and threw about them an atmosphere unrealistic and imaginative. The ideal of the classics was, to quote a phrase of Kyd's,

> Tragœdia cothurnata, fitting kings,
> Containing matter and not common things.

Where such differences existed, there was little chance of an early and direct influence of the classic model upon popular practice. There was, to be sure, an English imitation of classical tragedy, but from the first translation of Seneca in 1559 to *The Misfortunes of Arthur* in 1587 it remained in academic isolation.

This academic tragedy is often spoken of as Senecan and there is good reason for this, since the Latin tragedian Seneca was at once the inspiration and the model of Renaissance tragedy. This was due not only to the Renaissance mastery of Latin and comparative ignorance of the Greek tragedians, but also to the fact that much in the tone and temper of Seneca, his sensationalism, his didacticism, and his stress upon the tragedy of the individual, appealed with special force to the age of the Renaissance. It is an open question whether the plays that pass under the name of Seneca were ever acted on the Roman stage; it seems more likely that they were composed for recitation to a private audence. Yet the men of the Renaissance took it for granted that they were stage-plays and strained their powers to rival them. A crop of Senecan imitations broke out in Italy and France where they founded lasting schools. In England they failed to supplant the native tradition; yet they exerted, none the less, a profound influence on the development of English tragedy.

A brief review of certain Senecan characteristics may be of service. In the first place the themes which Seneca selects from Greek legend are highly sensational; they deal with murder and revenge, with adultery and incest. Such themes, especially when attached to characters of high estate, were, according to Renaissance conceptions, the proper and peculiar topics of tragedy. Seneca's Ghosts and Furies found a ready response in the minds of that superstitious and wonder-loving age. Yet Seneca's main interest is less in the sensational action than in the passions and sentiments of his characters, in their emotional response to the events in which they are involved. Crude as much of his work seems to us, Seneca is a pioneer in the field of psychological drama. His heroes indulge in long self-revelatory soliloquies and take part in the epigrammatic speech-and-reply in alternating lines which goes under the name of *stichomythia,* a feature of his style eagerly imitated by his followers. Seneca's poetic style seems today artificial, sophisticated, sometimes bombastic, often too heavily didactic. Yet such characteristics rather pleased than offended Renaissance readers, who loved language for its own sake, and rejoiced in the Latin brevity and point of Seneca's epigrams and moral maxims. Sidney could find no higher praise for a contemporary drama than to say that it climbed "to the height of Seneca his style." Seneca's insistent and undramatic moralizing was readily accepted by an age which believed, to quote George Chapman, that "elegant and sententious excitation to virtue and deflection from her contrary" were "the soul, limbs, and limits of an autentical tragedy." Finally Seneca's technique of construction is simple and regular, and so the easier to imitate. His plays fall easily into the orthodox five acts; he begins the action near the crisis or catastrophe and so escapes the difficulty of a complicated plot. There is little action on the stage; much that is necessary to the play is merely reported in high-flown epic strain by the Nuntius.

Seneca's contribution to English tragedy as seen in the work of his early imitators and to a less extent in later Elizabethan drama may be briefly summarized. In the first place he offered a pattern of construction, the regulation five-act division with comparatively little action upon the stage. Along with this goes naturally his messenger to report off-stage action, as the wounded soldier does in *Macbeth,* and the Nuntius in Chapman's *Bussy.* His Chorus moralizing upon the action and predicting its outcome takes the place of the Presenter in medieval drama, and carries over into Elizabethan plays, as, for example, in *Romeo and Juliet.* Elizabethan tragedy takes over certain typical Senecan characters, notably the Ghost, to start the action by crying for revenge, a figure which appears in *The Spanish Tragedy* and in *Hamlet.* Another stock Senecan figure is the confidant, a friend or nurse, to whom the protagonist may unbosom his or her thoughts, emotions, and purposes; Hamlet's Horatio and Juliet's Nurse derive from Seneca. Seneca's preference for startling and sensational themes authorized, if it did not originate, the Elizabethan delight in bloody action. The disciples of Seneca followed his practice in concentrating on such themes and banishing the comic interludes of native drama. This was a feature that they were unable to transfer to later tragedy; the old tradition of mingled tragedy and farce was too strong for them. They did succeed, however, in establishing a convention characteristic of Seneca, though not universal in his Greek masters, that a tragedy should terminate in death, conventionally the death of the hero attended by as many other deaths as possible. They set themselves to reproduce in English certain characteristic features of Seneca's style, the resounding declamatory soliloquy, the sententious epigrammatic dialogue, the dominant didactic note. Finally and most important, perhaps, the English Senecans attempted, at first with small success, to shift the interest from outer to inner conflict, from battles and murders to the emotions and passions of the mind. In so doing they paved the way for the "soul-tragedies" of Shakespeare.

A trio of early plays represents this academic Senecan school. The first of these is *Gorboduc, or Ferrex and Porrex,* 1561–62, the work of Norton and Sackville, two young members of the Inner Temple, one of the great London law-schools. Produced at the Christmas feast in the great Hall of the Inner Temple it met with such success that it was promptly repeated in a demand performance before the Queen. Dull as it seems to the modern reader, its importance in the development of English tragedy can hardly be overestimated.

In the first place the authors, though good Senecans, were yet independent enough to abandon Seneca's classic themes and take as their subject a story from legendary British history. It is that of old King Gorboduc, who divided his kingdom in his lifetime between his sons, Ferrex and Porrex. Civil war followed, and Ferrex, the elder, was slain in battle by his brother; the Queen in revenge murdered Porrex; the people revolted and killed both King and Queen. The nobles then suppressed the revolt; but the kingdom was left desolate without an heir and open to the threat of foreign invasion. Here one would imagine was opportunity for plenty of action; yet not a thing happens upon the stage but talk, interminable speeches in council and long reports of action off-stage. The theme is treated in true Senecan fashion: it falls into five acts, each preceded by an allegorical dumb-show and followed by a chorus of "ancient men of Britain" to comment on the action. The elaborate dumb-shows, later a frequent feature in Elizabethan drama, were borrowed from Italian pageants; the chorus is strictly Senecan, as are the Nuntius who reports the death of Ferrex, and the lady who laments the murder of his brother. Most important of all for the future of English drama, this play is composed in blank verse, a metre which some years before Surrey had introduced into English as a fit medium for the translation of Virgil. Sackville, a poet of real genius, no doubt recognized the superior merit of this form over the rhymed doggerel of the popular drama in lifting tragedy to Senecan heights. From the time of *Gorboduc* blank verse became the customary form for Senecan tragedy, after Kyd and Marlowe, for the true Elizabethan.

The success of *Gorboduc* in courtly and academic circles was immense. It was promptly printed and reprinted and set the fashion for a series of such plays. Encouraged by the success of *Gorboduc* Robert Wilmot and four other young gentlemen of the Inner Temple composed another Senecan play performed before the Queen in 1566. This was *Gismonde of Salerne,* based upon a tragic Italian love-story told by Boccaccio. Gismonde, the widowed daughter of Tancred, Prince of Salerne, takes against her father's will a lover; Tancred discovers the amour, puts the lover to death, and sends his heart in a golden cup to Gismonde who thereupon takes poison; smitten with remorse Tancred kills himself. Here is a thoroughly romantic theme, but the Senecan influence was still strong in the Inner Temple, and the play is cast in the strict Senecan mould. We have the five acts, a moralizing chorus of men of Salerne, mythological figures, Cupid to start the action and the Fury, Megæra, to rouse Tancred to revenge, along with a plethora of speech-making and almost no action, though to be sure Gismonde does drink the poison and die upon the stage. Still in the bonds of didacticism the authors treat the story as a text for a sermon against unlawful love; the play ends with a compliment—perhaps too flattering—to the Queen's maids of honor, virtuous and chaste. It is written in rhymed couplets, but many years later, 1591, Wilmot revised and published it as *Tancred and Gismunda* in the blank verse which Marlowe had by that time established on the public stage.

Academic Senecan tragedy culminates in *The Misfortunes of Arthur,* 1588, a play composed by Thomas Hughes and his fellows at Gray's Inn and presented before Elizabeth with elaborate dumb-shows devised by Francis Bacon and other members of Gray's. Following the example of *Gorboduc* Hughes selects a theme from British legend, the death of King Arthur. But his Arthur is far removed from Tennyson's blameless King; guilty of incest with his sister, he falls by the hand of their son, Mordred, who rebels against his father, seduces his queen, Guinevere, and dies in battle under his father's sword. The theme resembles some features of the story of Œdipus as dramatized by Seneca, and the play itself is pure Senecan in form and, interestingly enough, in diction; many of its lines are nothing but translations from Seneca, selected from one or another of his plays and ingeniously combined into a Senecan mosaic held together by a thin plaster of Hughes. The play opens with the ghost of Gorlois, the victim of Arthur's father, crying for revenge upon the cursed house of Pendragon; it is equipped with a chorus, the Nuntius to report action, and three confidants to draw out the emotions of the three chief characters, Arthur, Mordred, and Guinevere. It seems strange that so completely artificial a play should have been composed and presented after the revolution wrought by Kyd and Marlowe; but we must remember that this was written for a courtly audience, where the ideals of the New Learning and the worship of Seneca still lingered.

There are other plays of this school, some few preserved, many no doubt lost. Throughout its career it was strictly an academic and courtly form of drama; there is no record whatever of a performance of a play of this school to a popular audience at a public theatre. The influence of Seneca upon Elizabethan tragedy was immense, but it was transmitted to the drama of the people by poet-playwrights who had studied Seneca at school. Straight Senecan drama in English had but a brief temporary period.

Another influence, wholly distinct from the classical but quite as important in its transforming effect upon the native drama, also made itself felt in the period of transition. This may best be described as the quest for romance. In choice of theme, method of treatment, and manner of expression, it differs alike from the native tradition and the classic convention. Where the native was homely and realistic, the romantic influence led the playwright to distant, mysterious, and charming times and lands, to Cathay and to Arcady. Where the classical influence was largely formal, the romantic was essentially one of tone and temper. Seeking above all to touch and kindle the imagination it employs to this end all the devices of medieval romance: knight-errantry, distressed damsels, unhappy lovers, magicians, and strange transformations. To these it adds supernatural elements from popular superstition, witches, fairies, and wandering ghosts. The ghost, to be sure, appears in Senecan tragedy, but there is a vast difference between the ghost of Tantalus in the *Thyestes* and the "perturbed spirit" of Shakespeare's *Hamlet*. The first is a conventional piece of dramatic machinery; Shakespeare's Ghost wafts across the stage a chill breath from another world than ours.

The underlying cause of this romantic impulse was a transformation of English life in the sixteenth century from a medieval to a Renaissance civilization. There was an immense widening and enrichment of the life of man here and now upon this earth. Instead of longing for Jerusalem the Golden, man turned his eyes to the newly discovered lands across the Atlantic. English adventurers fought to share the treasures of the Indies with the power of Spain; while English commerce pushed into strange seas and brought home spoils from every quarter. Along with this material enrichment went a great intellectual advance due in the first place to the invention of printing; poems, histories, and romantic tales that had once been in the possession of the favored few in rare manuscripts were translated, published, and spread abroad. For those who could not read, the theatre became what the old liturgical drama had once been, a vehicle for the transmission of strange and wonderful story.

The quest for the strange, the beautiful, and the romantic found an increasing fit and lovely expression in the lyric-dramatic poetry that is the peculiar glory of Elizabethan drama. The native drama, to be sure, was not without its songs, but these were for the most part simple ballad snatches intercalated in the action; the dialogue still clung to the old doggerel of the medieval drama. The sixteenth century, however, saw an almost complete transformation of English poetry; new forms, the sonnet and blank verse, came in with the courtly poets in Henry VIII's reign; new motives, especially Petrarchan love-longing, crept into English poetry; old tales were retold in new measures and with a new desire for beauty of expression. It is not at once, to be sure, that this new poetry conquers the field of the drama; in fact it is not until the amazing outburst which follows the appearance of Spenser's *Shepheardes Calendar*, 1579, that the transformation of the drama into the "full-mouthed utterance of the early gods" is quite complete.

The sources tapped by this romantic impulse were varied and manifold. They may be summed up in a statement in a contemporary polemic against the new drama, Gosson's *Plays Confuted*, 1580: "the *Palace of Pleasure*, the *Golden Ass*, the *Æthiopian History*, *Amadis of France*, the *Round Table*, bawdy comedies in Latin, French, Italian, and Spanish, have been thoroughly ransacked to furnish the playhouses in London." To these we should add for completeness, Chaucer, whose works were drawn on again and again by Elizabethan dramatists. Gosson's list will repay examination: The *Golden Ass* of Apuleius and the *Æthiopica* of Heliodorus are the most romantic bequests of Graeco-Roman culture to modern times; *Amadis* and the *Round Table, i.e.,* Malory's *Morte D'Arthur,* are treasuries of chivalric romance; the *Palace of Pleasure* is Painter's anthology of Italian tales of passionate love and death; the "bawdy comedies" of Gosson's angry phrase are the countless plays in the Romance languages that were translated, imitated, and adapted for the Elizabethan stage.

It is well-nigh impossible to define precisely and separately the effect of the romantic impulse upon tragedy and comedy in the period of transition, partly because of the few examples out of the great number of plays produced that have come down to us—of sixty plays at Court between 1570 and 1585 only the titles are preserved; even more because the writers of these plays made no sharp distinction between these forms, but were inclined to blend them in what a playwright of the time called "tragical comedy." In other words they chose for the most part a serious, or even a tragic theme, handled it in such a fashion as to provide a happy ending, and lightened it with farcical action often provided by the Vice taken over from the native tradition.

An interesting example of this method is seen in the early *Calisto and Melibea,* printed by Rastell about 1530. A dramatization of the famous Spanish dramatic novel *Celestina,* it is the first attempt in English to present upon the stage a story of passionate and guilty love. Yet it is characteristic of the uncertainty and hesitation of the time that the author altogether eliminates the tragedy of the original and substitutes for it "a moral conclusion and exhortation to virtue"—to quote the words of the rambling title—wherein the lady is saved at once from lawless love and from a tragic fate; in spite of his choice of theme the author was still bound by the chains of didacticism. Something of the same reluctance to yield fully to the romantic impulse is seen much later in *Gismonde of Salerne.* It remained for Shakespeare to create a perfect sympathy with his star-crossed pair in *Romeo and Juliet.*

Plays based on medieval romance seem to have been especially popular at Court in the 1570's, but only their titles—*The Knight of the Burning Bush, The Solitary Knight,* and such like—remain. A good example of this dramatized romance is *Sir Clyomon and Clamydes,* printed as late as 1599, but probably written some thirty years earlier. This absurd play tells at tedious length the adventures of two young princes, the White Knight and the Knight of the Golden Shield. They traverse unknown lands, the Forest of Strange Marvels and the Isle of Strange Marshes; they appear at the court of Alexander the Great, who seems rather out of place in this medieval medley; they encounter flying serpents and wily magicians; they love two princesses whom in the end they marry after one of the ladies has followed her lover in the guise of a page. All this is pure romantic stuff, but the author has not been able to shake himself free from native tradition. He introduces the allegoric figures of Rumor and Providence, and as a concession to popular taste the Vice, Subtle Shift, to provide farce-comedy. It was plays like this and others of the same type, *Common Conditions,* 1576, and *The Rare Triumphs of Love and Fortune,* played in 1582 before the Queen, that provoked the indignant rebuke of Sidney for their indecorous blending of comic and serious matter—"horn-pipes and funerals," says Sidney—and their utter disregard of the unities of time and place. Later they became the butt of ridicule in such artistic, not to say sophisticated, plays as *The Old Wives' Tale, ca.* 1591, and *The Knight of the Burning Pestle, ca.* 1607. The Elizabethan audience had been well trained in the intervening years.

The best example in this period of a play drawn from the "bawdy comedies" of Italy is *The Supposes.* The author, George Gascoigne, was a typical Elizabethan, scholar, soldier, courtier, and man of letters, poet, satirist, and playwright. A student at Gray's Inn, he produced, probably for the Christmas festival in 1566, a translation of *I Suppositi* (*The Substitutes*), a comedy by the Italian poet, Ariosto. Ariosto's play, which has been called the first modern comedy in the vernacular, was, like most Italian comedies of the Renaissance, modelled upon Plautus and Terence, but it was much more than a pale imitation of Latin comedy. It complicated the action, set the scene in contemporary Italy, eliminated the classic figures of the slave, the harlot, and the pander, and built up a plot upon the theme of a true, if furtive, love-affair. Also, departing from the convention of his day, Ariosto discarded verse—though he later rewrote the play in metre—and composed his dialogue in vigorous idiomatic prose. Gascoigne followed Ariosto's example, and substituted for the doggerel verse of contemporary English comedy an easy, rapid and sparkling prose.

The Supposes is the first example in English of prose comedy, and its success paved the way for the prose of Lyly, Greene, and Shakespeare. For *The Supposes* was a remarkably successful play; it was thrice reprinted, and restaged at the University of Oxford in 1582. The reason for this success is plain; the play was something quite new on the English stage. It told an entertaining story of true love, crossed and thwarted, but crowned at last by marriage; it complicated the action with the old classic devices of mistaken identity, surprise, and reversal in a way unknown before in English comedy; it eliminated low farce and obscenity—*The Supposes* is a remarkably clean play—and set the scene in the romantic Italy so dear to the hearts of Elizabethan Englishmen. One might almost venture a guess that Gascoigne's play set the fashion of that localization of action in Italy prevalent in English romantic comedy down to the time when Ben Jonson's desire for realism led him to shift the scene of his revised *Every Man In His Humour* from Italy to London. An additional proof of the influence of *The Supposes* upon later drama is seen in the fact that the unknown author of *The Taming of a Shrew, ca.* 1589, lifted its story to serve as the sub-plot of his play, and that Shakespeare went back to *The Supposes* for additional details when he transformed the earlier work into his gayest farce-comedy, *The Taming of the Shrew.*

Gascoigne's play like its Italian original is an interesting blend of the classic with the romantic. This is especially true in the choice of theme, a tale of true love. Popular comedy had avoided this motive almost as if it were taboo; classical comedy was inclined to treat it with a certain Latin cynicism. The difference between *Calisto* and *The Supposes* is a sign of the growing freedom of English comedy and its readiness to treat the theme of love as a source of mirth and as a thing of beauty. There is, to be sure, little of beauty in *The Supposes*. It lacks the charm of poetry; that was still to come. English comedy had to wait until Spenser taught the poet-playwrights to sing.

The infusion of classic and romantic elements represents what was going on in English drama during this period of the transition. The old popular drama still held the stage, but it was being re-shaped, and enriched, by these new influences, the classic mainly for form, the romantic for tone and temper. All that was needed was a group of young poets to fling themselves upon the old drama and transform it into the new and true Elizabethan. In the fifteen-eighties such a group arrived in London, and found ready for them actors, theatres, and audiences which had grown up with the transitional drama.

CHAPTER THREE

ACTORS AND THEATRES

MEDIEVAL drama was essentially an amateur affair presented first by the clergy and later by trade guilds. Elizabethan drama, while it retained its amateur standing in academic performances at schools and colleges and Inns of Court, and in the participation of lords and ladies in masques and entertainments, was, in its public aspects, almost wholly professional. In Chaucer's time, while large sums of money were spent on pageant performances and one craft vied with another in sumptuous expenditure, there was no direct charge to the audience for witnessing the performance. Actors, it is true, were paid for their exertions, but the performer was really a fisherman or a butcher, a tailor or a goldsmith, not a professional entertainer. By Shakespeare's time, audiences paid to witness plays in public theatres which earned ample incomes for managers and share-holders, and the business and art of acting had become a profession providing an adequate livelihood. Moreover, since during the transitional period plays changed as well as the theatrical conditions under which they were produced, the methods of staging and presentation also underwent a transformation. Any study of Elizabethan drama which did not take into account the circumstances under which its plays were presented would be not only misleading but fruitless. If we must guard against divorcing plays from the theatre, we must be equally wary not to interpret the work of the great Elizabethan playwrights in the light of our acquaintance with the modern drama or our knowledge of the circumstances under which plays are now presented on Broadway.

The transition from amateur to professional may most easily be marked by considering the rise of the professional actor. It has already been noted that local players of Miracles, as in the case of the late *Ludus Coventriae,* sometimes presented their cycle away from home and became thereby an embryonic stock-company, amateur but paid for their services. When it grew apparent to them that there was a conflict between their acting and their local trade duties, that it was possible to earn a living wage and in a new and uncrowded activity, the step to professionalism was easy. Moreover, once a general interest had been aroused in the drama and the presentation of plays became profitable, the ever-present minstrels, mountebanks, and acrobats were quick to turn from juggling, jesting, and gymnastics to acting. Rivalry between amateur and paid entertainers or combinations for mutual assistance stimulated the process of professionalism. We have seen that *The Castle of Perseverance, ca.* 1450, was carried from place to place by a troupe of travelling players who drummed up trade by announcing performances a week in advance. A little later the actors of *Mankind* felt no compunction in interrupting their play to pass the hat, and professional comedians were assisting in the banquet-interlude, *Fulgens and Lucres, ca.* 1497.

This development of acting nevertheless exposed the early groups of players to a new danger, as is shown by an Act of 1545. Since the strollers had deserted their regular trades and were no longer members of craft guilds, they were listed as vagabonds and masterless men and hence were subject to arrest and imprisonment. The more fortunate escaped this precarious position by putting themselves like the minstrels under the patronage of important personages, which made them automatically "servants" and freed them from the stigma and the perils of vagabondage. This process was accelerated by later statutes of 1572 and 1596. It had begun a century earlier, for we hear of companies protected by the Earl of Essex, and Richard, Duke of Gloucester, later Richard III, in 1482; and the earls of Northumberland, Oxford, Derby, Shrewsbury, and Lord Arundel had actors in their service before the fifteenth century closed. Henry VI had "pleyars of the Kyngs enterluds" at his Court as early as 1494 and paid them an annual wage, and similar royal patronage was granted by his successors as late as the reign of Elizabeth.

Since the connection between patron and company was partly nominal, it was natural that the acting groups when they were not on duty as members of a household should eke out their income by travelling. In 1559 Robert Dudley, later the Earl of Leicester, wrote a fellow-nobleman requesting his friend's license for "my servants" to play in Yorkshire, and fifteen years later he secured from the Queen permission for them to act in London and elsewhere, despite local rules to the contrary, so long as their plays met the approval of the Master of the Revels. Other noblemen who had companies followed suit, so that by the end of the century there were always two or three groups playing in London and a number of less distinguished companies touring through the country. They presented their plays in great halls and banquet chambers, on village greens, and, most important of all, in inn-yards.

The inn-yard had proved from early times a most satisfactory place for the presentation of plays. The restrictions of a room were absent; there was no chance for the audience to scatter when it came time to levy contributions. It is interesting, for example, that *Mankind,* which includes in its dialogue directions for gathering money, had its stage set in the courtyard of an inn. It is hardly necessary to point out that since the inn was a center of social life as well as a haven for travellers, it made its own contribution to the audience and the festive atmosphere of the theatre. As time went on, certain inns—in London, the Bell, the Cross Keys, the Bull, the Bel Savage, and the Boar's Head (not, however, Falstaff's Boar's Head in Eastcheap)—were specifically dedicated to dramatic purposes, partially reconstructed, and even, somewhat misleadingly, referred to as theatres. Three were destroyed in the London fire of 1666, but in 1668 Samuel Pepys visited the Bull, and the Boar's Head Yard may still be reviewed by the curious in Whitechapel.

Those Elizabethan inns in which actors' companies presented plays were usually made up of a collection of buildings grouped around a hollow square, which formed the court-yard, entered from the street by a single archway. Inside around the yard ran a series of galleries opening on the adjacent rooms of the inn. Opposite the entrance the players set up a scaffold projecting from the building into the yard, and backed by a curtain hung from the gallery immediately over it, which could be utilized for balcony scenes or the walls of a beleaguered city. Behind the curtain was "behind-the-scenes"; in other words, actors came on stage through the curtains from their dressing and property room in the inn. At the entering archway stood a "gatherer" who collected the admission fee, usually a penny, to the flagged quadrangle where the "groundlings" stood. No doubt other "gatherers" within the court pointed out the advantage of paying further pennies for particularly desirable positions. Members of the audience who had the money for more commodious arrangements hired rooms in the inn and sat on benches or stools in the galleries, whence they could look down on groundlings and the stage. The Elizabethan theatre was anything but aristocratic. Class distinctions were certainly important, but all classes were there from nobles and sober citizens and their wives to prentices, pickpockets, and harlots; and the wide scope and variety of Elizabethan drama is mainly due to the heterogeneity of the enthusiastic playgoers at these professional performances in innyard or theatre.

In 1575 London had no regular theatres, that is, no buildings designed and constructed primarily for the presentation of plays. Nothing shows more clearly the growth of the professional drama than the fact that eight playhouses rose within the next thirty years, some of them so large and handsome as to evoke the unqualified admiration of travellers from the Continent. The first was built by James Burbage for his fellow actors of Leicester's company in 1576, and was called simply the Theatre; the site chosen was in Shoreditch, outside the city limits to the north, advantageous because of its proximity to the public playground, Finsbury Fields, yet not within the jurisdiction of the Common Council. The city officials from the beginning, unlike the Queen and her court, were chary of public play-acting, partly on moral grounds, more definitely for fear of three menaces: fire, sedition, and the plague. These were no idle fears. Fire was a constant danger to old London, which was at last almost wiped out by the great fire of 1666. The two largest theatres, the Globe and the Fortune, were burnt to the ground in 1613 and 1621. Plague was endemic in London; the deaths from this source averaged forty to fifty a week. When they rose above this number, the theatres were closed until it seemed safe to reopen them. The disorderly groundlings sometimes stormed the stage or indulged in rioting among themselves. One theatre, the Phœnix, was almost destroyed by rioting apprentices in 1617. The Curtain, so called from the estate on which it was erected close to the Theatre, was built in 1577. Soon after another structure was opened at Newington Butts, marking a shift of locality to the south of the Thames; but this was never a popular theatre, since it was an uncomfortable mile beyond the river. The Rose, built in 1587 by Philip Henslowe, who became the most important theatrical proprietor of the age; the Swan, 1595, of whose stage we have a somewhat puzzling picture; and the Globe, erected in 1599 from the timbers of the demolished Theatre by the sons of James Burbage, Cuthbert and the famous actor, Richard, with five members of their company—Shakespeare among them —as share-holders, were all situated on the south side of the Thames in the district known as the Bankside, also beyond city jurisdiction. Later public theatres were the Fortune, 1600, and the Red Bull, *ca.* 1605, north of the city limits, and the Hope, 1613, once more on the Bankside.

Besides the public theatres, there were so-called private theatres, a somewhat misleading designation since they housed professional actors and were open to the public. The term was apparently chosen mainly to appease the London authorities, for some of these theatres, unlike the public ones, were within the city limits. Moreover, the distinction attached to the word "private" no doubt attracted a more select and higher paying clientele. Used first by children, they came to serve as winter quarters for adult actors. In 1596, for example, James Burbage purchased certain rooms in a building in Blackfriars, once the property of the Dominican monks, and made them over into a theatre. The Privy Council promptly forbade the public use of Blackfriars, but, after the death of James, Richard Burbage leased it to the manager of the Children of the Chapel. It was not until 1608 that Burbage's company was able to use it as a winter home. Other important indoor theatres were in a building near St. Paul's Cathedral, another at Whitefriars, the Cockpit or Phœnix in Drury Lane, and the Salisbury Court Playhouse; all but the first were west of the city walls and north of the Thames.

The companies who played in the Elizabethan theatres are too many and various to discuss in detail, but it will be useful to sketch briefly the development and organization of two of them, and the names of the Burbages and Henslowe suggest the delimitation. With the Burbages we naturally associate Shakespeare; with Henslowe, Christopher Marlowe and a large group of later playwrights. The company of which Shakespeare was a member bore various names at different times as the patron, his rank, or his office changed. It may have begun as the Earl of Leicester's Men; after his death in 1588 its principal actors joined a group under the patronage of Lord Strange and for a time acted at Henslowe's theatre, the Rose. In 1593 Lord Strange became the Earl of Derby, and for a short time the company took over the new title, but he died the next year, and another patron had to be found. This was Elizabeth's cousin, the Lord Chamberlain, Henry Carey, and it is as the Lord Chamberlain's Company that until 1603 it is best known, for though Carey died in 1596, his son, Lord Hunsdon, shortly succeeded to his office. In 1603 the theatrical companies came under the direct patronage of the royal family, and the Lord Chamberlain's Men became the King's Majesty's Servants, a title which they retained until the closing of the theatres in 1642. The principal playwrights associated with this company were Shakespeare, Jonson, Beaumont and Fletcher, Massinger, and Davenant; its best known actor was Richard Burbage, who interpreted the principal roles in Shakespeare's plays, both comedies and tragedies.

The other major group was that controlled by Philip Henslowe, in association with his son-in-law, Edward Alleyn, who rivalled Burbage as the star of the day. Besides the Rose, built and leased out by Henslowe, they controlled the Fortune and the Hope, and managed the companies under the patronage of the Lord Admiral and the Earl of Worcester; these became respectively after 1603 Prince Henry's and Queen Anne's Men. Alleyn played the principal characters in Marlowe's tragedies, and later dramatists associated with Henslowe's companies included Chapman, Dekker, Middleton, and Thomas Heywood. Much of our knowledge of Elizabethan theatrical conditions derives from the valuable records kept by Philip Henslowe.

The Elizabethan theatrical company, especially such a group as the Lord Chamberlain's, was co-operative, self-governing, and self-perpetuating. It consisted of a certain number of full members who owned shares and divided profits, and leased, or, as in the case of the Globe, built a theatre; hired men paid a fixed salary to play minor parts; and apprentices, notably the boys who played all the female roles on the Elizabethan stage—there were no professional actresses until Restoration times—trained in the routine, as they would be in trade, by their individual masters, who hired them out to the company. The important members of the company played more or less definite "lines." Burbage, as a star, interpreted, we know, such roles as Richard III and the title-parts of Shakespeare's great tragedies; Shakespeare, as an actor, we principally associate with old men or kingly parts; Will Kemp and Armin were comedians. Playwrights were, as a rule, much more definitely associated with particular companies than is the case today. Plays were written for a particular troupe and frequently at their direction. A playwright often read the first acts of a projected play to the leading members of a company at a supper after their afternoon performance. He would listen to their criticism, accept suggestions, and promise to complete his work at a certain date. Surviving manuscripts show that plays were often revised in or after production. All in all, the major adult companies were strong organizations, which so long as they submitted to the rigorous restrictions by which the Master of the Revels forbade plays meddling with matters of Church and State, were free to produce what they pleased as they pleased.

With the children's companies who presented plays at Paul's or Blackfriars it was an entirely different matter. These companies grew out of the choir-schools of the Chapel Royal, of Windsor, and of St. Paul's, and were under the direct control of a master who had the right to impress children for singing and acting. The master supported and trained them, produced the plays, and received the money from performances. For a time the "little eyases," as Shakespeare makes plain in *Hamlet*, acting largely at the private theatres and at Court, vied in popularity with their elders; they must have been unusually competent, for they elicited the charming courtly comedies of Lyly, and performed such tragedies as Chapman's *Bussy* and Marston's *Sophonisba*. Some of these children, Nat. Field for instance, later became leading actors in adult companies.

We may now turn to a consideration of the physical structure of the theatre itself. The public playhouses were by no means alike in size or shape; yet there is substantial agreement about the basic plan of a typical public theatre. Since it is vastly different from anything we have today, since the methods of staging vary substantially from ours, and since both theatre and staging exerted a strong influence on the art of the playwright, it is essential to have a clear picture of the most important features.

The Elizabethan theatre evolved from those structures which had previously served most often and conveniently for the presentation of plays, the inns. Except for the Fortune, however, they did not retain the square or rectangular courtyard or pit, but were roughly circular or polygonal. The alteration was no doubt suggested by the bear- and bull-baiting rings on the Bankside, and assisted the hearing and vision of spectators in pit and gallery by bringing them nearer to the stage. As pictured in contemporary London maps the typical theatre justifies Shakespeare's description (*Henry V*, Prologue) of "this wooden O." Around the inside were three tiers of galleries, roofed over with thatch or tile; the center was uncovered and open to the weather. As in the inn court-yard, the audience entered through a door opposite the stage, except, perhaps, for a few especially favored who might use the players' entrance to the tiring-house or dressing rooms at the rear. A penny to a "gatherer" allowed the groundling to stand in the pit; and an additional charge of a penny or two permitted the more select spectator to climb stairs and sit on stool or bench in one of the galleries.

Halfway into the pit there projected a platform upon which most of the action of the play was presented. It is important to realize that the spectators were not only in front of the stage as in a modern theatre but actually on three sides of it. At the rear of the platform was an inner, or alcove, stage separated from the front by a traverse, or draw-curtain, and flanked by doors which allowed the actors to enter directly onto the plat-

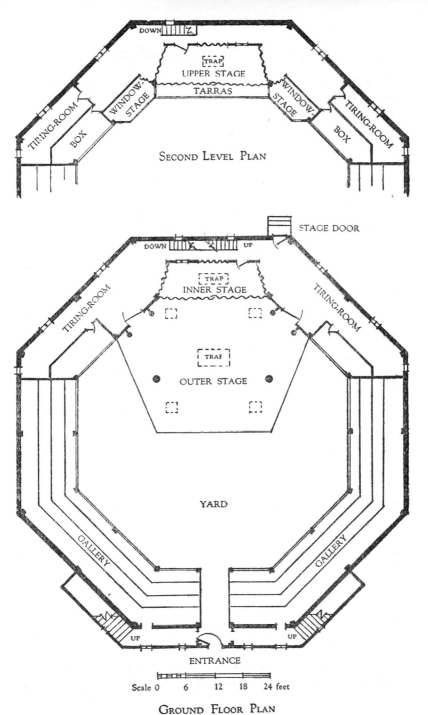

SECOND LEVEL PLAN

STAGE DOOR

TRAP
INNER STAGE

TIRING-ROOM

TIRING-ROOM

TRAP

OUTER STAGE

YARD

GALLERY

GALLERY

UP

UP

ENTRANCE

Scale 0   6   12   18   24 feet

GROUND FLOOR PLAN

FLOOR PLANS OF THE GLOBE PLAYHOUSE
Drawn especially for this book by John C. Adams

form from the tiring-house. Over the alcove-stage was an upper stage; it also had a curtain which could cut it off from the view of the audience when it was not in use, and in front of the curtain a balcony or "tarras" projected slightly over the platform. Occasionally it may have served as a music room, or for spectators presumably more interested in being seen than in seeing what went on in all sections of the playing space. Other spectators were sometimes allowed to sit on the platform-stage itself and must have been an unholy nuisance both to actors and audience. It is a pity there is no evidence that they ever fell through the various traps in the floors of all the stages. The upper stage, including curtained space and balcony windows on each side of it, over the doors to the main stage, was reached by interior stairs. Projecting from above the balcony-stage over a large part of the platform was a roof variously called the "heavens" or the "shadow" and on part of it a garret or "hut," which extended back over the third story of the tiring-house. The "shadow," usually supported by pillars, served in part to protect from the elements actors on the main stage. Moreover, through it heavy properties or even an actor impersonating a god—the ancient *deus ex machina*—might be let down to the platform. From the "hut" flew a flag on fair days to indicate, along with frequent trumpet blasts, that a play was to be given that afternoon. Sunday performances, though intermittently prohibited, continued till 1603.

The earliest private playhouses were apparently mere adaptations of rooms for the presentation of plays by the Children of the Royal Chapel or by Paul's Boys; there was a platform-stage backed by a curtain and artificially lighted, and seats in the hall, rather than standing-room, accommodated the more luxurious auditors. Beginning with Burbage's Blackfriars, however, the reconstruction included galleries, and no doubt alcove and balcony-stages not essentially different from those in the public theatres, though the galleries may have been less in number and the "interior" stages larger. The ceiling, of course, supplied the function of the "shadow," and an upper room that of the "hut." The public and the later private stages were therefore not essentially different; after 1608 the same plays were

frequently given both outdoors and in, and there does not seem
to be evidence of necessary adaptation because of the transfer.
Performances at Court, of course, were given indoors. There
dramatic entertainment was of two kinds: elaborate disguisings
and pageantry emphasizing music, dancing, and spectacle for
which special settings and properties were devised for the amateur participants;[1] and more regular plays presented by professionals ranging from simple Interludes on simple platforms to
more complicated drama with ornate multiple settings. After
about 1580, when the regular theatres and their practices had
become established, theatricals at Court were more and more
dominated by professionals called in to give special performances on variable temporary stages much resembling those in the
private playhouses though with more expensive decoration, fur-
nishings, and properties.

No one has ever been more aware than Shakespeare, actor
and poet-playwright, with his constant contrasts between seem-
ing and being, illusion and reality, that the theatre is "of imagination all compact."

> If we shadows have offended,

says Robin Goodfellow,

> Think but this, and all is mended,
> That you have but slumber'd here,
> While these visions did appear.

Fifteen years later, "these our actors" are still "spirits," and the
"insubstantial" pageant of *The Tempest* has faded, leaving "not
a rack behind," except perhaps the memory of a dream. It was
natural that the Elizabethans should emphasize the illusory quality of the drama, for its whole tradition had been one which
demanded and evoked the willing suspension of disbelief. Actors
and playwrights could count on audiences willing to use their
imaginations, to "eke out our performance with your mind"; to
help build "cloud-capp'd towers" from the suggestions which
they offered. We are still alive to this spell, but not often as
yielding. "Show me," says the recalcitrant modern spectator;
"convince me in spite of myself!" And so we try to make a play

[1] For a discussion of the masque, see pp. 286–90.

as much as possible like life, our actors must appear natural, and we put both action and actors within a picture-frame to be sufficiently confined. The Elizabethans were different. They said to the playwright, "Start us off; tell us a story"; to the actor, "Indicate grief; we know what grief is; we'll do the rest." Instead of demanding a designer to realize on the stage a room or a forest, they said to playwright and actor and the theatre itself, "Suggest it; a table is a room, a tree a forest." It is often the realer way. "Scenery," say the Chinese, "is as large as your imagination."

Primitive medieval drama demanded no more than two things of a stage: a neutral playing-space if the action was clear enough to require no localization and, if necessary, certain definite sections of the stage set up to represent specific places. When these are added, the stage, still retaining the neutral space, becomes multiple by the simultaneous presentation of various localities, no matter how far apart they were in actuality. The simple Interludes needed nothing but a platform; the dialogue of the actors did the rest. The elaborate Miracle play, presenting the Bible story from the Fall to the Last Judgment, with its shift from hell to earth to heaven, needed localization. On the fixed stages were various "mansions," as many as the cycle required, symbolically represented in a line or semicircle as a standing scene, hell a gigantic mouth at one end, heaven a raised portion with perhaps a throne for the Trinity at the other. In between were all the necessary "mansions" representing various places on earth, Rome, Jerusalem, the Sea of Galilee. Actors went from one "mansion" to another as the play demanded. Down-stage was still neutral for unlocalized incidents or comic interpolations. When Miracles were acted on a series of pageant-wagons, this meant merely that each pageant had its separate "mansion" and neutral space; in other words the standing scene was divided into its components, and each section was mounted on wheels. Properties, costumes, and action could be realistic, conventional, or symbolic.

As the drama became professional, as actors ceased to be butchers and bakers and chose to earn their living by acting, the neutral tended to supersede the simultaneous stage. Of course the Miracles continued to be presented with standing scenes or pageants well into Shakespeare's lifetime and were even moved ponderously to adjacent towns, but itinerant companies could not carry about the elaborate paraphernalia necessary for simultaneous presentation and not sufficiently adaptable to the conditions or places in which they were to play. At Court where more spectacular drama was possible, and in the early private theatres where children presented courtly plays, multiple setting might linger longer, and it did not entirely disappear from the public stage, but for the simplicity required by strollers the neutral stage with easily portable properties was more practical. The platform erected in inn-yards was a neutral stage. And as this process continued, the curtain became more and more important.

It is essential for any understanding of Elizabethan staging to remember that the curtain used by inn-yard players was not a front curtain but at the rear of the platform and that it served at first merely to screen the actors' dressing-room and to provide a place for their entrance onto the stage. It was the curtain and the inn-yard which gradually transformed the method of staging. The inns were permanent structures, and the section back of the platform served as a permanent façade. The balcony over the curtain could represent the upper room of a house. It was not long before the curtain itself could be drawn to reveal a lower room. And these back-stages were not neutral, they could represent *different* places, but they represented *definite* places. When the public theatres were built, the inner and upper stages, cut off from platform and from the spectators' view by curtains, became permanent features.

Nothing more clearly shows the difference between the Elizabethan and the modern stage than the position and use of the curtain. Most of our plays are presented behind drawn up curtains; the Elizabethan plays were acted largely in front of curtains, either closed or drawn aside. Most modern plays are punctuated by curtains lowered in front of them to indicate structural units, to allow for scene changes, or to provide intermissions; in Elizabethan plays the act unit is relatively unimportant, the "two hours traffic of our stage" was almost continuous, and the curtain was used during the action itself to increase the playing space, to allow dramatic disclosure, or to designate a specific locality. The Elizabethan stage, then, is not ours, nor is it with certain exceptions simultaneous. It is basically a combination of open unlocalized stage, and permanent localizable recesses. It is unlike the multiple stage in that it represents one place at a time; it is unlike our picture-frame stage in being able to represent at any one time whatever place the playwright suggests and the imagination of the audience can accept. The places may be definite or indefinite and in either case are quickly and easily transferable. In short the Elizabethan is the most free and fluid stage that has ever been devised.

If the Elizabethan stage was free and fluid, one must be wary of thinking of it as bare. In our sense of the word, it had little or no scenery, but to assist the imagination, elaborate and expensive properties were used: Tamburlaine's chariot, Don Horatio's arbor, fountains, trees, and thrones. Costuming was extravagant. Plays were acted, with certain adaptations, in contemporary dress, and Elizabethan garments were gorgeous in color and fantastic in cut. Henslowe, who seldom spent more than £8 for a play, squandered £20 for one cloak. Properties and costumes combined to make effective spectacular shows and splendid processions; and masques became a feature of some plays, dancing and music of many. Battles and trial scenes, royal audiences and mob scenes were played on an open platform but they did not leave it bare. Elizabethan drama is full of noise and bustle, of constantly moving and colorful action.

Most of this action took place on the front stage which was neutral ground; localizations in modern texts—a street, the Senate House, etc.—are the work of modern editors. The playwright could, of course, by the nature of the action or properties, or by allusions in the dialogue, immediately localize neutral ground; if he did not, it could be any place, indoors or out. The alcove and balcony-stages, and their adjacent doors and windows could more easily become definite places. The alcove, since it was concealed by a curtain, could be set with properties to indicate indoors, a study, a bed-chamber or prison, a cell for Prospero, a tomb for Juliet. When the curtain was drawn aside, the action could remain within the alcove, or could spread to the main stage, which then immediately took on the new locality. As soon as the curtain closed and the actors left the stage, it again became neutral ground. Most of the heavy properties, unless easily removable in full view of the audience, had to be within the curtained sections of the stage. Moreover, the inner stage could be used for discoveries, disclosures, tableaux, and stage-pictures. The doors from tiring-house to main stage were local if the stage was local; otherwise they served merely as entrances and exits for the actors. Upper windows were almost necessarily local, the upper stage usually so, representing upper rooms or balconies, monuments or towers or city walls. All parts of two stories became the playing space for Elizabethan drama and constituted the stage proper. Indeed, gods descending from the "shadow" and ghosts rising from traps added heavens and the subterranean. Over the diverse and shifting playing space, with scene changes indicated by exits and entrances, the Elizabethan play swept smoothly, swiftly, and practically continuously to its conclusion.

Acted on such a stage by companies so constituted, the Elizabethan play was naturally conditioned by its theatrical environment. It was the playwright's task to compose for this stage and these actors, and the conditions under which his play was to be presented determined in part his dramatic technique. How was he affected in his plan and writing by this kind of theatre and company?

Certain features are immediately obvious. He could have as many scenes in his plays as he wished, and he could place them wherever he wished, even on the sea-coast of Bohemia, which has no sea-coast. Action could still be fluid and continuous, no matter how many times he shifted places, no matter whether places were localized or not, real or imaginary. He did assist the audience by indicating in his dialogue where the action was taking place if it was a matter of importance, and he usually ended scenes with rhymed tag-lines, after which the stage would be momentarily bare. He could not, like a modern playwright, work up to a "curtain" because the greater part of the action was preferably on the main stage, close to the audience which surrounded it. Moreover he had to provide for proper exits. For example, characters in Elizabethan tragedy have a high death-rate, especially at the end of the play; bodies on the front stage must be removed; usually there is a funeral procession. Comedies, especially those with marriage-endings, frequently conclude with an exit dance.

It is not remarkable that Elizabethan drama is on the whole a poetic drama. Elizabethans—it is typical of the Renaissance everywhere—had fallen in love with language, with words, with speech of all kinds, homely and conceited, old words and new words, short words and long words, poor words and rich words. The young student of Elizabethan drama, having learned that the pun is the lowest form of humor, is often bothered by the plays on words he discovers there. The pun to an Elizabethan was not merely a joke; it was a rhetorical device by which he managed to say two or three things at once. Wit combats, badinage, thrust and parry are everywhere in Elizabethan drama. So are orations, elaborate descriptions, delicate sentiments, philosophical discussions. But if love of words and of their rhythms is a part of the inheritance of the English Renaissance, it was also fostered by the stage. Here were actors not cut off from the audience by orchestra-pit and proscenium-arch, but in the midst of a word-loving audience. All eyes were on them; all ears strained to hear. They were not puppets seen through a picture-frame but in intimate physical contact. Words accompanied by easily visible gestures and expression went home with extraordinary force and directness, whether they were high astounding terms or mere gags. And so Elizabethan drama is in its best sense a wordy drama. The playwright was not afraid of soliloquies; soliloquies properly used told the audience what was going on inside of a character, what he would not or could not say to anyone else. This was not a realistic stage; an aside was perfectly acceptable. Moreover, a speaker might very well be nearer to his audience than to the actor who was supposed not to overhear him. The variety and scope of the language, the emotional rhythms of poetic speech of the Elizabethan drama were partly the result of the Elizabethan theatre.

One other point may well be made. The Elizabethans loved stories, and their stage was ideally equipped to tell them in action. Since the scene could be shifted at will, and action was swift and continuous, it was not necessary to stick to one story. The playwright could tell two or three. If he was a poor crafts-man, he could amuse his audience even if his method was entirely episodic. If he was an artist, he would carefully preserve cause and effect in his handling of multiple plots, and connect the stories to each other by the inter-relationship of characters, and by parallel and contrast. This was a stage which cried out for the narrative method, and the stories became the more real and effective because the characters were seen literally in the round.

If the stage played a vital part in determining the dramatic method of the playwright, he was also strongly influenced by the company for which he was writing. We shall never know how widely this influence operated, but there is no doubt of its force. A dramatist working for a definite group cannot compose in a vacuum; his play must fit his actors. The lovely lyrics scat-tered through Lyly's plays were written for singing children. How much are Marlowe's supermen due to the titanic Alleyn? Certainly Shakespeare knew his tragic heroes were to be played by Burbage. It is important to remember that while Will Kemp was a member of the company, Shakespeare created for him such parts as Costard, Bottom, and Dogberry; rustic, blundering, unlearned characters at which Kemp was adept. When Robert Armin took his place, however, the comedy role changed. Armin was brilliant, witty, himself a man of letters; as a result we have Touchstone and Feste, court-jesters, "not altogether fool." Do we owe the Fool in *Lear* to Armin's expressed dissatisfaction with the very minor Clown in *Othello*? Moreover, these com-panies were fairly stable in size; the number of characters in a play was in part determined by the number of actors in the company. No doubt many characters in Elizabethan plays, absent in the sources, owe their origin to the need for utilizing the full talents of the company. The personnel may well have forced the playwright into minor stories and plot complications which structurally seem unnecessary or superfluous, simply to provide them all with opportunities.

All these forces interact. The companies produced the theatre; the kind of stage affects the work of the playwright. The playwright, conditioned by both theatre and company, may by the nature of his art modify both stage and acting. The Elizabethan audience played its part in creating Elizabethan drama. It is a complex problem. Unless we bear in mind these interactions; unless, more specifically, we understand the theatrical conditions under which Elizabethan playwrights worked, we have no basis for the assumption that we understand their plays. The freedom, the swift variety, the boundless scope in matter and manner, the universality of thought and expression which characterize the dramatic art of the English Renaissance and make it vital, vivid, and moving today stem alike from actor and theatre and poet-playwright. Since the purpose of this book is primarily to serve as an introduction to the work of dramatists whom we can still read, we must not forget that they could not have existed without player and playhouse. "Masters, you are all welcome," even though you can be heard no more.

CHAPTER FOUR

THE FORERUNNERS: LYLY, PEELE, GREENE, KYD, MARLOWE

ELIZABETHAN drama as we know it was created by a group of young playwrights, sometimes known as the university wits. Beginning their attack on the London stage in the early eighties, they carried it by storm and held the boards for a full decade until one by one they dropped out of the scene. Their plays were the popular successes when young Shakespeare came to London and must have been an amazing revelation of the power and beauty of the new drama to one who, as a boy in rural Stratford, had seen only survivals of the old Morals and Interludes presented by travelling companies. These new playwrights did not constitute a school with some definite formula for the creation of a new drama. Each was an individual genius and contributed something of his own to the popular stage; there is a vast difference between the courtly comedies of Lyly and the heroic tragedies of Marlowe.

Yet there is an essential similarity between them that goes far to unify their work. They were all born poets, makers, inventors; not one of them was content to follow the beaten path of traditional drama. They were all artists in words, consciously engaged in devising for the drama a better medium of expression than it had hitherto possessed. They were all imbued with the spirit of romance, seekers after the strange and lovers of beauty. Furthermore they had all enjoyed a sound classical education— all but Kyd were university graduates—which gave them a command of classic sources, an acquaintance with classical models, and an admiration for the polished dialogue of comedy and the stately speech of tragedy in the classical masterpieces. They were, however, loving students rather than slavish imitators of that drama like the young gentlemen of the Inns of Court; they borrowed freely from their models, but rather for the purpose of enriching and improving popular drama than of transforming it into an imitation of the classics. An explanation of their free handling of the revered classic models is found in another common bond which unites the members of this group. They were all professional dramatists writing for the public stage at a time when this career offered a man of letters the quickest and the surest reward in ready cash. But this reward could only be obtained if their plays were successful upon the stage, and of success or failure London was the final arbiter. To gain their daily bread these playwrights would have been forced even against their will to make large concessions to the demands of the public. Yet it is more than doubtful if there was any conscious yielding on their part; they were themselves members of the public for which they wrote, men about town for the most part, gay Bohemians and haunters of taverns. They shared the tastes of their public, but their education and their inborn talent enabled them to guide, purify, and elevate these tastes till at last they trained an audience ready to receive and applaud the work of Shakespeare.

The oldest of this group and the first to achieve success was John Lyly, 1554?–1606. A graduate of Oxford, he captivated the town and court in 1578 with his prose novel, *Euphues, i.e.,* the wellbred man. The story of *Euphues* is a mere peg on which to hang a series of discourses on education, polite behavior, and courtly love, but the style, a clever amalgam of various literary affectations, was new and fascinating. Fifty years later Blount, the editor of a collection of Lyly's plays, declared: "Our nation are in his debt for a new English which he taught them. . . . All our ladies were then his scholars; and that beauty in court which could not parley Euphuism, was as little regarded as she which now there speaks not French"—this at a time when the French Queen, Henrietta Maria, was setting the fashions at Court.

Yet even the success of *Euphues* was insufficient to support Lyly; he turned to the theatre, and became playwright-in-chief to the company of boy-actors at Paul's. The courtly note of Lyly, the least popular-minded of his group, is seen in his choice of form: "Soldiers," he says, "call for Tragedies, their object is blood: courtiers for comedies, their subject is love." Courtly love,

then, is the central theme of nearly all of Lyly's plays. It is, to
be sure, a rather cool and unemotional love, a graceful fancy
rather than a consuming passion. His aim, he tells us in the Prologue to *Sapho and Phao,* was: "to breed (if it might be) soft
smiling, not loud laughing: knowing it to the wise to be as great
pleasure to hear counsel mixed with wit, as to the foolish to
have sport mingled with rudeness." Rudeness, in fact, the old
profanity and foul language, Lyly banished from his work. As
a substitute he offered "counsel mixed with wit," advice on the
good life, couched in the witty epigrammatic phrase which
would provoke "soft smiling" rather than the loud guffaw. If
today Lyly's "counsel" seems outmoded, his "wit" thin, his
frequent puns absurd, we should remember that all this was
new on the Elizabethan stage. Lyly was the first English playwright to recognize in his first play, *Campaspe,* 1584, that
innocent love may be a matter for pleasant entertainment, and
the entertainment he offered his audience sprang in the main
from the polished, not to say sophisticated, dialogue.

The action, in Lyly's plays, is anything but exciting. His plots,
drawn for the most part from classical myth or legend, are simple
and regular, but so slight that to fill up his orthodox five acts he
has constant recourse to intercalary scenes in which minor characters divert the audience with song, with dancing, or with
mockery of some ridiculous butt. These characters, often enough,
are drawn from contemporary English life, and there is also
occasional, more or less veiled, allusion to contemporary characters, to the Queen herself as Cynthia in *Endimion,* to Philip
of Spain in *Midas.* As a result we often get a curious amalgam
of the classical, the romantic, and the realistic.

In one of his most characteristic plays, *Galathea, ca.* 1585, the
scene is laid in an English county, Lincolnshire, but an English
county that lies under the curse of Neptune, who can only be
appeased by the yearly sacrifice of a fair virgin to a sea-monster,
the "Agar," or tidal wave, a well-known local phenomenon. To
save their daughters from this fate two fathers disguise them as
boys, and the disguised girls promptly fall in love with each
other. To complicate matters, Cupid appears on the scene and
inflames Diana's nymphs, who are ranging in these English

woods, with a passion for the disguised girls. Diana in anger seizes Cupid, clips his wings, and breaks his arrows. He is freed at last by the intercession of Venus, who likewise persuades Neptune to remit the virgin tribute and promises to gratify the mutual love of the girls by changing one of them—which one she doesn't say and it doesn't make any difference—into a boy. As if this were not enough, Lyly introduces three shipwrecked English boys, one of whom takes service in turn with such contemporary characters as an Alchemist and an Astrologer, and all these unite to sing Hymen at the wedding of the girl and the transformed boy. Here, to be sure, we have what Lyly himself called a "gallimaufrey," a hodge-podge of unrelated elements; yet the result is not without its charm.

Not much can be said of Lyly's power of characterization. His people for the most part are stock types, the lover, the beloved, the coy mistress, the friend, and the intriguer; his women are graceful but almost lifeless figures. The only exceptions to be made in this matter are the eccentric and humorous characters that take part—usually a very minor part—in the action, such as the cynical Diogenes in *Campaspe* and the boastful Sir Tophas in *Endimion*. To these we must add the roguish witty page who appears repeatedly in these plays, a very fit role for one of Lyly's boy-actors. In these characters we get a trace at least of native English realism. Lyly was essentially a courtly dramatist; yet his plays, presented in public as well as at the Court, exerted a great and lasting influence upon popular comedy. They were immensely successful at the time, promptly printed and reprinted, and even revived when Shakespeare and Jonson were doing their best work. He completes the fusion of the native, the classical, and the romantic which had been slowly going on during the period of transition. He set a pattern of witty speech and repartee in lively prose as the true vehicle of comic dialogue, and he naturalized the gods and myths of ancient Greece upon the Elizabethan stage. No less a genius than William Shakespeare was content to learn from Lyly, to borrow his characters of the braggart knight and the mocking page in *Love's Labour's Lost,* and to carry to perfection his prose dialogue in the repartee of Benedick and Beatrice, of Orlando and

Rosalind. Such a masterly blend of graceful fancy and sturdy realism as *A Midsummer Night's Dream* could hardly have been written if Lyly had not shown the way in *Galathea* and *Love's Metamorphosis.*

George Peele, like Lyly, was an Oxford student and seems to have been known as a poet while still in college. Like Lyly he soon turned to the London stage; his first known work, *The Arraignment of Paris,* was performed by the Chapel Children before the Queen in 1584. This is not so much a play as a pastoral pageant. It deals with the well known story of the award by Paris of the golden apple to Venus, but Peele converts it into a splendid flattery of Elizabeth: Paris is arraigned before a court of the Olympian deities for a partial decision; the apple is reclaimed from Venus, and formally presented to the nymph Eliza, "a figure of the Queen," a match for all the goddesses in power, wisdom, beauty, and chastity. It would seem that such a panegyric would have established Peele as a Court poet, but there is no record of another play by Peele before the Queen. Henceforward all his plays were written for and produced by professional companies on the public stage.

Not much that is certainly Peele's has come down to us, but the little that is left shows an extraordinary variety; he tried his hand at nearly every sort of play current on the stage. *The Battle of Alcazar* is a hasty dramatization of the famous fight in Morocco where Sebastian of Portugal and the English adventurer Stukely were slain; *Edward I* is one of the popular chronicle plays; *David and Bethsabe* is an interesting experiment in casting a Bible story into Elizabethan dramatic form; the old realism of the Miracles is lost in a flood of Elizabethan declamatory rhetoric.

Peele's masterpiece, *The Old Wives' Tale,* is the one example of his work as a writer of comedy that remains to us. This delightful play is a mad melange of folklore and romance with a dash of personal and literary criticism thrown in by way of spice. It opens with three serving-men lost in a wood; they are met by Clunch, the smith, who takes them to his home, where after supper his wife begins a "merry winter's tale" to pass the time. It is of a wizard who stole a king's fair daughter and of her brothers' search for her. Hardly has the tale been started before the characters of the story appear upon the stage to act their parts. The action is a tangled web, a little difficult to follow in reading, a sheer delight when played in the open by a troupe of pretty girls at a Bryn Mawr May-day. The dialogue is as neatly blended as the story: the conjuror spouts blank verse; most of the characters talk a simple homely prose; and the action is interrupted by a handful of charming lyrics. At the end a grateful ghost, following a wandering knight who has bestowed burial on his body, kills the conjuror, frees the princess and her brothers from enchantment, and disappears into the ground. The tale is told; it is almost day; the old wife is nodding at the fire, but she rouses to give her guests a cup of ale and a toast before they leave.

Peele, of course, is laughing at the absurd romantic plays of wandering knights and lovelorn ladies which cluttered the stage of his day, but he is himself a romantic who thoroughly enjoys the stuff he laughs at, a realist as well, who knows and loves his simple English folk and their strange jumble of superstitions. Had Peele been able to write more such plays, his place in English comedy would have been far higher. There is, however, a good deal to show that Peele went to pieces in the wild life of Elizabethan London. *The Merry Jests of George Peele,* a chap-book published some ten years after his death, depicts him as a haunter of taverns, a dangler after courtesans, and a common cheat. We need not believe all the tales, but that Peele should have been chosen as their disreputable hero is not without significance. One cannot imagine such a set of shady stories attaching themselves to the courtly Lyly. In 1596 Peele sent a begging letter to Lord Burghley; two years later Meres noted that he was dead "by the pox."

It is no easy matter to determine Peele's contribution to the swiftly advancing Elizabethan drama. Had we a complete collection of his work, such a judgment would be easier, but much that he wrote has apparently been lost. If, as some believe, he was at least part author of a lost *Titus Andronicus,* the old *King Leir,* and *The Troublesome Reign of King John,* he was in a very true sense one of Shakespeare's predecessors, since the master thought well enough of all these plays to recast them for his company.

In spite of our imperfect knowledge of Peele it still seems possible to note in what fashion he assisted in the transformation of the native drama. He familiarized the audiences of the public theatres with classic myth and legend; his plays are packed with allusions to all the gods of Olympus. In sharp contrast to this parade of classic lore is his fondness for the homely and familiar sides of English life. This is shown not only in *The Old Wives' Tale,* but even more plainly in the Robin Hood episodes of *Edward I.* A somewhat blatant chauvinism, as in his outrageous treatment of Eleanor of Castile in this play, is the reverse of that spirit of conscious national pride that marks the years just before and after the defeat of the Armada.

Finally, and most important of all, Peele was a real poet and helped to touch the native drama with some sense of beauty. One finds throughout his work a genuine delight in words for words' sake, a joy in the art which plays with words in such a way as to convey their beauty to the hearer. Peele, we know, had read Spenser; he lifts a simile from *The Faerie Queene* to adorn a speech in *David and Bethsabe.* He was writing blank verse when Marlowe was still at College. His verse, to be sure, never attains the strength and splendor of Marlowe's; it tends too often to sink into a somewhat sugary sweetness. The truth is that Peele was a lyric rather than a dramatic poet; the songs in his plays are often the best things in them; there are few lovelier lyrics in Elizabethan drama than the song with which Bethsabe opens the play that bears her name:

> Hot sun, cool fire, temper'd with sweet air,
> Black shade, fair nurse, shadow my white hair.

Younger and shorter-lived than Peele, Robert Greene, 1558–1592, is a far more considerable figure in the literary life of his time. Like Lyly and Peele he was university bred. Soon after taking his first degree at Cambridge he seems to have travelled in Italy where, if we may trust his own words, "he practised such villainy as is abominable to declare"; *"Inglese italianato, diavolo incarnato,"* says an Italian proverb of the time, but there is no need to believe Greene quite so black as he loved to paint himself in his last wretched years. On his return he plunged at once into the life of the university wits in London as a "penner of love-pamphlets." His first work, *Mamillia*, 1583, written in imitation of Lyly's fashionable Euphuism, is the first of a long series of love-stories, of studies of roguery in the city, and of thinly veiled confessions of his own sinful life. Some twenty-seven such prose tracts were published during Greene's career. Yet he found time to go back to Norwich, his birthplace, marry, beget a son, desert his wife and child, and return to the group of young playwrights who were conquering the London stage.

The first of his plays, *Alphonsus, King of Aragon*, ca. 1588, is a patent imitation of Marlowe's epoch-making *Tamburlaine*. The hero, like Tamburlaine, fights his way up from low estate, bestows crowns and kingdoms on his soldiers, and finally weds the daughter of his enemy. The play is incredibly bad, so bad indeed that some have supposed it rather a parody than an imitation of Marlowe's play. The action is absurd; the blank verse, Greene's first attempt, stumbles and staggers. The most interesting thing about it is Greene's clever exploitation of the resources of the new theatre. It opens with a stage-direction: "After you have sounded thrice [the three trumpet calls that announce the beginning of a play] let Venus be let down from the top of the stage"; it closes with another: "Exit Venus, or if you can conveniently, let a chair come down from the top of the stage and draw her up"—evidently Greene was not sure how far he could trust the machinery. The Ghost rises and sinks through a trap-door; a brazen head spouting fire is disclosed "in the middle of the place behind the stage," *i.e.*, in the alcove stage; and the action proceeds to the sound of drums, trumpets, and all the Muses "playing on sundry instruments." Tamburlaine's chariot drawn by the pampered jades of Asia is paralleled, or parodied, by the entrance of Alphonsus under a canopy "having over each corner a king's head crowned"—a bloody head of course. It must have been quite a show.

His second play, *A Looking-Glass for London and England*, ca. 1590, written in collaboration with Thomas Lodge, another poet-playwright of the group, is an attempt to domesticate the Miracle on the Elizabethan stage. It is the story of Jonah and the threatened destruction of Nineveh. The sins of Nineveh are held up as a mirror and a warning to contemporary London; the play is as didactic as any old Moral. There is genuine, if rough and homely, English humor in the comic scenes played by Adam the clown, a real advance over the blustering heroics of *Alphonsus*.

Greene's next play, *Orlando Furioso, ca.* 1591, seems to have been planned as a conscious burlesque of two great theatrical successes of the eighties, *Tamburlaine* and *The Spanish Tragedy*. A villainous character, Sacripant, is a sort of pseudo-Tamburlaine. He indulges in wild dreams of love and conquest, but comes to an early end, slain in single combat by Orlando. This hero runs mad like Hieronimo, but his madness is absurd rather than tragic. He tears a shepherd limb from limb—off-stage of course—enters with a leg upon his shoulder, and routs a troupe of soldiers with this "massy club." He equips a company of country folk as soldiers with spits and dripping-pans, and after a victory with this motley host, bestows the accolade of knighthood upon his love, Angelica, whom he mistakes for a squire. It seems unlikely that so clever a man as Greene should have taken such stuff seriously; probably he aimed to get a laugh out of his audience by a parody of popular plays. If we had nothing more of Greene than these plays, his place in English drama would be almost negligible; but he went on to write two more which are, each in its own way, landmarks in the development of romantic comedy.

Friar Bacon and Friar Bungay, ca. 1591, is the first well planned and skilfully executed romantic comedy in English. It is essentially romantic since its two themes, magic and true love, are drawn from the domain of romance, and the artful interweaving of these themes proves Greene's growing skill as a playwright. Possibly the theme of magic was suggested by the stage success of Marlowe's *Dr. Faustus;* yet Greene's play is neither an imitation nor a parody. On the contrary Greene, whose talent was naturally for comedy, was quick to see that a play with a happy ending could be wrought out of the old folkbook of Friar Bacon, which tells how the famous magician repented of his evil ways and died in the odor of sanctity. Yet since a play based solely on this story would be quite devoid of plot interest, Greene wove into it an invention of his own: the passion of Prince Edward for fair Margaret, the betrayal of the Prince by Lacy, the friend he had engaged to woo the maid for him, the mutual love of Margaret and Lacy, the wrath of the Prince, and his final forgiveness of the lovers. All this is good old ballad stuff, as is Lacy's trial of Margaret's constancy, and their reunion when Margaret is about to enter a nunnery. These scenes, quite new and fresh in English comedy, give the play its special and delightful charm. Yet the Bacon story, too, must have made a strong appeal to an Elizabethan audience. Friar Bacon is a genuine Englishman; he triumphs over a boastful German magician; he plans to fence England with a wall of brass against foreign invasion; and he ends the play with a prophecy of the glories of Elizabeth. Into these scenes Greene introduces two comic characters: Miles, the blundering mischief-making Clown, a development of the old Vice, who is carried off to hell at the end on the back of a roaring devil; and Ralph, the King's Fool, a prototype of Shakespeare's Feste and Touchstone. Both these characters are as English as roast beef; there is nothing in their speech or action of Lyly's sophisticated courtly wit. Notable also is Greene's exploitation of the three stages of the Elizabethan theatre. It seems likely that, in the scene where Bacon reveals Lacy's treason, the Prince and Friar are seated on the outer stage, the magic glass into which they look has been disclosed on the inner stage, while on the upper stage Lacy, Margaret, and Friar Bungay are actually performing the action that the Prince is supposed to see in the glass.

Friar Bacon was a very successful play; it was promptly printed and reprinted. More than that, it was acted repeatedly by at least three different companies, produced at Court in the last years of Elizabeth's reign, and revived under Charles I. Today it is probably, after *Dr. Faustus,* the best known of pre-Shakespearean plays.

James IV, ca. 1591, has sometimes been called Greene's masterpiece. It is, to be sure, the most independent work of Greene as a dramatist, and it has a unity of theme and treatment that is absent even in *Friar Bacon.* Unfortunately it has come down to us in so badly garbled a form that it is hard to pass a final judgment on it.

What Greene tried to do is clear enough. He took from a collection of Italian tales a romantic story of wifely love, persecuted but triumphant, transferred the tale, with sublime indifference to the facts, to a period in Scottish history—the protagonist, James, is supposed to be the Scottish king who fell at Flodden—and set the whole in a strange fantastic framework. In the Induction Oberon, King of the Fairies, encounters Bohan, a Scottish knight who, finding "the court ill, the country worse, and the city worst of all," has retired to live in an empty tomb. After some dancing and bits of magic Bohan bids Oberon come with him "to the gallery," *i.e.*, the upper stage, and see a story acted that will demonstrate the wicked folly of the world. Here the play proper begins. Briefly it runs as follows: James of Scotland, married to Dorothea, the King of England's daughter, falls in love with Ida, daughter of a Scottish countess, and seeks her for his mistress. When she refuses, he plans to have the Queen murdered so that he may wed her. Learning of the plot, the Queen escapes disguised as a squire, but is overtaken by a hired assassin, is dangerously wounded, and left for dead. Rescued by a Scottish knight, she is conveyed to his house, where his wife falls in love with her. The King of England, angered at the report of his daughter's murder, invades Scotland and carries all before him. Hearing this, the Queen, who has never ceased to love her guilty husband, reveals her sex to the lady who loves her, proceeds to the camp, stops an imminent battle, forgives her husband, and reconciles the two kings.

Here we have something new in English drama, the germ of what was later to emerge as full-fledged tragi-comedy. Compared with the masterpieces of Shakespeare, and Beaumont and Fletcher, *James IV* is a rather feeble piece of work, but Greene deserves no little credit for his introduction of this genre upon the English stage. And he deserves more than a little credit for his characterization of the two ladies who figure in the play, the chaste and gentle Ida and the devoted Dorothea. Along with Margaret in *Friar Bacon* these ladies form a very charming trio. More fully realized, lifelike, and credible than the shadowy women of Lyly's plays, they strike a note of true romance and are in a sense the forerunners of such romantic heroines as

Rosalind, Viola, and Imogen. In these last plays—and it is by these alone that Greene should be judged—the romantic scene has shifted from strange lands to the British Isles, and a breath of country air, of country sports and dances, of country lads and lasses, blows across a stage that in Greene's day too often re-echoed to the rant of foreign potentates.

Greene's career as a dramatist was of the briefest; there is no extant play of his that we can date before 1587, nothing later than 1591. In his last years he seems to have quarrelled with most of his friends, broken with the actors whom he had always despised, and sunk to the company of the lowest dregs of London. Some time in August, 1592, he indulged in a banquet of Rhine wine and pickled herring, and his constitution, en-feebled by years of debauchery, succumbed completely. He died on September 3, 1592, and was crowned on his death-bed with a garland of poet's bays. Greene is a pathetic rather than a tragic figure: a sentimentalist, a waverer between high ideals and low living, a fluent pamphleteer and a true poet. As a playwright, the author of the first romantic comedy and the first forerunner of tragi-comedy holds an assured place in the history of Eliza-bethan drama.

When we turn from Lyly, Peele, and Greene to Kyd and Marlowe, we cross the borders where Elizabethan tragedy begins. Tragedies had been performed in England before this time, but they were either the academic plays of the Senecan school, like *Gorboduc*, or such parodies of tragic action as appear in *Horestes* and *Cambises*. Kyd and Marlowe were the creators of true Eliza-bethan tragedy. Their plays held the stage when Shakespeare came to London, and it was from them that he learned the rudi-ments of his art as a tragic dramatist.

Thomas Kyd, 1558–1594, was the son of a London scrivener, that is, a notary and writer of legal documents. He attended the Merchant Taylors' school, one of the best in England. There is no evidence to show that he studied at either university; yet he had a sound classical training—"Seneca," says his latest editor, "was always at his fingers' ends"—and he had a fair knowledge of French and of Italian. We know nothing of his connection with the theatre; his one great epoch-making play, *The Spanish*

Tragedy, was produced probably in 1586–87, possibly some years earlier. It was published without his name, and it is only by a casual reference in Heywood's *Apology for Actors,* 1612, that we are assured of his authorship. Only one other play is known certainly to be his, a translation of Garnier's *Cornélie,* a drama of the fashionable Senecan school.

There are, however, other plays, ascribed with more or less certainty to Kyd, that deserve mention. One of these, *Soliman and Perseda,* is a romantic tragedy of chivalry, true love, and a murderous Sultan. It is not improbably by Kyd; at least it dramatizes in five long acts the play that is supposed to be staged in the last act of *The Spanish Tragedy.* Of more importance is *Arden of Feversham,* the oldest surviving and perhaps the most powerful of Domestic Tragedies, in which it seems possible that Kyd had a hand. Finally there is some reason to believe that he was the author of the lost play of *Hamlet* on which Shakespeare's masterpiece is founded. If Kyd wrote all, or, indeed, any of these plays, he deserves a higher rank among Elizabethan tragic dramatists than is generally allotted him.

The last year of Kyd's life was darkened by a strange catastrophe. His papers were seized in a search ordered by the Privy Council to discover the author of current anti-alien propaganda. Among them was a document denying the divinity of Christ, enough at that time to convict the writer of that "deadly thing, atheism." Under torture Kyd declared that the document belonged to Marlowe and had got among his papers when they both occupied one room. Marlowe was arrested and released on parole, but Kyd was a ruined man. In a pathetic letter addressed to the Lord Chancellor, Kyd said that his patron had cast him off and that he was "utterly undone" unless some help were given him. Apparently no aid was given, and in the next year he died in poverty, a sorry end for the first English tragic dramatist.

The Spanish Tragedy was an extraordinarily successful play. It got into print in 1592, before Kyd's death, and a flock of editions followed, the last quarto appearing in 1633. One would have supposed that by then the taste for such primitive tragedy would have died out, but Kyd's play seems to have had something of the perennial drawing-power that exists in *Uncle Tom's*

Cabin on the American stage. There are no records of its early performances, but in 1592 Strange's company played it again and again to crowded houses. It was revived by the Admiral's company in 1597, and in 1601 and 1602 Henslowe paid Jonson handsomely for additions to the play. As late as 1614, after Shakespeare's tragedies had been on the boards for years, Jonson defined an old-fashioned play-goer as a man who would swear that *"Jeronimo (i.e., The Spanish Tragedy)* and *Andronicus* are the best plays yet."

The reason for this success can be quite simply stated. *The Spanish Tragedy* is a blend of classical theory and popular practice; it contains something for all the varied tastes of the time. From Seneca Kyd drew a sense of structure, a division of the play into acts and scenes, no mere dramatized narrative, but a plot carefully built up with beginning, middle, and end, motivation, suspense, counter-action, and catastrophe. Kyd borrowed also some characteristic bits of Senecan technique, the revengeful Ghost who opens the play, the Chorus, the epic reports as by the classical Nuntius. All these, of course, delighted the scholars in his audience, as did the Latin quotations and paraphrases of the classics scattered liberally through the play. The extreme sensationalism, the grim pursuit of revenge, the madness of the hero, the murders and the mutilation were all justified by the example of Seneca and were no doubt approved by the scholarly as well as enjoyed by the ignorant audience. From Seneca, too, Kyd gets his sense of style. He sternly excises the old popular horse-play and buffoonery; what humor remains is grim and quite in keeping with the action. The stately tirades, the *sententiae*, the many classical allusions, all show Kyd aiming at something far above the popular drama of his day. Finally, although in incomplete and faltering fashion, Kyd, like Seneca, attempts to excite interest in the tragic conflicts within his characters; Hieronimo's grief, his passion for revenge, his intermittent madness, and his exultation when his revenge is achieved: all this is the center of interest of the play. Ambition, love, and hatred are the emotions that influence the actions of the main characters; and these characters, in spite of a somewhat stiff drawing, are real people, not allegorical symbols. This is especially true of Bel-imperia, the proud and passionate heroine, and her brother, Lorenzo, the first Machiavellian villain in Elizabethan tragedy. Kyd's characterization of the protagonist is not so successful; Hieronimo is too full of words; and in the present text the outline of his figure has been further blurred by later "additions" which emphasize his madness. It remained for Shakespeare to achieve his supreme triumph in the character of a revenger hesitant upon the brink of madness, but Kyd at least pointed the way to this achievement.

From popular practice, on the other hand, Kyd drew his sense of the need of action on the stage; the most important events of his play are not reported, but represented before the eyes of the audience. One scene, especially, the murder of Horatio and the discovery of his body by his father suddenly aroused from sleep, so impressed the public that it is referred to over and over in the popular literature and drama of the time, and is pictured in the rude wood-cut which adorns the title-page of a late edition. Kyd presents the whole story in action; in fact he tells too much: the sub-plot, laid in Portugal, might well be dispensed with. Yet it is clear that Kyd had an extraordinary sense of stage effect: the discovery of Horatio's body, the hanging of the tool villain, the meeting of Hieronimo with the father of another murdered son, the bloody handkerchief, and the sudden and spectacular catastrophe, including the presentation to the actors and the audience of the body of the murdered man, the cause of all this woe, pack the play with thrills.

One other often neglected point may be touched upon: Kyd's sense of dramatic realism in speech. Much of the play, to be sure, is written in the high-flown style which he affected in imitation of his classical model; on the other hand there are scenes in simple homely prose; there are flashes, too, seldom but striking, of real dramatic utterance. Bel-imperia's cry, "O, save him, brother"; Hieronimo's "Alas, it is Horatio"; his muttered "go by, go by" as he slinks away from the presence of the King; his fateful words to Lorenzo, "I'll play the murderer, I warrant you" —these and many more show a dawning sense of effective dramatic speech. Kyd was no great poet; he was certainly a born playwright.

Christopher Marlowe, 1564–1593, "the Muses' darling," the most brilliant and interesting of all the university wits, was the son of a Canterbury citizen and his wife, the daughter of a clergyman of that Cathedral city. He has been called a cobbler's son; the fact is that his father belonged to the respectable and important guild of tanners and shoemakers. He studied at the King's School of Canterbury, and in 1581 he became a scholar on Archbishop Parker's foundation at Corpus Christi College, Cambridge. Holders of the Parker scholarships were supposed to be candidates for posts in the Church of England, and Marlowe must have been considered such a candidate, for after taking his B.A. in 1584, he continued to hold his scholarship. It seems probable, however, that he was already turning to the golden paths of poetry. His translation of Ovid's *Elegies*, poems so warmly erotic that they were condemned to the flames in 1599 by the Archbishop of Canterbury, may well be a work of his undergraduate days. His tragedy of *Dido, Queen of Carthage*, later revised by Nashe and performed by the Chapel Children, may have been written for a college performance. Certain it is that in the second stage of his university career he absented himself for considerable periods of time from the college walls. By doing so he forfeited his claim to the degree of Master of Arts, and it would certainly have been denied him but for the interposition of the most powerful body in England, the Queen's Privy Council. Apparently a rumor had been current in Cambridge that Marlowe was planning to leave England for Rheims, the training school of Jesuit missionaries. The Council denied this report, affirmed that he had done the Queen good service "in matters touching the benefit of the country," and insisted that he receive the degree "this next Commencement." The college authorities obeyed—they dared not do otherwise—and Marlowe became a Master of Arts in July, 1587. Exactly what the nature of his "good service" was, it is impossible to say; probably it was some form of counter-espionage connected with the Jesuit missionaries in the anxious year that preceded the Spanish Armada.

From 1587 to his death in 1593 Marlowe seems to have lived in or near London; his first play, *Tamburlaine*, was acted in 1587, and its instant success led at once to a second part. He was in touch with literary and even political circles in the capital; he certainly was acquainted with Chapman, Nashe, the poet-scholar Thomas Watson, and perhaps with Shakespeare. He was patronized by Thomas Walsingham, a kinsman of the Queen's great minister, and was on intimate terms with Raleigh and the free-thinking circle that gathered around that famous Elizabethan. On the other hand Marlowe was associated with far less respectable characters. It was asserted that he knew one Poole, a forger imprisoned in Newgate, who taught him how to coin money. This charge may be false, but it is certain that Marlowe was a prisoner in Newgate in September, 1589, on a charge of homicide. In the spring of 1592 Marlowe put the fear of death into a couple of London constables who placed him under bond to keep the peace. Finally Marlowe's three companions on the last day of his life were one and all very disreputable people: Poley was a spy, an informer, and apparently a man of most immoral life; Skeres was known as a pickpocket; and Frizer had been engaged in various shady transactions. These are not exactly the sort of men with whom one would expect the scholar, poet, playwright, and friend of Raleigh to spend a long day eating and drinking in a village tavern. Yet this certainly was the case.

The events leading up to Marlowe's death are a tangled web of politics, charges of blasphemy, and personal quarrels ending in manslaughter, or murder. They have so often been misrepresented that they seem to call for a brief report. The story of Kyd's arrest and his denunciation of Marlowe has already been told, and, if Kyd's accusation were not enough, Baines, an informer, filed about this time a long series of charges against Marlowe as a man of dissolute life, "utterly scorning both God and his ministers," a persuader to atheism, and a favorer of papists. The Council issued a warrant for Marlowe, but on his appearance, instead of being jailed, he was simply ordered to report daily till "licensed to the contrary." It would seem as if the Council was not gravely concerned with the charges against the poet; they had at that time weightier matters on their hands. To avoid the plague then raging in London Marlowe went to the little village of Deptford just down the Thames. Here on May 30, 1593, he spent the day at Dame Eleanor Bull's tavern with Frizer, Skeres, and Poley. They dined, supped, and presumably drank together in a private room, where a quarrel broke out about the reckoning. Marlowe, we hear, sprang from the couch where he was lying and fell upon Frizer, then sitting on a bench between Skeres and Poley. He snatched a dagger from Frizer's belt and cut him over the head with it. Unable to escape, Frizer grappled with Marlowe, caught his wrist, and drove the dagger into his head above the eye, "of which wound the aforesaid Christ. Marlowe instantly died." These details—and they are all that we know of the bloody business—come from the Coroner's verdict on the killing.

The story has been suspected on various grounds; yet it was plausible enough to be accepted by the Coroner's jury and to secure Frizer's pardon from the Queen on the ground of self-defense. Walsingham, Marlowe's patron, must have believed it, for he retained Frizer in his service. The slayer of Marlowe led a long and prosperous life and died in 1627 as a highly respected church-warden. Marlowe himself was hastily thrust underground in a churchyard at Deptford.

Since there were no Elizabethan newspapers, the violent death of a leading dramatist, which would make the headlines today, seems to have passed almost unnoticed. Five years later, 1598, Francis Meres in his *Palladis Tamia* reported: "Christopher Marlowe was stabbed to death by a bawdy serving man, a rival of his in his lewd love." This was a most unfortunate statement, for it was generally accepted as true and, until the discovery of the documents in the case, it was told and retold with manifold variations by historians, poets, and novelists. Sex, it appeared, had caused the untimely death of a great poet, and the false story of his end was used to point a moral and adorn a tale. Marlowe's contemporaries, however, the men who knew him best, seem wholly ignorant of this report; Peele, Nashe, Chapman, and Drayton all lament Marlowe's untimely end; none of them alludes in any fashion to his alleged "lewd love."

The final impression one gets of Marlowe, now that most of the facts are before us, is clear and definite. He was a young rebel who broke from the ordered conventions of Elizabethan life. He threw away his chance of promotion in the Church, and scoffed at the literal acceptance of the Bible story. He was hot-tempered and violent, but possessed a charm that recommended him to the friendship of all sorts of people; "Kind Kit Marlowe" an unknown contemporary called him. Marlowe is the only one of all his fellow poets to whom Shakespeare directly alludes, for Marlowe is the "dead shepherd" of a well known line in *As You Like It*. Arrogant, self-confident, and independent, he shattered the conventions of Elizabethan drama and opened the way for new and better plays.

Marlowe began his attack on the drama with *Tamburlaine*. That it was a deliberate attack upon accepted conventions is plain from the defiant words of the Prologue:

> From jigging veins of riming mother wits,
> And such conceits as clownage keeps in pay,
> We'll lead you to the stately tent of war,
> Where you shall hear the Scythian Tamburlaine
> Threatening the world with high astounding terms
> And scourging kingdoms with his conquering sword.

In the first line Marlowe proclaims his scorn of the rhymed doggerel of the old Morals and Interludes, poor stuff composed by writers who had nothing but their "mother wit," their simple common sense, to fall back on, none of the scholar's resources of which he, Master of Arts of Cambridge, is proudly aware. In the second he denounces the idle jests ("conceits") of the popular clowns. Instead of these Marlowe offers his hearers a play of heroic action by a famous conqueror. And this action, this character will be embodied and revealed in the heroic blank verse of the Senecan drama raised to the highest pitch of poetic declamation. Here was innovation with a vengeance, but it was splendidly successful. The novelty, the music of the verse, the acting and thunderous declamation of Alleyn, greatest actor of the day, took the town by storm. Marlowe's first play was epoch-making in the development of Elizabethan drama.

Tamburlaine has been called a dramatized epic, a plotless succession of scenes centering about the hero. That is hardly a fair criticism; knowing Marlowe's sources we can see how he selects, omits, and arranges to gain the effect he aims at. The character of Zenocrate, for example, is Marlowe's creation from a mere hint in history, and it is this invented character that allows Marlowe to show another side of the protagonist than that of the merely ruthless conqueror. It is true that there is but one vital character in the play, Tamburlaine himself. That is Marlowe's special and peculiar technique, the centering of all action about the protagonist, a technique that he retained till almost the close of his career. This character, to be sure, is static; there is little difference between the hero of the first and the last acts except that at first he aspires and at last attains; yet in this character Marlowe embodies, as no one had done before and few were to do after him, the two-fold spirit of the Renaissance, its lust for power which found "sole felicity" in the "sweet fruition of an earthly crown," and its worship of a beauty unat-tainable even by the "highest reaches" of man's art.

> If all the pens that ever poets held
> Had fed the feeling of their masters' thoughts,
>
> .   .   .   .   .
>
> If all the heavenly quintessence they still
> From their immortal flowers of poesy,
>
> .   .   .   .   .
>
> If these had made one poem's period
> And all combin'd in beauty's worthiness,
> Yet should there hover in their restless heads
> One thought, one grace, one wonder, at the least,
> Which into words no virtue can digest.

The prologue to the Second Part of *Tamburlaine* shows the poet no longer in a mood of defiant protest but rejoicing in "the welcomes Tamburlaine received" and prepared to give his friendly audience more of the same. Superficially the second part is a repetition of the first, a long succession of wars and conquests. Essentially it is something more; there is emotional expansion. Such crises as the death of Zenocrate and the failure and the punishment of the hero's son represent internal struggles and reactions, till at last the death of the protagonist ends the play with the proper tragic catastrophe when "Tamburlaine the scourge of God must die." Moreover, there is an exploitation of the resources of the Elizabethan theatre; the curtain of the inner stage is drawn to reveal Zenocrate "lying in her bed of state," while music plays for her death. There is a splendid procession of Kings crowning the son of Tamburlaine's victim, Bajazeth; before long we see these same Kings harnessed to the car of Tamburlaine, who scourges them across the stage. The Governor of Babylon is hanged in chains upon the city walls—that is, from the upper stage of the theatre—and shot to death by a general volley. The resources of the early playhouse must have been strained to provide such spectacles, but it was quite worth while; Henslowe's *Diary* shows that years after the poet's death the play was a drawing card at the Rose, and Henslowe was quite willing to pay out good money for the breeches of crimson velvet and the coat with copper lace which Alleyn wore as Tamburlaine.

The Tragical History of Dr. Faustus followed, probably, close upon *Tamburlaine*. Any attempt at a critical appreciation of this wonderful play is confronted with peculiar difficulties. It was immensely successful upon the stage, but it was not printed until 1604, eleven years after Marlowe's death. Twelve years later another edition appeared, adding about 550 lines to the brief text of the first. To make confusion worse confounded we know that in 1602 Henslowe paid two of his hacks £4 for additions to *Dr. Faustus*. Even in its first printed form, then, we are not sure that we have Marlowe's play unmixed with baser matter. The second edition adds much that cannot possibly be his, but does, none the less, give us some fresh passages that seem to come from Marlowe's pen. The play as it has come down to us resembles nothing so much as a Gothic church, partly in ruins, partly patched up by later and inferior work, brick and plaster for carved stone. Even so, however, it is possible to discern the outlines of the original structure.

The tragic tale of Faustus which Marlowe dramatized falls naturally into three parts: the temptation and fall of the hero; his life as a wonder-working magician; and his death and damnation. The play follows closely along these lines with, as it stands, a great admixture of comic horse-play, fiercely denounced by critics, but as experience in recent revivals has shown, very successful on the stage. A structural weakness in the story carries over into the play; the beginning and the end are the high spots, alike in the tale and in the drama. How is the intervening space to be filled up except with wonderful works of Faustus the wizard? Goethe, centuries later, solved the problem by intro. ducing the tragic theme of Gretchen's fatal love for Faust, but Marlowe, who disdained the dalliance of love, was content with the single apparition of Helen. Possibly the interval was filled in the original with narrative and descriptive passages, some of which may still remain. Possibly the tricks played by Faustus on the Pope represent Marlowe's bitter anti-clerical antipathy. It is only at the beginning and end, however, that we catch the clear, uninterrupted voice of the poet-playwright.

In some respects *Dr. Faustus* is a curious blend of old and new. The Good and Bad Angels, like the Seven Deadly Sins, are an inheritance from the Morals; the Chorus is a Senecan note. Yet essentially it is a true Elizabethan play, the first great poetic tragedy in the English language. For *Dr. Faustus* rises above *Tamburlaine* in that it is a soul's tragedy. Again Marlowe centers all action about a single character, but here the character is not static; it changes with the action. Faustus, dominated by the lust for knowledge, is tempted, falls, exults in his new power, fears, wavers between repentance and despair, sinks deeper into sin, and dies at last in horror. And beside this tragic hero stands the grim figure of Mephistophilis, not the comic devil of the Morals, but a bitter and malignant spirit, "deprived of everlasting bliss."

Marlowe's ruined play has an almost universal appeal. Faustus, in a sense, is Everyman, every man who has renounced his faith for the lust of the flesh and the pride of life. Yet one may wonder whether the character is not also a self-revelation of the poet. Like Faustus Marlowe was a scholar and a student of theology who turned his back upon the God revealed in the religion of the day. The bitter gibes reported as part of Marlowe's daily conversation may have sprung from an unhappy mind; the material hell to which Faustus is borne away seems little other than a symbol of the spiritual anguish of the poet. One drop of Christ's blood would save the soul of Marlowe as of Faustus, but the defiant poet will not, cannot, turn to Christ.

Like *Tamburlaine* (Part II), *Dr. Faustus* makes use of the resources of the Elizabethan stage; the curtain is drawn in the last scene to disclose the horrors of hell, painted, perhaps, upon a canvas background. But the special delight of the Elizabethans were the devils who ran about the stage spouting flame and scattering fireworks. In fact, a legend sprang up that at more than one performance of the play a veritable devil straight from hell appeared upon the stage. No wonder that *Dr. Faustus* was so popular that it outlived the Puritan Commonwealth and was still performed in the days of Mr. Pepys.

The Jew of Malta, Marlowe's third play for the Admiral's Company, was written some time after the death of the Guise, December 23, 1588, mentioned in the Prologue, but no earlier edition is known than that of 1633. There seems to be no direct source of this play; the intricate plot is certainly Marlowe's deliberate and conscious invention.

Less interesting to the reader than either *Tamburlaine* or *Faustus*, *The Jew of Malta*, none the less, is most important in any study of Marlowe the dramatist. We see him here moving towards the school of Kyd. As in his earlier plays the action centers around one leading character, written for and acted by Edward Alleyn; but this character is now involved in a long series of plots and counterplots, skillfully woven together to form a whole. We have no longer a mere succession of events arranged in chronological order as in *Tamburlaine*, nor a grouping of scenes as in the fragmentary *Faustus*, but an elaborate plot packed with startling incidents and culminating in a sensational and theatrically effective catastrophe.

Moreover, Marlowe, defiant as usual of tradition, introduces another innovation into English popular drama. The central figure of this play is a deliberate and unmistakable villain. He is a Machiavellian, as Machiavelli was understood, or misunderstood in Elizabethan England, self-centered, treacherous, and revengeful. No such protagonist had yet appeared on the English stage. As in the case of *Tamburlaine* this innovation was at once successful. Henceforward the villain-hero is a familiar figure in Elizabethan tragedy. Aristotle indeed forbade such a character as the hero of tragedy, and Aristotle was an orthdox authority, but Marlowe cared as little for orthodox esthetics as for orthodox theology.

Whether Aristotle's dictum is universally binding might well be questioned in view of Shakespeare's achievement in *Macbeth,* but it is plain that Marlowe does not successfully challenge it. The *Jew of Malta* is anything but a great tragedy. Perhaps melodrama is a better term, for there is little in the character of Barabas to evoke the sympathy due to the truly tragic hero. This is owing in the main to the degeneration of his character as the action develops. Magnificently presented in the opening scenes, the Jew wins our interest and to some extent our sympathy in his contest with his Christian persecutors; had he been content to rest after the recovery of his forfeited wealth, we should have had a quite satisfactory story of the triumph of the underdog. But this is not the kind of play that Marlowe meant to write. No sooner has the Jew regained his wealth than he begins to plot revenge against his Christian enemies using as his tool his dear daughter. Shocked by her lover's death, brought about by her father's machinations, the girl flies for refuge to a nunnery, whereupon Barabas calmly poisons her and all the other nuns. Henceforward his career is a mere struggle to evade the consequences of his crime, a successful struggle until at last, installed as governor of Malta by the Turks, he plans treason to his new masters, and perishes by a Christian counterplot.

This degradation of the protagonist is sometimes ascribed to the botching of Marlowe's play by later revisers; but whatever allowance is made for revision, it is clear that such a degradation was part of Marlowe's plan. The great soliloquy of Barabas in which he proclaims himself an inhuman villain:

> As for myself I walk abroad a-nights
> And kill sick people groaning under walls:
> Sometimes I go about and poison wells . . .

occurs early in the second act and is composed in unmistakable Marlovian verse. Indeed, fragments of Marlowe's poetry shine from time to time through the prosaic dialogue of the last scenes. Probably Marlowe planned a play on the triumph and downfall of a Machiavellian villain, embodied in the figure of the popularly detested Jew; his own hatred of Christian hypocrisy made it impossible for him to confront the Jew with worthy antagonists, and therefore the final result was bound to be little other than the play as it stands, a tangle of plots and counterplots with the villain-hero sinking steadily deeper into crime, till at last he meets his fate. This fate by the way is skillfully adapted to Marlowe's stage: Barabas is standing *"above,"* i.e., in the balcony; at *"a charge,"* i.e., a cannon fired behind the stage, a trap in the balcony opens, and he falls through it into a caldron concealed behind the curtain of the inner stage, which is then withdrawn to show him entrapped in a fiery pit. One can well imagine the loud applause of the first audience at this *coup-de-théâtre.*

Marlowe introduces another technical device into the construction of this play, new, it would seem, in Elizabethan drama. He sets the story of his protagonist against a background of history, the various Turkish attacks on Malta. The confiscation of the Jew's wealth with which the action starts is due to the Turkish demand for arrears of tribute; the return of the Jew in triumph to the town is as guide to an invading Turkish host. Some illusion of reality is thus given to the almost incredible events of the play, another evidence of Marlowe's increasing mastery of dramatic technique. Evidently this was a device which Shakespeare admired, for he used it more than once, especially with admirable skill in *Othello.*

Edward II belongs to that genre of Elizabethan drama known as the History or Chronicle. This type, of which Bale's *King John* had been an early anticipation, had sprung into popular favor in the late eighties with the outburst of national feeling already noted (p. 29). The early examples were for the most part carelessly constructed plays, a mere succession of scenes exhibiting the lives of English kings. In Marlowe's hands the genre is transformed into tragedy of character. The fate of Edward is not due to external circumstances, but to his own weak and wavering personality. The protagonist of this play is no superman like Tamburlaine, but a gentle monarch, victim of a fatal passion for an unworthy favorite, and pathetically incapable of coping with his responsibilities as king. Edward is not effeminate; he is capable of outbursts of anger, even of swift action. There is something in his nature which attracts sincere affection from those who know him best; even his cruel keepers pity him. Against such a king Marlowe arrays a group of turbulent nobles, proud of their birth, scornful of Edward's low-born favorite, and ready at any time to rise in arms to drive him from the king's side. Among these Mortimer stands out as a definite personality. One among others of the peers at first, he becomes before the play closes an ambitious, ruthless Machiavellian, seeking to confirm his sole power by an intrigue with the foolish Queen, by a harsh mastery over her young son, and finally by the murder of Edward himself. Mortimer is a cousin-german of Barabas and like him he comes to a sudden and violent end.

For the story of *Edward II* Marlowe turned to Holinshed, the standard authority in his day for English history, but he omits, condenses, and rearranges his material in order to obtain a swift and effective dramatic sequence. This free treatment of his source is especially noticeable in his handling of the relation between the Queen and Mortimer. It may be questioned whether he has successfully motivated the change from the devoted Queen of the first acts to the adulterous paramour of the close, but at least he has given a continuity and causal connection to these two phases of her character. Along with this freedom in handling his material goes Marlowe's increased mastery of dramatic construction. Regarded simply as a piece of stage-craft *Edward II* shows a distinct advance over *The Jew*. The theme is single, the struggle between the King and his lords, a struggle which rises and falls in a series of wave-like progressions. The protagonist wins and loses by turns until at last he is decisively overcome and forfeits both his crown and his life. Then swift retribution overtakes the guilty party, as the heir to the throne assumes the royal power, sends Mortimer to his death and the Queen to prison. The play closes on a major note as a new era begins with promise of better days. This is a much-admired device of Shakespeare's; he uses it not only in his chronicles, *King John* and *Richard III*, but even in such tragedies as *Macbeth* and *Hamlet*.

Lovers of poetry will naturally prefer *Tamburlaine* and *Faus-*

tus to *Edward II;* there are no such lyric passages in this play as Tamburlaine's appeal to beauty or the invocation of Helen in *Dr. Faustus.* Marlowe, the advancing dramatist, has learned to curb his exuberance. Much of the dialogue of *Edward II* consists of brief speeches and retorts between Edward and his peers; often there is little of poetical beauty in them, but they are good stage dialogue. The rhetorical tirades of *Tamburlaine* disappear; the longer speeches which Marlowe puts in the mouth of the King are essentially dramatic. It seems that in this play Marlowe is on his way to achieving the supreme gift of the poet-playwright, that of dramatic utterance, the speech exactly fitting the speaker and the situation. Gaveston's scornful retort to the barons debating on the manner of his death:

> I thank you all, my lords, then I perceive
> That heading is one, and hanging is the other
> And death is all;

and Mortimer's proud farewell to his mistress:

> Weep not for Mortimer,
> That scorns the world and as a traveller,
> Goes to discover countries yet unknown,

can hardly be bettered in Shakespeare.

Marlowe was certainly the original author of *The Massacre at Paris,* a play dealing with the contemporary civil war in France. Unfortunately the text has been so badly damaged that it is hard to recognize his hand except in some speeches by the villain-hero, the Duke of Guise. His presence as collaborator has been conjectured in a number of anonymous Elizabethan, even in some of Shakespeare's early plays, especially in the Second and Third Parts of *King Henry VI.* Most of this is pure guess-work. Marlowe's amazing success provoked a host of imitators; echoes of his "mighty line" reverberate through early Eliza-bethan drama; repetitions, imitations, and parodies of his char-acteristic images and phrases meet us at every turn. Modern conceptions of an author's right to his words and of the sin of plagiarism were quite unknown to the Elizabethans, who stole from one another without the slightest hesitation. It is wiser to limit our judgment of Marlowe to the four great plays which we know assuredly were his.

Marlowe's contribution to Elizabethan tragedy is too varied and potent to be summed up in a paragraph; yet a few phases may be pointed out. In the first place there is in all of Marlowe's work a sense of power, a vigorous driving energy, conspicuously absent in the work of earlier men. Himself a child of the Renaissance he embodies in his creations the lust for power so characteristic of that age. His ideal, at least in his early plays, seems to have been the Renaissance prince, a Richard Crookback or a Cæsar Borgia. Hence comes his glorification of such a figure as Tamburlaine with his wild desire

> To ride in triumph through Persepolis.

There is in Marlowe little or none of that sense of nationality and patriotism so strong in Shakespeare. He could never, one believes, have written a play like *Henry V;* he is the individualist of the Renaissance expressing himself in the words of Richard Crookback:

> I have no brother; I am like no brother;
> And this word love which greybeards call divine
> Be resident in men like one another,
> And not in me—I am myself alone.

This stormy individualism of Marlowe's impregnates later Elizabethan tragedy and begets a group of villain-heroes or of strong men fighting, often in vain, against an overwhelming force. Elizabethan drama differs from the Greek in many ways; in one especially, its insistence on the right of the individual to push on to his goal.

Yet there is something more in Marlowe than the mere lust for power. There is the Renaissance sensitivity, its passion for beauty. It is this passion which gleams through the gorgeous pageantry of *Tamburlaine* and finds supreme expression in the vision of beauty incarnate in Helen,

> . . . fairer than the evening air
> Clad in the beauty of a thousand stars.

Marlowe's sensitivity linked with his dramatic art enables him to seize on and express passions which presumably he never felt: the terror of Faustus awaiting damnation, or the greed of Barabas gloating over his gold. It is this sensitivity to passion and to passionate desire that makes Marlowe's heroes, even the pathetic Edward, real and living beings, something other than the stiff figures of academic tragedy. Here too we recognize in later tragedy the authentic gift of Marlowe. With all its faults and extravagance and careless work Elizabethan drama is keenly sensitive to human passion and to its destructive effect upon the lives of men.

Finally Marlowe was a poet. He was a born poet who only by degrees made himself a master playwright. Moreover he was the first great English poet to make use of the drama as a medium of poetic expression. In Marlowe's day for the first time there were theatres where plays could be produced, and skilful actors to declaim a poet's verse. Marlowe's great contemporary, Spenser, was for the most part out of England during the dramatic activity of the eighties, and Spenser's genius was anything but dramatic. Yet Spenser's influence on the new drama has already been pointed out, and the young poet in Marlowe came more readily under Spenser's spell than any of his contemporaries. Marlowe, of course, was quick to perceive that the linked sweetness of Spenser's stanzas was utterly unsuited to the stage, and he turned naturally and rightly to that form of verse which had been recognized from the time of *Gorboduc* as the fittest medium for poetic tragedy, the so-called blank verse. He was not the first to adopt this metre; Peele certainly, Kyd possibly, had used it before him, but neither Peele nor Kyd was Marlowe's peer as a poet. Marlowe made himself almost at once a master of this difficult metre, so easy to write, so hard to transform into poetry. It is not too much to say that this noblest of all English verse forms is essentially the creation of Christopher Marlowe. Shakespeare was to expand its range, but in this, as in so much else, Marlowe was the master from whom Shakespeare learned the secret of his art.

And it was not Shakespeare alone who learned this art of poetic-dramatic expression from Marlowe. Elizabethan drama as a whole is essentially poetic drama, and all the best of Elizabethan dramatic poetry is in Marlowe's measure, in blank verse. It is true that, as time passed, playwrights abandoned the long declamatory tirades of *Tamburlaine* and modified the measure into something more nearly resembling the customary speech of men; Marlowe had done that himself in his last play. But at the close of the era when the secret of poetic blank verse was lost and a halting metre hardly distinguishable from prose took its place, the drama withered to decay; it was at its last gasp when the Puritans administered the *coup-de-grâce* by closing the theatres. Poetry, a poetry of power and of passion, was Marlowe's greatest gift to Elizabethan drama.

In Marlowe's work we see the culmination of the long period of transition in the development of English drama, the final union of classical art with native life and vigor, heightened with a strong infusion of the romantic. It is impossible to say what Marlowe might have accomplished had he lived out Shakespeare's span of life. That he was pushing on to greater things is plain from the extraordinary advance of *Edward II* over *Tamburlaine*. Yet it seems fairly certain that he would never have attained the breadth and sweep and infinite variety of Shakespearean drama. He lacks Shakespeare's gay fancy, his broad humor, his delight in the words and deeds of common men and women, his vigorous patriotism—above all, his lofty ethics. Marlowe is a rebel, glorious to be sure, but after all a rebel, titanic, not divine.

CHAPTER FIVE

THE HENSLOWE GROUP: CHAPMAN, DEKKER, HEYWOOD

DURING the years 1594–1600 while Shakespeare was establishing himself as the most popular of living playwrights, it appears that his company, the Lord Chamberlain's Men, depended very largely upon his rapid production of masterpieces to lure London audiences to the Theatre. Presumably they had a repertoire of old plays, like Kyd's *Hamlet,* and some new plays by other authors, but until Jonson began to write for them in 1598 it is impossible to name a living author other than Shakespeare who was supplying them with plays.

It was a very different case across the river on the Bankside, where the rival company, the Lord Admiral's, led by Alleyn and backed by the financial resources of Philip Henslowe, gathered around them a small army of playwrights who fabricated plays for them in a fashion that might almost be called mass production, seventeen new plays in one year, 1597–98, twenty-one in the next. For the affairs of this company we have the invaluable record of the so-called Henslowe *Diary* and the miscellaneous Henslowe papers still preserved in Alleyn's College of God's Gift at Dulwich.

Henslowe's activities in connection with theatres, actors, and playwrights throw much light upon the commercial side of English Renaissance drama. A poor and apparently uneducated youth, he began his rise in the world in true Elizabethan fashion by marrying the rich widow of his first master. With her money he launched into the busy life of London, and rose to be church-warden and Groom of the Chamber under Elizabeth, a very respectable citizen indeed. In 1587, fired perhaps by the success of Burbage's Theatre, he conceived the idea of building a playhouse on the Bankside, and by the end of that year the first of the Henslowe theatres, the Rose, was ready for occupation.

When Shakespeare's company shifted to their new playhouse, the Globe, on the Bankside, Henslowe crossed the river and built the Fortune, "the fairest playhouse in this town," in the district that Shakespeare's fellows had abandoned, and some years later, 1613, he erected another, the Hope, on the site of the old Bear-garden on the Bankside. All these playhouses he rented out to theatrical companies. Henslowe's more intimate connection with actors and playwrights began in 1592 when his step-daughter, Joan, married Edward Alleyn. He and Alleyn, whom he calls affectionately his son, were from this time on closely associated in the financing and production of plays, and it is in this year, 1592, that the *Diary* begins.

This most interesting of Elizabethan theatrical documents is not really a diary at all, but a miscellaneous account-book in which Henslowe jotted down memoranda of all sorts from medical prescriptions to business transactions. Its special interest to students of the drama lies in the fact that he methodically entered in it his receipts at the performances of individual plays, name and date recorded, his advances to the company to buy new plays, and his personal loans to needy playwrights and actors, more than once to get them out of jail.

Henslowe's method of securing his rent from a company occupying one of his theatres was to contract with them for getting a percentage, usually fifty per cent, of the receipts of the galleries, where the better paying part of the audience sat. This percentage might be increased if the company got into his debt; it was seldom, if ever, diminished. Further, he was always ready to advance cash to secure for the company a new play on the promise that the manuscript would be ready at a fixed date. He seems, on the whole, to have dealt generously with what was often an embarrassing situation, but it is plain how his control over the company must have been increased by this method. Other practices of his tended still more to increase this control. From time to time he signed a contract with a needy actor binding him to play only with a company which he was financing; he went even further and bound an author by contract to write plays for the Admiral's Company only. Before Henslowe's death, 1616, things had gone so far that the old man evidently considered himself the master of the actors; he speaks more than once of "my company," and in the last year of his life there was a bitter protest on their part against what they termed his "oppression and dishonesty." It was fortunate for Shakespeare and his fellows that they were from the beginning independent of such a backer.

Some examples of the process of play-manufacturing by writers and acquisition of a play by the company may be cited to illustrate the usual procedure of the Admiral's Company. Thus on April 4, 1601, Samuel Rowley, a member of the company, writes: "Mr. Henslowe, I have heard five sheets of a play of the Conquest of the Indies and I do not doubt but it will be a very good play; therefore I pray you to deliver them [the writers] forty shillings in earnest of it and take the papers into your own hands, and on Easter Eve they promise to make an end of all the rest." We note here the preliminary hearing by one of the company of part of a proposed play, his approval of it, and his call on Henslowe for an advance payment to the authors, accompanied with the advice that Henslowe secure the manuscript by way of preventing the authors from pocketing the "earnest" and selling the completed play elsewhere; and finally the promise to finish the play by Easter. Occasionally Henslowe advanced money to help a writer out of trouble and deducted it from a future payment for work done and delivered. Thus on February 4, 1598, he paid £2 to discharge Dekker out of jail and later paid him only £4 for his play Phaeton.

Three authors were engaged on The Conquest of the Indies. This is by no means an unusual number. Henslowe's accounts show everything from single authorship to collaboration by two, by three, by four, and even by five—the lost Cæsar's Fall.

The Diary and the Henslowe papers give us the names of over twenty playwrights working for the Admiral's Company and drawing pay from Henslowe. Many of them are very minor figures; few readers have even heard the names of Hathway, Rankins, and Massey. There are others better known: the poet Drayton; Chettle, who from 1598 to 1603 was one of the busiest and neediest of Henslowe's hacks; Anthony Munday, poet, playwright, and government agent. Other still more famous names appear from time to time, notably those of Ben Jonson and Webster, whose best plays were written after they had severed their connection with Henslowe. There are, however, three playwrights of the Henslowe group who, both for the Admiral's and for other companies, did work of sufficient importance to deserve attention here.

The first of these is George Chapman, 1560–1634, better known as the translator of Homer than as a playwright. His plays, however, are by no means negligible; they illustrate certain phases of Elizabethan drama, reveal early foreshadowings of at least two Elizabethan genres, and very definitely establish Chapman as a dramatist with ideas and ideals of his own. Already known as a poet by his *Shadow of Night*, 1594, he appears as one of the Admiral's playwrights on February 12, 1596, when his *Blind Beggar of Alexandria* was performed as a new play at the Rose. It made an instant hit, running for over twenty-two performances before April 1597, a record surpassed by only three of the Admiral's plays at that time. A reader today finds it rather hard to account for this success; the play seems a mere jumble of farcical incidents. There is reason to believe, however, that the extant text has been so cut and altered that Chapman himself would hardly recognize it. What he planned apparently was a tragi-comedy of love and war diversified by the "variable humours" of the title character. These "humours" caught the fancy of the audience, and the romantic action was almost eliminated. What the Rose's audience wanted was clowning.

Chapman's second play, *An Humourous Day's Mirth*, 1597, is a better play. It anticipates Jonson's method of a slight and single plot whose various incidents serve to demonstrate the varied humours of the characters. To carry such a plot through, an intriguer is needed to start the action and devise the complications. Here the role is filled by the witty Lemot, the King's "minion," who plots mischief out of sheer delight in mischief-making, even when his intrigue involves his royal master. Around him play a group of humour characters: Labervele, the jealous old husband; Countess Moren, the suspicious old wife; Dowsecer, the melancholy scholar; and Florilla, the false Puritan, with Bible phrases on her lips and lust for the pleasures of the world in her heart. Chapman, the humanist, had only scorn for the Puritan assumption of peculiar virtue. The main value of the play lies in its daring and novel attempt to put over an exhibition of fantastic and amusing characters. There had been nothing quite like this in English drama before; there were plenty of counterparts later. Jonson, we know, worked hand in hand with Chapman in his Henslowe period, and it was Jonson who definitely established the Comedy of Humours on the Elizabethan stage.

Chapman's name occurs for the last time in the *Diary* in July 1599. Shortly after this he seems to have transferred his services to the newly organized company of the Chapel Children playing at Blackfriars. He took along with him the manuscript of a play for which he had already been paid by Henslowe, *All Fools*, or, as it is called in the *Diary*, "The World Runs on Wheels," and "now [*i.e.*, by change of title], All Fools but the Fool." This is Chapman's masterpiece in comedy. It is an extremely clever combination of two Terentian plays, the *Heautontimoroumenos* and the *Adelphi*, plus a purely English underplot dealing with the humours of a jealous husband. Chapman's greatest weakness was in plot construction; here with the Terentian pattern before him he carries through a complicated intrigue with marked success. He is not content merely to follow his pattern; he alters the whole situation to make it correspond to English life: the courtesan of Terence becomes a secret wife, and the intriguing slave a scholar bitten with a lust for managing other folks' affairs. In characterization as in plot *All Fools* shows a great advance over Chapman's earlier work. The main action is motivated by the contrasted characters of the worldly-wise, opinionated Gostanzo, his rakish son, and the kindly, easy-going Marc Antonio. In the underplot the jealous Cornelio is a swiftly sketched humour, as is the gallant courtier Dariotto, the object of his suspicions. In contrast with his earlier work the greater part of *All Fools* is written in a smoothly flowing blank verse; prose is reserved for passages of farcical or satirical character. It is an interesting illustration of the changing taste of the day that a witty page, a genuine Lyly figure, parodies Lyly's euphuistic style in a manner that must have delighted a Blackfriars audience.

Chapman's later comedies, *May Day, ca.* 1602, a clever adaptation of a famous Italian comedy, *Monsieur D'Olive,* 1604, an entertaining compound of romance and satire, and *The Widow's Tears, ca.* 1605, a cynical dramatization of the Ephesian widow story, were all written for the Children at Blackfriars. So were two others which deserve special mention.

The Gentleman Usher, ca. 1602, is an interesting example of the type of theatrical entertainment offered the audience at Blackfriars. It is a curious medley of diverse elements which the playwright's art has managed more or less successfully to harmonize. The first two acts are largely taken up with music and spectacle, a formal masque and a comic dance. Then the main action begins, founded on the old motif of rivalry in love between an aging father, here a Duke, and his son, the Prince. The Prince wins the friendship of the gentleman usher, the comic character for whom the play is named, and employs him as his ambassador to Lady Margaret. The scenes in which the Prince and Margaret in turn play upon the good nature and conceit of the usher approach as nearly to high comedy as anything outside of Shakespeare in Elizabethan drama. Graver matter follows: the Prince and Margaret celebrate a secret marriage with a ceremony of their own devising. Later surprised by the Duke the Prince flies, pursued by Medici, his father's villainous favorite. On a false report of the Prince's death Margaret disfigures her face with a poisonous ointment to escape a forced marriage with the Duke. Here, indeed, is a tragic situation, but a solution quickly follows. A wonder-working doctor restores the lady's beauty; the favorite is driven with shame from the court; and the Duke blesses the union of his son and Lady Margaret.

Here at an early date is a distinct anticipation of romantic tragi-comedy as Beaumont and Fletcher were to perfect it. Leading characters come near to death, but escape by something like a miracle; the villain himself is let off with banishment. Something like this can be found in many later plays; what cannot be found there is Chapman's sweet and sober poetry, and his independent thought. Here alone in his comedies appears the note of defiance of convention and of self-reliance, a characteristically Renaissance blending of pagan stoicism and Christian ethics.

Eastward Ho differs in almost every possible way from *The Gentleman Usher*. It is a collaboration on Chapman's part with John Marston and Ben Jonson, both then writing for the Children at Blackfriars. It represents a striking departure from the usual repertoire of the company. That had been composed in the main of romantic comedies, diversified by humour characters and personal satire. There is not a trace in it before *Eastward Ho* of the realistic comedy of contemporary English life. It seems likely that this departure was caused by the success of a series of plays mainly by Dekker and Middleton produced by the rival children's company of Paul's. One of these in particular, *Westward Ho*, 1604, by Dekker and Webster, suggested the title of the new play for Blackfriars. Eastward is the antithesis of Westward, and the new play was to be the very antithesis of the satiric, cynical, and laxly moral plays of the rival company. Yet it would vie with them in presenting a realistic picture of bourgeois London, stressing the industry and probity of the London merchant and pointing out the dire consequences of departure from his normal standard of morals.

The plot of *Eastward Ho* anticipates Hogarth's famous series of prints, "Industry and Idleness." The goldsmith, Touchstone, has two apprentices, Quicksilver and Golding. Quicksilver apes the fashions of the London gallants, runs into debt, gets drunk, is discharged, and ends in jail. There he repents and is freed by the compassion of his old master. Golding, the industrious apprentice, rises rapidly to be a freeman of the city and a deputy alderman who at one time sits in judgment on his former fellow. Touchstone also has two daughters. Gertrude scorns the city, desires at any cost to be a lady, marries a worthless knight who promptly deserts her, and is reduced to pawning her petticoat and silk stockings. Her sister, Mildred, a very colorless character, marries the virtuous apprentice, and in the end rescues Gertrude from distress.

Into this main plot there is woven a minor action exploiting contemporary interest in the colonization of America. Gertrude's knight has put all the remains of his fortune into a voyage to Virginia where he hears gold is more plentiful than copper in England. After a wild drinking party he takes a boat on the Thames to go down-stream to his ship; but he and his companions are wrecked in a storm on the river and the Virginia voyage ends ere it has begun. This sub-plot is certainly the contribution of Chapman, whose interest in discovery and exploration appears in his poem *De Guiana* and his *Masque of the Middle Temple.*

Into this sub-plot there crept a couple of clauses, apparently from the pen of Marston, which brought down a storm on the heads of the authors. Describing Virginia to the would-be voyagers Captain Seagull asserts that they will find there "a few industrious Scots." "But as for them," he continues, "there are no greater friends to Englishmen and to England, when they are out on't, in the world than they are. And for my own part, I would a hundred thousand of 'em were there, for we are all one country now, ye know, and we should find ten times more comfort of them there than we do here." A meddling Scot reported this jest to the King, and James exploded in wrath. Chapman and Jonson were thrown into prison—Marston seems to have escaped—and the report ran that they should have "their ears cut and noses" as a punishment for *lèse-majesté.* Fortunately the storm blew over; Chapman and Jonson had English friends at Court who thoroughly enjoyed the gibe at the Scots, and the authors were set free. At a banquet which celebrated their release Jonson's old mother showed him a paper "full of lusty strong poison" which she meant to have mixed in his drink, if the reported mutilation proved a fact, and, to show "that she was no churl, first to have drunk of it herself." The whole affair casts an illuminating light on the relations of the stage, the Court, and the censorship in the reign of James. A long career on the stage, both in its original form and in later adaptations, testifies to the theatrical success of this good old play.

Chapman's extant tragedies are of a later date than his comedies; like Shakespeare he seems to have entered into his tragic period in the early years of the seventeenth century. They differ strikingly from his early comedies. These evidently he wrote with an eye to stage performance; his tragedies, with one remarkable exception, are rather dramatic poems than stage-plays. They serve as a vehicle for the expression of his thought, his stoical philosophy, and his profound concern with the tragic conflict between the rights of the individual and the claims of the State. Four out of the five deal with characters and events in contemporary France and form a peculiarly individual group of plays. They are not chronicle histories of the old type; in a sense they are problem plays, set in the land across the Channel, perhaps because Chapman felt that he could speak his mind more freely on French than on English policies and statesmen. This was an error, as he was to discover to his cost before his work was completed.

The first of this group, *Bussy D'Ambois*, was acted by Paul's Boys about 1604. This, Chapman's tragic masterpiece, had a success such as none of his other serious plays ever attained. The reason is not far to seek. Using as his material the legend that had gathered around the flamboyant figure of Louis de Clermont d'Amboise, Seigneur de Bussy, soldier, duellist, and lover at the court of Henri III, Chapman built up his play along lines derived from Kyd and Marlowe. From Kyd he learned the technique of skilful construction by which the various incidents in the hero's career are woven into a unified pattern. From Kyd, too, come the sensationalism, the warning ghost, the scenes of torture and of murder, and the spectacular invocation and appearance of the devil Behemoth. From Marlowe, on the other hand, Chapman, himself a poet, caught poetic inspiration, flowering in long declamatory tirades adorned with epic similes. Like Marlowe a lover of the classics, he rounds out his "full and heightened style" with reminiscences of classic drama, sometimes even with direct translation of an appropriate bit of Seneca.

Chapman's hero, Bussy, is a direct descendant of Marlowe's supermen, one of the Titan brood of Elizabethan drama. Like Marlowe's early dramas *Bussy D'Ambois* is a one-star play; the masterful personality of the hero dominates all the action. Yet there is a real difference between Bussy and Tamburlaine or

Faustus. They are simple characters dominated by one passion, their eyes fixed on one goal; Bussy is the incarnation of Chapman's idea of the self-sufficiency of the virtuous man. The virtue of Bussy, duellist and adulterer, seems a little strange to us, but he embodies the Renaissance conception of *virtu*, "the sum of all bodily and mental excellencies." Chapman transformed a swashbuckler of the French court into a type of the self-reliant individualist at war with the world; the tragedy consists in his defeat by the powers of the world, a defeat as unexpected as it was incomprehensible to him. Alone of Chapman's tragedies, *Bussy* attained an instant and lasting success on the stage. It was revised and revived for a new company at Whitefriars, where Field acted the chief part. Later he carried the play over to the King's Men, who performed it at Court just before Chapman's death. It was promptly revived after the Restoration; Mr. Pepys saw a performance on December 20, 1661, when the part of Bussy was played by "that best of actors, Charles Hart."

The *Revenge of Bussy, ca.* 1610, the sequel to this play, is a more original, but far inferior drama. It is rather a revelation of Chapman's independence of thought than of his skill as a playwright. It is an emphatic protest against the established convention of the revenge tragedy, more particularly against the character of the revenger, half-mad like Hieronimo, hesitant like Hamlet, dominated by blood-lust like Vendice. As a contrast Chapman creates the character of Clermont D'Ambois, the "Senecal man." Charged by his brother's ghost—in a scene reported, not presented—with the duty of revenge, he accepts the charge, but will perform it in his own way with neither haste nor passion. When finally he comes face to face with his brother's murderer, he forces him to fight, strikes him down, and exchanges forgiveness with him. There follows a new and surprising departure from the convention. Heretofore, the revenger, enmeshed in the intrigue which accomplished the revenge, perished along with his victim. Such an end was unfitting, Chapman felt, for his ideal hero, so he devises for him another exit. No sooner has his mission been achieved than Clermont learns of the death of his friend and patron, the Duke of Guise, murdered by the King's command. Rather than linger in a world where such a deed was possible, Clermont dies like a Roman stoic by his own hand. This brief outline gives some conception of the action; only a careful perusal can give any notion of its grave and serious tone. It is weighted down with long philosophical and ethical tirades, most of them put into the mouth of the hero, some uttered in quite surprising fashion by very minor characters. One wonders whether such a play ever succeeded on the Elizabethan stage. Chapman himself was more than satisfied with it; he dedicated it in a formal epistle to a "right virtuous and truly noble knight" as containing "excitation to heroical life."

Between *Bussy* and its sequel, *The Revenge,* Chapman wrote for the Children at Blackfriars, 1607–08, a two-part play of a very original kind. It was a dramatization of the downfall and death of the Duke of Biron, the companion in arms of Henry of Navarre, condemned and executed as a traitor by his sovereign in 1602. No foreigner of that day was better known to Englishmen than Biron, and the parallel between Biron's fate and that of Essex naturally aroused special interest in England. It was daring enough of Chapman to dramatize a story involving the state policy of Henry IV and to bring the King himself upon the stage, but he went farther than this. To amuse his audience with a bit of Court scandal he introduced a scene in which Henry's Queen boxed the ears of Henry's mistress. The French Ambassador protested, and the English government acted promptly. The play was suspended and the chief actors jailed, while the guilty author fled to shelter. But Chapman was not to escape unpunished. He was proud of his work, and wished to see it in print; before publication, however, it was necessary to secure the license of the Master of the Revels, and his Deputy, Sir George Buck, looked long on the manuscript with an unfriendly eye. When at last it issued from the press, 1608, under the title of *The Conspiracy and Tragedy of Charles Duke of Byron* it appeared in a sadly mutilated form. A whole act dealing with Byron's interview with Queen Elizabeth had been cut out and replaced by a mere report of the embassy. The offensive scene between Henry's Queen and his mistress was of course cancelled, leaving a yawning gap in the action. Chapman protested in vain and in his dedication of the play to Sir Thomas Walsingham, Marlowe's old patron, he spoke sadly of the printed book as "these poor dismembered poems."

Poems Chapman calls the two parts of this play, and it is an apt description, for *The Conspiracy and Tragedy* is, perhaps, the most poetic and least purely dramatic of all Elizabethan stage-plays. There is almost no action; there is a complete absence of the Senecan machinery, the ghost, the tortures, and the bloodshed of *Bussy*. In the main the play is composed of excessively long speeches, soliloquies, debates, and choral comments, in which Chapman, often with profound thought and not seldom with noble beauty of expression, slowly evolves his theme.

That theme may be stated as the conflict between two ages, the Renaissance with its spirit of unbounded aspiration, and that of the New Monarchy, with its insistence on order and obedience. In *The Conspiracy and Tragedy* these two are incarnate in the persons of Byron, the warrior noble of the Renaissance, and King Henry IV, who regards his power as bestowed on him by God as a sacred trust. A conflict between these two representative figures, especially when the noble was swollen with self-confidence and the King determined on obedience, was inevitable; it reaches its tragic conclusion in the ruin of the individualist in the grip of inexorable law. Child of the Renaissance though he was, Chapman looks forward to and approves the coming triumph of the New Monarchy. That he was not blind to the dangers implied in this triumph appears in the last of his plays based on French history, *The Tragedy of Chabot Admiral of France*. This play, written shortly after 1611, was not printed till 1639, five years or so after Chapman's death, and then in a form revised by Shirley. Yet even through Shirley's additions and changes one can recognize Chapman's ground plan and see him dealing once more with the Byron theme, the conflict between a subject and a king. In this case, however, the subject is a loyal servant insisting only on justice and the king an arbitrary despot requiring blind submission. As before, the subject perishes in the conflict, but here the monarch learns too late the loss he and his kingdom have sustained. *Chabot* is at once a sequel to the *Byron* plays and a warning to absolute monarchs which Chapman's own kings, James and Charles, might well have heeded.

Chapman was a poet before he was a playwright; yet with the exception of his translations from Homer it seems clear that his best work was done for the stage. By mere necessity he was compelled in drama to lay aside the heavy mantle of pseudo-prophetic inspiration and to speak so as to be understood by the plain people of the pit. This is especially true of his comedies, and an unbiased judgment may well pronounce them better plays than the tragedies on which he prided himself. As a comic dramatist Chapman breaks decidedly with the native English tradition; he has little of the sheer realism of so many of his contemporaries and he discards the conventional clown. There is often a rather charming blend of the classic and romantic in his comedies, best seen perhaps in his masterpiece, *All Fools*. A genial good humor preserves him as a rule from the angry satiric note of Ben Jonson; he is readier to laugh at than to strip and lash the follies of mankind. He is no master of dramatic construction, but his management of single scenes is often excellent; he has a quick eye for an effective situation and exploits it in brisk dramatic dialogue. At his best Chapman is no unskilful hand at characterization: Gostanzo is a more credible character than his prototype in the Latin comedy; Bassiolo, the gentleman-usher, and Monsieur D'Olive, the foppish courtier, are little comic masterpieces. The prose of Chapman's comedies is racy and idiomatic, but there is a special excellence in his mastery of a blank verse so easy and flexible that it can drop into conversational dialogue and rise without an effort to pure poetic heights. In the central scene of *The Gentleman Usher* Chapman seems a forerunner of the easy grace of Fletcher.

Chapman's tragedies all deal with historic characters and events. Yet Chapman is so far from following the native tradition of truth to history that he allows himself at times such divergence from historic fact as to provoke contemporary remonstrance. If he had any model for these plays, it may have been Jonson's *Sejanus*. This Roman tragedy, produced in 1603 by Shakespeare's company, was a hopeless failure. Chapman, however, highly approved of it and prefixed to the first edition a long, barely intelligible poem in which he praises it as something "dear and rare." Jonson himself asserts that *Sejanus* preserves the tragic qualities of "dignity of persons, gravity and height of elocution, fullness and frequency of sentence." These are the qualities that Chapman admired in tragic drama and his tragedies, especially the *Byron* plays, are heavy with them. To enjoy these plays we must read them not for exciting action or for lively characterization, but for original and independent thought often expressed in grave and noble poetry.

Thomas Dekker, 1572?-1632?, is perhaps the most appealing figure among the lesser dramatists of Shakespeare's day. All that we know of his character as it is revealed in his work increases our desire to know more of the man; but a cloud obscures the most important events of his life. He speaks of London as his birthplace but the date of his birth is unknown; nor do we know certainly the date of his death. Nothing is known of his education except that he was not a university man; he may have attended a London grammar school since he shows a good command of Latin. A Londoner born and bred, he spent his life in the pursuit of letters in London. Our first knowledge of him comes from Henslowe's *Diary*, where on February 3, 1596, a revival of the *First Part of Fortunatus* is recorded. This is presumably Dekker's *Old Fortunatus*, and a "revival" would seem to show that Dekker was already one of the crowd of playwrights working for the Admiral's Company. His name appears for the first time a year or so later, January 8, 1598, when Henslowe advanced twenty shillings to "by a booke of Mr Dickers." This advance is followed in less than a month by an ominous entry: "lent unto the company to discharge Mr Dicker out of the Counter [a London jail] the some of 40s." Dekker's prodigious energy as a playwright and pamphleteer—he had a hand in over forty plays and wrote some twenty prose tracts—seems to have been matched only by his inability to save what his industry procured. There are frequent entries in the *Diary* of loans begged from Henslowe, and his connection with the theatre was broken in 1613 by a six years' imprisonment for debt. After his release he began work again as a playwright and prosewriter; he worked mainly in collaboration with younger dramatists, wrote the Lord Mayor's pageants in 1628 and 1629, and disappears from view in 1632.

Dekker's career as an author falls roughly into three periods: his early plays, 1596–1604; his prose period, 1606 to 1610; and his later work in drama and in prose. During the four years from 1598 to 1602 Dekker was one of the busiest of Henslowe's hacks; he was always ready to lend a hand in the hasty preparation of plays for the Admiral's. These dealt with British history in the form of the popular chronicle, with classic story—a lost *Troilus and Cressida*—, with Domestic Tragedy—*Page of Plymouth* in collaboration with Ben Jonson—, and even with the old-fashioned sacred play—a lost *Jephthah* with Anthony Munday. His surviving plays up to 1600–01 are in the field of romantic comedy with at times a dash of the old native realism.

The *Fortunatus* of 1596 does not seem to have been very successful; it was performed only six times and disappeared from the Admiral's repertoire. In November, 1599, Henslowe advanced £5 in earnest of the "whole history of Fortunatus." The "whole history" was, no doubt, a revision combining the original first and second parts. A month later Henslowe paid Dekker £2 more for "the end of Fortunatus for the Court." It was, we know, played at Court on December 27, 1599, and it is in this form that it has come down to us.

It is unfortunate that we do not have the two-part play in its original form. Dekker's amalgamation of the two plays and his further alterations of this "whole part" for the Court performance have quite obscured his original dramatization of the pleasant old story of Fortunatus and his sons with the purse of gold and the wishing cap. Whole sections of the action seem to have disappeared to make way for the Prologue at Court, for the masque-like effects of the Vice and Virtue scenes, and for the long closing scene in which Virtue kneeling before Elizabeth exclaims:

> I am a counterfeit, you are the true.

The result is a badly constructed but delightful play. It is an old-fashioned piece of work for 1599 when Shakespeare was writing his perfect comedies. It harks back to Greene in its dramatization of folk-tale; the prose with its puns, its paradoxes, and its quick-fire repartee suggests Lyly brought up to date for the popular theatre. The special charm of the play lies in its lovely verse.

Even before Dekker began his revision of *Old Fortunatus,* he was at work on what is now his best-known play. On July 15, 1599, Henslowe advanced £3 "to buy a book of Thomas Dickers called the Gentle Craft." This is *The Shoemaker's Holiday,* played at Court on New Year's Day, 1600, and published that same year with the double title, *The Shoemaker's Holiday, or The Gentle Craft.* In this delightful play Dekker turns from the fairy-land of *Fortunatus* to Elizabethan London. The action plays about the figure of a London shoemaker, Simon Eyre, who by a happy combination of industry, good-luck, and high spirits rises to be Lord Mayor, and ordains Shrove Tuesday a holiday for all London prentices. To add variety to so simple a tale of a citizen's progress Dekker interweaves two pretty, romantic love-stories. The first tells how a noble youth loves the Lord Mayor's daughter, woos her in secret, disguised as a Dutch shoemaker in Eyre's shop, weds her, and secures a pardon from the King—just the kind of tale to gratify an audience of London citizens. The second has a touch of pathos: Ralph, one of Eyre's shoemakers, is pressed for the wars in France; his young wife, deceived by a false report of his death, reluctantly consents to wed a London gentleman, but is snatched from him at the altar by the returned Ralph and a group of Eyre's workmen. For once in his life Dekker exercised control over his material and wove all the threads of his plot together into one harmonious pattern.

It is not the story, however, entertaining as it is, that gives this play its perennial charm. It is rather the abounding joy of life in general, of Elizabethan London life in particular, that flows from Dekker's heart and brain to find full and unrestrained expression in the character of Simon Eyre. Shrewd, honest, kindly, and democratic in Elizabethan fashion, Simon's special characteristic is an exuberant flow of speech, larded with tag-ends of proverbs and humorous abuse, and marked by a trick of repetitions that ring like a triple peal of bells. Well matched with him is his wife, Dame Margery, the would-be shrew, controlled and kept in place by Simon's firm hand, but rejoicing in the hood, the periwig, and the mask that mark her rise in social status; the "world's calling is costly," she says, "but it is one of the wonderful works of God."

Behind these figures and those of Eyre's singing, jesting workmen lies the London of Dekker's day. It would be hard to find another Elizabethan play where the background of contemporary life gives so strong a sense of atmosphere, an atmosphere of Old and Merry England at its jolliest. There were other and darker days to come in Dekker's London, and he was to tell of them in later work. Meantime this play of his joyous youth remains his unchallenged masterpiece.

Some time in 1601 Dekker was engaged on a play which, had it been finished as he planned it, would have been, perhaps, the most interesting of all his early work. The theme was the rescue of a bride from the lustful clutches of King William Rufus by her father and the bridegroom, Walter Tirrell, popularly supposed to be the slayer of Rufus in the New Forest. It seems as if Dekker had planned something like Greene's *James IV;* one cannot be quite sure of this, however, for while Dekker was still at work he was induced to take part in the War of the Theatres (pp. 137–9) and to reply in a stage-play to Jonson's *Poetaster.* Working against time to get this reply in rehearsal as soon as possible, Dekker had the unhappy idea of inserting it into his unfinished tragi-comedy. The result is *Satiromastix, or the Untrussing of the Humorous Poet,* one of the most incoherent plays in Elizabethan drama. It must have been effective on the stage, for it was produced not only by the Chamberlain's Company, but by Paul's Boys in their private theatre. It was promptly printed, 1602, and seems to have brought the so-called War to a laughing conclusion.

A change seems to come over the tone of Dekker's plays after *Satiromastix.* So far they had been essentially romantic; even the realistic scenes of *The Shoemaker's Holiday* show a dash of romantic lightness and gayety. His shift to a somewhat sordid realism had, perhaps, a double cause. The theatrical fashion was changing; romantic comedy was yielding on the one hand to

tragedy, on the other hand to a realistic and often satirical portrayal of contemporary middle-class life and manners. There is
little in Dekker's work to show that he had either desire or
capacity for tragic drama; much, on the other hand, to show a
keen observation of contemporary life which needed only a push
to drive him along the road of realistic comedy. This impulse
may well have been given by his association with Middleton.
Better born, better bred, a stronger and a harder genius than
Dekker, Middleton was well qualified to influence his gentle
friend. He and Dekker had worked together on the lost play,
Cæsar's Fall, in 1602, and his influence on Dekker is plainly
visible in a couple of plays: *Westward Ho,* 1604, and *Northward Ho,* 1605, in which Dekker collaborated with Webster. It
is not easy to assign particular scenes of these plays to their
respective authors; fortunately it matters little, for neither of the
plays is a credit to either of the authors. Reference has already
been made to *Westward Ho* as provoking a dramatic rebuke by
Jonson, Chapman, and Marston. *Northward Ho,* in turn, is a
reply to *Eastward Ho* with some lighthearted raillery of Chapman. There is little of Dekker's gay humor in these plays, and
less of his poetry than in any of his earlier work.

Early in 1604 Henslowe paid Dekker and Middleton for work
on *The Honest Whore.* This fascinating play appeared in two
parts, the first in 1604, the second, though no doubt written soon
after the first, not until 1630. Dekker's name alone appears on
both title-pages: Middleton may have contributed a scene or two,
but both plays are essentially Dekker's; he has assimilated Middleton's influence and used it here for his own purposes.

Like many popular Elizabethan plays *The Honest Whore* is
a story in dramatic form rather than a well-built play. In fact
it is three stories running side by side and only brought together
at the very end. The first of these is a romantic tale of two young
Italian lovers, Hippolito and Infelice. They are separated by a
family feud and only reunited after the lady's recovery from a
deathlike swoon caused by a sleeping-potion. Dekker seems to
be rearranging the plot of *Romeo and Juliet* to turn it into a
tragi-comedy. To this theme he adds the story of Bellafront,
the courtesan. She falls in love with Hippolito mourning over

the supposed death of his lady, offers herself to him, is moved
to repentance by his bitter denunciation of her trade, and resolves to return to her father. In the comic realistic under-plot,
an amusing inversion of the patient Griselda theme, a shop-
keeper's wife tries in vain to break the patience of her long-
suffering husband. She finally hits on the desperate expedient of
having him carried to Bedlam as insane. Here all the characters
assemble: Hippolito and Infelice secretly married, the repentant
wife come to free her patient husband, and, quite surprisingly,
Bellafront playing the part of a madwoman. The Duke, Infelice's
father, has also come there to see a show of lunatics, a popular
Elizabethan indoor sport. There is a general *éclaircissement,* the
lovers are pardoned, the wife regains her husband, and by the
Duke's command, Bellafront is made an honest woman by marriage to her first seducer, Matheo.

Like most sequels the Second Part falls below the First. The
same characters reappear, but now in changed roles. Hippolito,
who had converted Bellafront, now seeks to make her his mistress; Bellafront, the former courtesan, becomes the virtuous
wife; and the shop-keeper teaches a second wife the duty of
obedience. What gives interest and distinction to this sequel is
Dekker's extraordinary power of vivid characterization. Bellafront is a more vital character than in Part I; her role is that of
a patient Griselda but she plays it with a fine, instinctive loyalty
to the husband who abuses her and the father who has disowned
her. Matheo, a somewhat shadowy figure in Part I, comes to life
here as an Elizabethan gallant of the wildest type, a swaggerer
and a gambler, who pawns the clothes off his wife's back, robs
pedlars on the highway, and faces the gallows with a cynical
jest. A new character in this part is Orlando Friscobaldo, Bellafront's father, who watches over her in the disguise of an old
serving-man. His behavior is fantastic, but his speech reveals a
warm heart behind his gruff and forbidding exterior. He is a
Simon Eyre grown old, but still with Simon's inexhaustible
vitality and his kindly sympathy for those in trouble. All in all
The Honest Whore is the high-water mark of Dekker's work as
a popular playwright.

From 1606 to 1610 Dekker devoted himself mainly to the

composition of prose pamphlets. One of these, *The Gull's Horn-book,* in modern phrase, *An A. B. C. for Simpletons,* may be specially recommended to students of Elizabethan drama. One chapter in particular, "How a Gallant should behave himself in a Playhouse," offers a striking picture of the indignities which playwrights and actors suffered at the hands of the impudent pretenders to fashion who sat on stools upon the stage.

In 1610 Dekker joined once more with Middleton in *The Roaring Girl,* a play introducing a notorious figure in contemporary London, Mary Frith, alias Moll Cutpurse, a virago who dressed like a man, wore a sword and used it, and consorted with the scum of the city. It is characteristic of Dekker that he presents her as a woman more sinned against than sinning, "a roaring girl," indeed, but an honest one, as ready to help lovers in distress as to browbeat a bully. A pair of plays about this time, 1610–1612, show Dekker experimenting in various styles. The first, *If It be not Good, the Devil is in It,* is a dramatization of the folk-tale of Friar Rush. By way of variety Dekker next offered his audience a tragi-comedy in the fashionable Beaumont and Fletcher style, *Match Me in London.* This was not Dekker's line and he made a sad mess of it.

On his release from prison in 1619 Dekker returned to the theatre, but there is no extant play of this time which can be identified as his unaided work. On the contrary we find him now working in collaboration with younger playwrights. Where a stronger and more careful hand devised the plot, Dekker was always ready to contribute scenes of lively action. This is particularly clear in *The Virgin Martyr,* 1620, in which he collaborated with Massinger. The theme, the legend of St. Dorothea, was probably chosen by Massinger, of all Elizabethan playwrights the most interested in the doctrine and ritual of the Roman Church. The careful construction is his, as are quite certainly the beginning and the end of the play. Dekker fills in with some boisterous comic scenes in prose and with some exquisite poetry that passes between the Saint and her guardian angel.

In the following year he joined with Ford, just beginning his career as a playwright, and with the actor-dramatist William

Rowley, in *The Witch of Edmonton*, 1621. This is an interesting example of the Elizabethan theatre functioning like the newspaper of today in bringing the latest sensation before the public, for it is based on an account of the trial of Elizabeth Sawyer burnt as a witch earlier in the year. But it is much more than the hasty dramatization of a recent happening; it is a real play and a fine one. Along with the story of the witch there runs a domestic tragedy in which a young man murders his wife. This plot is probably Ford's invention, but Dekker intervenes to create the figure of Susan, the murdered wife, one of the simplest and sweetest girls in Elizabethan drama. His great contribution, however, is the character of Mother Sawyer, the wretched old woman hounded by slander and persecution into a compact with the devil. Dekker was enough of his time to believe in witchcraft; he was far beyond his time in the pity that he felt for the witch. Her defense against the charges brought against her is instinct with Dekker's sympathy for the poor and miserable.

Dekker seems to have liked working with Ford, for in 1624 there are records of several plays, most of them lost, of their joint authorship. In one of these, *Keep the Widow Waking*, they joined with Webster and Rowley to huddle up in a month a play that linked the incongruous themes of a scandalous marriage and a recent matricide in London. The only surviving play of this year of collaboration is *The Sun's Darling*, "in the nature of a masque," "often presented at Court and played at the private theatre, the Cockpit, with great applause." This charming dramatic poem—it is a pageant rather than a play—traces the career of Raybright, child of the Sun God, through the four seasons of the year. It is crowded with masquelike elements, songs, dances, and apparitions of the Sun in splendor. In such a work one cannot expect real dramatic action or strong characterization, but it is pleasant to find in the Dekker scenes of this, his last known work for the stage, a late flowering of his happy humor and his lilting lyric.

It is hard to form a final judgment of Dekker as a dramatist. There is so much in his work to delight us that it is easy to dwell upon his charm and overlook his weakness. On the other hand if one examines his plays closely, it is only too easy to point out his failures. Perhaps if one takes into account the circumstances under which his work was done, one may arrive at a fairly impartial conclusion.

Dekker was a professional Elizabethan playwright. Not only that, but he was from the beginning one of Henslowe's hacks, trained in the journeyman's craft of revision, collaboration, and hasty production. He never quite broke free, as Chapman and others did, from these bonds; to the end of his life we find him collaborating with other men to dramatize swiftly a contemporary sensation. It is hard to believe that under these circumstances he had any real pride in his art. As a professional playwright he naturally was inclined to make use of well-tried effects, sleeping-potions and feigned madness in serious plays, disguise and comic patter in his lighter work. His gravest fault is an amazing carelessness of construction; a crowded and tangled action is often brought to a swift and huddled close. Few of his fellow playwrights had any special reverence for the dramatic unities, but Dekker strays farther than most of them from the important unity of theme. No playwright with an artist's conscience would have shoved his satiric retort to Jonson into the framework of a romantic tragi-comedy.

Yet the merits of Dekker as a dramatist are far from inconsiderable. No one has spoken of him without dwelling on the beauty of his verse, but it has not always been observed how easily and naturally this verse often attains dramatic expression. Song is a natural and fitting decoration of Elizabethan drama, and Dekker's lyrics are among the sweetest in the chorus of Elizabethan song. Nor in praising Dekker's poetry should we overlook his command of a vigorous and racy prose. One of Dekker's characteristics is his keen observation of contemporary life. He knew his London as well as Jonson and loved it better, for there is none of Jonson's lofty scorn of human follies in Dekker's work; a romantic at heart, he tempered his comment on life with a kindly humor. He had a genuine if intermittent power of characterization; many of his characters are mere conventional dramatic types, but the best are vividly realized and strongly presented, the London shop-keeper, the long-suffering wife, and the swaggering gallant, all drawn from the life, creatures less of poetic imagination than of sympathetic observation. He is not a great dramatist, but certainly a delightful poet-playwright.

Like Dekker, Thomas Heywood, *ca.* 1570–1641, began his dramatic career as one of Henslowe's hack-writers, but behind this industrious and successful playwright there lay a background very different from that of Dekker. Born of a respectable family in Lincolnshire, he enjoyed a University education at Cambridge. He speaks in his *Apology for Actors,* 1612, of the "tragedies, comedies, histories, pastorals and shows publicly acted" during his residence there by "graduates of good place and reputation." Evidently he carried away from college a delight in the drama, but he gained also a wide knowledge of the classics, which was to furnish material for many plays and prose works, and to win for him in later years the title of "a learned author," the last epithet, perhaps, which one would ever apply to Dekker.

Our first knowledge of Heywood's connection with the theatre comes from Henslowe, who in October 1596 made an advance payment for "Hawodes booke." In 1598 he bound himself under a penalty of £40 to play only in Henslowe's theatre for the space of two years. Like Shakespeare, Heywood was actor as well as playwright, and his firm command of sure-fire stage-effects comes, like Shakespeare's, from his familiarity with them upon the boards. Heywood continued to act long after his two-year contract with Henslowe expired. It is possible that he left the stage about 1619, but he certainly did not cease to write. In 1624 his *Captives* was licensed for the Lady Elizabeth's Company, and later we find him closely associated with Queen Henrietta's Men and furnishing a couple of plays to the King's Company. When he published *The English Traveller,* 1633, he spoke of it as "one of among two hundred and twenty in which I had either an entire hand or at least a main finger." Evidently the score or so of plays that pass under his name today represents only a tenth part of his enormous output.

Besides his plays Heywood, like Dekker, wrote many prose tracts and treatises; unlike Dekker, however, the learned Heywood compiled for the most part histories and biographies. During the last ten years of his life he held the respectable position of City Poet to his beloved London and composed year by year the pageants for the Lord Mayor's shows. When he died in 1641, he was buried in the church of St. James, Clerkenwell, and the parish register records the funeral of "Tho. Heywood, Poet."

Publication dates in Heywood's case have as little bearing on the date of composition as in Shakespeare's; nor can we as in Shakespeare's work establish a fairly definite chronology by internal evidence. There is little sign of progress or development in Heywood's career as a dramatist. It seems best, then, in a review of his work to disregard chronological order and to group his plays under various classes, dwelling only upon outstanding examples.

We may begin with what is probably Heywood's first surviving play, *The Four Prentices of London,* probably written as Heywood says "in my infancy of judgment," *ca.* 1594. This absurd but amusing play is a dramatization of the heroic deeds of four London prentices who follow their father, the Earl of Boulogne, on the first crusade. After a series of fantastic adventures they are all crowned kings, while their sister, who has followed them in disguise, marries a Prince of Italy. There are certain features of this play that call for comment since they are more or less characteristic of the body of Heywood's work. In the first place it is remarkably old-fashioned; dramatized romances of chivalry like *Sir Clyomon and Clamydes* and Greene's *Orlando* were already going out of fashion, but they still appealed to a plebeian audience. It is not surprising that the aristocratic Beaumont ridiculed this play in *The Knight of the Burning Pestle* as the dear delight of such bourgeois souls as the Citizen and his Wife. The technique, too, is as old-fashioned as the theme. Heywood uses Dumb Shows, Choruses, and a Presenter to eke out the story. There is an immense amount of fighting, single combats in which the brothers "toss their pikes" —a stage-direction that Beaumont remembered—and mass battles between Crusaders and Turks. There is, of course, the Clown, half fool, like the old Vice, and a good deal of rather bawdy jesting. The dialogue consists in about equal portions of a stilted blank verse, and of the old traditional rhyming lines. Heywood was to do better work than this, but his conservatism and his sense of what his bourgeois audience would approve remained with him to the last.

Heywood's plays may be roughly divided into three classes: Histories, *i.e.*, dramatized narratives of historical or mythical actions; plays of romance and adventure; and plays dealing with contemporary life. The boundaries of these groups are not sharply defined, since the Histories sometimes deal with almost contemporary events, and romantic adventure is often given a vivid contemporaary background. Such a division will serve, however, for a summary review.

Two plays, each in two parts, handle episodes in English history. The first of these, *Edward IV, ca.* 1599, deals in conventional chronological fashion with the Wars of the Roses. The unusual feature is an under-plot of a type in which Heywood was later to do his best work, Domestic Tragedy. This is the pathetic story of Jane Shore, a citizen's wife, lured from her home to become Edward's mistress, later persecuted and driven to death in poverty by Richard III. Of all the writers who had told Jane's story Heywood alone dwells upon her final reconciliation with her husband; they die together in a scene where pathos comes dangerously near to sentimentality.

The second, *If You Know not Me, You Know Nobody, ca.* 1604, deals in the first part with the trials of Elizabeth under the reign of Mary Tudor, a topic very dear to the heart of a people who still cherished the memory of Gloriana. The second part dramatizes the career of Thomas Gresham, one of London's merchant princes, builder of the Royal Exchange, fondly believed by good Londoners the finest in the world.

The Rape of Lucrece: a true Roman tragedy, ca. 1607, is a chronicle history of Rome from the usurpation of Tarquin to his death in battle "with an arrow in his breast," a stage-direction that recalls one in *Cambises*, a generation earlier. The central scene of the rape is written with some degree of seriousness, but the tragic effect is quite ruined by a song in which the merry Lord Valerius, Horatius, and the Clown comment in a three-man catch upon the deed of shame. Valerius is a most entertaining anachronism; on every possible occasion he bursts into songs, Scotch, Dutch, and English, that vary from a catalogue of taverns, supposedly in Rome but plainly in Heywood's London, to a charming Elizabethan lyric: *Pack clouds away*. There must have been a well-voiced actor at the Red Bull for whom this part was specially composed. There is, of course, more to the play than the humours of the merry lord and the clown. There is swift and effective dramatization of the fall of the Tarquins with plenty of spectacle and fighting, and there is something like characterization in the figure of Brutus. Heywood is trying, with some degree of success, to do for a famous bit of Roman history what the writers of the Miracles did for the Bible story, to present it in such modern terms as to make it seem real to an illiterate audience.

The same may be said of Heywood's heroic attempt to dramatize the whole body of classical myth and legend from the birth of Jove to the siege of Troy. It took five plays to unroll this panorama of the past: *The Golden Age, ca.* 1611; *The Silver Age* and *The Brazen Age, ca.* 1612–13; and the long-deferred *Iron Age*, published in two parts, 1632. The series is packed with action presented in the manner of a chronicle play. The war between the Titans and the Gods is rationalized into a clash between two royal houses for an earthly kingdom. The labors of Hercules are unfolded in great detail, including his descent into Hell. When the dying hero lies upon his funeral pyre, "Jove above strikes him with a thunder-bolt: his body sinks and from the heavens descends a hand in a cloud that brings up a star and fixeth it in the firmament." "We all," says Nestor, uttering no doubt the conviction of the audience, "have seen Alcides deified."

The two parts of *The Iron Age* seem to have been especially popular. "These were the plays," says Heywood in an Epistle to the courteous reader, "often upon one stage publicly acted by two companies and have at sundry times thronged three several theatres with numerous and mighty auditories." There was good reason for this success: the theme itself, "the tale of Troy divine"; the love of Paris for Helen, and of Troilus for the faithless Cressida; and plenty of fighting ending in the general massacre of Priam and his family. There is a firm concentration upon the theme until halfway through the Second Part. Then suddenly the pattern changes, and we get a revenge tragedy of the type popular in the first decade of the seventeenth century. Cethus, a character who appears for the first time, starts an intrigue which brings about not only the deaths of Agamemnon, Clytemnestra, and Egistus, but a general mêlée in which all but one of the remaining heroes perish. Helen hangs herself, and Ulysses alone survives to speak the Epilogue.

The tragic matter is enlivened with plenty of comic foolery. There is the babbling clown and the railing Thersites. Above all, the audience is entertained with the amours of Jupiter. He comes, for instance, to the tower of Danae, not in a shower of gold, but disguised as a pedlar attended by the Clown. The Clown diverts the lady's guardians with gifts and patter while the God in a scene that pushes realism to the farthest limit gains access to her bed. The whole series is strikingly reminiscent of a medieval cycle, not only in its determination to tell the whole story, but in its episodic construction and its evident desire to instruct as well as to entertain.

Heywood, however, was too clever a playwright to adhere consistently to such old-fashioned matter. In his plays of romance and adventure we find him experimenting along other lines. *The Royal King and the Loyal Subject, ca.* 1602, is a tragi-comedy rather in the manner of Greene than in that of Fletcher. In fact a comparison with Fletcher's *The Loyal Subject,* 1618, affords an interesting example of the swift development of the genre. Both playwrights use the same source, but Heywood's play is a straightforward dramatization of the story plus a serio-comic subplot; Fletcher contrives a well-knit intrigue of disguise, suspense, and reversal with special emphasis on sex-appeal. It is a matter of taste whether one prefers the naïve simplicity of Heywood or the sophisticated art of Fletcher.

Before the close of his career Heywood contrived to acquire a degree of mastery of the new technique. Two late plays: *A Maidenhead Well Lost,* 1633, and *A Challenge for Beauty, ca.* 1635, show him attempting not without success to meet the taste of a more courtly audience than that of the Red Bull.

Two plays of adventure, both earlier than *A Challenge,* link this group with Heywood's plays of contemporary English life. *Fortune by Land and Sea, ca.* 1607, in collaboration with Rowley, is a pleasant blending of realism and romance. The somewhat complicated plot is set against a background of Elizabethan England; on the other hand the character and career of the hero are romantic enough. He avenges the murder of his brother, is concealed on his flight by a gentle lady, and escapes to sea. He becomes captain of an English ship, captures two notorious pirates, is knighted by the Queen, and comes home to marry his protectress.

The two-part play, *The Fair Maid of the West, or A Girl Worth Gold,* was published in 1631 "as it was lately acted before the King and Queen with approved liking." The First Part, Heywood's masterpiece in this genre, was written certainly many years before. It is a gallant play breathing the very spirit of a time when all the youth of England was on fire. The action starts at Plymouth where the fleet is assembling for the Island Voyage of Essex and Raleigh, 1599; it ends at the Court of Mullisheg in Morocco. In between we get the story of Bess Bridges, the girl worth gold. Seen first as a barmaid honest and beautiful, she later becomes mistress of her own tavern where she dons male attire and defeats a ruffian who has tried to bully her. On a false report of her banished lover's death she exchanges her inn for a ship, paints it black in token of her sorrow, and sets sail to war upon the Spaniards. After a series of adventures she and her lover meet in Morocco where the Turk, smitten with admiration of her courage and beauty, permits their marriage. The story is wildly romantic, but scene after scene is marked by a homely realism. The character of Bess, a true English girl, simple, frank, true in love, and chaste under trial, gives unity to Heywood's easy dramatization of a tale sure to enthrall an Elizabethan audience and still fascinating to the reader of today.

In striking contrast the sequel is conceived and executed in the spirit of tragi-comedy. It begins with a complicated intrigue in Morocco where the Turk has fallen in love with Bess, and his Sultana with Bess's husband. It ends in Florence where the married lovers, separated by a shipwreck, are again united after a sensational series of surprises and reversals. It is an amusing play, but it lacks the vigor and spirit of the First Part.

Of all Heywood's plays of contemporary English life the first, *A Woman Killed with Kindness*, 1603, is by far the best. Henslowe in a fit of generosity paid Heywood £6 for it and spent £7 on a velvet dress for the boy who played the leading woman's part. It is not only Heywood's best play, but the finest example of the characteristically native English genre, the Domestic Tragedy. Reference has already been made (pp. 29, 75) to this type of play and to a famous early example, *Arden of Feversham*, 1592, "a naked tragedy" which follows in close detail a story of adultery and murder related by Holinshed. With the wave of romanticism that swept over the English stage in the nineties this type of play seems to have disappeared, but towards the end of the century, coincident with the revival of tragedy and realistic comedy, it comes back again. In 1598–99, for example, Dekker had a hand in three such plays, all now lost; and a vigorous little specimen of this class, *A Warning for Fair Women*, was performed in 1599 by Shakespeare's company. These earlier examples of Domestic Tragedy are founded on actual fact and presented with a certain grim realism.

A Woman Killed differs from the convention in various ways, and the extent of the difference is the measure of Heywood's originality. The play is not founded on any happening in English life; on the contrary Heywood drew his material from a pair of Italian stories. He treated these with great freedom, shifting the scene to England, and setting the action against a background of English country life. More important still, he altered the dénouement from a husband's cruel revenge to Mr. Frankford's Christian forgiveness. Here is a complete break with the romantic convention, which, as in *Othello*, demanded death for the guilty wife, a shift to a treatment at once more realistic and more modern. That Heywood took his theme seriously is plain enough; his customary clown is absent and there is no lewd jesting over Mrs. Frankford's fall. He rises to an unusual height of poetic expression in the suitor's impassioned appeal and in the husband's final forgiveness of his wife.

The characters, too, are firmly realized. Mrs. Frankford is a gentle lady swept off her feet by a wind of passion which she has no power to resist. Wendoll, her seducer, is no intriguing villain; he is at once conscious of his guilt and greedy for his prey. The central character, of course, is that of the injured husband, and it is another mark of Heywood's originality that it is about the husband that he builds the whole action. The play opens with Frankford's marriage; the climax occurs when he discovers the guilty pair asleep together; and the end comes with his tender farewell to his repentant wife upon her death-bed. Kindly, generous, and unsuspicious, he is the very type to be betrayed by a false friend and a foolish wife, but he plays the hard role of the deceived husband with a simple dignity. One brief outburst of anger saves him from an almost super-human goodness; he dashes after the fleeing Wendoll with a drawn sword, and only the interposition of a servant stays him from an instinctive and bloody revenge. Here, surely, is an effective stroke of the born playwright.

It is unfortunate that the minor plot of this fine play should deal with a theme of over-strained romanticism. Yet it is charac-teristic of Heywood's method that this almost incredible story is given as realistic a background as that of the main action; the quarrel in the hunting field from which the sub-plot springs is as English as the dance of serving-men and maids at Frankford's wedding. The whole play, indeed, is a picture of English coun-try life, and the vigorous realism of the background joins with Heywood's thoughtful treatment to make *A Woman Killed* the most interesting to the modern reader of all Elizabethan domestic tragedies.

The English Traveller, written some time after 1625, is a belated and inferior example of this genre. At a time when the drama was largely dominated by masque-like elements Heywood attempted to renew interest in a simpler form. What he offers is, to quote his Prologue, "a strange play" without "song, dance or masque." The merit of the play consists in its characterization of the hero, a travelled and accomplished gentleman, and in its pleasant picture of life in a cultured English home. Heywood's share in *The Late Lancashire Witches,* a hasty dramatization along with Brome, of a reported outbreak of witchcraft, is very slight. It is confined to a few scenes which once more handle the theme of domestic tragedy. The sober sincerity of these scenes contrasts sharply with the coarse and riotous comedy with which Brome exploits the witchcraft story.

The Wise Woman of Hogsden, ca. 1604, stands alone in Heywood's work as a comedy of intrigue in the realistic manner of Middleton. The action is laid in the underworld of contemporary London. The central figure, the Wise Woman, fortune-teller, bawd, and baby-farmer, might well be a running mate to some of Middleton's rascals, but Heywood's kindly humor presents her as a benevolent old fraud. Her shrewd wit leads to the exposure of Chartley, "a wild-headed Gentleman" whose outrageous behavior furnishes the main action of the play. This "gentleman," a gambler, a wine-bibber, and a rake, is an interesting prototype of figures in Restoration comedy; but honest Heywood, in strong contrast to Restoration playwrights, delights his bourgeois audience by showing the young scamp brought to heel and forced to marry his deserted bride.

The Captives, or the Lost Recovered, 1624, might be included in this group, for it is an adaptation of Latin comedy, the *Rudens* of Plautus, to contemporary English life. On the whole Heywood follows the pattern of his source, but there was one incident in it that he could not use. For the Temple of Venus where two shipwrecked girls take refuge he substitutes a modern monastery, and a scurrilous Italian tale gave him the ingenious notion of developing a sub plot out of the immoral behavior of the monks. No doubt he knew that his audience would enjoy an exposure of monastic life and even condone the killing of a lustful monk by an irate husband. Heywood winds up the main plot in happy fashion; each of the captive girls is restored to her English father; each of them secures an English husband; and the reunited families set sail from Marseilles, where the scene is laid, to their English homes.

One late play by Heywood, *Love's Mistress, or The Queen's Masque,* published 1636, falls outside any of the preceding groups. This masquelike play met with extraordinary success. Queen Henrietta was so pleased with its first performance at

Court that she demanded another for the entertainment she gave the King on his birthday, for which Inigo Jones designed changing sets "for almost every scene." It was later produced by the Queen's Company at the Phœnix. It is an interesting example of the kind of entertainment that delighted a courtly public in the last years of Elizabethan drama. Apuleius, representing poetry and learning, presents a dramatic version of the Cupid and Psyche story to Midas, who stands for the general public, "best pleased with noise and show." These two figures might well stand for two opposing forces not only in the work of Heywood, but in much of Elizabethan drama: on the one hand the desire of the playwright to instruct the public, on the other his certainty that instruction must be sweetened to popular taste by a liberal dose of clowning.

Heywood leaves upon a thoughtful reader the impression of a very definite personality. Modest, industrious, and sound at heart, he is a true-born Englishman. He was not ashamed of his profession, for he believed that an actor might be as good a man as the severest Puritan. In no other contemporary dramatist do we find so simple a faith in the central Christian virtues, loving-kindness, pity, and forgiveness. Yet like a good Elizabethan he loved a jest and was not always averse to a very broad one. And with his humor went its sure companion, pathos.

As a playwright Heywood, though he lived on to the very close of Elizabethan drama, is in the main distinctly old-fashioned. He wrote as a rule for the conservative burgher class, substantial shop-keepers like the Citizen in Beaumont's play. Conservative himself, he knew what they liked and gave it them in full measure: story-plays with plenty of action, plenty of fun, and a recognizable background. Heywood is essentially a story-teller in dramatic form and a very good one; *The Fair Maid of the West* is the best adventure play in Elizabethan drama. He gives his audience plenty of laughs by his ubiquitous clown and he is a most inveterate punster. With few exceptions his plays have a background of contemporary English life; even when he is dramatizing alien matter, the characters are English. This is the native strain of realism so potent in Elizabethan drama; in spite of his learning there is little of the classic restraint or classic form in Heywood's plays. Yet it would be wrong to assume that Heywood lacked stage-craft. He has a real power of construction; his plots move swiftly to their appointed ends. He has a quick eye for effective situation and an actor's sure sense of what is telling on the stage. He writes at intervals a graceful song, but his dramatic verse is clear, fluent, and effective, rather than inspired.

It is impossible to take leave of Heywood upon even a mildly deprecatory tone. To the modern mind there is something more sympathetic in his best work than in that of many of his more brilliant contemporaries. His good humor, sincerity, and sentiment, his temperance and avoidance of romantic excess are all appealing qualities. *A Woman Killed* does not reach the tragic heights of *Othello*, but Mr. Frankford is a more modern husband than the Moor; Bess Bridges is to us a more attractive girl than the love-lorn heroine of *Philaster*. He is less cynical than Middleton, less didactic than Jonson, nearer to the common norm than Webster or Ford. A true Elizabethan, Heywood seems none the less to anticipate in his best work modern realism tinged with modern sentiment.

CHAPTER SIX

BEN JONSON

TODAY the name of Shakespeare seems to stand as the supreme representative of drama in the Elizabethan era. It was not so in his own day. His friend, and in some sense his rival, Ben Jonson, playwright and maker of masques, scholar and poet-laureate, seemed in contemporary eyes a more important figure. Shakespeare left no successor to his throne. Jonson, who survived Shakespeare for over twenty years, drew about him a school of young poets and playwrights proud to be sealed of "the tribe of Ben"; his influence on the tone and technique of contemporary and later drama is well-nigh incalculable. Shakespeare went quietly to his grave in rural Stratford, leaving over half his plays unpublished. In the very year of Shakespeare's death Jonson collected and published his plays, masques, and poems in a splendid Folio. His burial in Westminster Abbey was attended by a throng of peers and poets, and a memorial volume, *Jonsonus Virbius, i.e.,* Jonson recalled to life, appearing within a year, included tributes by almost all contemporary men of letters. Of Shakespeare's life we know little; Jonson has left in his conversations, letters, dedications, and personal poems, materials for a biography such as is available for no other Elizabethan dramatist.

Born in London, 1572, a month after the death of his father, Jonson traced his ancestry to the gentle family of Johnstone in southwestern Scotland. His widowed mother soon married a master brick-layer, whose one idea of providing for his stepson was to put him into his own trade. Before he succeeded in doing this, however, the boy managed to get some years of schooling at Westminster, where under the tutelage of the learned Camden he laid the foundation of a sound and varied scholarship. Poverty denied him a University education and forced him into brick-laying, a circumstance which his enemies in later life never allowed him to forget. A short spell of manual labor was enough for Ben, and he ran away to join an English army in the Low Countries where he distinguished himself by killing an enemy in single combat between the lines. His military service could not have lasted long, for we find him back in London and a married man in 1592, though what he had to marry on remains a mystery. He seems at one time to have joined a troupe of strolling players, and there is a well-authenticated tradition that he ranted through the role of Hieronimo in the ever popular *Spanish Tragedy*.

Our first certain knowledge of his connection with the theatre comes from Henslowe's *Diary*, where on July 28, 1597, there is an entry recording a loan of £4 to "Bengemen Johnson, player." The loan may have been made in anticipation of a return from Jonson's share in a new and promising play, *The Isle of Dogs*, begun by Nashe, finished by Jonson, and performed at the Swan with Jonson as one of the actors. Unfortunately this lost play provoked the authorities, who ordered the arrest of actors and author, so that Jonson got his first taste of prison fare, an experience that he was to renew more than once later on. Released in October, 1597, he approached Henslowe again and secured an advance of 20s. "upon a Bocke he was to write befor crysmas next." Jonson, however, was too independent and self-confident to bind himself to Henslowe as Heywood and others were doing. Early in 1598 he managed to place a play, *Every Man In His Humour*, with the Chamberlain's players. This production, in which Shakespeare, Kemp, and Burbage acted, was Jonson's first real triumph, but it was followed by an occurrence that threatened to cut short his career. In a duel with one of Henslowe's actors, Gabriel Spencer, Jonson received a wound in the arm, but countered with a thrust that killed his opponent. Henslowe wrote in grief and anger to Alleyn that he had sustained a "hard and heavy loss" in the death of Gabriel, "slayen by the handes of bergemen Jonson, bricklayer." Jonson suffered a short imprisonment, but escaped the death penalty by pleading benefit of clergy.

On his release from prison Jonson returned to Henslowe, who easily forgave Spencer's death and advanced him money upon a domestic tragedy and a chronicle play which he wrote in collaboration with Dekker and others. Meanwhile he was at work on another play for Shakespeare's company, *Every Man Out of His Humour,* produced in the autumn of 1599 at their new theatre, the Globe. It was by no means the success that his first play for them had been; and he turned to the newly organized Chapel Children at Blackfriars for whom he wrote *Cynthia's Revels* in 1600 and *Poetaster* in the spring of 1601.

Poetaster was the last gun fired by Jonson in the War of the Theatres—of which more hereafter. If, however, he expected to silence his enemies by this piece of heavy artillery, he was much mistaken. Such an angry outcry arose that Jonson felt called on to write an *Apologeticall Dialogue* which apparently he spoke in person on the stage. Unhappily this apology itself was so offensive that repetition was forbidden.

Shocked apparently by the failure of this play, Jonson declared his intention to "try if Tragedy have a more kind aspect"; we find him in 1602 writing further additions to *The Spanish Tragedy* and composing a *Richard Crookback* for which he received the handsome payment of £10 from Henslowe. *Richard Crookback* can hardly be the work that was in Jonson's mind when he declared in the apology that he was meditating something "high and aloof." That must have been his next play, *Sejanus,* produced in 1603 by Shakespeare's company. They seem to have done more than produce it. Jonson admits that, as acted, "a second pen had good share" in it, and his reference to this collaborator as "so happy a genius" may quite possibly refer to Shakespeare. If so, even Shakespeare's aid was not enough to win success for this portentous tragedy. Jonson, moreover, was in danger of something more serious than the public rejection of his play. The Earl of Northampton, who cherished a personal grudge against Jonson, summoned him before the Privy Council and accused him of "poperie and treason." Possibly Jonson's growing favor with the new sovereign, James I, helped in the dismissal of this charge. He had already been called on in collaboration with Dekker to provide the elaborate show which welcomed the King's formal entry into London, March 1604, and in the following Christmas holidays he joined with Inigo Jones, first English master of scene design, in presenting the first of a long series of masques at Court, that of *Blackness,* in which the Queen herself took part. Yet Jonson's favor at Court did not save him from imprisonment and the threat of mutilation in connection with *Eastward Ho.* Jonson came out of this affair with clean hands and was actually employed by the Privy Council in November 1605 to ferret out evidence in the unravelling of the Gunpowder Plot. Jonson's effort apparently failed, and he returned to his proper work as playwright.

His great comedy, *Volpone, or The Fox,* was produced by the King's Company early in 1606. It met with a success such as none of his plays since *Every Man In* had attained, and some months later during an outburst of the plague in London, it was presented at both Oxford and Cambridge, a very unusual concession on the part of the college dons to the popular drama.

The next ten years were among the happiest of Jonson's life. In high favor at Court he produced year by year, sometimes twice a year, his unrivalled masques. Free from dependence upon the actors he took his time in the composition of plays and brought out at longer intervals a succession of masterpieces: *Epicoene, or the Silent Woman,* 1609, for the Children at Whitefriars; *The Alchemist,* 1610, for the King's Men; and *Bartholomew Fair,* 1614, for the Lady Elizabeth's Company. This succession was interrupted by his tragedy *Catiline,* 1611, played by the King's Men and, like *Sejanus,* a failure.

In the spring of 1613 he visited France, acting as tutor to the son of Walter Raleigh, then a prisoner in the Tower. He must have been a strange tutor, for we hear that young Raleigh got him drunk and carted him about Paris in a wheelbarrow to the accompaniment of profane remarks; it is characteristic of Jonson that he was not ashamed to tell this story later. Jonson had temporarily broken with the King's Company after the failure of *Catiline;* but he returned to them with the last of his early comedies, *The Devil Is an Ass,* produced, 1616, at Blackfriars with an amusing Prologue begging the gentry who sat on the stage to allow the actors a little elbow-room for their performances.

In this same year, 1616, Jonson took the bold step of assembling all the plays he cared to acknowledge along with certain masques and poems, and publishing them in a volume entitled *The Workes of Benjamin Jonson*. There was no little laughter at the self-assurance of an author who called his dramas *Workes*, while those of other writers were only plays; but Jonson cared little for the laughter of the world. Secure in a pension of 100 marks—£66 13s. 16d.—granted him by the King, and in gifts from his friends and patrons—Pembroke, for example, gave him £20 every New Year's Day for the purchase of books—he withdrew altogether from the stage to devote himself to his studies. In 1618 he set out on foot for a visit to Scotland during which he spent a fortnight or so with the poet Drummond of Hawthornden. Drummond's record of Jonson's conversation is the most interesting bit of *personalia* that has come down to us from the Elizabethan age. Jonson talked apparently with the greatest freedom about himself, his work, and his contemporaries, and Drummond, not altogether a sympathetic listener, jotted down notes in a roughly abbreviated fashion that sometimes leaves the reader in doubt as to what Jonson really said. Many of Jonson's *obiter* need to be taken with more than the proverbial grain of salt.

The five or six years following Jonson's return from Scotland show him at the very height of his fame. He was invited to Oxford to receive the Master's degree as "a man of distinguished learning in humane letters." James wished to knight him, an honor which the poet prudently declined, but he held high court in the Apollo room of the Devil Tavern amid an admiring circle of young gentlemen, poets, playwrights, and politicians. A great misfortune befell him when in 1623 his entire library perished in a fire. A still greater blow was the death in 1625 of his kindly patron, King James. The new King, Charles I, though a lover of the arts, had none of his father's sympathy with learning, and when it came to a court masque preferred the spectacle provided by Jones to the poetry of Jonson. Willy-nilly he was driven back to the stage.

His return was marked by *The Staple of News*, performed by the King's Company at Blackfriars in February 1626, and soon afterward at Court, but Jonson was in no case to continue his career as a playwright. A stroke of paralysis in 1628 cut short his sessions in the Apollo room, and his next play, *The New Inn*, 1629, was written from a sick-bed. It was, to quote his own angry words, "never acted, but most negligently played by the King's Servants. And more squeamishly beheld, and censured by others, the King's subjects." Apparently a fashionable audience had displayed unusual dislike to the play. Charles, however, rewarded the unlucky poet with a gift of £100 for the promise made in the *Ode to Himself,* appended to the printed play, that he would henceforth sing the glories of the new sovereign. It was fortunate for Jonson that he did not live to see the tragic end of Charles's reign.

In the winter of 1631 Jonson was recalled to Court to join with Inigo Jones in presenting two masques. A quarrel, however, broke out between author and stage-designer in which Jones was so successful that he managed to terminate Jonson's connection with the Court Masque. Jonson tried the stage again with *The Magnetic Lady, or Humours Reconciled,* played by the King's Company in the autumn of 1632. It at least escaped the fate of *The New Inn,* but the actors gave offense in high places by the profanity with which they besprinkled the dialogue. In the next year, 1633, Sir Henry Herbert records a license for the last play by Jonson to appear upon the stage, *A Tale of a Tub,* but notes that the role of Vitruvius Hoop was to be struck out, "exception being taken against it by Inigo Jones . . . as a personal injury." In this role Jonson, still pursuing his quarrel with Jones, had revived with failing hand his old device of personal satire. The censored play was performed at Court in January 1634, and Herbert notes curtly, "not likte"—a sad close to Jonson's long career as professional entertainer.

Little remains to be said of Jonson's last years. Another stroke of paralysis confined him to his bed, but his brain was still active. He read and took notes on his reading, many of which are preserved in his *Discoveries;* he devised a pair of entertainments for the Duke of Newcastle, and even began another play, *The Sad Shepherd,* found unfinished among his papers. On August 6, 1637, Ben Jonson passed away, a lonely old man, penniless and in debt. He was buried in the Poet's Corner, and a subscription was started for a suitable monument to his tomb, but the troubles that shortly culminated in the Civil War put an end to this project. The only inscription on his grave was carved at the request of a friend: O rare Ben Jonson.

It seems advisable to deal first with Jonson's comedies in chronological order and to trace his development as a comic dramatist, for after all Jonson's fame as a playwright rests upon his comedies. Jonson told Drummond that not half his comedies were in print. It is reasonable to suppose that the lost plays belong to the period before the great success of *Every Man In*. There are extant, however, two comedies which almost certainly belong to this earlier period.

The first of these is *A Tale of a Tub*. Although this play was licensed and acted in 1633, there is good reason to believe that it is a play of Jonson's youth, *ca.* 1596. He must have given it a hasty revision and written in the role of Vitruvius Hoop at a time when age and illness made it impossible for him to compose a new play in which to attack his enemy, Inigo Jones. In a Prologue written for the Court performance Jonson frankly calls it a "ridiculous play"; he thought so little of it indeed that he broke his custom and failed to send it to the press; it was first published after his death in 1641. It is a lively and amusing realistic comedy, but Jonson's satiric vein is perceptible in his treatment of the country folk who crowd this play; he never shared Shakespeare's sympathetic delight in the follies of common people. On the other hand there is hardly a trace of the humour characters which he was to develop a little later.

The Case Is Altered, ca. 1597, a later and better play, reveals quite clearly Jonson's developing power as a comic dramatist. His name appears on the title-page of the first edition, 1609, but he never acknowledged it, and it was not included in any contemporary collection of his works. Yet internal evidence of the strongest kind points to Jonson, and no modern scholar doubts his authorship. The plot is a combination of two Plautine comedies: the *Aulularia* and the *Captivi*, telescoped to provide the more abundant action which the Elizabethan audience demanded. Jonson's developing skill in construction is shown in the deft fashion with which he weaves together his two bor-

rowed plots. The wooing of the heroine resembles that in a
romantic comedy of the type made popular by Shakespeare in
the last decade of the century, but the love-story is overshadowed
by a good deal of subordinate matter. There is the merry cobbler
Juniper, a very good role for a popular clown, but one quite
detached from the main action; there are intercalated scenes
ridiculing affectations in speech and behavior, and the first of
his dramatic attacks upon objects of his personal or artistic aversion in the caricature of Anthony Munday, his old fellow-worker
in Henslowe's play-factory. It is, after all, not surprising that
Jonson's mature judgment declined to acknowledge such an
assemblage of heterogeneous material.

Every Man In His Humour is the first play that reveals Jonson's definitely formed theory of comedy. To the modern reader
it is the best known of Jonson's plays, but as a rule only in its
later carefully revised form. A glance at the quarto, which presents the text as it was first acted, will show more clearly how
far Jonson accepted the dramatic conventions of his day and to
what extent he broke with them. Here the scene is laid in Italy,
as in so many Elizabethan comedies, and the main characters
have Italian names. Yet there is no attempt to impart Italian
color to the scene, and such characters as Cob and Tib are as
English in name as in behavior. The love-interest, slight as it is,
seems like a concession to public demand. A firm believer in
classic authority, Jonson follows in the main the conventions of
Latin comedy: he maintains the unity of time—the whole action
takes place in twelve hours,—of place—the scene throughout is
Florence,—and of decorum, since there is no intermixture of
serious matter; an impassioned defense of poetry, deleted in the
revised text, alone interrupts the comic tone.

Jonson's main break with the convention of his day was his
shift of interest from action to character portrayal. Then, as now,
a popular audience cared primarily for story, and Jonson was so
far willing to comply with the demand that he built up a slight
plot as a background against which his characters could display
themselves. There is, to be sure, a certain amount of action in
this play: the plots of the two old men, the embarrassments into
which they are plunged by the counter-plots of the young gen-

tlemen and their wily servant, and the final solution by the wise and witty Dr. Clement. Yet the story is of the slightest possible interest compared with Jonson's brilliant satiric character portrayal. This, as the title of the play shows, is an exposition of the humours of contemporary society.

The word "humour" derives from medieval physiology, according to which the temperament and consequently the behavior of a man was determined by the predominance of one or the other of the four fluids of the body: the blood, the choler, the black choler (hence melancholy), and the phlegm. Towards the end of the century, however, "humour" had become a mere catch-word to denote an individual whim or fancy. Thus Shylock replies to the question why he desires the pound of flesh: "Say it is my humour, is it answered?" Jonson's logical mind revolted against this abuse of the word; according to his Induction to *Every Man Out of His Humour*, the true meaning of the word is derived by metaphor from physiology: "When some one peculiar quality doth so possess a man that it doth draw all his affects, his spirits, and his powers . . . all to run one way, this may be truly said to be a humour." A Jonsonian humour, then, is an abnormality; a humourous character is an unbalanced one. Such a lack of balance may result in tragedy, as in the case of Coriolanus, a man dominated by choler. If, however, the humour be of a slighter quality as in Bobadil's vanity, Matheo's affectation, or even Thorello's jealousy, it affords natural material for satiric comedy.

This satiric quality is much more plainly visible in the revised form of the play in the Folio of 1616. The date of this revision is uncertain; but whenever it was made, Jonson had hardened and sharpened his theory of comedy. He equipped the new version with a defiant prologue in which he attacks the license of popular romantic drama: its violation of the unities of time and place, its excessive use of noise and spectacle. For these he would substitute "deeds and language such as men do use"—note the stress on realism:

> And persons such as Comedy would choose
> When she would show an image of the times
> And sport with human follies. . . .

Jonson's satiric purpose is clearly visible throughout the revision. The mere shift of the scene from Florence to London with its repeated touches of local color, brought the action home to the audience and made more effective his ridicule of familiar English humours. Along with the change of scene goes the rebaptism of the characters: the Lorenzos, father and son, become the Knowells; Thorello becomes Kitely; and the romantic Hesperida is new-born as plain English Bridget. Some of the altered names have an allegorical significance, a new trait in Jonson which emphasizes the didactic strain and connects him with the native tradition of the Morals. Thus Prospero becomes Wellbred; Mosca, Brainworm; and the meaningless Giuliano changes to Squire Downright to mark his humour. The main action of the play remains unchanged, but the dialogue, chiefly in prose, has been carefully rewritten, always with the purpose of making it more homely and realistic, and so enforcing its satiric quality. Only a line-by-line comparison of the two texts will assure the student of the value which Jonson placed upon this, his first great success, and the meticulous art with which he perfected it.

Jonson's second play for Shakespeare's company, published in 1600 under the title of *The Comicall Satyre of Every Man Out of His Humour,* seems to be an attempt to give dramatic form to the popular social satire in prose and verse which had just been suppressed by the ecclesiastical censorship. To shape this satire for the stage Jonson combined it with his own theory of humours realistically presented and composed a play in which story recedes to a vanishing point. Instead of the coherent plot of *Every Man In* we find here the presentation in successive scenes of a group of characters whose humours are so exaggerated that they become almost pathological specimens. They more than deserve the lash of satire so fiercely applied by two characters invented to serve as censors of their actions: Macilente, the envious man, and Carlo Buffone, the foul-mouthed railer. In the end this satire combines with the mishaps caused by their follies to drive them more or less out of their humours.

The inevitable failure of such a play so provoked Jonson that he hurried it to the press—it was the first play that he published—and gave it to the reading public "as it was first composed"; the title-page expressly states that the book contains "more than hath been publickly spoken." As if this were not enough, Jonson prefixed to the text a set of prose portraits of the chief characters, apparently on the ground that the first audience had found them not entirely intelligible. He printed also a long Induction which must have been heavily cut, if it ever was performed. Here Asper, who stands for Jonson himself, announces his determination to

> Strip the ragged follies of the time
> Naked as at their birth . . .
> . . . and with a whip of steel
> Print wounding lashes in their iron ribs.

Along with Asper two spectators, Mitis and Cordatus, discuss the essential quality of humour and the historical development of comedy. They remain after the Induction and serve as a sort of Chorus to comment on the action of the play. All this is interesting and valuable as throwing light on Jonson's conception of satiric comedy, but it is not in the least dramatic. *Every Man Out* is almost as heavy reading as it was poor theatre, but it is a veritable mine of information as to Elizabethan follies and affectations.

Jonson's next play, *Cynthia's Revels, or The Fountain of Self-Love,* shifts the attack from the humours of the city to the affectations of the Court. Like one of Lyly's plays it is set in a mythological frame-work; the court is that of Cynthia, the moon-goddess, also, as every one knew, a poet's name for Elizabeth herself. Cupid and Mercury take part in an action ending with a masque in which the pretenders to courtly manners are exposed in their true nature. This satiric, didactic play lacks the realism of Jonson's earlier work; the characters are, for the most part, sheer abstractions. Yet Jonson himself thought very well of it as a proclamation of the true ideals of courtly life; the Epilogue closes with a line supposed to express his own verdict on his work:

> By God 'tis good, and if you like't, you may.

No wonder that Jonson's enemies accused him of having drunk, like the courtiers in this play, from the fountain of Self-Love.

Poetaster, Jonson's next play, is his contribution to the so-called War of the Theatres. Much ink has been spilled by scholars over this war, sometimes represented as a sort of "blitzkrieg" involving most of the poets and playwrights of the day. As a matter of fact it was a tiny tempest in a small tea-pot, arising from a temperamental clash between two poets, Marston and Jonson, and exploited by the rivalry of theatrical companies. Writing for Paul's Boys Marston had introduced into his revision of *Histriomastix* a character that bore an unmistakable likeness to Jonson. Jonson replied by putting samples of Marston's affected diction, labelled "fustian," into the mouth of a fool in *Every Man Out.* Marston retaliated by introducing caricatures of Jonson into a couple of Paul's plays. Apparently he even attempted physical violence, for Jonson later told Drummond that Marston once drew a pistol on him and that he, Jonson, beat him and took it away. By this time the quarrel was the talk of the town, especially in theatrical circles, and Shakespeare's company, provoked perhaps by Jonson's desertion, and jealous of the success of the Chapel Children, the "little eyases" of *Hamlet,* arranged with Marston and that man of all work, Dekker, for a joint play, *Satiromastix,* attacking Jonson, to be produced at Paul's and at the Globe. Jonson got wind of this, determined to anticipate the attack, and in hot haste composed his *Poetaster.*

Not even the warmest admirer of Jonson can call *Poetaster* a good play. It was, no doubt, an ingenious idea to represent himself as Horace, poet and satirist, attacked by ignorance and envy and vindicated by his fellow poets at the Court of Cæsar. But this classic parallel to the contemporary situation is disturbed by alien elements: the appearance on the Roman scene of a Captain Tucca, promptly identified as a caricature of a living Londoner, "honest Captain Hannam," and by the bitter attack on a company of actors, evidently the Chamberlain's Men, then preparing, as most of the audience knew, to produce *Satiromastix.* There is an even graver fault, a lack of unity remarkable in such a classicist as Jonson; a large part of the play treats of Ovid's amour with Julia, a theme only loosely connected with the Horace plot, which as a matter of fact only gets started in Act III.

None the less *Poetaster* is an entertaining and amusing play. Jonson has returned to earth from the rarefied atmosphere of *Cynthia's Revels*. The portrait of Tucca is a vivid bit of realism; the satire on Crispinus-Marston is direct and pungent; and the judgment scene in which that wretched poetaster, condemned to swallow certain pills prepared by Horace, vomits up, straining and retching, choice gobs of Marston's vocabulary, is one of the most farcical in Elizabethan comedy. It seems incredible that after such treatment on the public stage Marston should ever have taken Jonson's hand again, but, as we have seen, within a few years they were collaborating on *Eastward Ho*. Perhaps the best thing in *Poetaster* is Jonson's portrait of himself as Horace, high-minded, free-spoken, and self-confident, a defender of the rights of poetry against the assaults of the vulgar herd. It is, to be sure, a flattering portrait, but it gives some notion of the author's high ideals.

Satiromastix, performed in the autumn of 1601, cannot have been completely written till after the performance of *Poetaster* because of its repeated references to characters and incidents in Jonson's comedy. Something has been previously said (p. 109) about this play; it is sufficient here to note the nature of its reply to Jonson. It is an amusing and by no means unskilful piece of work; Dekker manages to obtain a certain unity in this strange medley of tragi-comedy and personal satire by connecting the character of Horace-Jonson with the wedding feast of Terill. Horace is introduced in his study laboring over an epithalamium and murmuring rhymes: "game, dame, tame, lame," a scene which must have brought down the house. Later he makes trouble at a banquet by reciting a satire in genuine Jonsonian verse, and is tossed in a blanket by four ladies. Finally in the judgment scene before the King he is stripped of his satyr's garb ("satyr" and "satire" were often spelled alike and constantly confused by the Elizabethans) and crowned with stinging nettles instead of laurels. In spite of this horse-play the treatment of Jonson in *Satiromastix* is anything but contemptuous; the worst abuse of him is put in the mouth of Captain Tucca, a character calmly lifted from *Poetaster*, who had certainly abused Horace-Jonson violently enough in that play. On the other hand a real respect is shown for Jonson's wit and learning; and the qualities which he is bidden to discard are arrogance, self-love, and detraction, by no means an unfair accusation. It is quite probable that *Satiromastix* was more successful on the stage than *Poetaster;* at any rate it ended the War of the Theatres.

Volpone, or the Fox, 1606, marks Jonson's return to comedy after the failure of *Sejanus.* A comedy of a different sort from anything which he had yet written, it marks an immense advance upon his earlier work. Strange as it may seem, the dogmatic author of *Every Man Out* has renounced his creed that characterization is the essential of drama, and has written a play in which action predominates. The plot of *Volpone* is one of the best in English comedy and the plot is Jonson's own; there is no single classic source which furnished Jonson with a pattern for his play. All the suggestions that he picked from his wide reading are woven here into a harmonious whole, an action that advances swiftly, is checked, recovers, and ends finally in something that is more like a tragic catastrophe than the solution of a comic plot. Jonson himself was aware of this and justified it on the ground that he intended to "put the snaffle in the mouths" of Puritan critics who affirmed that playwrights never punished vice in their comedies. It is, in fact, vice rather than folly which is the object of Jonson's attack in *Volpone.* Apart from the minor figures of Sir Politic and his wife, survivors from the comedy of humours, and the contrasting but colorless characters of Celia and Bonario, all the actors in the play are vicious rather than foolish; avarice, lust, and overweening pride are the mainsprings of the action. Yet too much stress has been laid upon the semi-tragic temper of the play. It is after all a comedy, and stage performance brings out better than reading its delightful comic values.

Of all Jonson's comedies *Volpone* is the least realistic. The scene is laid in Venice, to the Elizabethans the most dissolute of cities; the characters, labelled with names from the old Beast Epic, the Raven, Crow, and Vulture, are rather types than individuals. An exception must, of course, be made for the central figure, Volpone, the Fox, a finely realized character whose master-passion is rather love of power than avarice and whose downfall is due to his insolent self-confidence in his ability to over-reach his fellow mortals. It is into his mouth that Jonson puts the finest poetry of the play, perhaps the finest that he had yet written, with the apparent purpose of lifting this figure above the plane of trickery and deceit on which the others move. Jonson's Volpone is a superb Elizabethan figure, "magnificent in sin."

Four or five years elapsed between *Volpone* and Jonson's next comedy, *Epicœne, or the Silent Woman.* The high favor he enjoyed at Court and the striking success of *Volpone* had so mellowed him that when he came to write a new play for a children's company, he did so in the best of humors. Whatever else *Epicœne* may be, it is Jonson's gayest comedy. The fun is riotous; the satire is impersonal and inoffensive; and, as Mr. Pepys was later to remark: "There is more wit in it than goes to ten new plays." So lively in fact is *Epicœne* that it has often been called a farce. It is much more than that, for the action springs naturally and rightly from the characters, and the manners depicted are those of Jonson's day with only the exaggeration permissible in satiric comedy. The truth is that *Epicœne* is a unique play, at once a comedy of humours and an anticipation of the coming comedy of manners.

Dryden remarked that the action of *Epicœne* is "entirely one"; there is no double plot as in *Poetaster,* no extraneous character like Sir Politic in *Volpone*; the various humours are skilfully woven into the tissue of the plot. The interest increases from act to act until the final surprise of the dénouement, the revelation of the true sex of Morose's newly wedded wife. The fun begins with the first surprise when the shy and soft-spoken bride reveals herself as a voluble and domineering wife; it increases step by step with the frantic efforts of Morose to escape from the bonds of matrimony, and it comes to an uproarious conclusion with the unmasking of the supposed girl. There can be no doubt of the stage success of *Epicœne.* Unlike most Elizabethan plays it passed from company to company; it was played at Blackfriars by the King's Men, performed at Court in the last year of Jonson's life by the Queen's Company, and revived with great success during the Restoration.

The Alchemist followed hard on the heels of *Epicœne*. Jonson caught some hints for the opening and closing of this play from the *Mostellaria* of Plautus, but its true source was his wide reading in the mystic lore of alchemy and his intimate acquaintance with the trickery and fraud—what we could call the "rackets"—of the London underworld. *The Alchemist* represents a distinct development of Jonson's art. Less light-hearted than *Epicœne*, it is a more vigorous piece of satire. Compared with the "Comical Satires" of his first period it is more objective and impersonal; one cannot identify any of the characters of this play with living contemporaries. Although he ridicules the various dupes of his impostors, Jonson's main object of attack is a great social evil, the profession and practice of alchemy in all its ramifications.

Alchemy, a strange compound of medieval philosophy, Renaissance science, and old-time roguery, had taken on a new lease of life towards the close of the sixteenth century. There was in part an economic reason for this. The influx of the precious metals from America had caused a steep rise of prices and a consequent demand for more money. Luxury-loving sovereigns lent a credulous ear to philosophers who professed their ability to transform base metal into gold. Elizabeth herself patronized Dr. Dee, one of the leading practitioners of the time; and in the very day of *The Alchemist*, Simon Forman, fortune-teller, dealer in love-philters, and seeker after the philosopher's stone, was a well known and widely patronized figure in London. Unfortunately the mysterious fashion in which alchemical research was conducted and the credulity of the greedy believers in this pseudo-science made the practice of alchemy a magnet to draw into its field all the rogues and fools of the day. It takes only a hasty reading of Jonson's play to see how much more than pure research was then connected with the profession of alchemy. A minor object here of Jonson's satire is the hypocritical zeal of Puritan extremists, following the lure of alchemy with dark designs on the whole fabric of Church and State.

Jonson had long outgrown his doctrinaire conception of the humours comedy when he wrote *The Alchemist*. There are, indeed, humour characters in this play, but they are represented

in action, not elaborately described, no longer mere embodi-
ments of a single trait, but very human people. Epicure Mam-
mon is one of the most fully realized characters in Elizabethan
drama; in greed and sensuality he resembles Volpone, but he is a
truly comic character whereas Volpone verges on the tragic.
Jonson's nice sense of discrimination is seen in the contrasted
characters of the shamelessly versatile Face and the solemnly
pretentious Subtle; even more clearly, perhaps, in the contrast
between the smooth hypocrisy of Tribulation and the blatant
zeal of Ananias. The dialogue is the quickest and liveliest in
Jonson's comedies. A reader is apt to be stunned by the pro-
fusion of technical terms of alchemy, but they were familiar
enough to Jonson's hearers, and no doubt in performance were
rattled off like stage patter.

The plot construction of *The Alchemist* is a marvel of ingenuity; thread after thread of contrasting colors is woven into
the pattern in steadily progressing movement. The final solution
is masterly; it is no sudden *coup-de-théâtre* as in *Epicœne*, but
the appearance on the scene of a character who might have
been expected from the beginning, the master of the house in
which the confederates have been plying their craft. And only
such a genial character as Lovewit could have outfaced the mob
at his door, condoned the tricks of his rascally servant, and won
the hand of the widow Pliant. His pardon of Face has been
blamed by rigid moralists, but it is a fitter conclusion for a
comedy than the severe sentence passed upon Volpone. In *The
Alchemist* Jonson attained the high-water mark of his achievement. Never again was he to write a play in which plot-interest,
lively dialogue, and realistic characterization were so perfectly
combined.

Yet his next comedy, *Bartholomew Fair*, 1614, is in its own
way a masterpiece, a riotous carnival of farcical action, humour
characters, and social satire. It was written for the Lady Elizabeth's Company at the Hope, a new theatre used alternately for
plays and bear-baiting. Jonson knew whereof he spoke when he
called it "as dirty as Smithfield [where the Fair was held] and
as stinking every whit," and he deliberately played down his
style to suit the rowdy audience. *Bartholomew Fair* offers all

that the author promises in his conciliatory Induction; it is "merry and full of noise," and introduces a group of the characteristic "Bartholomew birds" that haunted the Fair: "a fine oily pig-woman," "a strutting horse-courser," "a cutpurse serchant," and "as fresh a hypocrite as ever was broached, rampant." This last is the loud-mouthed, ignorant, and greedy Zeal-of-the-Land Busy, the vehicle of Jonson's bitterest attack upon the Puritan attempt to put down the sports and gayeties of Merry England.

What the play lacks, in striking contrast to its immediate predecessor, is plot, a connected story with beginning, middle, and end. The action displays a visit to the Fair by several distinct groups, who come into collision with each other and the showmen and booth-keepers with various comic consequences, but there is no one main thread to hold our interest, and the conclusion is hasty and huddled as in none of Jonson's earlier plays. In all probability the play acted better than it reads. The moving panorama of the Fair with its entertainments and its "enormities," the bustling action, sinking at times to absurdest farce, and the crowd of first-rate character parts, all combine to make it good theatre. Above all Jonson is here in the best of humors; his "whip of steel" is laid aside for gusts of Rabelaisian laughter.

Bartholomew Fair is the last of Jonson's great comedies. His next play, *The Devil Is An Ass,* 1616, seems a hasty assemblage of matter old and new to provide a play for the King's Men. The old matter is the legend of a visit by a devil to earth only to learn that earth's wickedness exceeds that of hell. In the play Pug, a foolish young devil, obtains Satan's permission to spend a day on earth, where he is baffled, beaten, and carried to jail as a thief. To avoid the disgrace of having a devil hanged at Tyburn, Satan and the Vice, Iniquity, enter Pug's cell and carry him off in a cloud of brimstone. The new matter is a comedy of intrigue centering about Fitzdottrel, a typical Jonsonian gull. The two themes are but loosely combined, and the whole play falls far below Jonson's best. There is no evidence that it ever was a stage success.

Of the three plays that Jonson wrote after his return to the stage, only one deserves careful consideration, *The Staple of News*, 1626. The object of Jonson's attack in this play is the new journalism embodied in the first English newspaper, *The Courant or Weekly News*. Its proprietor, an enterprising publisher, Nathaniel Butter, had secured a practical monopoly, in Jonson's word a "staple," of the printed news-letter, and his sensational and highly unreliable product had already attracted the attention of satirists. Jonson wove his satire on Butter and his staple into a plot based on the *Plutus* of Aristophanes. The main action deals with the rise, fall, and final redemption of Pennyboy, Jr., a gay young prodigal, and his affair with the Lady Aurelia Clara Pecunia, the personification of wealth. In Pennyboy's company the Lady tours London scattering kisses and favors. Together they visit the office of the Staple where Pennyboy meets Nathaniel, "a decayed stationer," *i.e.*, Master Butter, and purchases samples of his wares, the current news: the King of Spain has been elected Pope and Emperor; new engines of war, anticipations of bombs and submarines, threaten the peace of the world; a company of cooks is sailing to America to civilize the cannibals. The Master of the Staple tries in vain to win Pecunia away from Pennyboy, and his concern goes bankrupt, "all to pieces, quite dissolved."

To forestall criticism of his work Jonson introduces some impromptu critics. Four women, Mirth, Tattle, Expectation, and Censure, interrupt the Prologue, like the citizen in *The Knight of the Burning Pestle,* and take seats upon the stage to watch and judge the action. From time to time they voice their opinions: the play is a poor thing; there is neither fool nor devil in it; the news is "scurvy and stale." Finally they unite in a sentence denouncing the author as "a decayed wit, . . . forever forfeit to the scorn of mirth." These interludes in Jonson's raciest prose are packed with allusions to contemporary life: to the latest sensational play, *A Game at Chess;* "the blessed Princess Pocahontas"; and the current gossip of the London streets. They bring us back to real life from the semi-allegoric atmosphere of the play itself and add a special flavor to this neglected comedy.

The failure of *The New Inn,* 1629, was due, it would appear, less to the bad acting which Jonson blamed than to his own desperate attempt to combine two incompatible forms: romantic comedy and the comedy of humours. For the conventional love-interest of romantic comedy Jonson substitutes the theme of Platonic love which Queen Henrietta had made fashionable in courtly circles; and the romantic plot bogs down in long discourses on this topic. The comedy of the interplay of humours is far from amusing; Jonson's gift of satiric characterization is at its weakest in this play. The entertainment offered by this Inn is not likely to attract the reader; it can be recommended only to serious students of Jonson's work.

Jonson's last play, *The Magnetic Lady, or Humours Reconciled,* 1632, possesses a real unity of theme and form, for here he reverts once more to the old pattern of the comedy of humours. That he was conscious of this is plain from the words of the Induction: "The author beginning his studies of this kind with *Every Man In*—finding himself now near the close, or shutting up of his circle, hath phant'sied to himself in Idea this Magnetic Mistress." At the house of Lady Loadstone Jonson assembles "a diversity of guests, all persons of different humours . . . and this he hath called *Humours Reconciled.*"

Here, as in *Every Man In,* Jonson constructs a plot whose main purpose is to afford an opportunity for the display of humour characters. There, however, the plot was so slight as to be little but a background; here it is elaborate and highly complicated. It deals with the fortunes of two girls, the niece and the waiting-maid of Lady Loadstone. Around these girls hover the diverse humours of the play: the lawyer, Practice; the courtier, Sir Diaphanous Silkworm; the soldier, Ironside; and the usurer, Sir Moth Interest. Clever Mr. Compass plays off one humour against another, and finally wins the hand of the heiress. There is little fresh or new in these characters; Jonson contents himself with pushing old pawns about the board in a new gambit. One exception, perhaps, may be made for Mrs. Polish, the mother of the false niece, an amazing compound of volubility, religious cant, and downright fraud. *The Magnetic Lady* is a respectable and well-planned play, illuminated by some brilliant flashes of satiric description; the old comic fire, however, is burning very low.

The Sad Shepherd, or a Tale of Robin Hood consists of two acts and a fragment of the third along with prefatory "arguments" for all three. It was apparently written in the last years of his life, 1636–37, and may have been suggested by the success at Court in 1634 of the revived *Faithful Shepherdess*. His own connection with the Court had been broken by the failure of his *Tale of a Tub* and his quarrel with Inigo Jones. He perhaps hoped to regain favor by composing a pastoral play, yet one quite different from Fletcher's. In his talk with Drummond, Jonson had blamed the author of *Il Pastor Fido* for "making shepherds speak as well as himself could," and confessed that in his own *May Lord,* a lost play or poem, he had "brought in clowns making mirth . . . contrary to all other Pastorals." To break the convention that a pastoral play must eschew mirth and rely on high-flown sentiment Jonson laid the scene in Sherwood Forest and brought in Robin Hood and his merry men, the rustic shepherds of Belvoir, and such truly English figures as the witch, Maudlin, her familiar, Puck-hairy, *i.e.,* Robin Goodfellow, and her clownish son. From such characters we expect and get direct and simple English talk, varying, indeed, from the poetic utterance of Æglamour, the sad shepherd, to the homely speech of Robin's fellowship, and the laugh-provoking Northern dialect of Maudlin and her son. Here is the old realist of the early comedies striving with his last breath to transform the artificial pastoral into something fit for the native stage. It is a far cry from *The Faithful Shepherdess* to *The Sad Shepherd;* they have little in common but the name of pastoral. One can but regret that Jonson did not live to complete this charming fragment.

Jonson's tragedies, *Sejanus* and *Catiline,* were ranked by their author above his comedies, but the judgment of posterity has pronounced against him. Failures on the stage in their day, they exerted little of the influence of his comedies upon later drama; today they are seldom read except by scholars. The simplest reason for their failure may be found in Jonson's conception of tragedy. In the Preface to *Sejanus* he asserts that he has fulfilled the duty of a tragic poet in "truth of argument, dignity of persons, gravity and height of elocution, fullness and frequency of sentence." These are, indeed, admirable qualities in tragedy, but they are non-essential. Character and action such as to move inevitable pity and terror in the spectator are the prime qualities without which there can be no true tragedy, and of these, apparently, Jonson had no conception whatever.

Sejanus is a play of atmosphere, rather than of action or character. It reproduces the political life of Rome under the tyranny of Tiberius with an accuracy guaranteed by Jonson's elaborate apparatus of foot-notes. It has none of the anachronisms which startle us in *Julius Cæsar*; on the other hand it wholly lacks the interest of Shakespeare's play; the complicated action is, except for a student of Roman history, difficult to follow. And if the action lacks interest, the characters, at least the two chief characters, are incapable of provoking even a spark of sympathy; Tiberius is a monster of cruelty and dissimulation, Sejanus of cruelty and selfish ambition. Neither of them has a trace of the titanic qualities of the superman, which glow in the hero-villains of Marlowe and Shakespeare. The only sympathetic characters are the passive figures, the victims, or the commentators who replace to some extent the missing Chorus, and whose lament over the loss of liberty in Rome, where

> Knowledge is made a capital offence

and all free men have become

> The prey to greedy vultures and vile spies

has a startling significance today when applied to the subjects of the new totalitarian tyranny.

Catiline is in several ways a better play than *Sejanus*. It had a partial success upon the stage compared with the violence that *Sejanus* suffered; the first two acts, at least, pleased the audience, as Jonson tells us in his *Epistle to the Reader*, though he goes on to say that they were liked because they were the worst. Mr. Pepys's comment upon a Restoration revival might serve as the final judgment of the average spectator:

> —a play of much good sense and words to read, but that do appear the worst upon the stage, I mean the least diverting, that ever I saw in my life. . . .

Yet there is more to be said of *Catiline* than that it had a qualified success upon the stage. Jonson reverts here to the accepted
standard of the Senecan tragedy; he opens the play with the
ghost of Sulla rising to incite Catiline to the ruin of Rome, and
he equips each act except the last with a moralizing Senecan
Chorus. The first two acts which Jonson thought the worst are
at once the liveliest and the most original. This is especially true
of the second, which introduces two rival Roman ladies, wanton
and politically minded, and ends with the seduction by one of
them of the conspirator Curius, a scene which leads directly to
the ruin of the conspiracy. This act, for which Jonson received
only the faintest suggestion from his sources, is written in his
strongest vein of satiric comedy; one can only wish that Jonson
had followed his natural bent and written more such scenes.
Unfortunately his devotion to "truth of argument" got the better
of him; the last three acts are largely composed of direct translations from Cicero and Sallust. They are pieces of splendid
rhetoric; but it is strange that so practised a playwright should
have overlooked the crushing burden which these interminable
declamations imposed upon the endurance of the audience.

In spite of the divergence of tone between the first and the
last acts *Catiline* possesses a unity of action which is lacking in
Sejanus; there is but one theme: the conspiracy and its overthrow. The story is not only simpler, but more familiar and
therefore more intelligible. The characterization, too, is simpler
and more effective. The minor figures, Lentulus, Cethegus, and
the ladies, have been described as humour characters, but the
protagonist, Catiline, rises into something like heroic proportions. Compared with Sejanus, who falls without an effort at
self-defense, Catiline is a superman who takes arms against the
whole state of Rome, brings the Republic to the verge of downfall, and dies at last sword in hand, ruined less by his own fault
than by the weakness and folly of his confederates. If not a
sympathetic character, he is a tremendous force for evil.

It is no easy matter to pass an impartial final judgment on the
dramatic work of Jonson; it is particularly difficult for the young
student who comes to Jonson as a rule fresh from the masterpieces of Shakespeare. If it were possible to defer the study of

Jonson until after a course of reading in Dekker, Heywood, and minor Elizabethan dramatists, some valid appreciation of the great playwright's magnificent intellectual power might be more easily attained. For the appeal of Jonson is primarily to the intellect rather than to emotion. There is none of the magic of Shakespeare's verse in Jonson's plays; there is little of the charm of story that is found in the work of many minor Elizabethans; the theme of romantic love, for example, is conspicuously absent in his plays. The reason is plain: there was little of the romanticist in Ben Jonson. It would be absurd to deny him the title of poet; but he was a poet who set as his goal clear and correct expression of thought, chaste and polished form, rather than lyric rapture. In his plays the most poetic passages are rhetorical rather than passionate. A genuine Elizabethan, he unites two of the characteristic strains of Elizabethan drama: the native tradition of realism and the classical insistence on form. The romantic impulse with its exuberance and defiance of order he distrusted and defied. Yet Jonson was no slave to classical conventions; he was Elizabethan enough to mar too often the symmetry of his work by the introduction of alien material, like the Ovid-Julia story in *Poetaster*. Nor did he always obey the classic precept of restraint. His plays, and Shakespeare's, are the longest in Elizabethan drama, and his would suffer far less than Shakespeare's by drastic excision. Apart from his frequent draughts upon classic sources, the influence of classic rules and examples is most clearly seen in Jonson's plot construction. At his best he is the most skilful technician of Elizabethan playwrights. He scorned the device of the double plot to add the interest of additional action, strove for unity of effect, concentrated upon a single theme, and, though the illustrations of this theme might be diverse and manifold, wove them into a unified whole. Unlike Shakespeare, who made a practice of selecting a story from history or fiction and shaping it for the stage with special attention to the characters, Jonson's rule was to invent a plot to exemplify some dominant idea and then to devise incident to illustrate character. He is particularly successful in his solution of a comic complication, as in the close of *Every Man In* or *The Alchemist*.

Jonson's realism has a double aspect; it appears both in his treatment of character and in the background which he creates to lend atmosphere to character and action. The old charges that Jonson's characters are not human creatures but mere incarnations of some ruling passion will not hold good for any careful reader. It is true that in his first period he allowed himself too often to be carried away by his theory of humours, but even here we find such characters as Bobadil and Tucca, who seem to have stepped onto the stage from some low London tavern. In his masterpieces we meet a whole gallery of characters ranging from the gorgeous Sir Epicure to the greasy pig-woman of *Bartholomew Fair*; they are completely realized and drawn with an unerring hand. Jonson is most successful in his characterization of fools, fops, and hypocrites, perhaps because his satiric mind scrutinized them more closely than it did more estimable characters. Zeal-of-the-Land Busy has no fellow in English literature till we encounter the knavish hypocrites of Dickens. It has been remarked with truth that Jonson never created the character of a noble lady. This is not because he was unfamiliar with such characters; his poems and dedications show him on terms of intimacy with the noblest ladies of his day; but he judged rightly that there was no place for a Portia in *Volpone* nor for Rosalind in *Bartholomew Fair*. The characters of Jonson's plays are the proper people for critical satiric comedy.

Jonson's realism is most minute and convincing in his treatment of background. His comedies are invaluable social documents, since they present an unequalled picture of life in England during the great Elizabethan age. To take one example out of many, Shakespeare never so much as mentions the new fashion of smoking; Jonson's comedies are redolent of the pipe. Tobacco may be trivial, but there is more than smoke in Jonson's plays. There is not a folly, an affectation, or a fraud of his day that is not castigated by his satire; it ranges from new fashions in dress and speech to the proposed transmutation of base metals into gold and to grandiose schemes for reclaiming drowned lands. And all this matter is presented in "language such as men do use," in prose for the most part, or in verse that has little of the divine afflatus of poetry, but is only a more measured and rhythmical prose. Jonson is an earth-born Titan; like Antæus he draws strength from contact with the ground.

Classicist and realist, Jonson is a rebel against the dominant tendencies of his day. Yet unlike most rebels he is a conscious and conscientious artist; he knew what he was doing, surveyed his work, and with proud self-confidence pronounced it good. A just appreciation of his achievement demands from the reader some knowledge of the age for which he wrote, some notion of the underlying principles of the playwright's art, and, above all, a certain intellectual activity. The best of Jonson's comedies is no easy reading for an idle hour.

CHAPTER SEVEN

LATER COMEDY, SATIRIC AND REALISTIC: MARSTON, MIDDLETON, BROME

THE NATIVE tradition of realism held its own on the English stage even during the heyday of romantic comedy. It pushed scenes of realistic, often farcical, comedy into historical plays and set a contemporary English background to many a romantic theme. At times it was still capable of creating a play in which realism of background, character, and dialogue were predominant. An excellent example of this tradition is the amusing comedy, *The Two Angry Women of Abingdon, ca.* 1598, the only surviving play of Henry Porter. The plot deals with the bitter quarrel of two citizens' wives and their frantic efforts to prevent a match between the son of one and the daughter of the other. The true excellence of the play lies in its picture of middle-class life in the English countryside, the food, the drink, and the games. The characters exactly match the background; they are true English folk with no nonsense about them; the playwright laughs at them, but he quite sympathizes with them. There is no trace of condescension or of satire in his work, and this tone is characteristic of comedy before the advent of Jonson.

Satire, in fact, was late in entering Elizabethan comedy. It was not that the time was unripe for satiric comment. On the contrary the great increase of wealth with its corresponding spread of luxury, the steady drift of gentlemen from the simplicity of country life to the disorder of the town, the domination of the metropolis by a sophisticated and pleasure-loving court, all cried aloud for the lash of the satirist, as did the fanaticism, and its attendant shadow, hypocrisy, of the Puritan protest against this mode of life. In the last decade of the century satire found a voice. Beginning with the prose tracts of Nashe and Greene it broke out in verse in the early satires of Donne, *ca.* 1593. Lodge caught up the theme with *A Fig for Momus,* 1595, and suddenly at the very end of the century it seemed as if every one was writing satire. Hall opened the chorus; Marston responded; Guilpin echoed Marston; and Middleton turned from paraphrasing the wisdom of Solomon to join the strain.

Propriety was shocked by the savagery, bitterness, and often foulness of these chastisers of vice and folly. In June, 1599, the Archbishop of Canterbury forbade the future publication of satires and epigrams, and condemned to the flames all copies that could be seized of the work of Hall, Marston, Guilpin, and others. But the taste for satire had been created; it was too much in accord with the growing bitterness of the time to be snuffed out by ecclesiastical decree. Satire turned to the drama and mating with the comedy of humours created, tentatively at first and then with more assurance, a new phase of English drama, realistic-satiric comedy. Jonson's influence on this phase was very considerable; yet the new comedy differs from Jonson's in more ways than one. His is essentially a comedy of character; the new comedy is rather a picture of contemporary life with stress upon its darker shades. Jonson's work is characterized by an ethical earnestness, shown alike in the punishment of vice and in the exposure of folly. The new comedy, on the other hand, is often content to entertain with a tale of clever roguery triumphing over the accepted traditions; it is amoral rather than ethical; the element of satiric comment is always present.

The first and in some ways the most interesting of these new playwrights is John Marston. The son of a well-to-do lawyer and his Italian wife, Marston was graduated from Oxford and took up the study of law in London. That he soon abandoned this profession is shown by a pathetic clause in his father's will which leaves a collection of law books to the son "whom I hoped would have profited by them in the study of the law, but man proposeth, and God disposeth." The success of his satires led to a brief engagement with Henslowe. He appears in the *Diary*, September 28, 1599, under the disguise of "Mr Maxton, the new poete," engaged in collaboration with Jonson and others. One may well imagine that service under Henslowe would be intolerable to a gentleman of independent means; certainly Marston's connection with Henslowe was brief, for in this same year we find him working for Paul's Boys. He seems to have written exclusively for this company until the closing of the theatres in the plague year of 1603–04. When they reopened, Marston bought a share in the management of the Chapel Children, now the Children of the Queen's Revels, and continued with them through their stormy career, marked by such offences to authority as *Eastward Ho,* the *Byron* plays, and a lost comedy, *ca.* 1608, which provoked the special wrath of James and led to a brief imprisonment of Marston. Whether this indignity shocked Marston out of his career as satiric poet-dramatist or whether like Donne he experienced a religious conversion, we shall never know. All we do know is that he studied theology, married a clergyman's daughter, and for fifteen years served as rector of a country parish. He died in 1634 and was buried in Temple Church under a stone inscribed *Oblivioni Sacrum.*

Marston's first surviving dramatic work is his revision of *Histri-omastix, i.e,* a whip for players. This is one of the "musty fop-peries of antiquity" with which Paul's Boys, in default of a better repertoire, opened their season in 1599. The only interesting thing in the play is Marston's transformation of the character of Chrisoganus, originally a pedantic philosopher, into a satirist and playwright who bears a certain amusing likeness to Ben Jonson.

Marston's first original play, *Antonio and Mellida,* 1599, affords an interesting proof alike of his poetic talent, his sensitivity to stage-effect, and his imperfect mastery of dramatic form. The main plot is a romantic love-story, a Romeo and Juliet theme heightened by making the lovers princely children of rival and hostile states. Marston can hardly have taken the fantastic story seriously; his true concern is with the satire which he grafted so incongruously upon a conventional romantic theme. The play opens with an Induction in the manner of *Every Man Out* in which a group of actors discuss the roles which they are about to perform and comment satirically upon the impersonated char-acters. One of them, Feliche, serves later as the mouthpiece of the author, pouring out a flood of invective upon the humours: the lover, the flatterer, and the affected fool, who haunt the court. In the more serious scenes one catches from time to time the note of Marston's pessimistic dissatisfaction with the conditions of human life. What wrecks the play as a whole is the clash between the high-flown romanticism of the main plot and the savage bitterness of the would-be comic scenes. Marston had not yet learned to wed satire to realism.[1]

He was to do better in his next comedy, *Jack Drum's Entertainment, ca.* 1600. The scene is laid in England, and although the central theme is once more a story of lovers in distress, it is quite overshadowed by the satiric comedy that plays about a group of truly English fools. Marston is feeling his way towards a suitable dramatic vehicle for his satiric impulse. *What You Will,* 1601, is less realistic than *Jack Drum,* since it abandons an English setting to revert to the conventional Italian scene. On the other hand Marston now rejects the conventional love-story and substitutes for it a farcical plot which lends itself more readily to satiric infusion. Marston's satire, no longer detached and incidental, pervades the whole substance of the play, hurling darts of mockery at sentimental lovers, affected speech, foppery in dress, pedantic scholarship, and woman's inconstancy. Two characters serve in particular to voice Marston's satire, Lampatho, a beggarly, bitter railer, plainly a caricature of Jonson, and Quadratus, the "square" man, a witty, jovial critic of the follies of human life, an idealized portrait, perhaps, of the author himself. Slight as it is, this play represents Marston's achievement of a more harmonious combination than he had before attained of satire and dramatic action.

Marston returned to the stage after a pause of some years with renewed vigor. His *Malcontent,* 1604, is with the possible exception of *Antonio's Revenge,* the most significant, certainly the best acting, play that he had yet composed. It was, indeed, so good that it was seized upon by Shakespeare's company and staged at the Globe with an Induction written especially for this performance by Webster. The protagonist, Malevole, the malcontent, an incarnation of the pessimistic spirit of the time, is the center of a serious action far removed from the farcical plot of *What You Will.* The scene is laid in Italy at the court of a usurping Duke, where the deposed ruler, Malevole, disguised

---

[1] The second part of this play, *Antonio's Revenge,* turns from comedy and satire to sensational tragedy. It will be discussed later (pp. 210–11).

as a sort of licensed jester, "more discontent than Lucifer," initiates an intrigue which in the end restores him to the throne. The machinery of the intrigue creaks violently; at times it approaches tragedy only to swing back again when a supposed corpse is suddenly restored to life. Here as in the earlier plays the important element is the satire which ranges freely and with a bitterness that recalls the tone of Marston's early poems over the whole range of human life. There is a difference, however, and an important one. Satire here, as in the comedy of Jonson, is corrective. There is good as well as evil in the dissolute world which the satire surveys; Malevole has an honest friend at Court and a faithful wife in prison. All in all *The Malcontent* is Marston's most harmonious play; it was, no doubt, with a proud humility that he dedicated the printed version to his late enemy, Ben Jonson.

Parasitaster, or the Fawn, ca. 1605, is the most Jonsonian of Marston's comedies. The unusual first word in the title was probably suggested by Jonson's *Poetaster*; the second is Marston's own diminutive of fawner, *i.e.*, flatterer. This fawner, like the protagonist of *The Malcontent,* is a disguised Duke, but unlike Malevole, his humour is that of honeyed flattery. The murderous intrigues of *The Malcontent* are missing in *The Fawn*; the entire action remains in the plane of comedy. As in Jonson's early plays the slight plot is almost completely lost in the exploitation of a gallery of humour characters around whom the mockery of Faunus plays like a flame that lightens rather than destroys. Marston's satire has mellowed; the irony of Faunus is poles removed from the savage onslaughts of Malevole.

The Dutch Courtezan, ca. 1604, the least Marstonian of Marston's comedies, may have been provoked by the success in that year of Dekker's *Honest Whore* at the Fortune. One may well imagine that Dekker's romantic presentation of the courtezan aroused the satirist in Marston. Yet in this play realism triumphs over satire; Marston almost apologizes in the Prologue for not railing like other playwrights. The argument of the play, to quote Marston's own words, is "the difference betwixt the love of a courtezan and a wife . . . intermixed with the deceits of a wittie Cittie Jester." The action, as these words show, is on two distinct planes: the first serious enough, approaching at times the tone of tragedy; the second a lively comedy of intrigue. In both realism is predominant alike in characterization and in speech.

The four outstanding figures of the serious plot are Freevill, a young gallant; Beatrice, his betrothed; Franceschina, his discarded mistress; and his "unhappy"—we would say unlucky—friend, Malheureux. There can be no doubt about the vitality of the characters; they are not embodied humours, but genuine flesh and blood. Freevill is the carefree Elizabethan youth who discards his mistress with as little concern as he would toss away an old glove; his friend, "a man of snow," once induced to visit the courtezan, falls an instant and helpless victim to her charm. Even after he has been shocked into a realization of his folly by the harlot's demand that he kill his friend, he still persists in his pursuit, and it is not until her betrayal of him for the supposed murder that his eyes are opened. The women, too, are fully realized. Beatrice is all modesty, tenderness, and forgiveness, an admirable contrast to her lighthearted and mocking sister. Franceschina is Marston's masterpiece; her wantonness, her anger, insolence, and treachery are a startling revelation of the depth to which a woman may sink. Here is no romanticizing of the fallen woman, but the sternest realism.

The same realistic treatment of character prevails in the subplot. Mr. and Mrs. Mulligrub, the victims of the coney-catching Cocledemoy, are far from flattering portraits of honest London citizens; they are miserly, cheating, and revengeful, as well as foolish. Cocledemoy himself is no ordinary rogue; he is individualized as a debauched scholar in the familiar tradition of George Peele. Characterization is attained by dialogue rather than description; and the speech of these worthies is an admirable vehicle of self-revelation. One cannot soon forget the rogue's torrential flow of speech larded with foul oaths and scraps of Latin or Mrs. Mulligrub's protestation that she would not be so unkind as to leave her husband until he was well hanged. If Marston had always written like this, his fame as a dramatist would be higher than it is today. His reputation, such as it is, rests upon two comedies: the satiric comedy of *The Malcontent*,

the realistic comedy of *The Dutch Courtezan*. His two important tragedies will be considered later.

Marston remains a unique figure among Elizabethan comic
dramatists. His work both repels and attracts; it is certainly the
work of a man superior to the savage caricature of him in the
Poetaster by which he is unfortunately best known. One can
trace a gradual evolution from the discordant satire of his early
days to the realism and dramatic dialogue of *The Dutch Courtezan*. His prose is excellent; at its best, as in his comic scenes in
Eastward Ho, it attains a striking swiftness and pungency. His
poetry on the other hand is disappointing; one feels that he had
little control over his Pegasus. It soars at times into the upper air
only to stumble over very rocky ground. He uses the spur rather
than the bridle; the straining for effect is too evident, the labor
of the file unhappily absent. Yet even so Marston occasionally
attains inspired poetic utterance such as the judicious Jonson
and the sober Heywood rarely reached.

One leaves Marston with the feeling that he was a restless and
bitter spirit. He pierced the veil of illusion to the harsh realities
of life. After a short and brilliant career broken by quarrels, dis-
appointments, and imprisonment, he turned away from the world
and retired into religion. His epitaph sums up the Jacobean con-
tempt for the pursuit of Fame which had inspired earlier Elizabethan poets. Since life was not worth living, let it be buried and
forgotten. Yet no student of English drama is likely to forget the
author of *The Malcontent* and *The Dutch Courtezan*.

Thomas Middleton, 1580–1627,[1] one of the most prolific and
versatile of Elizabethan playwrights, presents an interesting contrast to his contemporary, Marston. The son of a London brick-
layer who boasted a coat of arms and wrote himself down
"gentleman," he studied at Oxford, and returned to London
about the close of the century to spend the rest of his life there.
From the beginning he was identified with the life of the metropolis, writing plays for various theatres, turning out pamphlets on
topics of contemporary interest, composing pageants and entertainments for civic festivals, and serving for some time as Chro-

[1] The date of Middleton's birth, 1580, has now been established by the
research of Professor Eccles.

nologer of the City. He lived twenty years or more in the suburb
of Newington Butts and was buried in the parish church there
on July 4, 1627. He knew his London as well as Jonson and
loved it far better than did Marston.

Middleton's earliest published work is non-dramatic: *Microcynicon*, 1599, is a youthful excursion into the fashionable field
of satire; *Father Hubbard's Tale* and *The Black Book*, 1604, are
prose tracts in the manner of Nashe, showing an intimate acquaintance with the seamy side of London life. Middleton's connection with the drama began under the shadow of Henslowe.
In May 1602 the *Diary* records his collaboration with Dekker,
Webster, and others on a lost play, *Cæsar's Fall*. Another tragedy, *Randal, Earl of Chester*, has also perished without leaving
a trace. Middleton soon deserted the Admiral's Men for the
fashionable Children of Paul's, a company for which Marston
and Dekker were already writing. The first play included in the
collected editions of Middleton, *Blurt, Master Constable*, 1602,
was acted by this company. Published anonymously it is probably the work mainly, if not entirely, of Dekker. Middleton collaborated with Dekker in *The Honest Whore* for the Prince's
Company and then settled down for some years of steady work
for Paul's Boys. For them he composed *The Phœnix; A Trick to
Catch the Old One; A Mad World, My Masters; Michaelmas
Term*; and, probably, *The Puritan*. All these are realistic satiric
comedies, all but *The Phœnix* comedies of contemporary London life. *The Family of Love* belongs to this group and may
originally have been a play for Paul's. For the Queen's Revels
Company he wrote *Your Five Gallants*, 1607, another realistic
comedy of London life, and a lost tragedy, *The Viper and Her
Brood*, 1606. Reverting to collaboration with Dekker he composed *The Roaring Girl*, 1610, for the Prince's Company. For
the Lady Elizabeth's Company he wrote the last and in some
ways the best of his realistic comedies, *A Chaste Maid in Cheapside*, 1611, and two years later the first of his plays to show the
unmistakable influence of the rising art of Fletcher, *No Wit,
No Help Like a Woman's*. Fletcher may have introduced him
to the King's Men, for whom he wrote *The Witch, ca.* 1615, a
tragi-comedy; *More Dissemblers Besides Women*, 1615, a com-

edy more or less in Fletcher's vein; and *The Widow, ca.* 1616, another Fletcherian comedy, first printed in 1652 as the joint work of Middleton, Fletcher, and Jonson.

About 1616 Middleton began his long and fruitful collaboration with William Rowley. They worked partly for the Prince's Company, of which Rowley was a leading member. To this group belong *A Fair Quarrel, The Old Law,* and a masque, *The World Tossed at Tennis.* Rowley, however, acted at times with the King's Company and for them he and Middleton wrote, or perhaps revived, *The Mayor of Queenborough.* For the Lady Elizabeth's Company they collaborated in *The Changeling,* a tragedy, and a tragi-comedy, *The Spanish Gipsy.* Meanwhile Middleton continued to write at intervals for the King's Men: *Anything for a Quiet Life,* in collaboration with Webster, a comedy; his sole unaided tragedy, *Women Beware Women;* and his famous political satiric comedy, *A Game at Chess,* 1624. The trouble in which this play involved the author seems to have put an end to his career as a playwright; a Lord Mayor's pageant, 1626, is Middleton's last work before his death in 1627.

The dates assigned to Middleton's plays in the preceding paragraph are largely conjectural since the chronology of Middleton's work is still far from clear. Many of his plays appeared in his lifetime without his name, or with only his initials, on the title-page; others were printed for the first time many years after his death; *The Witch* remained in manuscript till 1778. The authorship of various plays assigned to him has been challenged; his hand has been suspected in plays that are ascribed to other playwrights. Yet there is a sufficient body of undoubted work by Middleton to permit an appreciation of his peculiar characteristics and to note the development of his ingenious and flexible talent. It seems best to discuss his plays in certain groups, dwelling at some length only upon outstanding examples of each.

The first surviving play that can be attributed with any degree of certainty to Middleton is *The Phœnix,* published without his name in 1607. It is strangely old-fashioned for this date. The scene is laid in Italy, but the characters are unmistakably English. Strictly speaking there is no plot, only a succession of scenes in which Phœnix, son and heir of the Duke of Ferrara, wanders in disguise through the land exposing the evils of the time. These, needless to say, are English evils, the abuse of justice, the wantonness of city wives, and the custom, long thought to be especially English, of selling a wife in open market. The dialogue for the most part is a swift and telling prose, varied at times by passages of true poetry such as the apostrophe to Law and the pæan in praise of marriage. It seems as if Middleton had planned to write a realistic satiric comedy, but was still constrained by the romantic convention of the nineties.

A Trick to Catch the Old One is the first and one of the best of Middleton's realistic comedies. He comes back here from a conventional Italy to his own London. The satiric note fades out in his realistic portraiture, or, at most, is implied in the action rather than explicit in attacks by the author. *A Trick* is a carefully planned and well-executed comedy of intrigue. The hero, young Witgood, ruined by his extravagance and the usury of the "old fox" Lucre, his uncle, devises an ingenious trick to restore his credit by spreading the report of his approaching marriage to a rich widow. The alleged widow is his mistress, who plays her part so well that she is accepted as his prospective bride not only by his uncle, but by his uncle's bitter enemy and rival in the field of usury, Master Hoard. The strife between the two old rogues, each eager to plunder her supposed wealth, is skilfully exploited by Witgood, who gets back the titles of his land from Lucre and has his debts paid by Hoard in return for a release of his claim upon the widow. For Hoard in his eagerness to outwit Lucre has fallen into the trap and actually married the courtezan. The play ends with her vow to be a true wife; Witgood's renunciation of dice, drabs and drink; general forgiveness, and a banquet. This is a sop to bourgeois morality; the truth is that all Middleton's sympathy goes out to the clever young rogue who has outwitted the old ones. It is no small tribute to Middleton's art that Witgood's "trick" suggested to Massinger the device for that "new way to pay old debts" by which Wellborn in the comedy of that name gets the better of his uncle, Sir Giles Overreach.

There is no need to discuss in detail Middleton's other realistic comedies of London life; they follow the same essential pattern with various ingenious differences. In *Michaelmas Term* the main action reverses the theme of *A Trick*; the prime mover here is a London citizen, Quomodo, woolen-draper and moneylender, who reduces a country gentleman, Master Easy, to bankruptcy. At last, however, in an access of insolence which reminds one of Volpone's behavior, Quomodo feigns death to discover how his wife and son will take the news. His wife promptly marries Easy, and his foolish son lets the title to Easy's land pass into the true owner's hands. The play presents a lively picture of contemporary London life with special stress upon the devices, legal and illegal, by which city merchants strove to attain the property, and with it the social status, of country gentlemen. The main interest of *The Family of Love* lies in the prose scenes of the subplot, satirizing the hypocrisy of the heretical sect from which the play takes its name, whose members were generally believed to indulge in the practice of communal free love. *Your Five Gallants* is rather a dramatic exposure of certain shady sides of London life than a comedy of intrigue, with scenes laid in Paul's Walk, the Mitre Tavern, and various London streets and lodgings.

A *Mad World, My Masters* is a more ambitious piece of work, a comedy of intrigue with two independent plots, joined together by the presence in each of the courtezan, Gullman. The first of these deals with the pranks by which a roguish gallant, Dick Follywit, manages in various disguises to extract money and jewels from his rich but tight-fisted grandfather, Sir Bounteous Progress. In the end as evidence of his reformation he announces his marriage and introduces his wife, who is promptly recognized as the old gentleman's kept mistress, Gullman. There is no sufficient reason for Dick's sudden marriage with such a character other than Middleton's delight in presenting the biter bit. In the subplot the courtezan plays a more important part. Disguised as a religious virgin she is engaged by a jealous husband to keep his wanton wife in the path of virtue. Naturally enough she plays quite a contrary role and acts as a bawd to throw the lady into the arms of her lover. Later the repentant lover persuades the lady to remain true to her husband, who in turn casts off suspicion and embraces the lover as his true friend. The serious tone of these scenes contrasts rather incongruously with the witty comedy of the courtezan as a go-between, but it serves to show Middleton moving towards a graver treatment of human relations than appears in his earlier plays.

The last of these realistic comedies, *A Chaste Maid in Cheapside,* represents a considerable advance in Middleton's art both in plot construction and characterization. There are three distinct actions in the play: the tangled love affair of young Touchwood and Moll Yellowhammer; the liaison of Sir Walter with Mrs. Allwit; and the domestic troubles of Sir Oliver and Lady Kix. All three are closely interwoven and brought at last to a satisfactory solution. There is a flavor of romance in the story of young Touchwood and Moll, the chaste maid, but the tone of the play in general is rather sordidly realistic. The Yellowhammers are determined to force their reluctant daughter into marriage with Sir Walter, even after his liaison with Mrs. Allwit has been revealed, and to wed their foolish son, a Cambridge student, to the knight's supposed niece, really his Welsh mistress. The Allwit household, where Sir Walter has for years maintained a flock of bastards, presents a picture of hopeless degradation.

There is none of Jonson's moral indignation in Middleton's treatment of these characters; he is rather a dispassionate observer of things as they are, always ready to dispel the gloom by the introduction of highly farcical scenes, such as that in which the Country Wench leaves the searchers after forbidden meat in Lent with a bastard baby on their hands. The riotous revelry at the christening of Mrs. Allwit's latest child affords Middleton an opportunity for a burst of satire against the greedy and sensual Puritan gossips who gather at the feast, and the Latin logic-chopping of Tim Yellowhammer and his tutor provokes a laugh at academic pedantry. In variety and deft power of characterization this play surpasses most of its predecessors. The Kixes, who kiss and quarrel by turns as each blames the other for their lack of children, are swiftly drawn but lifelike figures. Middleton's supreme achievement in satiric comedy, however, is the character of the complacent cuckold, Allwit, with his smirking satisfaction in his wife's shame and his swift repudiation of the affair when his patron is no longer able to maintain him in comfortable idleness. It is, perhaps, a sign of Middleton's conscious effort towards something better than he had done before that in *A Chaste Maid* he abandons almost entirely the prose of earlier plays for an easy metrical speech.

It seems characteristic of the changing temper of the times and of the altered taste of theatrical audiences that early in the second decade of the century Middleton deserted the field of realistic comedy for romantic plays more or less in the style of Fletcher. A group of these, mainly written for the King's Company, are so unlike his early work and so inferior to the serious plays that he wrote about the same time in collaboration with Rowley that they may be briefly dismissed.

The first of these, *No Wit, No Help Like a Woman's* is an interesting example of Middleton's attempt to combine his own realistic portrayal of London life and Fletcher's comedy of intrigue. The main plot dealing with the troubles of the Twilight family is essentially a Plautine comedy transplanted to Elizabethan London. In the subplot the heroine dons doublet and hose and sets out to restore her husband's fallen fortune. She is one of Fletcher's girls, clever, audacious, and essentially virtuous, though she lacks the gayety and sprightly wit of Fletcher's brightest stars. *The Widow* is a comedy of intrigue in the fashionable Fletcher manner with the scene laid in Italy, and characters: a foolish old Judge with a wanton young wife, an amorous young gallant, a swaggering suitor, and a runaway girl in boy's clothing, who might have stepped out of any of Fletcher's comedies. The tangled action with its constant shifts and surprises, and its happy solution is miles away from the vigorous realism of Middleton's earlier work. *More Dissemblers Besides Women* is a more ambitious play than *The Widow,* but on the whole less successful. Once more Middleton leaves his London to lay the scene in Italy. The tangled plot resembles that of a Fletcher comedy, but the greater part of the play is written in a serious and rather formal verse without a trace of Fletcher's gayety. Another play for the King's Men, *Anything for a Quiet Life,* contains some amusing realistic scenes, but as a whole reflects little credit on either Middleton or Webster.

The Witch, a play of uncertain date for the King's Men, has received more attention than its intrinsic merit deserves, because of its peculiar relation to *Macbeth.* The character of Hecate, mistress of the witches, appears in both plays, and the songs, "Come away" and "Black Spirits," only named in Shakespeare's play, appear in full in Middleton's. It is now generally agreed that the character of Hecate, two songs, and a dance of witches in *Macbeth* are interpolations in Shakespeare's text made by Middleton at a time when he was called upon by the Company to lighten the grim tragedy. The central theme of *The Witch* is the tragic story of Rosamund, Queen of the Lombards, compelled by her brutal husband to drink his health from her slain father's skull, and revenging the outrage by a craftily planned murder. Unluckily Middleton turned this tale into a tragicomedy in which neither the heroine, her husband, nor her accomplice perish, although all come very close to death. The witch scenes have little bearing upon the action and are of a nature to make the whole business of witchcraft ridiculous and disgusting rather than terrible. Middleton was too much the realist to believe in it and too little of a poet to use it with Shakespeare's tragic power.

Middleton collaborated at times with various playwrights, but his best work, apart from his realistic comedies, was done during his long association with William Rowley, an actor-playwright known as the author of a bloody tragedy, *All's Lost by Lust,* and a comedy or two. He had a hand in various plays by Heywood, Dekker, and Webster, but his connection with Middleton was the longest and most fruitful in his career. An excellent actor, he had a quick sense of what was theatrically effective, and in his collaboration with Middleton we can trace his restraining hand on his partner's tendency towards exuberance and expansion.

Their joint work probably began when Middleton was writing and Rowley occasionally acting for the King's Men. With one exception, however, their plays were performed by other companies than the King's. This exception is the curious medley of history, tragedy, and farce, *The Mayor of Queenborough,* ascribed on the title-page to Middleton alone. Several scenes in the native tradition of low comedy, however, are quite plainly the work of Rowley, while occasional flashes of fine poetry reveal the hand of Middleton. *The Old Law,* published in 1656 as by Massinger, Middleton, and Rowley, is a far better play. It is an excellent example of the blend of comedy and romance which Fletcher had made popular, but the comedy is rather more boisterous and the romance more serious than in most of Fletcher's plays. The old law is an edict published by the Duke of Epirus condemning to death all men who have reached the age of eighty and all women at sixty, and the plot deals with the varied reactions of sons, husbands, and wives to this strange situation. The best character in the play is Gnotho, a rogue so anxious to get rid of his wife that he bribes the clerk of the parish to alter her birth date so as to hasten her death by the law. This role was probably written and played by Rowley; the more poetic passages are by Middleton, but it is impossible to divide the play scene by scene.

A Fair Quarrel is a serious, almost a tragic, play. Some boisterous comic scenes are by Rowley, as is the whole of the minor plot. Middleton had control of the main action which gives the play its name. This is a thoughtful and realistic treatment in dramatic form of the problem of the private duel, at that time troubling the upper circles of England. Bitterly opposed by the pacific King and prosecuted by the law, duelling had, none the less, increased to an alarming extent in recent years and was defended on the ground that it alone allowed a gentleman to protect his honor. Middleton's play is no propaganda against duelling; on the contrary the hero, Captain Agar, engages in a duel. His opponent, the Colonel, is a passionate adherent of the code; he draws his sword first at a fancied slur upon his reputation, indulges in foul language to provoke his adversary, and when that adversary strives for a reconciliation denounces him as a coward. The character of Captain Agar, on the other hand, is a masterpiece of firmly realistic portraiture; a young soldier, sober and self-reliant, he is, like Bunyan's Mr. Valiant-for-truth, "in a just cause as bold as a lion," but in a just cause only. A slanderous accusation of his widowed mother provokes him to challenge the Colonel; but an uneasy doubt, springing from what might be called an anticipation of the New England conscience, leads him to seek from her an affirmation of her honor. Her foolish mother-love, desiring at all costs to save her darling from danger, induces her to belie her truth, and daunts his courage. On such a ground he cannot fight; to the amazement of his friends and the scorn of the Colonel he stoops to beg

> Peace, constant amity, and calm forgiveness.

Even so there is nothing base in him; the taunt of "coward" with which he is answered comes as heaven's reward of his "excessive patience." "Now," he cries, "I have a cause"; and he strikes the Colonel down in fair fight. Yet his spirit is not wholly restored till he hears from his mother a confession of the falsity of her self-accusation. Had all Jacobean gentlemen resembled Captain Agar, there would have been little need of the King's repeated edicts against duelling.

The Spanish Gipsy, 1623, for the Lady Elizabeth's Company, has a special interest as showing Middleton's skill in dramatic construction and his firm grip on a serious theme. The play is almost entirely his; little can definitely be assigned to Rowley except a share in the gipsy scenes and the comic roles of Sancho and Soto. The plot is a deft interweaving of three separate strands: an exiled nobleman and his companions, returned to Spain in the disguise of gipsies; the love affair of Pretiosa, the gipsy girl, and Don John; and the tale of Roderigo's rape of Clara and his atonement by marriage. The second and third of these are based on two novels of Cervantes, *The Little Gipsy* and *The Force of Blood*. Middleton handles the love story with ease and grace, eliminating the killing that occurs in the source —death is out of place in tragi-comedy—and stressing the character of the witty and virtuous Pretiosa. The somber theme of rape is treated here with all due seriousness. Middleton in the main follows his source, but he makes several important changes. He discards the unpleasant incident of a child born to Lady Clara, and he indicates a prompt remorse on the part of Roderigo, a feeling deepened when he learns that the woman he has wronged is the beloved of his friend, Louis. This makes their marriage at the close more plausible and to the modern mind more acceptable. Middleton's strong realism appears at its best in his portrayal of Clara; her anguish, her demand for secrecy, and her final plea for justice are all held within the due bounds of a noble lady's character.[1]

Middleton's last play, *A Game at Chess*, first performed on August 6, 1624, achieved an instant success unparalleled in the history of Elizabethan drama. It ran for nine consecutive days and was reported to have brought the actors £1,500. Apparently it might have run indefinitely; it was necessary to go hours in advance to secure a place. This amazing success was due not to its merit as a stage-play, but to the skill with which it reflected in dramatic form an excited political upheaval.

The pacifist statecraft of King James was from the beginning disliked by the advocates of a firm foreign policy; but popular feeling had no weight with the King. Hoodwinked by the shrewd Spanish ambassador, Gondemar, he allowed his heir, Prince Charles, and his favorite, Buckingham, to proceed incognito to Madrid early in 1623, in order to bring to a final conclusion the long drawn-out negotiations for a marriage of the Prince to a Spanish infanta. It was Gondemar's hope and England's dread that this match would result in the Prince's conversion and in the re-establishment in England of the Church of Rome. There was a wild outbreak of joy when Charles and Buckingham, weary of long delays and the impossible conditions imposed by Spain, returned to England in October. Bells were rung, bonfires lighted, and banquets spread for all in the streets of London. The two young men seized the reins of power from the faltering hands of the old King and embarked upon a course that led straight to war with Spain. It was in such an atmosphere of anger, exultation, and hope that Middleton composed *A Game at Chess*.

The play is an elaborate allegory of the long trial of diplomatic skill between Spain and England, just ended, from the English

[1] The fine tragedy of *The Changeling* and Middleton's *Women Beware Women* are treated in Chapter IX.

point of view, in the complete victory of the good cause. The two nations are represented as the opposing pieces on a chess-board, the English, naturally, as the white, the detested Spaniards as the black. The tangled plot is hard to follow, and the identification of the various "pieces" is not always clear. But there can be no mistake about the villain of the play, Gondemar, who appears as the Black Knight, boasting of his intrigues against England and of the Spanish design of universal monarchy. To make assurance double sure the actor of this role "counterfeited his person to the life, with all his graces and faces"; wearing a cast-off suit of Gondemar's, he was carried across the stage in a litter like that which the ambassador's infirmity required him to use in London. Charles and Buckingham appear as the White Knight and the White Duke (the Rook) who visit the Black House and feign adherence to its cause only to win the game by declaring "check by discovery," whereupon the black pieces are hustled unceremoniously into the bag, a conclusion received, no doubt, with shouts of joy by a patriotic audience.

Naturally the Spanish ambassador, Gondemar's successor, entered an emphatic protest at Court, and James at once ordered the play stopped. Summoned before the Privy Council the actors defended themselves by showing that the play had been duly licensed by the Master of the Revels. Their defense was not accepted; they were not only forced to stop this play, but forbidden under bond of £300 to act "any play or interlude whatsoever, until his Majesty's pleasure be further known." The King's wrath was soon cooled, and the actors were allowed to play again—except the forbidden drama. Yet if the public could no longer see *A Game at Chess* upon the stage, it was soon easy for them to read it. Three quartos appeared early in 1625, surreptitiously printed without the name of author, printer, or bookseller upon the title-page. Manuscript copies of the forbidden fruit were in high demand; five of them are still extant, a record number for any Elizabethan play. It is still worth reading, not only for the political satire which brings it nearer to the plays of Aristophanes than any other English drama, but for the sheer beauty of the poetry which Middleton poured out so lavishly on this unique work. One passage in particular evoked the admiring imitation of the young John Milton:

> Upon these lips, the sweet fresh buds of youth,
> The holy dew of prayer lies, like the pearl
> Dropt from the opening eyelids of the morn
> Upon the bashful rose.

It is difficult to form any definite conception of Middleton's personality. We know a good deal about his life, little about the man himself. What we know is largely negative. He was not involved in violent quarrels, artistic, or personal; he was not imprisoned for debt; he was not bound to the service of any company either as actor or playwright. Ben Jonson stigmatized him as a "base fellow," probably because he had no friends at Court and no well-defined theory of dramatic art to uphold. Yet if Middleton had no theory of dramatic art he was, none the less, a true if unconscious artist. His art rested on the firm foundation of life as he saw it lived around him. He saw good in it as well as much evil, but refused either to sentimentalize or to denounce. He turned away from Elizabethan romanticism and set himself to mirror in his work the cool and scrutinizing temper of the new age. Middleton was, of course, a man of the age that his plays reflect. There is often a certain hardness, not to say cynicism, in his attitude towards moral questions, particularly towards those involving sex relations. Dekker for example neither could nor would have written the witty scene in *A Mad World* where the courtezan gulls the eavesdropping husband while his wife enjoys the embraces of her lover. Such a scene looks forward, as nothing else in earlier Elizabethan comedy, to the Restoration plays that make a jest of adultery.

Middleton's hand was not always true, but by a long process of experiment he perfected his art until it became an adequate instrument for the expression of his view of life. There is no falling off in Middleton as in Dekker, or even in Jonson. Beginning as a satirist in verse and prose, he developed steadily a strain of realism, "deeds and language such as men do use," that should have earned him the praise rather than the censure of Jonson. Satire falls into the background and becomes implicit in his comedy. Yet Middleton was no earth-bound realist; he was still Elizabethan enough to retain something of the poetic temper of that age. There is a marked increase in his work of limpid and often lovely poetry; it adds to his dialogue the heightening effect of verse, but is never too far removed from the speech of real life.

As a playwright Middleton's range is remarkably wide; he swings from the realistic comedy of London life to the play of intrigue in an imagined Italy, from the tragi-comedy of *The Witch* to the sober problem play of *A Fair Quarrel*. He is one of the best of Elizabethan story-tellers in dramatic form; his plays are never dull; he does not overweight them with Jonson's learning, nor let them dissolve into a shapeless congeries of scenes like Dekker at his worst. He is always master of his material, and once we accept the Elizabethan conventions of aside, disguise, and sudden conversion, his plots hang well together. On the other hand one misses in him the vivifying creative power that one finds at times in less skilful artists. A master of comedy he yet never managed to create such memorable comic characters as Bobadil and Simon Eyre. What one remembers best in Middleton is neither his poetry nor his characters, but his lively and varied picture of Elizabethan London with its rogues and harlots, its swindling shopkeepers and gay young gentlemen, its demure Puritans and swaggering soldiers.

The realistic satiric comedy of the Elizabethan age comes to an end with Richard Brome, a playwright whose work deserves more attention than it has usually received. The date and place of his birth are unknown. His name first appears in the Induction to *Bartholomew Fair*, 1614, where the stage-keeper speaks of Ben Jonson's "man, Master Brome." A copy of verses by Jonson prefixed to Brome's first published play, *The Northern Lass*, 1632, is addressed to "my old faithful servant . . . my loving friend . . . Mr. Richard Brome." An epigram (ci.) of Jonson's, inviting a friend to dinner, contains as an inducement the promise that his "man," presumably Brome, will read aloud to them "a piece of Virgil, Tacitus, Livy, or of some better book." It would appear from this that Brome was something better than a menial, possibly even Jonson's secretary. Nine years after

Bartholomew Fair we hear of him again; in 1623 Herbert licensed a new comedy called *A Fault in Friendship*, "written by young Jonson [the poet's son] and Brome." It is unfortunate that this play is lost, for the maiden effort of Jonson's son and his faithful servant would certainly be an interesting work. Another period of silence follows before a second record by Herbert throws a new light on Brome. About three weeks after the failure of *The New Inn*, January 1629, the King's Men produced Brome's *The Lovesick Maid* to such "extraordinary applause" that the gratified players made Herbert a special present of £2. Furious at his own failure, which he blamed upon the actors, Jonson was doubly enraged at his man's success and vented his spleen in the famous *Ode to Himself*, where in an attack upon the theatre he declared that

> Brome's sweepings do as well
> There as his master's meal.[1]

It is characteristic alike of Jonson's hasty temper and of his forgiving nature that in his published version of the *Ode* he altered these lines to read:

> There sweepings do as well
> As the best order'd meal.

The Lovesick Maid is also lost; it was followed, however, in the same year by another success, *The Northern Lass*, published in 1632, "as acted at the Globe and Blackfriars," with a group of commendatory verses prefixed. By this time Jonson had forgotten his outburst and wrote the commendatory lines recognizing Brome as a disciple who has climbed to success after a long "prentice-ship" in contrast to the crew of courtiers who "all write plays" without any knowledge of the craft. Other contributors to the chorus of praise are John Ford, probably the dramatist, and Dekker, who addresses Brome as his son and friend in a graceful set of verses, the last known utterance of the genial poet-playwright.

By this time Brome had established himself as a furnisher of

[1] The playwright's name, it appears from this and other contemporary allusions, was pronounced Broom.

plays for the King's Men, and he continued to write for them until about 1635. To this period belong, probably or certainly, *The New Academy, The City Wit, The Queen's Exchange, The Court Beggar, The Novella, The Weeding of Covent Garden,* and in collaboration with Heywood, *The Late Lancashire Witches.* In 1635 he signed a contract to write three plays a year for the King's Revels Company at Salisbury Court. For this company and for the Queen's players, with whom they united in 1637, Brome wrote *The Queen and Concubine, The Sparagus Garden, A Mad Couple Well Match'd,* and *The English Moor.* They also produced *The Antipodes,* originally written, as Brome himself tells us, for Beeston's Boys, a children's company playing at the Cockpit. It would seem that Brome had not lived up to the terms of his contract and was forced by the Queen's Company to turn his latest play over to them. He broke free, however, and from 1638 till the closing of the theatres wrote exclusively for Beeston's Boys, giving them *The Damoiselle, The Lovesick Court,* and his last play, *The Jovial Crew.*

Little is known of Brome's activities during the Commonwealth. In 1652 he published *The Jovial Crew* with a dedication "to the right noble, ingenious, and judicious gentleman, Thomas Stanley, Esq." In a charming blend of modesty and self-confidence, he recommends to his patron this product of his old age which "had the luck to tumble last of all in the Epidemical ruin of the Scene," calls himself "poor and proud," and suggests that since "the times conspire to make us all beggars, let us make ourselves merry." Next year, 1653, his friend Alexander Brome —no relation, by the way—gave to the world *Five New Plays: A Mad Couple, The Novella, The Court Beggar, The City Wit,* and *The Damoiselle* by Richard Brome. In a prose preface Alexander tells us that the author being dead "is of Falstaff's mind and cares not for honor." This fixes the date of his death in 1652 or 1653.

Only four of Brome's plays, not counting *The Late Lancashire Witches,* were published in his lifetime: *The Northern Lass,* 1632, *The Sparagus Garden* and *The Antipodes* in 1640, and *The Jovial Crew,* 1651. This is because Brome's plays were written for the stage and not for the closet. There is good evi-

dence to show that this hard-working playwright achieved theatrical success in his own day, and some of his plays carried over
into the Restoration. Pepys saw the *The Antipodes* in 1661 and
remarked that it contained "much mirth, but no great matter
else." He saw *The Jovial Crew*, "the most innocent play that I
ever saw," three times; on one occasion the King, The Duke of
York, and Madam Palmer, the King's mistress, were also in the
audience. In the next century this popular play was made into
an opera, 1731, after the style of *The Beggar's Opera*, and held
the stage intermittently down to the time of Charles Lamb. In
addition *The Northern Lass* was revived at least four times, and
the industrious Mrs. Behn adapted *A Mad Couple* under a characteristic Restoration title, *The Debauchee, or the Credulous
Cuckold*, 1677. This is no bad record for a minor Elizabethan
playwright.

Brome's success as a practising playwright in the last years of
Elizabethan drama was due to his diligence in following an
established and acceptable formula for realistic comedy and his
ingenuity in varying the pattern. He was ready, however, at the
call of the company he served to furnish plays of another genre.
The Queen's Exchange, 1631, for instance, is a tragi-comedy of
a strangely old-fashioned type. *The Queen and Concubine*,
founded upon the first tale in Greene's romance, *Penelope's
Web*, is a more up-to-date play, an interesting example of the
extravagance of action and absurdity of character into which
the Fletcher pattern of tragi-comedy was sinking. *The Lovesick
Court*, another tragi-comedy, is an amalgamation of the themes
of *A King and No King* and *The Two Noble Kinsmen*, eliminating in the process the tragic, or near tragic, elements in both these
plays. *The Novella*, on the other hand, is a gay comedy of intrigue; the interest lies in a clever and complicated plot packed
with disguises, surprises, and reversals.

To turn from these fantastic and second-rate plays to Brome's
realistic comedies is like getting back to actual life again. One
of the earliest and best is *The City Wit, or the Woman Wears
the Breeches*, a very amusing farce-comedy. Brome follows here
the pattern set by Middleton's early comedies, more particularly
that of *A Trick*. The hero, Mr. Crasy—not insane, but only

bankrupt—is a London merchant who sets out to retrieve his ruined fortunes by tricking his ungrateful friends and harsh creditors. He accomplishes this mainly by the aid of a supposed wealthy widow who goes through a marriage ceremony with a young citizen and then induces him to buy off Crasy on the grounds of a pre-contract. So far the plot develops along Middleton's lines, but Brome springs a surprise at the end when the "widow" pulls up her skirts to show her breeches and reveals herself as Crasy's faithful servant, Jeremy. This, of course, goes back to Jonson's *Epicœne,* but it has a special bearing on the plot since the mother of the bridegroom is herself a "breeches-wearing" woman. This is Mistress Pyannet—the magpie—the domineering wife of Mr. Sneakup, a woman gifted with an extraordinary flow of abusive speech, a Jonsonian humour pushed to farcical extremes. Incidentally various episodes emphasize the opposition between the City and the Court, and Brome, like a good Londoner, tips the scales in favor of the City.

The Weeding of Covent Garden is the most Jonsonian of Brome's comedies. The intrigue, more complex than in most of Jonson's plays, springs none the less from a group of Jonsonian humours: Mr. Crosswill, a self-willed and tyrannical father, anticipating Sir Anthony Absolute; Clotpole, a mere gull who, like Jonson's Angry Boy, longs to master the fashion of "roaring"; and Cockbrain, a Justice of the Peace, who wants to weed Covent Garden of its vices even as Justice Overdo in *Bartholomew Fair*—to whom he refers by name—strives to purge the Fair of its "enormities." The satiric note is stronger here than in most of Brome's plays, particularly in the character of Gabriel, Crosswill's son, who has lapsed into a Puritanic preciseness from which he is reclaimed only after a heavy drinking bout.

The Sparagus Garden is a sort of replica of *The Weeding of Covent Garden.* Once more the scene is laid in London, one whole act in the Garden itself. This was one of the suburban resorts, often mentioned in Elizabethan comedy, where citizens' wives came to feast on asparagus, then believed to be an aphrodisiac, to drink and dance, and often, it was suspected, to do worse. Jonsonian humours reappear in the two testy old Justices, whose long feud starts the main action of the play, and in a shrewish childless wife who longs for this and that, particularly to see a play, *"The Knight of the burning*—what dee' call 't." A very complicated intrigue ends in the marriage of the grand-daughter of one Justice to the son of the other, and a general reconciliation.

If these last two plays throw back to Jonson, *A Mad Couple Well Match'd* looks forward to Restoration comedy. Nowhere else in Elizabethan comedy do we meet so hopelessly debased a young ruffian as the leading gentleman of this play. He is Careless by name but much more than careless by nature. He casts off a girl that he has ruined, does his best to seduce the aunt who has restored him to his uncle's favor, slanders her when he fails in his attempt, and is at last rewarded by a marriage with a rich widow. She affects him—there can be no question of love in the matter—out of a pure spirit of opposition, and takes him as her husband in spite of his brutal warning, unmatched perhaps for plain-speaking in Elizabethan comedy, that she will not be able to satisfy his physical desires. These two are the mad couple and they are indeed well matched. There is another example, how-ever, less mad but quite as bad: the cheerful cuckold, Saleware, and his wife, Alicia, who is not only a wanton, but a liar and a mischief-maker. The play might well be called a bedroom farce for there are two bedroom scenes of rather startling realism. When one reflects that this comedy was produced by Queen Henrietta's Company, one can see how far the native tradition of realism differed from the fashion of Platonic love which the young Queen's patronage had introduced into the courtly com-edy of the day. *A Mad Couple* is a clever play, simpler in plot and swifter in action than most of Brome's comedies, and packed with effective situations.

It is a relief to turn from so coarse a play as this to a group in which there appear certain qualities of mind and heart that raise Brome above his fellows in the last period of Elizabethan comedy. The first of these is *The Northern Lass*. The success of this play, as the prose of Brome's dedication and Dekker's verses show, was due primarily to the character of the heroine, Constance. There is, to be sure, something else in the play: an entertaining intrigue, plenty of action, and a group of Jonsonian humours. But Constance is unique in late Elizabethan comedy, a wild-flower blooming in the dirty streets of London. She is a young girl from the Northern border brought up to London to be married off by her uncle. At his house she meets Sir Philip Luckless, falls in love with him at first sight, and in her simplicity takes his friendly courtesies for something like a definite proposal. Learning later of his coming marriage to a city widow, she sends him a pitiful little message signed only with her name, Constance. Unfortunately this is also the name of a woman of the town with whom Sir Philip had been but too well acquainted; he takes the note to come from her, and its only result is to hasten his marriage. It would take too long to unravel the tangled intrigue of the play; in the end Philip's marriage is shown to be null and void, Constance gets the man she loves, while the city wench is palmed off on the widow's foolish brother. It seems not unlikely that the roles of the northern lass and the city girl were played by the same actor, for the latter, like the true Constance, sings and, at need, speaks in the same northern dialect; they are never on the stage together except in the last scene, when the true Constance has not a word to say. It must have been an excellent part for a boy in Shakespeare's old company with a good voice and a pretty face; even to the reader there is something appealing in the quaint speech, snatches of song, love-longing, and modesty of Constance. She is a character such as Dekker might have drawn, and it is a proof of Dekker's admiration that he was prompt to claim her as his grandchild by his son, Dick Brome.

The Antipodes, the second of the group, has been called a delightful farce; it is more than that; it is farce directed to the ends of high comedy. The theme is the cure of various humours: old Joyless's jealousy of his young wife; the mad obsession of his son, Peregrine, with travellers' tales; and the melancholy of Martha, Peregrine's maiden wife. The means of the cure is an impromptu play enacted by the private company of the sport-loving Lord Letoy. The scene of this curative play is laid in the Antipodes to England where all things go by contraries. Peregrine is brought in a drugged sleep to Letoy's house, where he awakes in the firm conviction that he has been transported

to that strange land and that the action he sees upon the stage
is a real bit of Antipodean life. After a series of farcical scenes
played to a running accompaniment of witty comment by Letoy
and others, Peregrine is moved to take part in the action. He
crowns himself King of the Antipodes, makes various reforms
in the realm, and marries his own wife, introduced to him on
the stage as the daughter of the late Antipodean King. They are
put to bed together with all due ceremony; his madness and her
melancholy are promptly cured, and they become "her dear
Per. and his sweet Mat." The final cure is effected when Joyless
hears his wife repelling with firm dignity all Letoy's offers and
threats. Then it turns out that she is really Letoy's daughter; the
play and the feigned seduction scene have been her father's plot
to cure the Joyless family.

This is a bare sketch of the action, but no sketch can do
justice to the inimitable humor of scene after scene of the mock-
play: the ducking of a man scold; the beggar doling out alms
to a gallant gentleman; the lawyer refusing his client's fees; and
the girl entreating her granny to refrain from visiting the "satani-
cal pastime" of bear-baiting. Once the contrary nature of the
Antipodes is granted, all else follows with the logical consistency
of Gulliver's travels, but without a trace of Swift's misanthropy.
The dialogue is for the most part conducted in easy graceful
verse of more poetic worth than is usual in Brome.

In his last and gayest play, *The Jovial Crew, or the Merry
Beggars* Brome turns away from the town. A fresh breath of
country air blows through the playhouse while the story of good
Squire Oldrents and his merry daughters is unrolled. The
Squire, known far and wide for his benevolence, is plunged into
deep melancholy because of a prediction that his daughters will
be beggars. The girls, unable to endure the gloomy atmosphere
of a house that used to be so gay, make good the prediction by
running off with their lovers to join a band of gipsies. They are
introduced to the jovial crew and instructed in their new roles
by Springlove, the Squire's steward, who, following his custom,
has left his master this month of May to take the pleasure of
the open road. Presently they are joined by another couple,
Mistress Amie, who has eloped with her uncle's clerk, Martin,

to avoid a hated marriage. Martin proves a coward and a miser, so Springlove has little difficulty in winning Amie from him. Presently the whole company, gipsies and all, are caught in the nets of the law and dragged before her uncle, Justice Clack. Here it is discovered that Springlove is the Squire's son by a gipsy lass he had loved in his youth; Springlove marries Amie; the girls wed their lovers; the gipsies are given a free pass to wander elsewhere, and all ends well.

This is a tissue of romance, but it would not be a Brome play if it were not woven on a background of realism. There are such humours as the voluble Justice Clack, whose method is to punish first and then investigate; the lachrymose Talboys, Amie's first suitor; and the laughter-loving Hearty, who cheers the Squire with sack and song. Even more significant are the realistic touches that show the disgust of the girls and their lovers with the hardships and indignities of the beggar's life that seemed at first so carefree. The gipsies, too, are painted in colors worthy of Teniers; they are lousy, drunken, dissolute rogues, yet not ungrateful for kindness shown them. They are not nobles in disguise like the masqueraders of *Beggar's Bush* and *The Spanish Gipsy*, but flesh-and-blood folk such as haunted English highways in the days of Elizabeth and James. Their patter, their song and dances add atmosphere to the action, but it is true country atmosphere; the city gamesters, cuckolds, and harlots who swarm in Brome's earlier comedies are happily absent from this delightful play.

From the prologues and epilogues, the dedications, and the commendatory verses attached to Brome's plays it is possible to attain some conception of his personality. This faithful servant of Ben Jonson seems to have risen by hard work to a position where he could contemplate his achievement with a modest self-assurance. He was evidently on good terms with his fellows, the professional playwrights, but regarded with a touch of scorn the showy work of the courtly amateurs of his day. He maintains his independence and self-respect, and dies poor as he was born, but still, we may believe, as proud as he was poor.

Brome disclaimed more than once the title of a poet and preferred to call himself merely a "play-maker." He was, in fact, one of the last of the professional dramatic entertainers, furnishing actors and audience with what would please them best, even if at times he was obliged to step out of his own field of realistic comedy and attempt a transient success in other genres. For it is as a continuator of the tradition of realistic comedy down to the very moment of the closing of the theatres that Brome's work deserves study. Coming as he does at the end of the great age of Elizabethan drama he had at his disposal all the accumulated resources of the period, and he used them in a way that evinces ingenuity rather than originality. Like all his fellow playwrights he exploited Jonsonian humours, but managed on the whole to keep them somewhat nearer to real life than the fantastic figures of Jonson's early plays. He learned the art of complicated comic intrigue from Middleton and pushed it to a point where it often becomes a bewildering labyrinth of plot and counterplot. Brome's comedies are packed with action; a master of stage-effect, he borrows what he likes from earlier plays and deftly transforms it to suit his present purpose.

In the main Brome's comedy reflects the life and manners of a Caroline bourgeois London, a counterpart of Shirley's upper-class society. Brome was no more a gentleman than a poet; there is a coarseness of touch in his handling of this life that contrasts rather to his disadvantage with the moral earnestness of Jonson, and the cool impartiality of Middleton, his two most illustrious masters. If in the main his work continues an old tradition, it anticipates by this coarseness certain phases of Restoration comedy; the uxorious husband, the contented cuckold, the wenching gallant, and the wanton wife of many of his plays are prototypes of characters unhappily too familiar in the work of later seventeenth-century playwrights. Yet there is something more and better in Brome than this coarse realism; the man who drew the character of Constance, invented the absurdities of *The Antipodes,* and laughed with and at the strollers of *The Jovial Crew* certainly possessed a vein of tenderness and of gay clean humor.

A vein of satire runs through most of Brome's comedies, as a rule implicit in the action rather than explicit in the purpose of the play. He wrote no comedy with such patent satiric aim as *The Alchemist* or *A Game at Chess.* Yet it is easy to trace

Brome's dislike of Puritan preciseness and hypocrisy, of bourgeois affectation of upper-class manners, and of the noisy brawling of the London "roarers." As a vehicle alike of his satire and
of his realism, Brome employed for the most part a swift and
vigorous prose, stripped of the conceits and affectations of earlier
Elizabethans, and no doubt effective on the stage. Although no
poet he commanded an easy flow of verse which he employed
not without success in his more serious scenes. Occasional songs
are scattered through his plays, but with a few exceptions they
lack the charm and beauty of the Elizabethan lyric. As a matter
of fact the poetic Elizabethan drama was slowly dying in Brome's
day. What survived and still gives value in his work is the frank
and vigorous realism of popular Elizabethan comedy.

CHAPTER EIGHT

BEAUMONT AND FLETCHER

SOMETHING has been said in the preceding chapter as to the change in the national temper towards the close of the sixteenth century. Nowhere was this change more marked than in the relation between the Court and the nation as a whole. Under Elizabeth England had achieved a national unity hitherto unknown; the Queen herself was the incarnate symbol of this unity, and the Court that gathered round her, like the knight-errants of Gloriana, was the active expression of a proud and vigorous patriotism. A change, however, began to appear when the question of succession became prominent; the fall of the popular Essex rallied disaffection; and the last years of the Queen's reign were clouded with uncertainty and gloom.

The accession of James to the throne was received with a sense of relief as at least averting the possibility of civil war, but the new King never achieved the popularity of Elizabeth. His Scotch accent, his awkward shambling figure were openly derided; his policies at home and abroad were personal rather than national. He insisted in season and out on the divine right of kings, where Elizabeth had known how to temper her prerogative; he was extravagant where she had been sparing, quarrelled constantly with Parliament over money for his expenses, and tried so far as possible to rule without it. He sold knighthoods to whoever could afford the price and created favorites who in turn sold monopolies right and left. A pacifist at heart he at once concluded an unpopular peace with Spain; the long imprisonment and final execution of Raleigh, the last Elizabethan hero, marks his breach with the aggressive foreign policy of the Queen's reign. His attempt at religious toleration broke down completely and led only to renewed persecution of the extremists, Puritans and Papists alike. In short he succeeded in alienating one group after another and found himself ere long surrounded not by a united nation but by a frivolous, pleasure-loving, and extravagant Court, a center of intrigue and of social and political corruption.

As has already been said, the acting companies were taken under direct royal patronage at the beginning of the new reign, and so came, naturally, under the direct influence of the Court. Private theatres, catering to a more select and courtly audience, multiplied; playwrights were called on to devise the splendid court-masques, and masquelike elements began to appear in the popular drama. The influence of the Court upon later Elizabethan drama is unmistakable. It must not, however, be exaggerated; popular theatres like the Red Bull still drew crowds to see old-fashioned plays; satiric comedy and tragedy alike uttered their protests against the superficial brilliance and inner corruption of the age. Yet with the increasing separation between Court and nation a new type of drama appears and flourishes. In strong contrast to earlier Elizabethan drama it reflects not the national spirit, but the pageantry, the intrigue, political and amorous, the excitement and sophistication of life at Court. It might, in fact, be called a drama of escape since it ignores the undercurrents of unrest and disaffection which led in the next reign to revolution and civil war.

Of this courtly drama Beaumont and Fletcher, with their associates, followers, and imitators, were at once the creators and the great exemplars. In them their disciple Shirley found the "transcendent abilities" required to express "the air and insinuations of the Court . . . the virtues and passions of every noble condition, nay the councils and characters of the greatest princes." They were specially qualified for this expression, for both, by birth, training, and affiliation, were closely connected with the Court.

Francis Beaumont, born *ca.* 1584, sprang from an ancient family of considerable distinction; his father was Justice of the Court of Common Pleas; his mother, Anne Pierpont, was connected with a number of noble families. Along with two elder brothers Francis entered Oxford in 1597 as gentleman commoner, left without taking a degree, and was admitted, 1600, with special privileges to the society of the Inner Temple. In this center of literary and dramatic activity he seems to have lived until he set up housekeeping *ca.* 1608 with Fletcher on the Bankside. He had in all probability begun his career as a poet with *Salmacis and Hermaphroditus,* a poem in the fashionable erotic vein, published anonymously, 1602. He had also written a play or two, of which a word hereafter, before he began his famous collaboration with Fletcher. He belonged to the circle of poets and playwrights that gathered about Jonson at the Mermaid, and was chosen by his fellows of the Inner Temple to compose the magnificent masque which in conjunction with the members of Gray's Inn they presented, February 1613, in honor of the marriage of the Princess Elizabeth. About this time he married, broke off his connection with the theatre, and retired to the country, where he died in 1616. He was buried in the Poets' Corner of Westminster Abbey, not far from the grave of Spenser.

John Fletcher, born in 1579, was of an humbler family, but one which had good connections at Court. His father, Richard, a scholar and clergyman, studied at Cambridge, became President of Corpus Christi College, Dean of Peterborough, in which capacity he attended Mary Stuart upon the scaffold, Lord High Almoner to Elizabeth, and Bishop of London, living for many years in "her highnes gratious aspect and favor." Richard's brother was a diplomat; the poets, Giles and Phineas Fletcher were his nephews. It is interesting to compare the families of Beaumont and of Fletcher with those, for example, of Dekker and Heywood; little wonder that, in Dryden's phrase, "they understood and imitated the conversation of gentlemen."

Of John Fletcher's early life we know exactly nothing. He may have gone to his father's university; if so, he left without taking a degree. His father, the Bishop, died in 1596, heavily in debt, leaving eight young children for whose support powerful friends petitioned the Queen. It is probable that John turned early to the stage, but it is difficult to trace him there with any degree of assurance much before his collaboration with Beaumont. In 1607 he and Beaumont joined in commendatory verses prefixed to Jonson's *Volpone;* apparently the two young playwrights knew each other at that time; their first great joint success, *Philaster,* dates a couple of years later. When Beaumont retired, Fletcher attached himself to the King's Men; he collaborated in two plays, *Henry VIII* and *The Two Noble Kinsmen*, with Shakespeare, and till 1625, alone or in collaboration with younger men, was playwright-in-chief to that fine company. He died of the plague in 1625 and was buried in St. Saviours, Southwark, where today a painted window preserves his name and that of his friend and fellow-worker, Philip Massinger.

Only a few of the Beaumont and Fletcher plays appeared in print before Fletcher's death. A folio in 1647 collected thirty-four not previously published; a second folio, 1679, announcing fifty comedies and tragedies, actually contained fifty-two plays and Beaumont's *Masque*. To this number one or two more plays belonging to the group must be added. Both folios ascribe all the plays to Beaumont and Fletcher, but it is quite certain that the two playwrights wrote no such number either alone or in collaboration with each other. The collected plays represent, in fact, a whole library of Stuart drama with which one, usually Fletcher, or both of them were in some way connected. Scholars have puzzled for years and are still contending over the problems of dates and authorship. It will be quite sufficient here to deal with only certain representative plays: two substantially by Beaumont alone; two early plays by Fletcher alone; some characteristic examples of their collaboration; a few typical plays by Fletcher alone; and a specimen or two of his work in collaboration with others.

Fortunately the work of Beaumont is marked by such individual characteristics that it is comparatively easy to distinguish his hand from Fletcher's, although when they worked together it is not always possible to assign a play scene by scene to one or to the other. Beaumont's verse is more regular than Fletcher's, patterned apparently on the verse of Shakespeare in *The Merchant of Venice* and *Julius Cæsar*. It is marked by an abundance of run-on lines, and a frequent use of rhyme. As his mood changes from grave to gay, he shifts from verse to prose, which Fletcher seldom uses. A stronger mind, apparently, though younger than his friend, he seems to have been the guiding force in their collaboration. The serious, tragic, and pathetic scenes in their joint work are as a rule his; so too are the comic-satiric scenes, for Beaumont was a disciple of Jonson as well as a lover of Shakespeare.

It is this lighter side of Beaumont that appears in his first surviving play, *The Woman Hater*, produced by Paul's Boys, before they stopped playing in 1606. It is in the main a play of Jonsonian humour characters: Gondarino, the woman-hater, flying from Oriana, a mock man-hater, who pursues him out of sheer fun; Lazarillo, the epicure, following a dainty dish from house to house; Lucio, a would-be statesman, who gravely examines Lazarillo, accused of treason on less than no grounds. The construction, too, is Jonsonian, several intrigues neatly woven together and brought to a satisfactory conclusion, but it is a gayer, livelier play than any of Jonson's. It is full of laughing parodies of popular plays, some of Shakespeare's among others. The scene is laid in Italy, but the life portrayed is that of Stuart London with its courtiers, merchants, would-be fashionables, and political spies. All in all it is the play of a clever young man whose eyes are wide open to the follies of life.

A better and funnier play is *The Knight of the Burning Pestle*, written apparently for the Children at Blackfriars, ca. 1607. It is better because the gay satire is concentrated rather than diffused, funnier because instead of stock humour characters we find here real and ridiculous people. The courtly Beaumont naturally despised the manners of London citizens, more especially their taste in dramatic performances. The plan which he devised to bring them into ridicule is most ingenious. The Prologue has no sooner announced a play called *The London Merchant* than a grocer leaps upon the stage denouncing the topic and insisting on a play in which a grocer shall do "admirable things," like one of the prentices in a Heywood play. He is promptly followed by his wife, who has never seen a play before, but is none the less quite certain that their swaggering apprentice, Ralph, can play the chief part in a story of adventure. The suggestion is accepted—otherwise the worthy couple would have stopped the show; Ralph gets a costume from the players, and the grocer pays cash for special music for Ralph's scenes. All this seems absurd to us, but it is a bit of real life; plays in an Elizabethan theatre were more than once altered at the demand of the audience, and it was not uncommon for an aspiring amateur to take over a leading part.

What now follows is a most amusing hodge-podge. The originally planned play proceeds to tell how the prentice Jasper wins the hand of his master's daughter, Luce. It is at once silly and sentimental, a bourgeois parody of romantic love, enlivened from time to time by the outbursts of old Merrythought, Jasper's father, whose mouth is as full of snatches of old song as his belly is of old ale. But the progress of this action is constantly interrupted by the improvised adventures of Ralph. Fired by reading romances of chivalry, he sets out as the Knight of the Burning Pestle, a title ironically bestowed on him by the speaker of the Prologue. After a series of exploits reminiscent of those of Don Quixote he returns on the demand of the grocer to London to drill the train-bands and finally to stage a death-scene "with a forked arrow through his head," spouting a parody of *The Spanish Tragedy*. Both actions are punctuated by the running commentary of the grocer and his wife. He is a rather superior person; she, good soul, constantly mistakes the stage-show for reality and is moved to interfere in the action herself. They are, perhaps, the most delightful comic couple in Elizabethan drama. The play was, it seems, a failure at first; twenty years later when the difference between Court and city was more pronounced, it was revived with great success by the Queen's Company. Recent amateur performances have shown that Beaumont's gay burlesque still appeals today.

When we turn from Beaumont to his friend, we note at once various striking differences. In the first place Fletcher's verse-pattern is peculiarly his own. It abounds in extra syllables within and at the end of the line, which gives it an easy fluency, poles apart from the stiff rhetoric of earlier dramatic verse. It is marked by the constant repetition of words and phrases and by little tricks of apposition and alliteration; it must have been an easy verse for an actor to commit to memory. None the less Fletcher is a real poet; he has a lovely lyric gift and a happy faculty, particularly in farewell speeches, for the elegiac strain. He has none of Beaumont's keen power of observation, nor of his turn for satire and burlesque. Essentially a man of the theatre he never seems to have thought seriously of life; he confuses moral issues, he warps his characters out of shape to fit the purpose of his plots. What he cared for most and did best was to tickle his audience with a comic or thrill them with an emotional situation. A playwright of extraordinary skill he was an adept in devising a series of such situations, piling up the fun, or heaping up the agony, in an action that never stands still. A more original artist than Beaumont he brought to their joint work, no doubt, suggestions for plot, character, and situation, along with a keen sense of the theatrically effective which his partner's stronger mind and sense of construction whipped into shape. The Beaumont-Fletcher collaboration is far and away the best of a period when collaboration was a common dramatic practice.

The Woman's Prize, or The Tamer Tamed, of uncertain date, is a good example of Fletcher's early and unaided work. He hit on the happy idea of writing a sequel to *The Taming of the Shrew* in which the tables would be turned on Petruchio, the tamer, by a second wife. His bride, the lively Maria, swears for the honor of womankind so to deal with him that she will make him "easie as a child." First she bars him admission on their wedding night and backed by a troop of brawling city and country wives stands a formal siege. When he consents to conditions, she still continues to flout him. Every trick that he tries she meets and betters, till at last he feigns death and is brought before her in a coffin—an old stage device. Then she bursts into tears, not for his death, but for his foolish wasted life. That finishes him, and on his complete collapse she promises to be a loving wife.

The play does not read well; the jesting is rather broad for modern taste. In fact when it was played at Court in 1633 Herbert felt obliged to purge it of "foul and offensive matter." But it must have acted capitally. When Shakespeare's play was given at Court a couple of days before this of Fletcher's, Herbert records that Shakespeare's was "liked," but Fletcher's "very well liked." It is the swift action, the easy flow of dialogue, the sure command of stage effects that make it a good acting play. It stayed in the repertoire of the King's Men till the end; and was promptly revived in the Restoration theatre, when Mr. Pepys pronounced it "a very fine play."

The Faithful Shepherdess, 1608, is a very different play, so different indeed that if it were not signed by Fletcher it would be hard to prove it his. It is a pastoral play of shepherds and their loves, displaying all the forms of that passion from brutish lust to ideal devotion. There is a complicated plot but little action; instead of lively dialogue there is an over-abundance of long speeches composed for the most part in rhymed couplets which lend a further air of artifice to the whole. There is great play with magic herbs and a holy well; a satyr and a river-god take part in the action.

It is not surprising that the play failed when first performed. Misled by the title the audience evidently expected a play in the tradition of English realism, of "country hired shepherds in gray cloaks with curtailed dogs in strings." Missing the rural background of "Whitsun ales . . . and morris-dances," they flatly rejected Fletcher's artificial, if charmingly poetic, work. To justify himself he published it with commendatory verses by such acknowledged masters as Jonson and Chapman and painstakingly explained what he had tried to do. This play, he declares, is a "pastoral tragi-comedy" and he goes on to define both terms: a pastoral is, indeed, "a representation of shepherds" but "such as all the ancient poets have received them," *i.e.,* the shepherds of Theocritus and Virgil. "A tragi-comedy is not so called in respect of mirth and killing, but in respect it wants deaths which is enough to make it no tragedy, yet brings some near it which is enough to make it no comedy. . . ." Fletcher was a better poet than a critic, but what he was trying to say seems fairly clear. Tragi-comedy, as he conceived it, was not a mere juxtaposition of serious and comic scenes—that had been common in English drama from the time of the Miracles—but a clever blending of the two in which a tragic situation threatening death, the inevitable conclusion of Elizabethan tragedy, should be dispelled and brought to a happy ending. Thus in *The Faithful Shepherdess* there are tragic situations: a girl is struck down by her lover, who later tries to kill himself. But all ends happily: the estranged lovers are reconciled; the unchaste are purified; the very villain of the piece escapes with the mild punishment of exile.

It is true that there had been something like this in English drama before, notably in such plays as *James IV, The Gentleman Usher,* and *Measure for Measure,* but *The Faithful Shepherdess* is the first of a series of plays in which Beaumont and Fletcher established a type immensely popular in the last period of Elizabethan drama and the forerunner of the "heroic play" of the Restoration theatre. What distinguishes this genre from its predecessors is its sophistication, its high-flown sentiment, its use in serious themes of the devices of comedy, mistaken identity, for example, above all its deliberate rejection of the old tradition of realism. It may well be called a drama of escape since it carries us from the troubles of real life into an imaginary and fantastic world. To Fletcher's daring originality we owe the first attempt at this type; he needed the help of Beaumont to bring it to perfection.

This perfection was achieved in *Philaster, or Love Lies a-Bleeding,* written in collaboration for the King's Company, *ca.* 1609. It is from this admirably contrived play that the typical romantic tragi-comedy of late Elizabethan drama takes its rise. It would take too long to summarize the complicated plot, but a brief comment on some of its characteristic features may serve to demonstrate the nature of this genre. In the first place it discards the pastoral, which had proved so confusing to the audience at Fletcher's first attempt. It sets the scene in a distant and romantic land with no relation to history and little to contemporary life. The plot is not derived from any one source, but composed of situations, borrowed or invented, ingeniously woven together into an exciting story. It opens with a situation like that in *Hamlet,* with the hero, a disinherited prince, living in the court of an unfriendly king. A difference, however, develops at once, for this hero is deeply in love with the usurper's daughter. She returns his passion, and they make use of his young and handsome page to act as a messenger between them. The lady's affection for the page gives rise to a slander on her chastity, a slander too readily believed by the hero. In jealous rage he strikes both the princess and the page, is captured, and condemned to death by the usurper. After he is rescued by a revolt of the citizens, his secret marriage with the princess is revealed and all seems about to end well when the slanderous charge against the princess and the page is renewed. To clear the matter up, the usurper orders him stripped and tortured, whereupon it turns out that the page is a girl, hopelessly in love with the hero and serving him in disguise like Viola in Shakespeare's play. This revelation, borrowed perhaps from Jonson's *Silent Woman,* solves all difficulties. After the suspense and surprise of the last scene, the hero gets an untarnished bride and a devoted servant and, in addition, his lost kingdom back again.

To preserve the highly romantic atmosphere the authors refrain from any comic underplot; what fun there is consists in the jests of the courtiers and the riotous behavior of the revolting citizens, but there is far more sentiment than fun in the play. The action consists of a series of tense emotional situations playing in turn on such varied passions as love, jealousy, devotion, and self-sacrifice. Through these situations the characters are pushed like chessmen at the will of the authors. It is not too much to say that in *Philaster* plot determines character rather than character plot. Under critical examination the plot falls apart; on the other hand *Philaster* was not meant for critical examination, but for the theatre, and it was and long remained a theatrical success. The characters are types rather than realized human beings: the jealous hero, the chaste heroine, contrasted here with a wanton lady of the Court, the lovelorn girl, the blunt soldier friend, and the arbitrary tyrant. Such types keep reappearing in various forms and disguises throughout later tragicomedy since they lend themselves more easily to its purpose, to entertain, amuse, and thrill rather than to interpret life. The unreality of the whole is hidden by the veil of poetry which the authors throw about character and situation. When the page expresses willingness to die at the hand of his angry master in the lovely words that Beaumont put into Bellario's mouth, we forget for a moment that all the page need do is to reveal his true sex. That revelation, however, is carefully reserved for the last scene.

A King and No King, produced by the King's Company,
1611, is a better play than *Philaster;* it is perhaps not quite so
typical a tragi-comedy. It is almost entirely the work of Beaumont; Fletcher's part is limited to a few relatively unimportant
scenes. Probably for this reason it is a more serious play, approaching more than once a tragic intensity. One cannot take
the sorrows of Philaster seriously; there is no doubt of the anguish of Arbaces. The plot is simple and unified: Arbaces, a
victorious king, falls in love with a sister whom he has not seen
since her childhood; he struggles hard against this passion until
he discovers that she too loves him. Then, though conscious of
his sin, he resolves to push on through incest to suicide. At the
very end tragedy is averted in tragi-comedy fashion by a surprising discovery: Arbaces is not what he seems; he had been palmed
off on the late monarch as his child by a queen hopeless of issue.
Yet this queen, left pregnant at her husband's death, really bore
a child, none other, of course, than the supposed sister of
Arbaces. He is no king; she is the queen; and they are free to
marry. Some such solution has been, indeed, foreshadowed in
the action, but so skilfully that it is hardly to be detected by the
reader. It may be a question for a moralist whether a playwright
dare take up and then evade the theme of incest; there is no
question but that a strong and thrilling play has been made of it.

There is, fortunately, more in the play than this theme. There
is Beaumont's humorous comment on the follies of citizens who
might have stepped out of *The Knight of the Burning Pestle;*
there is his creation of Bessus, an admirable variation of the
stock *miles gloriosus.* In fact the characterization throughout is
firmer than in the earlier play. Arbaces is neither a tyrant nor
a sentimental lover but a strange compound of virtues and vices,
modelled, perhaps, on the author's conception of Alexander the
Great; he is valiant and vain-glorious, imperious and warm-
hearted, capricious in mood, but constant in affection. His supposed sister is a very gentle lady, adoring the reports she has
heard of her heroic brother, dismayed at his first strange treatment of her, and horrified into flight when she discovers a kin-
dred passion in her own breast. Mardonius is more than the
stock figure of the blunt soldier-friend. He loves his king, but

is not blind to his follies, dares to rebuke him, and scornfully refuses to become the tool of his master's guilty passion. There is a good deal of lively vigorous prose in the play, particularly in the mouth of Bessus. The poetry is Beaumont's best, rising and falling with the tenseness of the emotional situation.

Two plays by the collaborating authors are technically tragedies. One of these, *Cupid's Revenge*, of uncertain date but some time before 1611, may be briefly dismissed. Founded on two stories from the *Arcadia* and apparently mainly composed by Fletcher, it has been revised and altered till it is hard to follow the plot. To tell the truth it is hardly worth following; a fantastic story has been given a tragic turn—there are seven deaths in the course of the play—but the characters are stock figures, their actions unmotivated, and the whole tale, turning as it does on God Cupid's revenge for his desecrated altars, is so unreal as to forfeit all sympathy. Lovers of dramatic poetry may find a few pearls in the Beaumont scenes, but the play as a whole may be left to scholars concerned with the problem of collaboration.

The Maid's Tragedy, ca. 1611, on the other hand is a powerful and still interesting play. As in *A King and No King* the dominant hand is that of Beaumont, and it is his strength and seriousness that give tragic intensity to many of the finest scenes. There is no known source for the plot, and the theme that the authors invented is one that could only with difficulty be wrenched to the happy ending of tragi-comedy. It deals with the irreparable injury done the hero, Amintor, a brave young soldier, by a wicked king. Briefly the plot runs as follows: the king induces Amintor to break his engagement to Aspatia, the maid who gives the play its name, and to wed Evadne. On their wedding-night, she coolly tells him that she has been and means still to be the king's mistress, married only to conceal her shame. Amintor's loyalty keeps him from revenge, but he reveals the secret to Melantius, his wife's brother. Melantius, a stern soldier, has none of Amintor's loyalty; he forces Evadne in a thrilling scene to repent and vow to wipe off the stain upon their honor by killing the king. She does so and comes with bloody hands to Amintor to ask forgiveness and reconciliation. She finds him standing over the body of the love-lorn Aspatia, who has put on male disguise, forced a duel with him, and thrown herself upon his sword. Horrified by Evadne's deed he rejects her, whereupon she kills herself, and Amintor, looking upon the bodies of the two women whose fates were so involved with his, follows her in death.

Here certainly is a tragic ending; yet the final impression of the whole is far from the high seriousness of true tragedy. The hero is a sentimental rather than a tragic character; the motivation, especially in Evadne's sudden change, is uncertain; there is a constant striving for sensation in the ebb and flow of contending passions. Even Melantius, the strongest character, combines the craft of the intriguer with the fixed resolve of the sworn revenger. Needless to say there is much fine poetry in the play; the words of Amintor in the last scene reach a point of direct dramatic utterance unmatched elsewhere in Beaumont's work, and Fletcher contributes a lovely song. After all, it is unfair to compare such a play as *The Maid's Tragedy* with Shakespeare's masterpieces; they are for all time, this for the Stuart theatre, yet not without a lasting charm for the impartial reader.

We need not linger over the remaining plays of the collection in which Beaumont had or is thought to have had a hand. Only two of them perhaps may be recommended to the general reader: *The Scornful Lady*, a lively comedy of manners and intrigue, will be discussed later; *The Coxcomb, ca.* 1609, deserves a passing word. It is composed of two quite different strains. The first, from which the play takes its name, tells of a foolish gentleman who, out of an excess of courtesy, positively thrusts his wife into his friend's arms. It seems to be originally the work of Fletcher, but quite unworthy of him—it was later revised by Massinger. The second, mainly by Beaumont with some Fletcher touches, is a pleasant blend of realism and romance. It is the story of an innocent but foolish girl, Viola, who leaves her home at night to elope with her lover. Unfortunately he has been on a wild drinking party and does not even know her when they meet. Unable to return home she is robbed and bound by a thieving tinker, freed by a man who tries to seduce her, and befriended by a pair of milkmaids who place her with their mistress. Here she is found by her deeply penitent lover, and the play ends with her frank forgiveness. It is a romantic theme set against a background of genuine English realism. This realism and the exquisite poetry of the best scenes keep it from degenerating into false sentimentalism. It is pleasant to find Beaumont turning, if only for a time, from the heroics of tragi-comedy to such a gentle strain as this.

During Beaumont's lifetime Fletcher wrote two so-called tragedies single-handed, *Bonduca, i.e.,* Boadicea, *ca.* 1611, and *Valentinian,* a little later, both for the King's Men. The first of these is a tragedy in name only. There is neither tragic theme nor tragic hero. It is Fletcher's variation of the old chronicle play, dealing with the wars of Britons and Romans. He alternates in the old fashion serious and comic scenes; the serious, in fine swelling rhetoric dealing with the fame and fortunes of the leaders on both sides; the comic, jesting with the soldiers' greed for food and wenches. There is plenty of spectacle and sensation: the suicide of the British Queen and her daughters; the Roman death of Pœnius, and a tenderly pathetic scene in which the little British boy, Hengo, dies in his uncle's arms. This uncle, Caratach (the historic Caractacus) is, in a sense, the central figure of the play, the heroic fighting man who honors bravery even in his enemies. Were it his tragedy he would die at the end, but he comes off safe and yields to the Romans as a friend rather than a prisoner. It must have been a stirring play at the Globe, with something in it for all tastes from lofty declamation to bawdy jesting, but it is not one that a modern mind can take at all seriously.

Valentinian is a more ambitious work, Fletcher's sole unaided attempt at straight tragedy. It begins well with a series of firmly planned scenes leading through attempts at seduction up to the rape of Lucina, the chaste wife of the soldier Maximus, by the Emperor Valentinian. A strong contrast is drawn between the honest loyalty of the army, represented by Maximus and the heroic Æcius, and the dissolute court around the Emperor. His character is revealed when he replies to the despairing cry of his victim:

Justice shall never hear you; I am justice.

Unfortunately after the death of Lucina the tragedy degenerates into a series of startling sensations. Maximus, who by all conventions was bound to revenge his wife's dishonor and death, deserts the straight role of revenger for that of the Machiavellian intriguer. He brings about the death of his friend, Æcius, whose loyalty guards the Emperor, by denouncing him in an anonymous letter delivered to the tyrant. Then he incites two servants of the dead hero to kill the Emperor. They poison Valentinian, and there ensues a death scene which pushes sensationalism to the last limit as the agonizing tyrant is taunted by one of the servants who had taken the same poison before. Now that his revenge is attained, the proper thing is for Maximus to die too; he recognizes this and calls upon the departed spirits of his wife and his friend to see him "coming boldly" after them. Then with "Stay; I am foolish" his mind changes—a sudden reversal even for Fletcher—and he decides that he may better seize the empty throne. Chosen Emperor by the army, he weds the tyrant's widow and for some unknown reason reveals to her all his past actions. She promptly kills him with a poisoned wreath, and the play ends with her justification of this act. The last scene where the tragic interest should culminate is dominated by spectacular effects: a procession to the sound of trumpets, a singing boy descending from the clouds, and a dance of soldiers.

As tragedy in the true sense of the word *Valentinian* is a failure. Yet the play is not without its merits. The characters of Lucina, the tyrant, and old Æcius—a grand role for Burbage—are strongly drawn. There is an abundance—perhaps too much —of Fletcher's flamboyant declamation, and some of his loveliest songs. A reader willing to take fine poetry, sensation, and surprise in lieu of tragic theme and hero may still find entertainment in this forerunner of the Restoration "heroic play."

After Beaumont's retirement Fletcher's chief collaborator in the busy years of his activity as playwright-in-chief to the King's Men was Philip Massinger. They worked together on a group of plays that partake more or less of the nature of tragedy.

The False One, ca. 1620 for the King's Men, is an interesting example of their collaboration. It dramatizes Cæsar's stay in

Egypt and his amour with Cleopatra. Massinger begins and ends the play in sober fashion; Fletcher fills the central acts with Cæsar's passion for Cleopatra, and the Egyptian plots against him. He weaves in some serio-comic scenes about the renegade Roman, Septimius, the false one, who has murdered his old general Pompey, is despised by Romans and Egyptians, repents, turns bad again, and swears to murder Cæsar. No Fletcher play would be complete without a spectacle, and he introduces here the masque of Nilus and his wealth, cleverly devised to motivate Cæsar's momentary neglect of his mistress and her scornful reproach. All this is entertaining but hardly tragic; it remained for Massinger to bring the action back to the grand scale by showing Cæsar victorious over his enemies. Massinger was the younger artist, but his sense of temperance and order seems to have restrained Fletcher in this play from the indulgence in sensation that wrecked the structure of *Valentinian*.

A better and in some ways more interesting Fletcher-Massinger play is *The Tragedy of Sir John Van Olden Barnavelt*, 1619, a play for the King's Men. Its interest for the student of Elizabethan drama lies not so much in its story as in the circumstances under which it was composed, presented, and published. The trial and execution, May 13, 1619, of the great Dutch statesman had naturally aroused great interest in England, since he had played a leading part in the joint struggle of the two countries against the power of Spain. Accordingly the playwrights promptly dramatized the story of his fall and death. It is surprising that a play on a topic so closely related to the King's foreign policy was ever allowed upon the stage. It had, indeed, great difficulty in passing the censorship; long passages were deleted—"I like not this" the censor wrote at one place in the margin of the manuscript—; words and phrases were altered, including what seemed like an allusion to the recent execution of Walter Raleigh. It was, however, licensed and, a contemporary letter states, "had many spectators and received applause." How long it ran we do not know; probably like *A Game at Chess* it was suppressed after a few performances. Publication was forbidden, and the play remained in manuscript till 1883, when it was discovered and published. The manuscript now in the British Museum is a most interesting theatrical document, bearing as it does not only the censor's comments but the notes of that member of the company who prepared it for performance.

It seems likely that Massinger, always keenly interested in Stuart foreign policy (*cf.* p. 263) suggested the topic and that Fletcher agreed to lend him a hand in the haste of composition; the play was written, passed the censor, was rehearsed and staged in about three months after Barnavelt's death. The two seem to have worked in perfect accord; there is no such sharp division of their acts as in *The False One*. Massinger deals with the scenes of special political interest; Fletcher stresses the emotional and the realistic—a characteristic bit of his work is the scene in which three civic headsmen throw dice for the privilege of decapitating the hero. Between them they have given lasting value to what might have been a merely topical play. The struggle between the statesman jealous for local liberties and the soldier bent on maintaining national unity is treated in restrained and serious fashion, and Fletcher's elegiac verse rises to a high point in the last words of the protagonist.

Tragedy was not Fletcher's forte; even when working with such reliable partners as Beaumont and Massinger he was apt to weaken or to divert the tragic strain. It seems unprofitable to pursue his collaboration with Massinger still further in a group of plays: *Thierry and Theodoret, The Bloody Brother,* and *The Double Marriage.* All are highly melodramatic, enlivened often by gay comedy, and glorified by sudden outbursts of Fletcher's poetry. Compared with true Jacobean tragedy, that of Tourneur and Webster, for example, they fall sadly short of the mark, but they were in their time entertaining shows and are still good reading.

It is a relief to turn from such work as this to plays in Fletcher's true vein, tragi-comedy. Seven such plays: *The Mad Lover,* 1616; *The Loyal Subject,* 1618; *The Humourous Lieutenant,* 1619; *The Island Princess,* 1621; *The Pilgrim,* 1621; *Women Pleased,* revised 1619–22; and *A Wife for a Month,* 1624, seem to be his own unaided work. It is impossible to discuss all these; a pair of them may be selected as examples of the variety and range of this genre.

Setting aside *The Loyal Subject,* already referred to in connection with Heywood's earlier play, we may consider briefly *A Wife for a Month* and *The Humourous Lieutenant.* The first of these is a true tragi-comedy verging indeed towards tragedy. The usurping tyrant, Frederick, tries in vain to seduce the chaste Evanthe. In revenge he arranges a marriage between her and her lover, Valerio, but one which is to last for a month only, after which he is to die and she to remarry on the same conditions. To add an additional torture, Valerio is forbidden to lie with his wife or to tell her the reason of his abstinence on pain of her instant death. One can better imagine than describe the situation that arises when the longing bride seeks to embrace her husband and is put off with the false plea that he is impotent. The seemingly inextricable knot is severed by a *coup-de-théâtre.* Frederick sends a poisonous drug to his deposed brother, who is sunk in melancholy, but instead of killing him the poison cures him after a scene in which his shrieks of anguish almost match those of the dying Valentinian. Restored to health he heads a popular revolt which overthrows the tyrant; Valerio and Evanthe are united in a true marriage, and all ends well. Even the tyrant and the tool-villain escape with the mild sentence of confinement to a monastery. Modern critics have found the play shocking, but to shock, to startle, and to thrill was precisely Fletcher's aim, and he attains it in a brilliantly constructed, if totally unreal play.

The Humourous Lieutenant, on the other hand, stresses the comic element and blends it with a high romantic strain. The character who gives the play its name is a humour, but not one of Jonson's satiric creations. On the contrary he is very much alive, a jolly, boisterous, mirth-provoking soldier. Tortured by disease, he plunges into danger to seek death; cured suddenly by a wound, he becomes a rank coward; then he is persuaded that he is again sick unto death and charges once more into battle. This is no mere subplot but deftly interwoven with the main, which treats of love and war. The gallant prince Demetrius loves and is loved by Celia, a fair captive. During his absence at the war, the King, his father, lures her to Court and uses all his arts to seduce her. When she stands firm and mocks him, he procures a love-potion from a magician. Luckily for all concerned it is administered to the Lieutenant with the imaginable comic consequences: he courts the King, buys all the pictures of the King, kisses the King's horses as they pass him on the street. How did the potion come to the Lieutenant? That again is part of the romance. On his return from a victorious war Demetrius had been told by his father that the lady he loved, a creature far beneath him, had been put to death as a witch. Plunged in despair Demetrius cuts himself off from all company, and it is only the brave Lieutenant who dares disturb him. The Prince points a pistol at him; he falls in a swoon and is only brought to by a draught of the love-potion set down by mistake by the bawd who is bearing it to the King for Lady Celia. But the romance continues. Convinced of her virtue the King sends Celia to his son gorgeously attired and decked with jewels. He at once suspects her, and when she teases him about her reception at Court, denounces her as "a subtle Circe." She replies with a burst of anger that leaves him speechless. With much ado they are brought together again, and it then appears that Celia, captive though she was, is the lost daughter of a king conquered in war and courtesy by her lover, a recognition which, of course, brings about the happy ending.

As a mere story-play this is a masterpiece, but it is more than that. Fletcher's high-pitched declamation is exactly suited to the fantastic contests in arms and courtesy that fill up half the play; his art of dramatic dialogue is at its best in the scenes between Demetrius and Celia; his Rabelaisian realism lights up his portrait of the bawd, a prosperous promoter of the white-slave traffic. His characters, for once, are no puppets moving as he pulls the strings. Celia, above all, is Fletcher's most living and most lovable lady: tender, witty, chaste, and proud, a very woman. He who can take no delight in this play may as well turn away from Fletcher; he will find nothing better; in Fletcher's special blend of comedy and romance there is nothing nearly so good.

Massinger, of course, worked with Fletcher in tragi-comedy; their partnership was prepared to furnish the King's Men with any type of play required. There are about half a dozen tragi-comedies of their joint work, many of them apparently revisions by Massinger in the sixteen-thirties of plays that he had written with Fletcher years before; one must bear in mind the constant cry of the company for new plays or revisions of old ones. Perhaps the best of the lot is *A Very Woman*, licensed in 1634. As it stands, the greater part of the play is by Massinger, who handles the old theme, *souvent femme varie*, with dignity and restraint. Fletcher's gayety breaks through in the character of the bibulous and amorous Borachia and in scenes like that in the slave-market, which enliven his partner's graver work. It is a true tragi-comedy in that one of the fickle lady's lovers is brought near to death in a duel; the central story is truly romantic, and a well-built plot is carefully conducted to a happy ending.

Massinger was not the only playwright who helped Fletcher pour out plays. The master's study must in some ways have resembled the studio of his contemporary Rubens, where numerous disciples worked on the designs of that great painter. No one except Massinger seems to have worked more regularly with Fletcher than the actor-playwright, Nathan Field, the author of a pair of lively comedies and later collaborator with Massinger in *The Fatal Dowry*. Field seems to have written the first two one-acters, *The Triumph of Love* and *The Triumph of Honor* in the *Four Plays in One*. He and Massinger joined Fletcher in a group of plays of which only two need be mentioned, both produced by the King's Men about 1616. *The Queen of Corinth* is a strange combination of comedy and melodrama which might be compared with interesting results with the thoughtful play that the Middleton-Rowley partnership built up from the same material, *The Spanish Gipsy*. *The Knight of Malta* is a better piece of work; in fact it has a certain distinction as reaching perhaps the very height of sensation, surprise, and spectacle. The scene is laid in Malta, defended against the Turks by the knights of the order, but the action has more to do with the internal troubles than with foreign war. There is, of course, the lustful villain who accuses the heroine of treason; there is the blameless knight—played apparently by Field himself—who fights in her defense. Later the lady's husband charges her with loving the knight, as in fact she does, but chastely. She swoons, is given a sleeping potion by the villain's black concubine, and is laid for dead in a church vault. Here the knight opportunely comes to pray at her tomb, and to rescue the reviving lady whom later he restores to her penitent husband. One of Fletcher's scenes must have surprised the audience as it does the reader. The blameless knight tries hard to win a fair Turkish captive to his bed, and she repels him by holding before his eyes the sacred cross of the order and bidding him recall all that it means. Fletcher certainly gave Field a splendid chance to show his histrionic talent as newcomer to the King's Men in this scene, but the attempted seduction lacks any sort of motivation, and the knight's excuse after his repulse that he meant only to test his captive's virtue is incredible and unconvincing. The play ends with a magnificent spectacle in which the villain is formally degraded from the order, and the knight, hitherto a novice, takes the final vows of poverty and chastity. Few plays in the Beaumont-Fletcher corpus show more clearly than *The Knight of Malta* at once the merits and defects of the fully developed form of tragi-comedy.

It was only natural that Fletcher, the chief supplier of plays to the King's Men for ten or twelve years, should respond to their demand for comedy. In fact a large proportion of the plays in the Beaumont and Fletcher corpus belong to this genre. Fletcher's genius turned rather to comedy than to the graver vein of drama, and after Beaumont's withdrawal he devoted more and more of his attention to this field. Here as in tragi-comedy his originality, his sense of stage effect, and his mastery of a lively bustling plot are his distinguishing characteristics. He drew on Jonson for various humours but never allowed them to dominate the action; he cared little for consistency of character, and even less for a moral, explicit or implied. His comedies reflect in the main, whether the scene be laid in England or abroad, the manners of upper-class English life. Broadly speaking they may be divided into two groups: comedy of manners, where character, to some extent at least, starts the action and determines the solution; and comedy of intrigue, where character falls into the background and interest is concentrated on the ingenious complication and solution, with the attendant reversals and surprises, of an entertaining plot. No sharp division can be made between these groups; there is plenty of intrigue in the manners comedy, and even in the typical intrigue plays there are clearly defined characters.

The Scornful Lady, written apparently *ca.* 1610, for the Queen's Revels by Beaumont and Fletcher and later revised by Fletcher for the King's Men, is the earliest and in some ways one of the best of the comedies. It is essentially a Fletcher play. While their collaboration lasted, Beaumont was the dominating force in tragedy and tragi-comedy, but in this experiment in the comedy of manners his share is limited to a few, though quite important scenes. He opens the action, a duel between the sexes, with his admirable characterization of the lady who has doomed her lover to a year's exile because he has dared to kiss her in public. He ends the conflict when her jealousy of the lover's new-found bride impels her to lay aside her scorn and regain him by consenting to an immediate marriage. But the greater part of the action is by Fletcher. It not only consists of the duel between the lady and the lover with its plots and counter-plots, reversals and surprises, but also deals with the career of a scapegrace younger brother who turns the lover's house upside down during his absence and wins a rich widow away from a crafty usurer. The background of life in a pair of English country houses, the minor characters of the scapegrace and his riotous companions, the lover's steward who tries in vain to check them and finally joins in their revels, and a third young gentleman, a rejected suitor of the lady, who wins her gentle sister's hand by a most outrageous trick—all this is Fletcher's, as is the swift pace of the action and the lively dialogue swinging from verse to prose and back again and quite properly avoiding poetry. It is a capital acting play and won an instant and well-deserved success. It was played "with great applause" at Blackfriars, performed at Court on the very eve of the Civil War, and printed seven times in quarto before it was included in the omnibus of the Second Folio.

Wit without Money, *ca.* 1615, is a capital example of Fletcher's ingenuity in adapting Jonsonian humours to his own ends. Valentine, the leading character, is obsessed with the idea that a gentleman should live by his wits alone. He squanders his estate, ruins the prospects of his younger brother Frank, a gentle scholar, and rejects all efforts to recall him to a more ordered course of life, more especially that he should recoup his fortunes by marriage with a rich widow. He despises women in general and widows in particular. But the widow of this play, Lady Heartwell, has fixed her eyes upon him and finally takes him by surprise, while her witty sister wins the hand of the modest Frank. The scene is laid in London with a realistic background of London life, but with little of the satiric note of contemporary realistic comedy. There is some pleasant, not too exaggerated characterization. Valentine, in spite of his obsession, is a more lovable fellow than most of Fletcher's young gentlemen; there is a good character part in Lance, the outspoken old servant, and the two leading ladies are shrewd, humorous, and kindly. There is less talk of wenching and its physical consequences than usual in the easy flow of the dialogue. It would not be a Fletcher play if it were not packed with effective scenes. One that sticks in the memory is where Valentine strips himself to his breeches, empties his pockets, and makes his false friends pull off his boots, in order to restore the gifts that they have made him, and then, shivering with cold, turns to discover a bundle of rich clothes and a purse of gold dropped for his use by the loving widow's servant. All in all, *Wit without Money* is one of the most entertaining as it is one of the least fantastic of Fletcher's comedies. It seems to have been only fairly successful on the stage; but it was revived during the Restoration with a Prologue written for the occasion by Dryden.

Rule a Wife and Have a Wife, 1624, perhaps Fletcher's last comedy, has been called his "climax as a dramatist of humours and manners." It is indeed a masterpiece of construction, lively action, and well-drawn characters. There are two distinct plots, not juxtaposed, but neatly interwoven with contrasting effects of character and action. The minor plot on which most of the fun depends is an extremely clever dramatization of one of the *Exemplary Novels* of Cervantes. The original is a sordid story of a rogue's marriage to a harlot; Fletcher eliminates the baser elements and turns it into an amusing tale of diamond-cut-diamond. A greedy Spanish captain marries an attractive girl whose special charm is the fine house in which she lives, but it soon turns out that she is only a servant of the mistress of the mansion. On the other hand the splendid chain and jewel with which he wooed her are mere pinchbeck and earn for him the title of the Copper Captain. When he discovers the cheat and threatens her life, she pulls a pistol on him, and then pacifies him with a thousand ducats which she has got by pledging his copper trinkets to an amorous suitor of her mistress. Finally the Copper Captain and cheating maid-servant settle down in peace in the house of her mistress. The main plot on the other hand seems to be Fletcher's invention, or rather an inversion of an earlier theme of his. He had long since written *The Tamer Tamed;* this is the story of a high-flying wife broken to submission by the husband she had chosen for his sheepish simplicity to serve as a cloak for her gay extravagance. He suddenly reveals himself as an iron-willed master, drives out her guests, foils all her efforts to deceive him, and finally wins not only her obedience but her love: rule a wife and have a wife.

No summary can do justice to the high comedy of the clash of characters in this play. The intrigue is complicated and entertaining, but it springs from and is solved by the characters of the action. The dialogue is in Fletcher's liveliest verse, rising at times to something like poetry in Leon's assertion of a husband's rights and his wife's rebuke of a courtly suitor. It was produced by the King's Men within a few months of their scandalous success with *A Game at Chess* to which there is a jesting allusion in the Prologue, and twice performed at Court in that year. It was one of the most popular of Restoration plays, was revived by Garrick, who played the part of the Copper Captain, and held the stage well into the nineteenth century.

The Wild-Goose Chase, produced by the King's Men in 1621, was so acclaimed that, according to actors who took part in it, the author himself "in despite of his innate modesty" joined in "applauding the rare issue of his brain." No source is known except the author's brain. It is a very skilful tissue of old motives and well-tried stage-effects. The intrigue plays on the old theme of the pursuit of the reluctant male by the wily and determined woman. The scene is laid in Paris, but the characters and the atmosphere smack of the better-class society in Fletcher's London.

The Wild-Goose is Mirabel, a lively young gentleman, just returned from travel and quite determined not to keep his promise
of marriage to the fair Oriana. She in turn is equally determined
to win him, since "the reclaiming of him" will be an honor.
Needless to say, she succeeds in the last act after a series of
failures in one of which she appears as a girl driven mad by love,
an imposture which he detects and ridicules. The theme is
doubled by the successful pursuit of Mirabel's friends, Pinac and
Belleur, by the sprightly ladies, Rosalura and Lillia Bianca, who
alternately repel and allure the gentlemen.

There is enough firm character drawing to keep the play from
being one of pure intrigue. Mirabel anticipates the gentleman
rake of Restoration comedy; he is something more of a gentleman, perhaps, and less of a rake than most of them. The gentle
Pinac and the blunt Belleur are neatly contrasted, as are the two
girls who pursue and capture them. Oriana is not quite the sentimental heroine, not quite the witty intriguer, simply a young
woman out to get her man. Yet after all, the fun of the play,
more effective no doubt on the stage than in the study, consists
in the "chase" with its turns and windings and final success. It
was adapted for the eighteenth-century stage by Farquhar and
quite spoiled by a lavish dose of sentiment and moralizing; there
is nothing either sentimental or moral in Fletcher's comedy.

The Chances, on the other hand, represents the comedy of
intrigue carried to the extreme. Founded on one of the *Exemplary Novels* of Cervantes, it does little more than adapt for
the English stage the complicated plot of the Spanish story. The
only decided change is the farcical dénouement in the house of
a sham conjuror with mock devils, disguises, and discoveries,
which replaces the sentimental conclusion of Cervantes. There
is some effective characterization in the minor roles of the land-
lady, Dame Gillian, and the blustering Antonio, but these
humours do not in any way determine the action. An earlier
play than *Rule a Wife*, it sticks closer to the intrigue of its
source. The play starts with the nocturnal adventures of two
young gentlemen, students at Bologna, who come unexpectedly
into the possession of a new-born babe and a wandering damsel

both of whom they bring back to their lodgings, to Dame Gillian's disgust. The rest of the action deals with the reunion of mother and child and their restoration by the gallant students to the proper lover and father. It might be noted in passing that the conversation of these gentlemen, particularly that of the wenching Don John, is very highly spiced. That did not offend Fletcher's audience nor that of the Restoration, which saw a Buckingham version, but it was drastically purged in the alteration of David Garrick, who personated Don John. It is certainly a bit racy for modern taste.

To complete this group of comedies of which Fletcher was the sole author, one more play may be mentioned, *Monsieur Thomas*, of uncertain date. It is a most amusing compound of high-flown romance and extravagant farce. The romantic action deals with the rivalry in love between an old gentleman and his young friend for the former's betrothed, Cellide. Each wishes to renounce her for the other, and she quite properly is offended at their apparent disregard of her own wishes. All comes well at last when the younger man is discovered to be the long-lost son of his kindly patron. The farce deals with the strange dilemma of Monsieur Thomas, a mad-cap gentleman sent abroad to acquire polish, who, returning home, offends his lusty old father by an assumed civility and his sweetheart by his outrageous behavior. Out of sheer perversity he continues to provoke his father to the point of losing his inheritance while attempting to win his mistress by one wild prank after another. In the end, of course, his father recognizes him as a chip of the old block— *Father's Own Son* was an alternate title for the play—and the lady, a very lively lady, is content to take him for all his wildness. The two themes are neatly linked together, but extravagant sentiment and knockabout farce are juxtaposed rather than blended. It is still an entertaining play for a reader ready to admit a suspension of moral scruples as well as of disbelief.

In his mass production of plays for the King's Men Fletcher's chief assistant in comedy as in tragi-comedy was Massinger, and there are three plays which appear to be their joint work, to say nothing of others where Massinger seems to have retouched a

Fletcher play for a later revival. These are *The Elder Brother*, *The Little French Lawyer*, and *The Spanish Curate*. The last will serve as a good example of their method of collaboration.

Licensed in 1622, *The Spanish Curate* is founded on an English translation of a long Spanish novel. The source contains both plots of the play: the serious family quarrel, and Leandro's amour with the lawyer's wife. Both are handled with the greatest freedom by the playwrights, who eliminate the four deaths that occur in the source and bring both actions to a happy ending. It seems plain that a working plan was agreed on: Massinger to take the serious story and convert it into a tragi-comedy; Fletcher to turn the amour into a comedy of mingled humours and intrigue. The two plots are closely interwoven, and more than once Fletcher writes a short scene which links the major with the minor action, but the comedy is his alone and is an excellent example of his gayety, power of invention, and lively dialogue. He turns the rather dismal intrigue of the original, which involves the murder of the lawyer and the condemnation of the lover, into a laughing comedy which ends with the exposure of the jealous husband and the vindication of the lady's honor. The excellent acting part of the Curate is developed out of a mere sketch in the novel, while the comic role of his sexton, Diego, is a sheer creation. There is no trace in the original of the amusing scenes in which the Curate and Diego break down the resistance of their Puritan parishioners, of the preposterous will which the mock invalid, Diego, dictates to the lawyer, or of the banquet in which the lawyer turns the tables on his tormentors. Fletcher's lyric gift appears in the jolly part-song with which the parish thanks the Curate for his decision to remain and in the charming ditty to the lute with which the lover lures his mistress from her seclusion. It seems rather unfortunate that such good comedy should be overweighted by the unpleasant intrigue of Don Henrique and the wicked Violante, but the Blackfriars audience wanted grave matter as well as gay, and the collaborators were ready and willing to gratify them.

Fletcher's gifts as a dramatist were admirably suited to catch the carefree yet sophisticated tints which the gallants of the Stuart court desired in comedy. His easy style and lyric gift combined with his moral impudence and theatrical facility to evoke charm and laughter in plays which deal almost uniformly with the love-chase and the battle of the sexes. They were acted usually with great success in the reigns of James and the first Charles, and are indeed the first plays we meet which really foreshadow the comedy of manners of the Restoration, with which they were to share popularity. If the comedies of James Shirley remind us most of the plays which were to come, it must be remembered that it was Fletcher who first responded successfully to the new comic taste, and helped to crystallize the form of manners comedy and that Shirley was his successor and imitator. Essentially a man of the theatre, he listened to his time acutely and responded with skilful innovations and daring variations which captivated his listeners then, and still delight those who have ears to hear.

CHAPTER NINE

JACOBEAN TRAGEDY: MARSTON, TOURNEUR, WEBSTER, MIDDLETON, FORD

THE impetus to romantic tragedy given by the brilliant success of Kyd and Marlowe in the late fifteen-eighties seems to have waned and faltered in the last decade of the century. There is almost no sign in this period of an attempt by professional playwrights to follow in their steps. The truth seems to be that the Elizabethan temper with its high spirits, its love of life, and exultant nationalism was in no mood to welcome a type of play that peered into the darker depths of human nature. The change that came over this temper towards the turn of the century with the last unhappy years of the great Queen's reign is marked by the sudden emergence into popularity of satire, whether in the form of poetry or satiric comedy. Significant, too, is the simultaneous revival upon various stages of tragedy, heralded by the "additions" to *The Spanish Tragedy*, 1601, for the Admiral's, Shakespeare's recast of the old *Hamlet*, 1600–01, for the Chamberlain's Company, and Marston's sensational *Antonio's Revenge* for Paul's Boys in the winter of 1600. Here is the beginning of a stream of tragedies that was to flow unbroken till it ended with Shirley's *Cardinal*, 1641, on the very eve of the closing of the theatres. The distinguishing note of this later tragedy is its intense interest in the complex character of man, its realization of the baser and bestial elements in his nature, more especially that of sex in its destructive form, and a perception, amounting at times to defeatism, of the power of evil. A steady deepening of this note may be heard in Shakespeare's plays from the melancholy of *Hamlet* to the hopeless misanthropy of *Timon*; and Shakespeare's great tragedies, it must be remembered, fall within this later period.

Marston's *Antonio's Revenge* is a fitting introduction to these later tragedies. This is the second part of *Antonio and Mellida*, but spectators who came to see a continuation of that romantic love story must have been startled when the voice of the Prologue warned all men "uncapable of weighty passion" to "hurry amain from our black-visaged shows" and welcomed only "hearts pierc'd through with anguish." The play is an ingenious mosaic of all the deeds of craft and violence that had occurred in the tragedy of blood for the last decade. These deeds are arranged in a consistent pattern about the career of an incredible tyrant, Piero of Venice, who opens the play with a secret, black, and midnight murder, and ends it stabbed and tortured by a group of revengers. The ghost of a murdered man rises to incite his son to vengeance and appears in his widow's bed-chamber to warn her against marriage with his murderer. The avenging son plays the fool in the tyrant's court, defers an opportunity to kill his foe until he can obtain complete revenge, and stabs the tyrant's little son as a sacrifice to his father's ghost. The theme of sex is stressed in the contrast of the tyrant's lustful passion with the pure affection of his daughter, who dies of a broken heart on hearing a false report of her lover's death.

It is easy enough to laugh at the extravagance and unreality of *Antonio's Revenge*. Yet this play, an immediate success upon the stage, exerted a strong influence upon later and greater dramatists than Marston, Webster for example and even Shakespeare. It is not merely Marston's sensationalism that tells; it is his instinctive conception of the power of atmosphere: of darkness, "sooty coursers of the night," of "graves, vaults and tombs," of ghostly voices, to heighten a tragic situation, that serves as a stimulus to later tragedy. *The Duchess of Malfi* and *Macbeth* are better plays than *Antonio's Revenge*, but both of them owe something to the work of the young poet-dramatist.

It is a very different case with Marston's second tragedy, *Sophonisba, ca.* 1605–06. This is an essentially original work conceived on the grand scale. Choosing a famous dramatic theme from Roman history Marston challenges comparison with Jonson, whose *Sejanus* he had praised as above the reach of envy. Yet he is no follower of Jonson's historical method; he avows his purpose to work as a poet rather than a historian and to "enlarge" his theme. This enlargement is specially marked in his treatment of character; his old satiric note has vanished, and the chief characters of the play rise to heroic proportions. Perhaps Marston's immediate inspiration was Chapman's *Bussy D'Ambois;* certainly he follows Chapman in the epic narrations and similes of *Sophonisba*. Even more plainly is Chapman's influence to be seen in the "sententious excitation to virtue" which marks this tragedy. The gnomic verses with which the play is packed:

> Gods prosper more a just than crafty state;
> 'Tis less disgrace to have a pitied loss,
> Than shameful victory . . .

are specially directed against Machiavellianism.

Marston, however, is no more a slavish follower of Chapman than he is of Jonson. His whole treatment of the plot in its simplicity and directness compares favorably with Chapman's proneness to hold up action by moralizing comment, and there are scenes of swift dramatic dialogue unmatched by anything in *Bussy*. It is unfortunate that Marston's lofty conception of his theme is marred by an execution that makes it one of the most difficult of Elizabethan tragedies. In his straining for terse expression he too often defies the rules of syntax and the idioms of English speech, and clouds his thought in hopeless obscurity.

The bulk of Marston's work was in the field of comedy; all that remains of Cyril Tourneur's drama is two tragedies. Chronologically he is the first of Jacobean tragic playwrights. He was not primarily a man of letters, much less a professional playwright; on the contrary he was a soldier serving in the Low Countries, secretary to Sir Francis Vere, employed for a time by the United Provinces, and finally secretary to the Council of War of an English expedition against Cadiz. He found time, however, in a life of action to write a few poems and an occasional play.

We do not know the date of Tourneur's birth; there seems some reason to believe that it was about 1584–85. There is no evidence that he attended either university, but his work shows such familiarity with Latin that it seems probable that he finished the regular course in one of the classical grammar-schools. He belonged, it is clear, to a gentle family, serving the state in peace and wa. under the ægis of the powerful Cecils. Soon after the publication of his first poem, *The Transformed Metamorphosis*, Tourneur must have joined the English forces in the Netherlands. He probably took part in the bloody siege of Ostend, 1601–04, to which there are references in the elegy on Vere and in *The Atheist's Tragedy*. He may have returned to England with Vere in 1604, for in 1605 there appeared a prose tract, *Laugh and Lie Down, or the World's Folly*, signed C. T. This is not improbably his, but it adds little to his reputation.

It would seem as if from 1604 to 1613 Tourneur was resident in England. At any rate a succession of poetic and dramatic works ascribed to him appears at irregular intervals during this period. The first of these, *The Revenger's Tragedy*, generally accepted as his, was published in 1607. No author's name is given; the title-page states only that the play had been "sundry times acted by the King's Majesties Servants," *i.e.*, after May 1603. Somewhere between 1604 and 1607 the play must have been written and performed; a probable date is 1606. Two years after the publication of *The Revenger's Tragedy* there appeared *A Funeral Poem upon the Death of . . . Sir Francis Vere*. There is no author's name on the title-page, but the poem is signed at the end Cyril Tourneur.

The Atheist's Tragedy, or the Honest Man's Revenge, Tourneur's one signed play, was published in 1611. The title-page states that it had "in divers places often been acted." The phrase "in divers places" implies, at least, that this play had not been performed at the Globe, or Blackfriars, as *The Revenger's Tragedy* had been; it might have been produced by a minor company, possibly on a tour in the provinces. There is no satisfactory evidence as to its date; the year 1610 seems a probable conjecture. That Tourneur continued his work for the theatre is shown by the entry in the Stationers' Register, February 15, 1612, of "The Nobleman, a tragi-comedy written by Cyril Tourneur." It was twice performed at Court by the King's Men, but there is no evidence of its publication. It would have been interesting to see what the author of *The Atheist's Tragedy* could do in tragi-comedy. The death of Robert Cecil, May 24, 1612, was followed by Tourneur's *Character* of his patron. This brief prose work was not published until the present century, but it aroused considerable interest; four or five manuscript copies still remain. More important than the *Character* is Tourneur's last published work, *A Grief on the Death of Prince Henry*, entered December 25, 1612, as by Cirill Tourneur, along with two other elegies by Webster and Heywood. There is little sign of personal emotion in the poem; rather it attempts to reveal the kingdom's loss in the death of a prince idealized as "the Precedent" of all heroic virtues.

Only one more record remains of Tourneur's literary activity. On June 5, 1613, Daborne, one of Henslowe's hacks, wrote to his master that he had "given Cyril Tourneur an act of the Arreignment of London to write." This lost play seems to have been a dramatization of Dekker's prose satire, *The Bellman of London*, which a group of playwrights were whipping into shape for the stage. It is rather sad to find a man like Tourneur engaged in this sorry business; probably it was forced upon him by the poverty which, as frequent contemporary allusions show, was the usual lot of the unemployed soldier.

Fortunately, however, this period of unemployed poverty was brief in Tourneur's case. Six months later, December 23, 1613, there is a record of a payment of 40s. to him for carrying letters on his Majesty's service to Brussels. He must shortly have rejoined the English troops in the Low Countries, for a letter dated August 14, 1614 states that "Cirill Tourneur, in former times Secretary to Sir Francis Vere . . . is now gone to the army with his Colonel." In 1617 he was back in England and for some unknown reason was arrested and thrown into prison on a warrant from the Privy Council. Luckily his friend, Sir Edward Cecil, was also in England and in high favor at Court; in a month or so Tourneur was released on Sir Edward's bond. Nothing more is heard of the charge, which was probably dismissed.

A complete blank of eight years follows. Tourneur presumably returned to his military duties in the Netherlands, since it must have been during this period that he was in receipt of a yearly pension of £60 from the Dutch government. This he gave up in 1625 to attend Sir Edward Cecil on an expedition against

Cadiz. Cecil had been named Lord Marshall of the fleet, and he appointed his old friend Secretary to the Council of War and Secretary to the Marshall's Court. From the first of these posts Tourneur expected to draw the handsome yearly salary of £400. This, however, was too ripe a plum to be allotted to an old soldier; a fortnight before the expedition set sail, a Court favorite was named to take his place as Secretary to the Council. Tourneur retained his inferior post, attended his patron through the expedition, and watched its disastrous failure. The flag-ship, the *Royal Anna,* leaking like a sieve with half her crew dead or disabled, put in at the Irish port of Kinsdale on her return. There Tourneur was put on shore to die. His widow, left destitute, repeatedly petitioned the Government for redress. Penurious as usual in its treatment of soldiers, the Court evaded her plea on a technicality. No further records of the case exist; it is unlikely that Charles I, who spent money like water on masques, opened his purse to relieve a soldier's widow.

The circumstances of Tourneur's life seem to account fully for the brevity of his career as a playwright. His fame rests upon two plays, and even of these his claim to the first and greater, *The Revenger's Tragedy,* has been challenged. Yet there is no good ground for such a challenge except the striking difference in thought and style between the two plays. Change, however, whether development or retrogression, is no unusual feature in a writer's career, and a study of Tourneur's work as a whole seems to explain the difference between the plays. *The Revenger's Tragedy* was assigned to him in 1656 in "an exact and perfect Catalogue of all the plays with the Author's names," appended to Archer's edition of *The Old Law.* Ascriptions of authorship by book-sellers during the Commonwealth are notoriously unreliable; there was a general tendency to assign plays of uncertain authorship to outstanding names in the drama; it seems unlikely, however, that Archer should have assigned *The Revenger's Tragedy* to such a forgotten playwright as Tourneur without good evidence. In 1661 Kirkman, a passionate admirer, collector, and publisher of old plays, also assigned *The Revenger's Tragedy* to Tourneur, and Kirkman may be regarded as an independent witness to Tourneur's authorship.

The proper approach to *The Revenger's Tragedy* would seem to be, not backward from his one signed play, but forward from his first work, *The Transformed Metamorphosis.* This strange and repellent poem is a curious compound of contradictions. On the surface it is only another contribution to the tide of satiric verse. Unlike his predecessors, however, Tourneur does not stoop to single out individual objects of satire; the poem is singularly free from personal animus. What the young poet sees is a world corrupted by gold and lust, and lying under the shadow of death. But there is more in the poem than this general satire; appended to it is a bit of allegory quite in the manner of Spenser. Something of this curious juxtaposition—it cannot be called a blend—of Marston's obsession with vice, specifically with sexual vice, and Spenser's worship of chaste beauty, appears in much of Tourneur's work, more particularly in his first play.

The Revenger's Tragedy is an offshoot of the tragedy of blood, the dramatic form established by Kyd and perfected by Shakespeare. Yet its departure from the established convention is more remarkable than its adherence. The play completely eliminates the supernatural; man's world, as Tourneur saw it, was vile enough to demand the most ruthless purge without the interposition of a Senecan ghost. Absent too is the madness, real or feigned, of the revenger. For this hitherto effective trait Tourneur substitutes the ironic cynicism of his protagonist. Marston's influence predominates in the background of the play. The scene is laid, like that of *The Malcontent,* in an Italian Court, debased almost beyond the power of imagination, where the only prevailing motives for action are revenge, ambition, and lust. The startling stage-effects: the opportune crash of thunder, the blazing star that heralds the catastrophe, the dance of masquers that precipitates it, are signs of the sensationalism with which Marston inoculated later Elizabethan tragedy. Yet for a young dramatist Tourneur has an amazing sense of what will tell upon the stage. There is hardly a more effective opening scene in Elizabethan drama than that in which the wicked Court sweeps across the stage by torchlight while on the balcony above Vendice, holding in his hand the skull of his murdered lady, invokes Vengeance, the bounden servant of Tragedy. Nor is

there a more striking example of surprise and reversal than in
the closing scene where Vendice, incapable longer of recognizing
the presence of justice in the world, calmly avows to the new
Duke his murder of the old, and so brings upon himself the
well-deserved doom of his sadistic cruelty.

Tourneur is no master of dramatic construction. The action
proceeds by leaps and bounds rather than in a well-ordered
march to its goal. It is the single scene rather than the plot as
a whole which evokes the playwright's power; some of the most
effective scenes of the play have little or no bearing upon the
main design. Yet there is not a scene which does not add to the
atmosphere of evil, brooding over the whole action. There is a
unity of tone in this play which is remarkable in Elizabethan
tragedy.

It is a curious fact that Tourneur does not give proper names
to any of the courtly family who occupy the center of this play.
The Duke and Duchess appear only by their titles; their sons
are labelled rather than named, like figures in the old Morals:
Lussurioso (the licentious), Ambitioso, Supervacuo (the idle),
Spurio, the bastard. Possibly Tourneur meant them to stand as
incarnate representatives of the vices of this foul court. Another
member of this noble family, the "youngest dearest" son of the
Duchess, is neither named nor labelled; yet he is etched into the
picture with stronger lines than any other of the brood, a head-
strong, lustful, and insolent ruffian. The members of the revenger's family, on the other hand, are named and clearly characterized: Hippolito, his brother, an easy-going gentleman, who
finds it possible to live in favor at the Court and yet to follow
the revenger with doglike fidelity; Gratiana, his mother, a wax-
like character, easily taking upon her the impress either of evil
or of good; and Castiza, his sister, a type like Spenser's Brito-
mart of invulnerable and militant chastity. Tourneur's masterpiece, of course, is the character of Vendice. He is at once the
malcontent of stage tradition and the revenger of the tragedy of
blood. Yet he is more than a mere combination of two conventional figures; he is a man obsessed with a vision of the world
poisoned by lust and overshadowed by death. Such is his conviction of the rottenness of his world that he accepts the office

of pander in disguise to his mother and sister, since another, he thinks, might indeed work effectually upon them. His plea for wealth and state as against honor is not altogether feigned; it is thus that Vendice sees his world. So, too, with his brooding thought of death; the skull of his mistress suggests to him not so much the beauty that was hers or the happiness that he has lost, but the destined end of all mortality in "the steadfast and enduring bone." Such a skeleton at the feast would, he thinks, "fright the sinner"; but it does not fright Vendice from his own treasured sin, the purpose of revenge. There is a double and ironic meaning in the very title of Tourneur's play: *The Revenger's Tragedy* is not only the tragedy accomplished by the revenger, but the tragedy which overtakes the revenger in the corruption of his own nature.

What lingers in the memory after reading *The Revenger's Tragedy* is neither the tangled plot nor the repulsive characters but single scenes couched in dramatic poetry of extraordinary power and terrible beauty. The metrical movement is swift and flexible; the rhythm pauses and hesitates, only to burst out again in fiercer flow. Deeply influenced by Marston, Tourneur has none the less in this satiric tragedy completely purged his style alike of Marston's pedantry and Marston's filth; the diction of *The Revenger's Tragedy*, in spite of the theme of lust which recurs like a dominant motif in the play, is remarkably free from offense. Images of darkness, of poison, of steel, and the flame of fire furnish a fit atmosphere for a dreadful play, but one memorable as presenting a fiercely unhappy poet's outlook on life. *The Revenger's Tragedy* is the dramatization of the vision obscurely apprehended in Tourneur's first poem.

The Atheist's Tragedy differs so startlingly from Tourneur's first play that it is hard to believe the two were written by the same man. In a sense, indeed, they were not, for the Tourneur who composed this play was a very different man from the young poet whose bitterness poured into *The Revenger's Tragedy*. Somewhere in the four-year interval between the two plays Tourneur had undergone conversion. It is possible, in fact, to fix the date of this change of heart, for the elegy on Vere in 1609 shows Tourneur escaping from the sinister preoccupation with death which hangs like a cloud over *The Revenger's Tragedy* into a calm and firmly grounded stoicism. The seldom read Elegy seems to reveal, both in what it says and what it leaves unsaid, the change that had come over Tourneur. Sir Francis Vere had been the most famous fighter of living Englishmen; yet there is strangely little about the fighting man in the six hundred lines of the poem. Tourneur knew Vere as a soldier; he tells of his "smiling in the face of war," exactly as the hero of *The Atheist's Tragedy* was to smile at the scaffold and the axe; but he makes no reference to Vere's share in such famous expeditions as the attack on Cadiz and the Island Voyage. The main stress, repeated over and over, is laid upon the character of Vere, a character so portrayed as to resemble the ideal Stoic hero. Vere was, says Tourneur, sweet and temperate, self-sufficient, free from passion, moved by neither fear nor anger. It is the admiring contemplation of such a character that permits Tourneur to speak of his own "reposed state of soul." It was no "reposed state" that gave birth to *The Revenger's Tragedy.*

It was under the influence of such a conversion from a morbid contemplation of death to a calm acceptance of life that Tourneur composed his next play. The dramatic form that he selected was the tragedy of revenge, but he made a considerable modification of the received convention to shape this form to suit his purpose. *The Atheist's Tragedy* has, indeed, been called a "thesis play." The thesis is stated in the sub-title, *The Honest Man's Revenge,* and clinched in an italicized line at the very end. It is a dramatic protest against the growing materialism of the age that tended to deny the existence of any beneficent power above Nature. This Tourneur stigmatizes as Atheism, and he creates dramatic characters to display in action the inevitable consequences of this denial of God. The protagonist, D'Amville, the Atheist, reveals his character in the opening scene; he declares his belief that Death "casts up" the sum of man's joy, and it is therefore expedient for man to crowd his brief life with "fulness of delight." Man's only immortality is in his children; for them as for himself he must strive to gain the wealth which will secure them from "dishonest poverty," and in this pursuit of wealth all means are lawful. The rest of the play reveals scene by scene the consequences of this opinion: he perpetrates one murder, plots another, and attempts incestuous intercourse with Castabella, the unhappy wife of his son Rousard. Thwarted in his violent attack upon her, he begins to lose the grim determination with which he had pursued his ends, and is completely overthrown by the sudden death of both his sons. Fallen into a state of distraction, he appears before the tribunal where his nephew, Charlemont, is being tried on a false charge of murder, claims the right of executing him personally, and in the attempt to do so strikes out his own brains with the headman's axe. This is conceived as the direct act of God, and D'Amville's last words are a renunciation of his atheism: "there is a power above Nature."

D'Amville has a female counterpart in Levidulcia. Like him she follows Nature, but to her Nature means but one thing, the sexual impulse. Her amour with D'Amville's son, Sebastian, leads to a brawl between her husband and her lover in which both are killed. Then, most unexpectedly, she bursts into tears, talks of her lost honor, and stabs herself "to make the example move more forcibly to virtue." Her death is as theatrically effective as D'Amville's, quite as improbable, and, like his, motivated solely by the purpose of the play.

Opposed to these representatives of crass materialism stand the contrasting figures of Charlemont and Castabella. Charlemont is, perhaps, an idealized portrait of Tourneur himself, a brave young soldier, given to philosophic speculation. He belongs to the group of sons like Hamlet and Antonio who have a murdered father to avenge, but his father's ghost is a good Christian, who on first appearing to his sleeping son tells him of the murder but bids him "leave revenge unto the King of Kings." Nothing could demonstrate more clearly Tourneur's breach with the Senecan tradition than such an employment of supernatural machinery. On trial for murder, Charlemont makes no defense, but rather aspires to death as a happy ending to "the stormy troubles of this life." He attributes D'Amville's death to the judgment of Heaven and voices the lesson of the whole action in the line already referred to:

> Patience is the honest man's revenge.

He is a cold and unsympathetic figure, but a model of Christian stoicism, carefully designed to point the moral.

Castabella, on the other hand, apparently planned as a contrast to Levidulcia, develops in the course of the action from an allegorical embodiment of chaste love into a very real and womanly character. Her swoon at the sight of her supposed dead lover, her horror at the infamous proposal of D'Amville are characteristically feminine touches; so too is the air of maternal protection which she assumes towards Charlemont when she learns of his danger, and her cheerful willingness to die for a crime she has not committed so long as she may die hand in hand with him.

The setting of *The Atheist's Tragedy* contrasts as strongly with that of Tourneur's first play as does his treatment of character. Ostensibly laid in France it is in reality a play of English family life; the atmosphere is rather that of domestic than of Senecan tragedy. Tourneur has deliberately placed the scene of this play in a familiar background to bring its lesson more strongly home to the audience. The style, too, of *The Atheist's Tragedy* is in keeping with its didactic purpose. It is deliberately low-toned; the swift rush of *The Revenger's Tragedy* has been modulated down to a slow and regular movement that often is barely distinguishable from prose. It should not be inferred, however, that *The Atheist's Tragedy* is a prosaic play. On the contrary it often rises to heights of grave and thoughtful poetry. This is particularly true in the soliloquies of the villain and of the hero, where Tourneur gives full and fine poetic expression to the opposing principles that underlie their characters.

There is a general agreement that *The Revenger's Tragedy* is the better play of the two. Theatrically, no doubt, it is. The action is swifter and more sensational; the characters are more startling in their immediate effect. Above all the poetry is more moving, because more passionate. To put it briefly, *The Revenger's Tragedy* is a play created by a fiery if diseased imagination; *The Atheist's* is a drama soberly composed by a cool and restored reason. As such it has its value; it is good to see a mind of such power as that which created Tourneur's first play recovering from a nightmare obsession with lust and death. *The*

Atheist's Tragedy is evidence, too, of a reaction in later Elizabethan tragedy against the old convention of revenge and the new sensationalism.

Enough has already been said of Tourneur's work to preclude the need of a full reappraisal. Slight in quantity, it has, none the less, its own distinctive note. Never an originator, Tourneur was yet able to impart to tragedy something peculiarly his own. He stripped the Senecan drama of its supernatural trappings; he raised domestic tragedy to a loftier ethical pitch than it had attained before. Above all he poured into his plays the flood of his own poetic inspiration, bitter and fiery in *The Revenger's,* cool and thoughtful in *The Atheist's Tragedy.* Tourneur is, perhaps, the most subjective of Elizabethan dramatists; he is a poet expressing himself in terms of drama rather than a professional playwright.

There are year-long blanks in our knowledge of Tourneur's life, but with John Webster the blank reaches from the beginning to the end; we know neither the date of his birth nor that of his death; we know nothing of his family connections, nor of his education. All that we are sure of is derived from a few references in Henslowe's *Diary* and from the dates of his published plays; the rest is inference.

In his dedication of *Monuments of Honor* to a member of the Merchant-Tailors, Webster declares that he himself was "born free of your company." This would make Webster the son of a freeman of that guild, presumably a London merchant. The usual conjectured date for Webster's birth, *ca.* 1580, fits in well enough with the admission of a John Webster to the Middle Temple and also to the first certain record of his activity as a playwright. There are entries in Henslowe's *Diary* in May 1602, noting advance payments to a group of writers: Munday, Middleton, Drayton, Webster, and Dekker. These entries mark the beginning of Webster's connection with the theatre as an underling in the Henslowe play-factory. He continued working for Henslowe along with Dekker on *Lady Jane,* 1602, a two-part play, published, 1607, under the title of *Sir Thomas Wyatt.* He and Heywood received an advance for a play called "Cryssmas comes bute once ayear"—Henslowe's spelling is a pure joy—in

1602. After that he disappears from the *Diary*, and his next work is the Induction to *The Malcontent* in 1604. In the same year he and Dekker each contributed an Ode to *Ten Arches of Triumph*, an illustrated record of King James's ceremonial entrance into London in March of that year.

Dekker probably carried Webster along with him to work for the Children of Paul's, for whom they wrote *Westward Ho* in 1604 and *Northward Ho* in 1605. When this company ceased to play in 1606, Webster seems to have been out of work for a period of years. His next play, *The White Devil*, published 1612, was produced by Queen Anne's Company, probably in 1611–12 at the Red Bull. Apparently it was a failure, for in the address "To the Reader" which he prefixed to the published text Webster complains that it was "acted in so dull a time of winter, presented in so open and black a theatre, that it wanted . . . a full and understanding auditory." Submitting it with a certain confidence to "the general view," he apologizes for its deficiencies if judged by classical standards, admits that he has taken a long time in its composition, but suggests that what he has written slowly may last for years. The year of the publication of *The White Devil*, 1612, saw Webster contributing a set of verses to the *Apology for Actors* of "his beloved friend, Master Thomas Heywood." Later in the year he joined Heywood and Tourneur in mourning the death of Prince Henry. His *Monumental Column, erected to the ever-living memory of the ever-glorious Henry* is a sorry piece of work. Webster himself confessed it when he excused his "worthless lines" by the haste in which they were composed.

Webster was more successful with his second independent play, *The Duchess of Malfi*. Composed in 1613–14, it was produced by the King's Company at Blackfriars and the Globe with Burbage in the role of Duke Ferdinand, and Lowin, a famous actor of Shakespearean characters, in that of Bosola. It must have had a signal success, for we can trace at least two later revivals. It was not printed until 1623, when it appeared with commendatory verses by Middleton, Rowley, and John Ford.

Some time, probably soon after the success of *The Duchess,*

Webster wrote a play called *Guise,* now lost but referred to in his dedication of the *The Devil's Law-Case.* In 1615 he contributed a set of thirty-two prose sketches: *A Roaring Boy, A Waterman, An Excellent Actor,* etc.—to the sixth edition of the popular *Characters* of Sir Thomas Overbury. These lively sketches of contemporary types throw some light on Webster's partiality for bitter humor, equivocation, and pun. Certainly a considerable period of time intervened between *Guise* and his next play, *The Devil's Law-Case,* published in 1623 as "a new tragecomedy—as it was approvedly well acted by Her Majesties Servants. Written by John Webster." The date of its composition is uncertain, probably about 1620.

From 1620 for a period of five years or so Webster was very busy with playwriting. He joined hands with Middleton in *Anything for a Quiet Life, ca.* 1621; with Ford, Rowley, and Dekker in *Keep the Widow Waking,* 1624, already referred to (p. 113); with Rowley and perhaps Heywood in *A Cure for a Cuckold, ca.* 1625. Webster's share in *The Fair Maid of the Inn, ca.* 1625, is that of a partner in revision. There has been much difference of opinion as to the date as well as to the authorship of *Appius and Virginia,* published in 1654 as the work of Webster. The final conclusion seems to be that it is perhaps the latest work of Webster, *ca.* 1625–27. It belongs to this period of collaboration, and his partner in the play is undoubtedly Heywood. There is no sure evidence of his existence after 1625; he may have died in the great plague of that year.

Webster's work seems to fall into three distinct periods: the first of apprenticeship and collaboration, the second of independent work, the third a final period of collaboration in which, however, his contribution is definitely marked and individual. The early period includes a small share in *Sir Thomas Wyatt.* In the printed version of this archaic specimen of the chronicle play there are few clearly visible traces of Webster. The general characteristics of the two Dekker–Webster comedies, *Westward Ho* and *Northward Ho,* have already been described (p. 110). In *Westward Ho* his share is slight enough; there is not a single scene that can be assigned to him alone. Almost the same verdict can be rendered for *Northward Ho.* There are scattered traces of Webster in three or four scenes, but the play as a whole, in atmosphere, characters, and diction, is Dekker's.

It was while he was working with Dekker that Webster got the opportunity to do, so far as we know, his first piece of independent work. This was the Induction to *The Malcontent* as performed by the King's Company. They had by some means acquired an acting version of the play as originally performed by the Children of the Chapel at Blackfriars. To replace the vocal and instrumental accompaniment to the Children's performances, the actors engaged Marston to write in additional dialogue and hired Webster to compose an Induction of the type that Jonson had made fashionable in *Every Man Out* and *Cynthia's Revels*. In this a pair of gentlemen representing the audience take their seats upon the stage of the Globe, where they were by no means welcome, and chat with the actors, Burbage and others, before the play proper begins. They maintain the right of the audience to criticize; the actors uphold the privilege of the playwright to correct abuses by satire. The little sketch—it is nothing more—has significance only as it expresses Webster's dissatisfaction with the "uncapable multitude" who passed final judgment on the art of playwright and actor.

In his first great tragedy, *The White Devil*, Webster set his scene in that Renaissance Italy whose blend of beauty and wickedness exercised so strong a fascination on the simpler English mind. He chose for his theme a tragedy of real life which had startled even Italy in the last quarter of the sixteenth century. This was the adulterous passion of Vittoria Accoramboni and Paolo Orsini, Duke of Brachiano, beginning with the murder of her husband, maintained in defiance of Papal thunders, and ending after the Duke's death, possibly by poison, in the ruthless slaughter of Vittoria by his kinsmen. We do not know where Webster learned the story; at times he seems to have accurate information on minor details; at others he is far astray from the truth. *The White Devil* is Webster's interpretation of life in Renaissance Italy rather than his dramatization of a true history.

As a tragedy Webster's play has been extravagantly praised and as harshly condemned. It is from the point of view of dramatic construction that the attack has been fiercest; "ram-shackle" work, one critic calls it. This is too severe; the general outline of the action is simple and well planned. It begins in the first act with the intrigue between Vittoria and the Duke, runs through the murders that make their marriage possible, shows the gathering of forces against them, and closes with the murder of the guilty lovers. But this comparatively simple outline is obscured by much irrelevant matter: satiric interludes, spectacles like the election of the Pope, and incidents that have little or nothing to do with the main plot. It is in single scenes, or even in parts of scenes, that Webster's strength as a tragic poet reveals itself.

It is, however, in characterization that Webster excels. He has the Elizabethan gift of imparting life to the people of his plays; most of his characters, certainly all the chief actors, are not types, but individuals. Vittoria, the White Devil, is, perhaps, a unique figure in Elizabethan drama. Hers is a charm compounded of admiration and aversion; she is as beautiful as wicked and as brave as beautiful. It is her courage, whether facing her hostile judges, her jealous lover, or her assassins, that wins our sympathy. Yet she is no virago, but from first to last a very woman. Her ready wit, her outbursts of anger, and the proud resolution with which she meets inevitable death are characteristic traits of the great lady of the Renaissance. Brachiano, her partner in guilt, is a simpler character drawn with a few swift and telling strokes. Self-centered, insolent, and ruthless, he is redeemed from utter baseness by his passion for Vittoria. He has none of Vittoria's charm, but he evokes a reluctant admiration by the proud self-confidence which scorns alike the threats of the Medici and the curses of the Church.

There is a subtler and more complex characterization in Webster's treatment of Flamineo. In a sense he is another representative of the malcontent so frequent in later Elizabethan drama, and certainly Webster often makes him the mouthpiece of his own satiric outlook. But Flamineo is more than the conventional malcontent; he plays an important part in the action, bringing the Duke and Vittoria together in the beginning, reconciling them after their quarrel, and attempting after the Duke's death to blackmail his sister. He is hardened, and cynical; he shows no trace either of loyalty to his master or of family affection. Underneath his cold and selfish exterior, however, there lies a bitter and passionate spirit which more than once breaks through the outer crust as in the burst of rage that drives him, sword in hand, to murder his defenseless brother. Over against these characters Webster sets three others to represent the side of virtue in a world dominated by the power of evil: the devoted and self-sacrificing wife, Isabella; the noble mother, Cornelia; and the simple, honest soldier, Marcello. They all lose the game of life; one is poisoned, one stabbed, and one goes mad. That is Webster's view of the world, and it seems characteristic of his view that he is more interested in his evil than in his virtuous characters.

Webster achieves his characterization, for the most part, by direct dramatic dialogue. There is little in *The White Devil* of the Jonsonian device of describing one character by words put in the mouth of another. It is by speech exactly fitted to the situation that his characters reveal themselves. Brachiano's

> Have you proclaim'd a triumph that you bait
> A lion thus?

and Vittoria's

> I will be waited on in death; my servant
> Shall never go before me

are but two of the many examples that might be culled from the play. Had Webster always written thus, he would have been one of the greatest of tragic dramatists. Unfortunately he did not. Misled by his admiration of the "sententious chorus" of classical drama, he insists on padding his dialogue with moral maxims often voiced incongruously by other than moral characters. Even worse perhaps is his trick of holding up the action to insert an irrelevant or moral apologue drawn, it seems, from the note-book he kept.

Webster's verse is peculiarly his own. He owned no master; he left no disciples. He discards the conventional pattern of blank verse for an irregular, often a rough, meter that seems a conscious effort to approximate the realism of daily speech. Yet at times when he is greatly moved, the lines rise to a grave beauty unmatched outside of Shakespeare. It is essentially dramatic poetry; there is little of the lyric sweetness of Dekker in the verse of *The White Devil*. He avoids also the narrative declamation, an inheritance from Marlowe, that persisted as late as Chapman and Massinger, and attains his greatest heights in swift and sudden outbursts that illuminate the sober texture of his usual verse like stars breaking through a cloud. These outbursts, moreover, are wrung from his characters at some tense moment of their existence, often indeed in the face of death. Such lines as:

> We cease to grieve, cease to be fortune's slaves,
> Nay, cease to die by dying,

or

> My soul, like to a ship in a black storm
> Is driven, I know not whither,

represent dramatic poetry at its best, and it is the frequency of its recurrence in *The White Devil* that lifts this play from the plane of melodrama to that of high poetic tragedy.

For the story of his second tragedy, *The Duchess of Malfi*, Webster turned again to Renaissance Italy; but this time to a definitely recognizable source, the twenty-third tale in Painter's *Palace of Pleasure*, 1566–67. Briefly the story is as follows: The Duchess of Amalfi of the royal house of Aragon, left a widow at the age of twenty, contracted a secret marriage with her major-domo, Antonio Bologna. For some years their connection was unsuspected, but after the birth of a second child, the scandal grew so great that Antonio to avoid the wrath of her brothers withdrew to Ancona. Here the Duchess followed him, proclaimed their marriage, renounced her rank, and settled down to a private life. Shortly after the birth of a third child her brothers managed to have the lovers expelled from Ancona, and later from a second refuge in Siena. In an attempt to escape to Venice they were overtaken by an armed band in the service of the brothers. Antonio and his oldest child escaped, but the lady was taken to a castle in her duchy where, as it later transpired, she, her children, and her waiting maid were secretly murdered. A year or so later Antonio, ignorant of his wife's death and still hoping to appease the brothers, was stabbed to death in Milan by a certain Bozolo in their pay. The murderer escaped, and the blot on the scutcheon of Aragon was washed out in blood.

Such was the story, pathetic rather than tragic, that Webster set himself to dramatize. He handled his source something in the fashion with which Shakespeare treated the Italian tale of the Moor of Venice. He kept the general outline and even took over some minute details, such as the three children of Antonio and the Duchess. In spite of his general fidelity to his source, however, Webster makes considerable changes in the first and last acts. The first is largely devoted to the characterization of the chief figures, and it foreshadows tragedy by the angry warnings of the brothers against their sister's second marriage. The last act, almost entirely his invention, has been blamed as unnecessary; yet certainly no Elizabethan would have been content to leave the theatre after the death of the Duchess without seeing the due penalty exacted from her murderers. The confused series of accidents by which this judgment is accomplished is in perfect accord with the atmosphere of a play where so much seems to happen by blind chance.

Another departure of Webster from his source serves to give unity to the play, the continual presence of Bosola. He is introduced in the first scene; he acts as a spy upon the Duchess, discovers the birth of the first child, informs the brothers, becomes their tool in the arrest and murder of the unhappy lady, and in the last act serves as the instrument of retribution on the guilty pair. That he pays with his death the penalty of his own guilt must have been as satisfying to the Elizabethan spectator as it is to the modern reader.

More important than these changes in construction is Webster's shift in sympathy. In Painter the Duchess and her husband are violently denounced, she as a victim of "libidinous appetite," he as rashly presuming to match above his rank. Painter's point of view corresponds to that of Brooke, who told the story of Romeo and Juliet in didactic verse; Webster's to that of Shakespeare, who transformed Brooke's poem into romantic tragedy. Webster's sympathy from the first to last is with the Duchess, whom he portrays not as the slave to her passion, but as the innocent victim of her brothers' cruelty. Self-assured and light-hearted in her happy days she faces death with a fortitude that matches the active courage of her sister Vittoria. Born of a royal house she bears herself like one to the manner born.

> Whether I am doomed to live or die
> I can do both like a prince,

she says to the brother who has surprised her secret. Yet with pride goes a womanly tenderness that transfigures it. She is ready to ask pardon and kiss the hand of the brother who has pursued her with such malice; almost her last words are for the children whom she leaves behind. All the tortures, physical and mental, that are practised on her cannot bring her to despair; it is with gentle resignation rather than defiance that she meets her end. Her lover Antonio is a weaker character, but not altogether unworthy of his lady's love. His comment on her brothers' characters and upon Bosola show him not devoid of insight, and his gentle modesty in the wooing scene marks him as quite free from self-seeking ambition. In the end, like the Duchess, he meets death with resignation; he is, in fact, too much like her to be her savior in the storm that breaks upon them.

The Aragonian brothers represent two types of the Renaissance nobleman. The Cardinal is the fox, the crafty politician, cold-blooded, treacherous, and cowardly. His brother, "a most perverse and turbulent nature," is the wolf, insatiate in hunger for revenge. The madness that falls upon him after his savage torture of his sister is but the logical result of his unbridled passion. Webster does not motivate as clearly as he might have done the cause of the brothers' persecution of their sister. Ferdinand's reference to the "infinite mass of treasure" he had hoped for at her death is a misleading afterthought. The true motive lies far deeper, in the insensate pride which revolted against the staining of "the royal blood of Aragon" by a misalliance. That is a motive hardly comprehensible today; it was strong enough in the Renaissance for Webster's hearers to understand, if not to share it.

Bosola is a more complex character than either of the brothers. Born a gentleman, bred a scholar, he early became a retainer of the Cardinal and because of a murder performed at his behest spent some years in the hell of the galleys. Set free he has no recourse except to revert to his old post as a retainer. In this he resembles Flamineo of *The White Devil*, but he is a very different character. Flamineo is a single-minded self-seeker; Bosola presents a divided self; he accepts with reluctance the base employment of a spy on the Duchess, but is honest enough to earn his pay by doing his dirty work. He relieves his mind by outbursts of malcontent railing, but he is keen-sighted enough to distinguish good from evil. In his case there is no sudden conversion from evil to good; it is not until his discovery that his own death is plotted by the Cardinal that in despair he turns his sword upon his masters. Tossed between his knowledge of good and his practice of evil, his vision of human life is summed up in the words:

> We are merely the stars' tennis-balls struck and bandied
> Which way please them.

It is by a stroke of creative genius that Webster has evoked this strange and tragic figure from the hired assassin of his source.

It is by the poetry that one best remembers *The Duchess of Malfi*. It is a graver, sweeter utterance than the vigorous dramatic verse of the earlier play; there are few of the sudden flashes of inspired speech that burst from Brachiano and Vittoria. Often the tone seems rather elegiac than tensely dramatic. It would be hard to match elsewhere the plaintive sigh of the Duchess:

> O that it were possible we might
> But hold some two days' conference with the dead!
> From them I should learn somewhat, I am sure,
> I never shall know here.

In *The White Devil* life is something to be enjoyed to the full and fought for to the bitter end; in *The Duchess* Bosola, the fatal bellman, utters the poet's final conclusion on life:

A long war disturb'd your mind,
Here your perfect peace is sign'd.
Of what is't fools make such vain keeping?
Sin their conception, their birth weeping,
Their life a general mist of error,
Their death a hideous storm of terror.

To such a pit of pessimism had sunk the light-hearted drama of earlier Elizabethan days.

In a sense both these plays belong to the Elizabethan genre of revenge tragedy; but they wear their rue with a difference. In *The White Devil* there is, to be sure, a well-grounded motive for revenge, but the sympathy of the audience is directed to the guilty lovers rather than to the revengers. In *The Duchess*, on the other hand, there is no moral ground for the revenge wrought by the brothers upon a sister who, by Elizabethan standards, was reckless in her disregard of convention rather than guilty of crime. Webster in this play has broken even more decidedly than Tourneur with stage tradition. In his treatment of his source, particularly in his characterization of the chief figures, Webster shows an unexpected originality of thought and a fine grasp of material.

It seems clear that in the interval between his apprenticeship and his independent mastery Webster had been profoundly influenced by two contemporary playwrights, Marston and Shakespeare. The influence of Marston was on the whole unfortunate, since it tended to strengthen Webster's bent for satire. Marston's sensationalism too had its effect on Webster's work. The Ghost of Brachiano, who appears with a skull in his hand and throws earth upon Flamineo, is not the revengeful ghost of Senecan tradition, but a sheer theatric effect which has no bearing on the ensuing action. Shakespeare's influence is subtler and more pervasive. It is most noticeable, of course, where Webster directly borrows situations from his master; Cornelia's broken ejaculations over the body of her murdered son recall those of Lear over Cordelia. But there is more than this. The firm grip Webster takes on the action in his great scenes, the intense realism with which he brings character and passion before us are closer to Shakespeare than anything else in later

Elizabethan drama. Webster's great characters are like those of Shakespeare, neither wholly good nor bad, but all too human in their composite strength and weakness, wisdom and folly, passion and fortitude. The tragic world of Webster is not far removed from that of Shakespeare; it is a world where evil dominates, where innocence goes down in the struggle, yet one where through the clouds of night "the stars shine still."

What has been said of Webster's likeness to Shakespeare can be said only of his two tragic masterpieces. It is by them alone that he lives today. He still had years of dramatic activity before him, but his later work is on the whole inconsiderable in the final estimate of his achievement. *The Devil's Law-Case*, a strange and in many ways repellent play, is an example at once of Webster's strength and of his weakness. There is no direct source; the plot is a mosaic of incongruous matter. It is usually classed as a tragi-comedy but it is so only in the sense that *Measure for Measure* belongs to this genre; it is a serious, well-nigh tragic action violently wrested to a technically happy, though hardly satisfactory, conclusion. The last act, in which Webster borrows Fletcher's technique of surprise and reverse, is a bewildering complex of incidents; nowhere is Webster's weakness in construction more plainly visible. There are a few passages of strong dramatic dialogue; there are occasional flashes of self-revealing speech; and there is an ample sufficiency of Webster's moral maxims, but one looks in vain here for the fiery energy of *The White Devil* or the elegiac sweetness of *The Duchess*. *The Devil's Law-Case* is the work of a poet grown older, soberer, and, in truth, less inspired.

The plays of Webster's third period may be briefly dismissed. *A Cure for a Cuckold* was published in 1661 as the joint work of Webster and Rowley. Rowley's share is plain enough in the boisterous farce of the sub-plot, built up around a capital acting part for Rowley himself. The serious action is a domestic tragi-comedy quite in the later manner of Heywood; indeed it is possible that Heywood had a finger in it. The strong scenes in this plot are certainly by Webster and show his grasp on character and situation. Unfortunately in the last act his desire to introduce new and surprising motifs results in an almost inextricable confusion. *A Cure* is interesting only as it shows Webster capable of doing creditable work in other than tragic lines.

In his last surviving drama Webster fortunately deserts the technique of Fletcher to return to that of Shakespeare. *Appius and Virginia* is a sober tragedy of Roman history like *Julius Cæsar*. It was written in collaboration with Heywood, but how greatly the tragic genius of Webster predominated appears at a glance when this play is compared with Heywood's earlier *Rape of Lucrece*. Heywood's hand is visible in the familiar and bawdily jesting Clown, in the realism of certain scenes, and in a final touch of sentimentality in the forgiveness of Virginius and the penitent suicide of the villain. To Webster, on the other hand, we owe the fine opening with its swiftly sketched figure of the hypocritical Appius, the masterful quelling of a mutiny by Virginius, and the trial scene in which he kills his daughter. The play as a whole has a more regular and more unified effect than Webster's earlier dramas. This may perhaps be due to the controlling influence of Heywood; it is not Heywood, however, but Webster who utters the sober and lovely poetry of the play. A short passage may give some idea of Webster's latest music. Virginius bids farewell to the daughter he is about to sacrifice:

> Let me forget the thought
> Of thy most pretty infancy, when first
> Returning from the wars, I took delight
> To rock thee in my target; when my girl
> Would kiss her father in his burganet
> Of glittering steel hung round his armed neck,
> When I first taught thee how to go, to speak;
>
> .   .   .   .   .
>
> And when my wounds have smarted, I have sung
> With an unskilful yet a willing voice,
> To bring my girl asleep.

It is good to end a survey of Webster's work on such a note.

Little as we know of Webster's life, it is yet possible to form some conception of his character and personality. He was industrious and admired industry; he was on good terms with the actors and with his fellow craftsmen; yet he stood a little aloof from them, rejecting with a touch of pride the offer of commendatory verses for *The Devil's Law-Case*. He was a conscious artist who knew what he wanted, though more than once he was forced into what must have been repugnant work. It was only for a brief period in the middle of his life that he seems to have been free to stand alone and to turn out the slowly pondered work that was taking shape within his mind. He was no great scholar but he brooded over his few books until phrases, images, and maxims from their pages were transmuted into the poetry of his plays.

As an artist he cannot well have been quite happy or satisfied. For one thing he never learned the first principles of his craft, sound construction and clear motivation. Perhaps this was because he went to school in the Henslowe factory, where speed rather than quality was the rule. Moreover, as a playwright Webster was what we might call a split personality; intellectually he admired the "divine rapture" of the classic drama with its "sententious Chorus" and its "weighty Nuntius"; yet he could not for his life have written a play like Jonson's *Sejanus*. He was at heart an emotionalist, not in the blithe spirit of the early Elizabethans, rather in that of the Jacobean poets and playwrights who beheld the early glory fading. The world that Webster saw, when unhampered by the necessity of collaboration, was an evil one. Fate rather than a divine providence seems to rule it; the innocent are helpless victims in the net of circumstances. The guilty perish too, but that is because to Webster the shadow of death hangs over human life. Yet in spite of this gloomy outlook Webster is not a hopeless or discouraged poet. The world of human life is to him intensely interesting because of the characters that have their being there. And one human quality above all others makes these men and women sympathetic, the quality of courage to defy or to endure. It is from this profound sympathy with doomed and struggling men and women that Webster's power of creative characterization springs. Along with it goes the intensely dramatic poetry in which these characters reveal their nature. For Webster's characters and more especially for Webster's poetry we can pardon many a fault in technical construction, many a moralizing and sententious interruption. After all, great poetry is not so common in the world, not even in the world of Elizabethan drama, that we should cavil over the robes it wears.

Middleton's two tragedies, *The Changeling* and *Women Beware Women,* seem to have been written during Webster's last period and may be noticed here.

The Changeling, 1622, the masterpiece of Middleton's collaboration with Rowley, is founded on a collection of "thrillers," entitled *God's Revenge Against Murder.* The comic sub-plot loosely attached to the main action is plainly the work of Rowley, who seems also to have written the first and last scenes of the play. These open and end the tragic action, and if they are Rowley's, he wrote them under Middleton's direction, for it is to the greater dramatist that we must ascribe the masterly recasting of character and events in the source.

There is nothing in Elizabethan tragedy quite like *The Changeling.* The usual atmosphere of tragedy, the sense of hostile fate that crushes the innocent along with the guilty is wanting here; no fate of empires or of noble houses is involved; nothing but the destiny of two characters, De Flores and Beatrice-Joanna. Upon these two Middleton concentrates with a tragic intensity unmatched outside of Shakespeare. Outwardly De Flores is a familiar type, the broken gentleman serving as a nobleman's retainer, but none of his fellows in Elizabethan drama is so wholly dominated by one master passion, a humour in Jonson's sense turned to dreadful tragic purpose. His one motive in life is his desire for Beatrice; merely to look on her he submits to scorn and insult; to possess her he commits murder as coolly as he would take a glass of wine; to avoid the loss of her, when once possessed, he kills her and himself. In the source De Flores is a gallant young gentleman, an old suitor of Beatrice, but there is nothing romantic or appealing in Middleton's character. His ugly visage is the sign-manual of his distorted mind.

Beatrice too is the creature of one passion, the fierce desire to have her will, at once, regardless of all consequences. Unlike the realist De Flores, she never faces the consequence and is loath to pay the necessary price. To escape a hateful marriage she determines on the death of the proposed bridegroom; the easiest way to accomplish it seems to be to hire De Flores, and to win his service she stoops to flatter the man she loathes. After she has paid, reluctant and struggling to the last, the price that he exacts, she sacrifices the honor of her handmaid to conceal the loss of her own, and to avoid detection she acquiesces without remorse in the murder of the wretched girl. At the end, confronted with proof of her liaison with De Flores, she betrays him with as little reluctance as she had hired him. There is a progressive moral degeneration in Beatrice from the proud virgin of the first act to the cowering adulteress of the close; yet her last words show no consciousness of guilt; it is fate, she thinks, not her own self-will, that has thrown her into the clutches of the man who has ruined her. It is this unhappy falling off—"beauty changed to ugly whoredom"—not merely the main role of the underplot—that gives its title to the play.

Middleton's firm realism appears not only in his treatment of these characters, but also in his handling of the dialogue. A true poet, he curbs his genius here to strict dramatic utterance. In the great scene where the relentless will of De Flores storms the weak barriers of Beatrice's defense, he puts into the mouth of the speakers language—"a woman dipped in blood," "foul villain," "my fair murdress"—that brings the situation directly before us. Yet there is no prosaic realism here; throughout he heightens the effect by poetic phrasing:

> Let me go poor unto my bed with honor

and

> Can you weep Fate from its determined purpose?

He did not often write thus, but here at least he touched the height.

Women Beware Women shows Middleton's reversion after his collaboration with Rowley to his proper field of satiric comedy, but comedy now tinged with irony and leading to tragic issues. A well-constructed plot interweaves two distinct actions: the incestuous amour of an uncle with his niece, and the semi-historic story of Bianca Capello, the beautiful Venetian, the mistress and later the wife of the Grand Duke of Tuscany. The link between the two actions is the widow Livia, who plays the role of the intriguer in a comedy. The theme of the play is the degeneration and collapse of a whole society; not a single character escapes the moral taint, except a Cardinal, who appears at the end to sermonize. Yet Middleton's attitude here, as in *A Chaste Maid,* is rather that of the passionless observer than of the tragic poet. In subtle characterization as in skilful plotting *Women Beware Women* is one of Middleton's best plays, but it falls below *The Changeling* in tragic intensity. Unrestrained by Rowley, Middleton indulges in long speeches, soliloquies, and harangues that cover pages of the text. Yet none of his plays is so richly stored with passages of lovely verse; poetry, irony, and delicate portraiture usurp the place of swift dramatic action.

We know a little more about the life of John Ford than we do of Webster's, not because he was a greater or more famous poet, but simply because of his social status. After the brilliant success of two such gentlemen as Francis Beaumont and John Fletcher, a crowd of courtiers, especially in the reign of Charles I, hurried onto the stage and into print. It is with these authors that Ford, who began work as a playwright rather late in life, is connected chronologically, but the serious thought and grave beauty of his verse link him more closely with the great tragic writers of the reign of James, with Shakespeare, Tourneur, and Webster.

John, son of Thomas Ford, a Devonshire gentleman of good family, was baptized on April 17, 1586. He may have studied at Oxford; he certainly entered, a boy of sixteen, the Middle Temple, where his uncle, Sir John Popham, the Lord Chief Justice, was the most distinguished member. The atmosphere of the Inns of Court at the turn of the century, gayly social, literary, and dramatic, was only too likely to lead a young gentleman of poetic tastes away from the study of legal technicalities. Young Ford, apparently, was far from a satisfactory student at the Middle Temple. He was expelled in 1606 for non-payment of "buttery" bills—charges for food and drink—and was restored only on the payment of a fine of 40s., no inconsiderable sum in those days. Some years later, 1617, his name appears in a list of young members of the society who had "conspired" to wear the hats of gentlemen rather than the caps of scholars at meals and at divine service, a demonstration of rebellion against established order which the authorities took quite seriously. His father, who died in 1610, left him a bare £10, compared with £10 a year to his two younger brothers, a token apparently of parental dissatisfaction.

Strangely enough considering the affiliations of the Inns of Court with the Elizabethan stage—Shakespeare's *Twelfth Night* was performed in the hall of the Middle Temple in the very year of Ford's entrance into the society—there is no evidence of Ford's early interest in contemporary drama. He made his début as a poet in 1606 with an elegy on the Earl of Devonshire, Charles Blount, the lover, and later the husband of Penelope, Lady Rich, Sidney's Stella, "that glorious star" to whom Ford dedicated the poem. Ford was not at all troubled by the long adulterous connection of Penelope and Charles, for he declares himself the "honorer and lover" of her "noble perfections." In the same year he broke into print again, this time with a prose tract, *Honor Triumphant, or the Peeres Challenge,* a defense in high-flown style of four fantastic propositions: "Fair lady was never false," and the like, maintained by four noble challengers at a tilting before King James and the visiting King of Denmark. It was dedicated to the Countess of Pembroke and the Countess of Montgomery, wives of two of the tilters, the "incompairable paire of brethren," William and Philip Herbert. A prose tract, *The Golden Mean,* by John de la Fforde, 1614, has been ascribed to him; he was certainly the author of a lost work, *Sir Thomas Overbury's Ghost,* 1615, apparently mistaken for a play by various scholars. No play on the Overbury murder could have been licensed for the stage at a time when the trial of his supposed murderers, the Earl of Somerset and his wife, was actually in progress. Ford's interest in the case is shown by his verses *A Memorial to That Man of Virtue, Sir Thomas Overbury,* prefixed to several editions of Overbury's posthumous poem, *The Wife.* It was not until 1620 that Ford once more appeared in print, this time in *A Line of Life,* a rather heavy ethical treatise, the work of a scholar, but a scholar who is interested in the life around him, as is shown by his references to such contemporary figures as Essex, Marshall Biron, and Sir Walter Raleigh.

Ford's career as a dramatist begins in 1621 with *The Witch of Edmonton,* already noticed, in collaboration with Dekker and Rowley. The success of this play, which was presented at Court by the Prince's Company "with singular applause," evidently turned Ford's attention to the theatre, and from this time to the end of his life his work consists solely of plays and a few poems in praise of fellow playwrights.

The first period of Ford's dramatic activity is wholly taken up with his collaboration with Dekker, recently released from prison and busily cobbling up plays for any company that would buy them with any writer who would help him finish them. In 1624 he and Dekker turned out no less than four plays. The first of these, *The Sun's Darling,* for the Lady Elizabeth's Company, has already been discussed. The lost *Fairy Knight* was licensed in June for the Prince's Company; the lost *Keep the Widow Waking* was huddled up with the aid of Webster and Rowley for the Prince's Company in September; and the lost *Bristowe Merchant,* apparently a domestic tragedy, was licensed in October for the Palsgrave's Company. This may have been too hot a pace for a gentleman of the Middle Temple; certainly there follows a pause of four years.

The Lover's Melancholy, 1628, Ford's first unaided play, was produced by the King's Men at Blackfriars with the full strength of the company—seventeen actors' names are printed in the first edition. Ford published it in 1629 with a graceful dedication to his cousin, John Ford, and to "all the best of the noble society of Gray's Inn." Speaking as a gentleman amateur rather than as a professional he says that this play, "the account of some leisurable hours," may be the last as well as the first of his to appear in print. But Ford's success emboldened him to continue; his lost *Beauty in a Trance* was played by the King's Men at Court in 1630; *The Broken Heart* was also produced by the King's Men, presumably in the winter season of 1632–33. Ford must have been a hard-working as well as a successful playwright at this time, for 1633 saw the publication of two more tragedies, *Love's Sacrifice* and *'Tis Pity She's a Whore.* An anonymous tragi-

comedy, *The Queen, or the Excellency of her Sex,* published in
1653, has been reclaimed on strong internal evidence for Ford.
The Chronicle Historie of Perkin Warbeck appeared in 1634
with a dedication to Jonson's friend and patron, the rich and
drama-loving Earl of Newcastle. *The Fancies, Chaste and Noble,*
ca. 1636, was published in 1638. Ford's last play, *The Lady's*
Trial, was acted at the Cockpit in 1638 and published in 1639.
Nothing more is heard of Ford after this year. There is a tradition that he retired to his native Devonshire, but it is a tradition
only.

The active life of Ford as a playwright, apart from his early
collaboration with Dekker, extends over a period of some ten
years, 1628–38. The exact chronological order of his plays
within this period is by no means certain, and it seems best to
treat them according to their respective genres. In his early work
with Dekker, Ford seems to have alternated between the realistic
treatment of his collaborator and his own interest in romantic
themes. His contribution to *The Witch of Edmonton* is confined to those scenes which deal with the domestic tragedy of
Frank Thorney. It is characteristic of Ford that the protagonist
is a youth, driven by what he calls his fate, first into a bigamous
marriage and then into the murder of an innocent and unresist-
ing wife. Yet he is not portrayed as a deliberate villain; he is
forced by circumstance into actions for which in the end he
repents, and Ford shows a certain sympathy for the unhappy
man. In *The Sun's Darling,* where Ford's work seems to overshadow that of Dekker, both theme and treatment are as far
removed as possible from the native tradition of realism.

It is only natural, then, to find that Ford began his career
as an independent playwright with a purely romantic play, *The*
Lover's Melancholy. This is a tragi-comedy somewhat in the
Beaumont-Fletcher style, but marked by a gravity and sweetness of expression notably absent in later Fletcherian work. The
scene is laid in an imaginary Cyprus, and the characters bear
such Arcadian names as Palador, Parthenophil, and Cleophila.
The plot is a matter of slight importance; what counts is the
courtly atmosphere, broken at times by the intrusion of a set of
comic figures, but in the main sustained and gracious. Above

all, it is the music of Ford's verse, slow-moving, with pauses, echoes, and repetitions, that makes *The Lover's Melancholy* a delightful play. Ford is here rather the poet than the playwright; the action is slow in starting and often halted and confused by irrelevant intrusions. Yet in certain scenes where he is deeply moved by the situation, we feel already the hand of a master of his craft. The dénouement in particular is treated with a sober grace that is far removed from the sudden surprises and reversals common in most tragi-comedy. The source of Ford's interest in the strange characters of this play is, as a marginal reference (III, i) shows, Burton's *Anatomy of Melancholy*, 1621. This fascinating literary-medical study of abnormal mentalities exerted an influence upon the early seventeenth century comparable to the work of Freud today, and Ford more than any other Elizabethan dramatist responded to its appeal.

The Broken Heart is a better play than *The Lover's Melancholy*, but like its predecessor it remains for the most part on the same plane of unreality. The scene is laid in Sparta; a Prince of Argos and a conqueror of Messene are among the characters. These lands are not, however, the city-states of ancient Greece, but the kingdoms of Sidney's Arcadia; the name of Ford's Spartan king, Amyclas, for example, is lifted directly from Sidney's romance. On the other hand the dominant theme of the play: the separation of true lovers by the forced marriage of the lady to an unworthy mate, her lover's persistent claim upon her, and her resolute denial, was drawn from real life. Ford says as much in his Prologue:

> What here may be thought fiction, when time's youth
> Wanted some riper years, was known a truth.

The "truth" to which Ford alludes is the well known story of Philip Sidney's passion for Penelope Devereux, the unhappy wife of the brutal Lord Rich, rehearsed in Sidney's sonnet-sequence, *Astrophel and Stella*. Yet *The Broken Heart* is not merely a dramatic version of Sidney's poem; it takes the situation given in *Astrophel and Stella* and develops it to a tragic conclusion. For *The Broken Heart* is a true tragedy. In the Prologue Ford warns

his auditors not to expect the "apish laughter" of comedy, and
no other play of his is so free from the comic interludes which
too often jar upon his tragic strain. The plot is single: the
revenge of Orgilus for the thwarting of his marriage and the
consequent misery of his beloved Penthea. With this action is
interwoven, by way of contrast, the passion of Ithocles, who had
forced Penthea, his sister, into her unhappy marriage, for the
Spartan princess. It is the successful issue of this passion that
finally drives Orgilus to the murder which he considers no more
than an act of just revenge. This is a revenge play without a
villain; sympathy is almost equally divided between Orgilus and
Ithocles, whose wrong, committed before the action of the play
begins, is more than atoned for by the penalty, loss of love and
life together, which he is forced to pay.

The characters, like the scene, are in a sense Arcadian, but
Ford has created them with an imaginative power that raises
them far above the shadowy figures of Elizabethan romance.
Orgilus, with his brooding sense of wrong, his persistent claim
upon the lady he has lost, his vengeance, and his proud acceptance of his doom, is a very human figure. So too is Ithocles, the
noble soldier, whose courage leads him to defy the Prince of
Argos. Bassanes is a humour character, driven mad by jealousy
and restored to sanity when the cause for this passion is removed.
The princess, Calantha, is at once a strong and gentle figure.
She, like Penthea, dies of a broken heart, but with her it is the
sudden snapping of a cord unnaturally strained. Penthea is a
subtler piece of characterization. Introduced as the sad but
obedient wife of a jealous husband, she develops in the great
scene with Orgilus (II, iii) into a character of admirable purity
and sweetness. Her attitude of resolute chastity is exactly that of
Stella in Sidney's poem; she confesses her love, but repels her
lover. As the action proceeds, however, she rises to a height far
beyond that of Stella. Since she was in spirit the wife of Orgilus,
her forced marriage has branded her with the guilt of adultery,
and she implores her brother to put a swift end to her martyrdom
by death. It is characteristic of her tenderness that she not only
forgives him, but becomes his intercessor with the princess. That

task accomplished she has nothing left to live for; sleeplessness and voluntary fasting drive her down to melancholy madness and to death.

The Broken Heart is written entirely in verse. Ford was a true poet, and in this play he manages blank verse with admirable effect; when the action rises, the verse quickens into vigorous dramatic diction. Ford has few of those swift revelations of character in a phrase so frequent in Webster; yet he is a true dramatic poet. At times his verse has a hard metallic ring, as in Calantha's judgment on Orgilus:

> Bloody relater of thy stains in blood.

At times it seems to throb with emotion as in Penthea's lament after her repulse of her lover:

> He sigh'd my name, sure, as he parted from me:
> I fear I was too rough. Alas, poor gentleman,
> He look'd not like the ruins of his youth,
> But like the ruins of those ruins.

After all *The Broken Heart* is not a dramatic poem, but a play written for the King's Men at Blackfriars. It is in many ways a characteristic Blackfriars play with music, vocal and instrumental, and with ingenious use of spectacle.

Love's Sacrifice seems logically to follow *The Broken Heart*. It is an inferior play; yet it represents a certain progress in Ford's career. He has left the Arcadian scenes of his earlier plays to place the action in contemporary Italy. Bianca, Duchess of Pavia, resembles in name and rank Bianca Capello, Duchess of Florence, who had already appeared on the English stage in *Women Beware Women*. But there is more than this; the atmosphere of *Love's Sacrifice,* redolent of lust and blood, is nearer to that of *The Revenger's Tragedy* than to the somewhat rarefied air of *The Broken Heart.* Here is real life, the real life at least of Italy as English playwrights conceived it.

In spite of its atmosphere, however, *Love's Sacrifice* is not a revenge tragedy. It might more fitly be called a problem play, and the problem springs from the Astrophel-Stella story on which Ford seems to have been still brooding. Stella had confessed her love for Astrophel and had granted him every favor, except the last. Ford's answer to the question whether she had still retained her honor would surely have been in the affirmative. Suppose, however, that the situation had developed beyond the point where it was dropped in Sidney's poem: suppose that Stella's husband had given way to jealous rage, had laid violent hands on the lovers, and in so doing had brought about their deaths and his own. What then would have been the final verdict? Ford's answer is given in the dénouement of the play.

The main plot may be briefly summarized. The gallant courtier, Fernando, is desperately in love with Bianca, wife of the uxorious old Duke. She repels his advances so resolutely that he at last vows he never will renew his suit. Then with a sudden revulsion of feeling she comes to him by night, confesses her love, and offers herself to him, but only on condition that if he accepts her sacrifice, she will kill herself before morning. Convinced of her earnestness he masters his passion, and they part vowing to remain "chaste lovers." The continuance of this relation, however, was impossible in such a Court as that of Pavia. Urged on by a sister, jealous of Fernando's love, and by an Iago-like secretary, the Duke surprises the lovers, sends Fernando to prison, and in a fit of rage kills Bianca. Later in an interview with Fernando the Duke is persuaded of her innocence and orders a splendid funeral for the lady. When the doors of the vault are opened, Fernando is disclosed wrapped in a funeral winding-sheet; he forbids the Duke to enter a place sacred to Bianca's memory, and on the Duke's threat of violence takes poison and dies. Thereupon the Duke, lamenting the double loss of a chaste wife and an "unmatched friend," kills himself; love's sacrifice is complete.

Fantastic as the action is, a connection like that of Fernando and Bianca had been glorified in Sidney's poem and had been raised into a cult in the court of Charles I by the young Queen's patronage of Platonic love. Ford's conclusion seems to be that such a connection, though innocent in itself, was bound to provoke misconception and in the end to precipitate tragedy. With that it might be well to leave the fruitless discussion of the playwright's ethics. If the discussion, however, is shifted from ethics to esthetics, it is impossible to pronounce any but a severe judgment on *Love's Sacrifice*. The construction is confused and muddled; the offensive minor action of Ferentes, who gets three ladies with child and is murdered by them in a court masque, is probably meant to contrast with the idealized passion of the hero. There is little of Ford's poetry in this unpleasant play. On the other hand there is a large amount of prose rather carefully distributed among the villainous and comic characters. It is as if Ford by the use of this medium was endeavoring to shift the action from the high plane of *The Broken Heart* to one more nearly approaching common life.

In *'Tis Pity She's a Whore*, on the other hand, Ford attains his highest point in tragedy. Like *Love's Sacrifice* this play has a realistic background, that of an Italian city in the late Renaissance; but now Ford is no longer dealing with a fantastic problem but with a truly tragic theme. The repulsive nature of the theme, incest, and the unfortunate title of the play have done much to prevent an impartial estimate of the play's merits. These are, in fact, extraordinary. Never since Webster's *Duchess of Malfi* had a tragic poet struck with such power the strings of pity and of terror; never again in the brief period that remained to Elizabethan drama was a playwright to do so. The theme is handled with a high seriousness that contrasts strongly with the evasion of its consequences in *A King and No King*. It is, perhaps, this very seriousness that has led critics to cry out that Ford condones the sin and to cite as proof Giovanni's sophisticated defense of his action. It is not by single speeches, however, but by the conduct of the whole action that the standpoint of the author should be judged; and Ford's conduct of the action is clear enough. The sin of Giovanni and Annabella leads to bitter remorse on her part, to madness and to murder on his. That Ford sympathizes with the guilty lovers is clear; without such sympathy there could have been for him no tragedy; but to sympathize is not to condone.

The construction of the action shows Ford at his best. The minor actions of Soranzo and of Bergetto are woven into the main pattern; both are suitors for the hand of Annabella. Soranzo

is a villain who tries by threats and torture to drag out Annabella's secret. The harmless fool, Bergetto, is killed by a third
suitor who mistakes him for Soranzo, and the killer is pardoned
by a Prince of the Church because he is "nobly born." It is in
such a world that the brother and sister draw towards and
cling to each other.

The keynote of the play is struck in the opening scene in
Giovanni's avowal to his father confessor of his guilty love. The
character of Giovanni, the brilliant youth driven beyond self-
control by passion, is revealed alike in his words and in the
horrified reaction of the Friar. After a brief pause to introduce
Annabella, comes the great scene of the mutual confession of
love by brother and sister. It is one that might easily have been
ruined by the least taint of lubricity, but there is here only the
deadly earnestness of consuming passion; Annabella's "Love me
or kill me, brother" is echoed by his "Love me or kill me, sister."
The choice seems to lie between love and death; they chose love,
but the inevitable consequence is death for both. In the catastrophe Giovanni, driven to madness, kills his sister to save her
from Soranzo's vengeance, enters with Annabella's bleeding
heart upon his dagger—a dash of Marstonian sensationalism—
stabs Soranzo, and falls under the swords of hired assassins. Annabella's last word had been a plea for heaven's mercy; his, still
clinging to his infatuation, is a wish that he might rejoin his
beloved; the action closes on the note with which it opened, and
the final comment is that of the Cardinal: " 'Tis pity."

The fusion of high imagination and realism which Ford
vainly attempted in *Love's Sacrifice* is perfected in *'Tis Pity*. The
passion of the lovers stands out in bold relief against a background of everyday life: street brawls, marriage intrigues, and
lessons on the lute. Here are such characters as the babbling
Bergetto, the bawdy nurse, Putana, and the crafty servant, Vas-
quez. For their talk Ford uses prose, for the speech of the lovers
poetry of a high dramatic quality. Strip *'Tis Pity* of its poetry
and it sinks into little better than a story of abnormal lust.

These three plays, *The Broken Heart*, *Love's Sacrifice*, and
'Tis Pity complete Ford's contribution to Elizabethan tragedy.
After *'Tis Pity* he seems to have shifted to other genres. *The*

Queen, of uncertain date, is a tragi-comedy more or less of the Beaumont and Fletcher pattern, with a strong infusion of Burtonian melancholy. In *Perkin Warbeck,* Ford returns to the old-style chronicle play; "studies of this nature," says his Prologue, "have been of late out of fashion and unfollowed." What attracted his attention to this genre was his interest in the character of the pretender to the English throne. Ford chose to consider Perkin as a case of abnormal self-delusion, and represents him as a man so convinced of the truth of his claim that he plays at all times and with complete assurance a kingly part. Even when facing shameful death he retains a high nobility of soul, for death is "but a sound, a name of air, a minute's storm." It is the same spirit with which Ithocles and Orgilus meet their ends, and it is a striking evidence of Ford's creative imagination that he could transform the sorry rogue of his sources into so brave and self-assured a character. *Perkin Warbeck* is a creditable play, but it rises to real height only in the scenes which concentrate on the protagonist. It is, in fact, a psychological study thrown into dramatic form.

The two comedies that close Ford's career present a rather difficult problem. Differing so markedly as they do from all his earlier work they challenge an answer to the question why he chose this form of comedy and what end he proposed to himself. Perhaps an answer may be found in his friendly rivalry with Shirley and in his admiration for Jonson, "the best of English poets." Like Shirley's best work these plays are social comedies; the scene is laid in Italy, but characters and situations are essentially upper-class English, and like Jonson's comedies they are meant to carry a moral.

The Fancies, Chaste and Noble reveals Ford's predilection for a theme challenging the conventional morality of his age. The aging and impotent Marquis of Siena has gathered about him a bevy of young girls, the "Fancies," commonly believed to be little better than his private seraglio. As the action proceeds, however, it appears that common report is altogether wrong; the "Fancies" are "chaste and noble" ladies, nieces of the Marquis whom he is training for their entrance into courtly life. In the final scene the marquis throws off the cloud of secrecy which has aroused suspicion, and the play ends with a pair of weddings. The implied moral is that appearances are deceitful. This is a well-worn commonplace, but Ford presents the obverse of the old proverb: all that glisters is not gold. He shows that metal thought base may prove pure ore; the "Bower of Fancies" is an innocent school of manners; and two suspected ladies turn out to be above reproach.

The *Lady's Trial* is a better but on the whole a disappointing play. The central theme, the vindication of a slandered lady's honor, is well adapted to a problem comedy, but it is obscured by the strange behavior of the chief characters. It is no common play of the innocent wife, the crafty intriguer, and the jealous husband; Ford's characters, Spinella, Auria, and Aurelio, rise high above the stock types in a comedy of intrigue. Their speech, except for a rare flash of direct dramatic expression, is remark-ably like a play of Browning's, less for what it says than for what it leaves unsaid, to be apprehended by the understand-ing reader. Ford's thesis seems to be that unfounded suspicion is as blame-worthy as slanderous accusation. If the main action could be detached from the rest of the play, it would stand as a final proof of Ford's originality and of his subtle characterization. Unfortunately it is interrupted repeatedly by the intrusion of a minor plot and the pranks of a group of Jonsonian humour characters.

Compared with most of his contemporary dramatists John Ford emerges as a rather definite personality. He was a gentle-man, something of a scholar, and an amateur rather than a pro-fessional playwright. In the Prologue to *The Lover's Melancholy* he speaks with an artist's scorn of

> Some that of late have made
> The noble use of poetry a trade,

and he more than once refers to his plays as the products of a leisure hour. An often quoted couplet from *The Time Poets*, 1656,

> Deep in a dump John Ford was got
> With folded arms and melancholy hat,

doubtless preserves a tradition of his reserved temperament. Yet he seems to have lived on good terms with his fellow playwrights, and his elegy on Jonson expresses high admiration of the old master. Amateur artist as he was, Ford stands high above the mob of gentlemen who wrote for the stage in the last days of Elizabethan drama. For one not unimportant thing he was a poet. The music of blank verse discovered by Marlowe and perfected by Shakespeare had later been ruined by increasing changes which destroyed the pattern and reduced it to a jangle of sweet bells out of tune. In Ford alone of Caroline playwrights do we catch an echo of the old strain, graver, more subdued, and with a certain dying fall:

> Parthenophil is lost and I would see him;
> For he is like to something I remember
> A great while since, a long, long time ago.

Ford's verse is neither declamatory like that of the imitators of Marlowe, nor conversational like that of the school of Fletcher. Perhaps in pattern it is nearest to the verse of Beaumont.

There is, moreover, a higher quality in Ford's dramatic poetry than his skill in the handling of blank verse. It is imbued with a sentiment that contrasts strongly with the striving of his contemporaries for witty epigrammatic expression. In the Prologue to *The Lady's Trial*, Ford protests against this modern mode:

> Wit, Wit's the word in fashion, that alone
> Cries up the poet.
>
> .   .   .   .   .
>
> The Muses chatter that were wont to sing.

A romanticist at heart, Ford keeps turning back to the storied past; he would sooner

> Sigh out a lamentable tale of things
> Done long ago, and ill done,

than "venture on a jest that can rail on another's pain." Throughout Ford's work there runs a strain of melancholy brooding that may be summed up in the half-title of his best-known play, *'Tis Pity*.

After all, however, Ford is not a dramatic poet, but a poetic dramatist, and it is as a dramatist that he should be judged. The usual charge brought against him, that he contributed to the decadence of the Elizabethan drama, may be dismissed. There is nothing to show that Ford was either a popular or an influential dramatist. His plays were not welcomed with a chorus of commendatory verses by fellow playwrights, nor were they in sufficient demand to warrant a reprinting. The sensationalism of his plays is a characteristic of Elizabethan drama from Kyd and Marlowe through Marston down to the end. Spectacle and the introduction of masquelike features of song and dance were well established on the stage before Ford set pen to paper. He used them as his fellows did, sometimes as in the last scene of *The Broken Heart* with a splendid effect. The real onus of the charge against Ford is, of course, the morbid atmosphere of his plays and their repulsive themes. Certain exceptions have to be made; there is nothing morbid about *Perkin Warbeck*, nothing repulsive in the theme of *The Lady's Trial*. As a result, these plays are as a rule set aside from the rest of Ford's work, while the heaviest guns are levelled at *'Tis Pity* and *Love's Sacrifice*, with an occasional shot at *The Fancies*. But it is a mistake to divide the work of a poet-playwright into praiseworthy and blamable sections. As a matter of fact there is a certain consistency in all the work of Ford, no matter into what dramatic genre a given play may fall. The thread that binds them all together is his interest in abnormal characters, and his curiosity in the outcome of unconventional relations. It is a mark of Ford's originality and of his independence of the dramatic fashions of his day that he chose to deal with such characters and such situations.

The three tragedies that form the central core of Ford's work reveal this dominating interest. In *The Broken Heart* Penthea becomes the victim of an obsession that she is guilty of adultery because of her loveless marriage. The problematic relation of Bianca and Fernando in *Love's Sacrifice* has already been discussed and Ford's attitude to this relation explained. In *'Tis Pity* the unnatural relation is pushed to the extreme in the incestuous love of brother and sister. If incest be a theme debarred from tragedy, this play suffers under an inhibition that would exclude also master works of Euripides, Racine, and Shelley. If the theme be allowed, the one further requirement is that the dramatist treat it with high seriousness and demonstrate its tragic consequences. This, certainly, Ford has done; it is a squint-eyed criticism that accuses him of justifying the sin by putting into the mouth of the sinner, a perverted character, a dramatically appropriate defense of his perversion. Less need be said of his other plays, but in them also Ford has left the impression of his own peculiar, curious, and powerful mind.

If the oft-quoted couplet (p. 249) gives anything like a true report of Ford's peculiar temper, it explains as nothing else does the chief weakness of his plays. The man who sat brooding alone with folded arms had none of Shakespeare's frank enjoyment of the follies and absurdities of ordinary mortals. The characters that alone interested Ford were gently born and bred; yet he had none of Fletcher's gay delight in the wanton excesses of the cavalier. The merry Muse of Comedy shrank away from the reserved and lonely aristocrat, John Ford. Yet since the conventions of the day demanded buffo roles for certain actors and funny scenes for the audience, Ford reluctantly pursued her, and dragged her by the hair, as it were, upon the stage. Little wonder that she emitted shrill and indecent screams. It is characteristic of the man that in the one play which he wrote with his "best of art" there is neither "apish laughter" nor "jests fit for a brothel." Fortunately for the reader the comic scenes elsewhere are so loosely connected with the main action that they may be passed over lightly with less than no loss. What remains after such omissions is more than worth while: lovely poetry, subtle psychology, and a profound pity for the unhappy lot of man.

CHAPTER TEN

THE CURTAIN FALLS: MASSINGER, SHIRLEY, DAVENANT; COURT MASQUES, SUMMARY

THE last period of Elizabethan drama coincides almost exactly with the reign of Charles I from 1625 to the outbreak of the Civil War and the closing of the theatres in 1642. One by one the old masters of the drama disappear from the scene. Fletcher died in the plague of 1625; Middleton shortly after in 1627. Apart from his *Staple of News*, 1626, Jonson's infrequent comedies were failures. There is nothing of Webster's that can be dated with any certainty in this period.

New names begin to appear: Brome, already treated elsewhere, maintains in workmanlike fashion the convention of realistic comedy; Ford comes to his own in a group of tragedies that belong in tone and temper to the Jacobean age. Shirley, whose activity exactly corresponds with this period, reflects on the one hand the tragi-comedy of the school of Fletcher, and on the other anticipates the advent of Restoration comedy. Davenant is more interesting as the transformer of the Elizabethan into the modern stage than as a playwright proper. The curtain is slowly falling as the great spectacle of Elizabethan drama draws to an end.

Perhaps the most characteristic mark of this period is the growing dependence of the drama on the Court and on courtly circles. The old public theatres, the Globe, the Fortune, and the Red Bull, still continued their activities, but it is noticeable that by far the majority of the new plays in this period were produced at the so-called private theatres. The prevailing high prices of admission tended to debar a large part of the old Elizabethan audience and to limit the attendance to wealthy groups. As a natural result the Caroline drama ceased to be national in the sense that the earlier Elizabethan had been. The rift in national unity already apparent in the reign of James deepened and widened as the catastrophe of civil war approached, and the drama, with a few exceptions, took its stand with the Court. The old chronicle play had long lost its appeal: its place was taken by a tragi-comedy especially concerned with court intrigue and the rise and fall of court favorites. Along with this comes the rise into prominence of a comedy of manners that sets its scenes in a better class of society, the lords and ladies, or at least the well-to-do and cultured citizens, of Shirley's plays. The satire of this comedy is directed on the one hand against the vulgarity of shopkeepers and merchants, and on the other against the foolish simplicity of country gentlemen and their wives.

It is wrong to label this period, as has often been done, with the stigma of moral degeneracy. The tone of courtly society was probably purer in the days of Charles than in those of his father, and Shirley's comedies are less gross than those of Middleton and cleaner of speech than those of Jonson. The tragedy of Massinger and Shirley is less extravagant and impossible than that of many earlier Elizabethans. Yet beyond a doubt the period is one of decline from the height reached by Shakespeare, Jonson, and Beaumont. The romantic impulse fades away and with it the inspiration of poetry. Playwrights seem to have lost the secret of writing good blank verse, and the prosaic rhythms of their dialogue are a poor substitute for the lovely music of the older masters. The closing of the theatres was after all the natural termination of a drama which had lost its universal appeal and become the mere diversion of a social class.

Philip Massinger was baptized at Salisbury, November 24, 1583. He was the son of Arthur, a gentleman in the confidential service of the Earls of Pembroke, patrons of literature and the drama. Arthur sent his son to Oxford, where young Philip stayed for three or four years, leaving without a degree about the time of his father's death in 1606. It is reported that he neglected the study of philosophy, *i.e.*, the formal logic taught at the universities, and "gave his mind more to poetry and romances." Certainly he gave his mind also to the study of the classics, for Massinger's plays show a remarkable familiarity with Latin prose and verse. In addition he seems to have acquired at Oxford or later a good reading knowledge of French and Spanish.

Presumably Massinger left Oxford to try his fortune in London, but we know nothing of him there for six or seven years. When we catch sight of him, it is in rather unhappy circumstances. In 1613 the actor Nat. Field, Daborne, one of Henslowe's hacks, and Massinger were under arrest, probably for debt. The three addressed a note to "our most loving friend, Mr Philip Hinchlow, esquire" requesting an advance of £5 on a sum of £10 still due on a play on which they were collaborating with Fletcher. Field remarks that he cannot play until released, which seems self-evident, and Massinger adds a pathetic postscript: "I have ever found you a true loving friend to me, and in so small a suite, it beeinge honest, I hope you will not fail us." It is pleasant to know that their "most loving friend" did not fail the distressed prisoners; a receipt still exists in which the go-between acknowledges the receipt of £5 "for the use of Mr Daboerne, Mr Feeld, and Mr Massinger."

In 1613, then, we find Massinger engaged along with Fletcher in furnishing plays for a company supported by Henslowe. In 1616 Massinger's friend, Field, became a leading actor in the King's Company, and from this time on for a period of six or seven years Massinger was working in close collaboration with Fletcher, sometimes along with Field, as in *The Knight of Malta* (pp. 201–2'), on plays for that company. In 1619 he and Field felt strong enough to produce without Fletcher's assistance a tragedy, *The Fatal Dowry*, for the King's Men. A few years later, *ca.* 1621–22, Massinger wrote for the same company his first unaided play, *The Duke of Milan*. Encouraged by its success he now began his career as an independent playwright; he seems to have written *The Maid of Honor*, of uncertain date, for a company playing at the Red Bull, where *The Virgin Martyr*, in which he joined with Dekker, had already, 1620, been produced. For the Lady Elizabeth's Company he wrote three plays in quick succession, *The Bondman*, 1623, *The Renegado*, 1624, and *The Parliament of Love*, 1624.

Soon after Fletcher's death in 1625 the King's Men recalled Massinger and from that time till his own death he was the playwright-in-chief of their company. He had already written, 1625–26, for Queen Henrietta's Men his most famous play, *A New Way to Pay Old Debts,* and a year later he gave that company his charming comedy, *The Great Duke of Florence.* Except for these two all the rest of Massinger's plays were produced by the King's Company. His last extant play, *The Bashful Lover,* was licensed for them in 1636. He seems to have written two others, now lost, after this date. One of them, *The King and Subject,* was submitted, 1638, by the Master of the Revels to King Charles for perusal, and the angry monarch wrote against a passage where the King of the play asserted his right to tax the subject arbitrarily: "This is too insolent and to be changed." Massinger did not live to see the final break between King Charles and his English subjects. He died quite suddenly in 1640. The King's Company gave him a formal funeral and laid him to rest, according to a contemporary poet, in the same tomb with his old master, Fletcher, in St. Saviour's, now Southwark Cathedral.

Massinger began his work for the theatre, as we have seen, under the wing of Fletcher; most of his collaboration with his master was in the latter's special field of tragi-comedy. It follows naturally that a good part of Massinger's independent work was also in this popular genre. Yet he is by no means a mere imitator of Fletcher; even in his tragi-comedies there is an absence of Fletcher's sensationalism, a dignity of speech and conduct, and a moral earnestness that mark them as his own. These characteristics appear more or less clearly in all his tragi-comedies, as an examination of some typical plays will serve to show.

The Bondman was in some ways his most successful play. It was promptly produced at Court and, unlike most of his plays, it attained a second edition. When it was revived by Betterton during the Restoration, the leading character became one of that great actor's favorite roles. Pepys saw it again and again; "there is nothing more taking in the world with me than that play," he notes. In one adaptation or another it lived through the eighteenth century and was played at Philadelphia in 1795 under the catching title of *The Female Patriot.*

The reason for this success is plain: *The Bondman* is a play on the grand scale, combining the ever popular themes of love and war. Laid in classic Sicily, the action has for a background the victory of Timoleon, one of Plutarch's heroes, over the invading Carthaginians. As an episode in this war Massinger introduces, quite unhistorically, a revolt of Sicilian slaves, planned and led by Marullo, the bondman, not so much for the sake of liberty as to win possession of his adored Cleora, a Sicilian lady. When, however, she comes into his power, he assures her of a love so pure that he will guard her from all outrage and return her unspotted to her betrothed, Leosthenes, a soldier with the army of Timoleon. When the revolt is crushed, Marullo is seized and condemned to death on the cross. Cleora's intercession for him and her visit to his prison provoke still more the wrath of the already jealous Leosthenes. The case comes to trial before Timoleon where Marullo reveals himself as Pisander, a noble Theban, who had disguised himself as a slave to live near Cleora. Leosthenes, on the other hand, is convicted of a breach of vows to Pisander's sister, a lady serving Cleora in a slave's disguise, and the play ends with a double marriage and the pardon of the slaves.

Fantastic as the action seems, it is given power and dignity by the sober eloquence of the dialogue and by the characterization of the two chief roles. Cleora is a noble lady whose patriotism moves the cowardly Sicilians to aid Timoleon in the war, and whose transfer of affection from Leosthenes to the bondman is no sudden act but carefully motivated. The bondman himself is drawn on the heroic scale; his disguise for love's sake goes back to incidents in the *Arcadia;* his unselfish passion and lofty bearing anticipate certain features of Restoration drama. The lingering influence of Fletcher appears in the farcical episodes where the slaves maltreat their late masters and more especially in a very broad scene where a wanton lady seduces her step-son.

Of all Massinger's tragi-comedies *The Maid of Honor* is the best example of his skill in construction, his decisive, if limited, power of characterization, and his moral earnestness. Starting from a mere anecdote and a long oration in Painter's *Palace of Pleasure (Camiola and Roland)*, he has built up a well-made play with various additions of his own to intensify and vary the dramatic interest. The rich widow of the source becomes the charming maid of the play, and the affection existing between her and the hero adds a love-interest to the action. The Duchess of Siena, whose sudden passion for the hero explains without excusing his desertion of the maid, is a new figure in the story. Most important of all, the surprise ending in which the heroine takes the veil is Massinger's improvement of the tame and impotent conclusion of the source.

There is in this play, too, a realistic treatment of character which raises the figures above the idealized or merely typical characters of most tragi-comedies. The four suitors of the maid are sharply distinguished: the foolish Sylli, a humour character; the insolent royal favorite, Fulgentio; the devoted and humble Adorni; and the impetuous and fickle Bertoldo. Camiola, the maid, is Massinger's masterpiece. She is no creature of impossible virtue, but a very human woman, modest, loving, and brave. Her peculiar characteristic is a confident self-respect which enables her to withstand the frown of the King and to plead her cause before hostile judges with complete assurance. What she lacks, and it is a want that seems to spring from Massinger's own temperament, is a strain of feminine tenderness. No tragi-comedy in Elizabethan drama is marked with so strong a note of moral earnestness. This appears especially in an alteration of the source which furnishes the key-note of the play. There is no reference to the Knights of Malta in Painter; Massinger's bestowal of their cross upon Bertoldo makes his suit to Camiola a breach of vows; a dispensation may indeed be obtained, but

> When what is vowed to heaven is dispensed with
> To serve our ends on earth, a curse must follow.

It is Camiola herself who speaks thus; yet in her eagerness to free her lover from prison and win him for herself she forgets this truth, and the curse that she has foreseen follows, her betrayal and the wreck of all her hopes. The play does not end as a typical tragi-comedy might, with a reconciliation of the lovers, but with Bertoldo's repentance and with her renunciation of the world. The grave beauty of the verse with which the priest inducts Camiola into the religious life brings to a fitting end a play in which tragi-comedy is stretched to the very verge of tragedy.

Only four plays by Massinger can be classed as comedies, and the first and the most famous of these, *A New Way to Pay Old Debts*, is a serious drama rather than a comedy in the ordinary sense of the word. The success it attained at first was due in part, at least, to its presentation of the detested Sir Giles Mompesson, an upstart tool of Buckingham, in the person of the protagonist, Sir Giles Overreach. After its revival in the mid-eighteenth century it became the vehicle for a succession of great actors and has outlived on the stage all other Elizabethan plays except some of Shakespeare's.

There is nothing especially new or original in *A New Way*. It is an amalgam of tested stage devices skilfully combined by a master craftsman. The trick by which Wellborn obtains money to pay his debts from an uncle who has ruined him is that employed by Witgood in Middleton's *A Trick to Catch the Old One* (p. 161). It may be noted, however, that Massinger substitutes a noble lady for Middleton's courtezan and throughout raises the atmosphere far above the sordid city intrigue of the older play. Jonson rather than Middleton is Massinger's model in *A New Way*. This appears most plainly in the various humour characters that enliven the serious action, characters labelled, as in Jonson, by distinguishing names: Greedy, Marrall, and Furnace, the cook. More important is the fact that here, as in Jonson's *Volpone*, Massinger has chosen as the theme of a serious comedy the exposure and overthrow of a villain on the grand scale, and has made the villain's overweening self-confidence the prime cause of his downfall. Yet again there is a striking difference between these plays: Jonson sets the scene in Venice and heartily enjoys the tricks that Volpone plays upon the rascals that surround him. Massinger on the other hand lays the action in the England of his own day, all but identifies his leading character with a notorious contemporary, and for the devices by which the upstart Sir Giles has attained wealth and power has nothing but unbounded scorn.

A New Way is a comedy of intrigue. The intrigue, to be sure, is rather mechanical; there is a little too much of the familiar

Elizabethan conventions, the aside and the overheard conversation. The plot, indeed, starts with a whisper whose purport is only gradually revealed. On the other hand there is an admirably realistic presentation of life among the gentlefolk of the English countryside, disturbed and threatened by the intrusion of a rich and ruthless city usurer; Sir Giles has bought his knighthood and seeks to wed his daughter to a lord. Most of the characters who take part in this life are rather conventional types; it would be hard to find a tamer pair of lovers than young Allworth and his Margaret. Wellborn, in the ever-popular role of the prodigal who redeems himself by his wit and high spirit, is clearly drawn, but Massinger concentrates all his powers upon the person of Sir Giles. One trait in particular distinguishes him from the familiar usurer of comedy, his savage courage; Sir Giles is the wolf incarnate. On the whole it may fairly be said that *A New Way* is a play for the theatre rather than the study; its remarkable career upon the stage testifies to Massinger's excellence as a professional playwright.

The City Madam is in a sense a companion-piece to *A New Way*, a realistic comedy of contemporary life. Here the satire is directed, as the title shows, against the vanity of citizens' wives who strive to ape their betters at the Court. The theme recalls one of the motifs of *Eastward Ho* (pp. 99–100), but the milieu differs. Instead of the modest shop of Touchstone the scene is laid in the home of a merchant prince, Sir John Frugal; and it is his wife who serves as the butt of Massinger's attack. In a complicated intrigue, Sir John's brother, Luke, at once hypocritical and avaricious, is made to reveal his true nature as well as to humble the pretensions of the city madam. The device by which this is accomplished had a special interest in the days of early American colonization. Sir John and two friends disguised as Indians from Virginia present themselves to Luke, temporarily in possession of his brother's wealth, and persuade him to hand over Lady Frugal and her daughters to be offered as human sacrifices to the Devil whom the Indians are supposed to worship. The scene in which Luke's perfidy is exposed is sensational and spectacular beyond what one expects in realistic comedy, but this was a Blackfriars play and that audience had to be satisfied.

With all its faults there is good acting stuff in *The City Madam,* and in one adaptation or another it held the stage well into the nineteenth century.

The Great Duke of Florence differs widely from these realistic comedies. "A comical history" Massinger calls this play, and that is an exact description. An old legend that passed for authentic has been re-shaped into romantic comedy. This is the tale of the Saxon King Edgar and his faithless friend, Ethelwald, who, sent to report on the beauty of a prospective bride for the monarch, brought back a false report, and married the lady himself. All the early versions of the legend bring it to a tragic conclusion, but in the last decade of the sixteenth century, an unknown playwright worked it into a play, *A Knack to Know a Knave,* and gave it for the first time a happy ending. Massinger no doubt knew this play and hit upon the happy idea of re-working its scattered historical episodes into a comedy of the latest Fletcherian fashion.

He retains the original motif, the deception of a prince by his trusted friend, but all else is changed. The Saxon King becomes an Italian Grand Duke; and a complicated intrigue develops about his supposed desire to marry the lovely Lidia, the messenger's sudden passion for her, and the true and tender affection that really exists between the lady and the Duke's heir and nephew, Giovanni. This theme of a young and virtuous love is a new note introduced into the tale and gives rise to the most charming scene in the play, where Lidia obtains from the angry Duke a full pardon for both Giovanni and the messenger. *The Great Duke of Florence* is an admirable example of Massinger's art, not only of construction but of characterization: Giovanni is a finished portrait of the modest and accomplished prince, and Lidia the most charming of Massinger's young women. The dialogue is couched in easy, fluent verse that strikes more often than in Massinger's other comedies the true poetic tone.

It was, of course, only natural that Massinger during his long connection with the King's Company should from time to time supply them with a tragedy. Tragedy, to be sure, was not exactly Massinger's forte: he lacked both the piercing insight into human nature and the poetic expression of passion that go to make a tragic dramatist. What he did for the most part was to take old and tested themes, re-shape them in well-ordered form, and heighten them with a dash of the surprise and sensation that he took over from tragi-comedy.

This, at least, is certainly the case in *The Duke of Milan*. The main source is the old story of Herod's infatuation for his wife, Mariamne, of his jealousy, leading in the end to her murder, and of his subsequent remorse and madness. This tragic theme has repeatedly been presented in dramatic form, but no one has taken such liberties with the source or recast it so completely to suit contemporary taste as Massinger. In the first place he shifts the scene to Renaissance Italy, the natural background for later Elizabethan tragedy, and Herod of Jewry becomes Duke Sforza of Milan. Still more important for the conduct of the action, he invents an intriguer, Sforza's trusted friend Francisco, to heighten the Duke's jealousy and push him on to murder. This character, plainly taken over from Shakespeare's Iago, has, however, a stronger motive for action than any of Iago's. It transpires in the last act that Sforza had long since seduced and deserted Francisco's sister, so that his plot against the Duke is motivated by revenge. And this revenge is accomplished in a most sensational fashion; disguised as a Jewish doctor and his servant, brother and sister paint the hands and lips of the dead wife with poison; Sforza, madly believing that she still lives, covers them with kisses and falls dead. This startling scene, lifted from the anonymous *Second Maiden's Tragedy*, 1611, ends the play with an effective *coup-de-théâtre*.

Perhaps the chief defect of the play is the absence of a tragic hero. Sforza, the protagonist, is an impossibly inconsistent character; his dotage in the first act exceeds that of Antony; his behavior before the Emperor is that of a brave and prudent statesman, but he has only to meet the Duchess again to relapse into insensate folly. He is an effective stage figure, but far from a convincing or sympathetic character. None the less *The Duke of Milan* is a play that does credit to Massinger's workmanship. The three strands: the Herod story, the Italian setting, and the revenge intrigue, are woven together into a well-constructed whole. The action moves steadily on from scene to scene with little interruption or relapse into comic interlude. The dramatic dialogue, for the most part grave and dignified, rises into real eloquence in the strongest scenes.

Had *Believe as you List* come down to us in its first form, we should have had perhaps the most interesting and appealing of Massinger's tragedies. But the history of this play is one of the strangest in Elizabethan drama. Some time in 1630 Massinger planned a play to rival *A Game at Chess* (pp. 168–70) in voicing a national protest against a peace with Spain which abandoned the cause of Elizabeth of the Palatinate, sister of King Charles. When, however, he submitted his manuscript to the Master of the Revels, Herbert, who well remembered the scandal caused by Middleton's play, noted in his Office Book: "This day I did refuse to allow of a play of Massinger's because it did contain dangerous matter as the deposing of Sebastian, King of Portugal by Philip . . . there being a peace sworen twixte the Kings of England and Spayn." What Massinger had written was evidently a play telling the story of a man who claimed to be the Sebastian of Portugal who fell at Alcazar (p. 67) and whose kingdom was thereupon annexed by Philip of Spain. Such a claimant had indeed appeared in 1598, had been hounded from place to place by Spanish intrigue, and was finally seized and condemned to the galleys. Massinger's purpose, as Herbert perceived, was to draw a pathetic parallel between this Sebastian and Elizabeth's husband, Frederick, whose kingdom had been overrun and whose appeal for aid from England had been rejected.

On Herbert's refusal of a license Massinger subjected his play to a thorough revision and sent it to him again. This time it got by; on May 6, 1631, Herbert wrote on the submitted manuscript: "This Play, called Beleive as you liste may be acted." Acted accordingly it was by the King's Company, but there is no sign that it met with any great success. It was not published —quite possibly publication was forbidden—and it remained in manuscript for over two hundred years. It turned up at last in a sadly mutilated condition and was printed for the first time in 1849.

Even in the present imperfect form of the play it is possible to recognize what Massinger attempted and what he achieved. In revision he shifted the scene back to classical times; his Sebastian becomes Antiochus of Asia dethroned and persecuted by Rome, which now stands for Spain. In defiance of historic truth Massinger presents the tragedy of Antiochus in such a way as to suggest the tragic story of the supposed Sebastian. The Prologue confesses that the play draws near "a late and sad example" which "may move compassion."

Apart from its political significance *Believe as you List* has genuine dramatic and poetic value. The protagonist, Antiochus, a passive rather than an active hero, is a truly noble character, eloquent, patient in suffering, and confident in his assertion of his rights. His character is heightened by contrast with that of his persecutor, the Roman Flaminius, a true Machiavellian, ready to lie, to threaten, and to murder, in order to forward the policy of Rome. It is characteristic of Massinger's belief in poetic justice that in the last scene Flaminius is disgraced and imprisoned on the charge of taking bribes—a turn of events especially pleasing to patriotic members of the audience who recognized in Flaminius the portrait of a hated Spanish statesman.

Massinger published *The Roman Actor* in 1629 with a dedication stating: "I ever held it the most perfit birth of my Minerva." It follows that this play serves better than any other to express the author's conception of tragedy. Like most of his contemporaries he no doubt regarded tragedy as the highest form of dramatic art, and *The Roman Actor* is a pure tragedy with no trace of the comic scenes and humour characters which Massinger admitted into other serious plays. Moreover, it is a play on a theme drawn from classic history: Massinger comments in the dedication on the "gravity and height of the subject." Like Jonson Massinger was a devoted student of the classics, and a play like *Sejanus* may well have seemed to him a graver and loftier work than *Othello* or *Macbeth*. Like Jonson, too, Massinger was a careful architect of plot, and *The Roman Actor* is a masterpiece of construction.

The hero of the play is the famous actor, Paris, put to death by Domitian because of his supposed intrigue with the Empress. The action is composed of a number of episodes from the reign of Domitian so arranged as to bring out the contrast between the integrity of the actor and the nobility of a group of Stoics on the one hand, and the licentiousness and cruelty of Domitian on the other. Each act is a little unit in itself, building up to the final catastrophe. In the first Paris defends drama and the actor's art before the Roman Senate. In the second and third he performs at Court two playlets—dramatizations of episodes from Horace and Ovid—with such skill as to arouse the passion of the Empress. She arranges a private interview with him, "courts him wantonly," and is just breaking down his resistance when they are surprised by the Emperor. Domitian then commands a third performance, *The False Servant*, in which he takes part and kills Paris with his own hand by way of doing him honor in his death. In the last act Domitian is murdered by the Empress in revenge for the death of Paris.

There was, moreover, a special reason why Massinger should prefer this play. He was always a champion of the theatre, and the story of Paris offered him an opportunity to defend his art against the growing hostility of the Puritan party. This had lately, 1625, found voice in a summons to Parliament to "take once more into consideration this matter of stage-plays and . . . to restrayne them for ever hereafter." The eloquent defense of the drama uttered by Paris is perhaps the finest example of Massinger's dramatic rhetoric, and stage history shows that this speech was more than once singled out and recited by great actors. The contrast between the honest actor and the wicked ruler illustrates Massinger's belief that the drama should not merely entertain but teach a moral lesson.

Earnest and dignified as this play is, it is apt to leave a reader rather cold. Paris hardly evokes the sympathy due to a tragic hero; the Stoics who appear in the historical episodes are chorus figures rather than real characters; the Emperor, his wife, and the courtiers who surround them are almost incredibly vicious. A warm human interest is definitely wanting in *The Roman Actor*. For that we must turn to an earlier work by Massinger.

The Fatal Dowry, the joint work of Massinger and Field, published in 1632, must have been written long before, since Field was dead in August 1620. There is no known source for the twofold action of this play. The incident which starts the plot: the refusal by creditors to allow the burial of a bankrupt and the voluntary imprisonment of his son to secure a decent funeral, is told by Valerius Maximus of Miltiades and his son Cimon. It is possible that the second theme of the play: the condemnation of a guilty wife by her father and her execution by her husband, comes from a Spanish source; the insistence upon the point of honor by the husband seems peculiarly Spanish.

The scene is laid in Burgundy, but there is nothing specifically French or foreign in the atmosphere, and the characters are wholly English. Charolais, the hero, is the most finely conceived and fully realized character in all of Massinger's plays. The son of an old general and himself a soldier from his youth, there is nothing of the swaggering fighter in his nature. On the contrary he is modest, easily rebuffed, and ready to suffer rather than resent wrong, always provided that it inflicts no stain upon his honor. For this gentle soldier is dominated by a self-respecting pride as sensitive as an ascetic's conscience. His every action is dictated by his sense of that personal honor in which "all his life's joys and comforts were locked up." Yet there is nothing extravagant in his speech; he is no talker; he simply acts as honor bids him.

His friend, Romont, is the bluff, outspoken soldier common in later Elizabethan drama; but he is perhaps more realistically presented than any other of his class. His ruling passion is his devotion to Charolais, the son of his old commander. More active and self-assertive than his friend, it is his task to defend him from attack and to push him into action, and for this he is ready to risk even a breach of their friendship. He is loyalty incarnate in an outwardly repellent form.

Minor characters of less importance in the action are on the whole clearly depicted. Beaumelle has been criticized as "thinly drawn," but to have made her a stronger character would have turned the tragedy into hers rather than her husband's. This is, indeed, exactly what happened when Rowe adapted this play to the sentimental taste of the eighteenth century and re-baptized it *The Fair Penitent*. It is the very frivolity of Beaumelle that makes her illicit amour consistent and credible. It is only when her eyes are opened by her fall that she becomes for the one scene of her trial and death a pathetically tragic figure, bold enough to have been a strumpet, yet daring not to live one.

The Fatal Dowry is a tragedy less of stage types than of life-like men and women. This may be due to the influence of Field, but the hand of Massinger is seen in the firm construction of the play and in the ethical earnestness of its tone. Despite his evident sympathy with Charolais, Massinger will not glorify him as a romantic hero or condone his self-willed exaction of justice. The death of Charolais and the banishment of Romont serve as a "sad precedent" to teach the world that private wrongs are not to be redressed except by duly constituted judges.

Massinger was not a man of letters who also wrote for the stage, like Greene or Jonson. He was a professional playwright and nothing else. It is by his success, then, as a dramatist that he should be judged. In his own day he seems to have barely derived a living from his plays. The truth is that Massinger was in various ways out of touch with his time. He was in constant opposition to the pacificist policy of the Stuarts and was more than once in trouble with the censor on this account. He was no less opposed to certain features of the Government's internal policy, to the granting of monopolies by which Court favorites were enriched at the expense of the public, and to the levying of arbitrary taxes. He was too serious to condone the extravagance and frivolity of the Court. On the other hand he disliked the rise to social and political power of the wealthy citizen class and he dreaded the increasing attack of the Puritans upon the theatres. He was, in other words, an outspoken English conservative.

As a playwright, too, Massinger is, on the whole, conservative. There is little in his work of the spectacular and masque-ike element so conspicuous in Caroline drama. He was, to be ,ure, a disciple of Fletcher, but he lacked Fletcher's love of fun and easy disregard of morals. On the other hand, he was an admirer of Jonson, whose work was already ceasing to attract the public by the time that Massinger established himself as an independent dramatist. Jonson's influence appears not only in the humour characters so frequent in Massinger but in the careful construction of his plays and still more in the critical morality that pervades them.

In his long and busy career Massinger wrote every type of drama known to his day. Yet he is not really successful in either of the extremes, passionate tragedy or laughing comedy. He is at his best in serious drama, whether it be called comedy, as *A New Way*, or tragi-comedy, as *The Maid of Honor*. Here his artistry, his interest in ethical problems, his turn for dramatic argument stand him in good stead. His partiality for trial scenes and formal speeches is characteristic of a playwright interested rather in discussion than in action. He has been called the stage-poet, but he has, in reality, less claim to this title than his master, Fletcher, or his contemporary, Ford. His verse is even, regular, often stately and impressive, but it lacks lyrical charm and dramatic fire. He is rather the master-craftsman of drama than the dramatic poet. His judgment in selecting an interesting theme, his skill in presenting it in dramatic form, his command of effective situations and playable characters give him a high rank among Elizabethan dramatists. The continued success upon the stage of certain of his plays long after those of his contemporaries had vanished from the boards testifies to the achievement of this serious, conscientious, and self-respecting artist.

James Shirley, Massinger's successor as chief dramatist to the King's Company, came rather late to the business of playwriting. The son of a London merchant, he was baptized on September 7, 1596. He enjoyed four years of classical education at the Merchant Tailors' School, and then entered St. John's College, Oxford, but left it for St. Catherine's, Cambridge. The story goes that Laud, then presiding at St. John's, informed Shirley, who was studying for church orders, that he could not consent that a man disfigured with "a large mole on his left cheek" should ever "take the sacred functions upon him." Apparently the authorities at Cambridge were not so scrupulous, for after leaving that university he became a parish priest in or near St. Albans. It is supposed that he left the Church of England for that of Rome; certainly he gave up his parish, and after a few years came to London, ca. 1625, where he "lived in Gray's Inn and set up for a play maker."

His first play, *Love Tricks, or the School of Compliment,* was produced early in 1625 by the Queen's Company at the Phœnix, a private theatre. It is an absurd medley of intrigue, pastoral, Jonsonian humours, and satire, but it seems to have hit the public taste, and its success definitely established Shirley as a playmaker. His biography from this time until the closing of the theatres consists of little more than the chronology of his plays.

Shirley was so prolific a playwright that the mere enumeration of his plays with their dates would occupy too much space here. He maintained his connection with the Queen's Company for a dozen years or so, furnishing them with tragedies, comedies, and tragi-comedies as they required. *The Wedding* was the first of his plays to appear in print, 1629, heralded by commendatory verses by Ford and others. His first typical comedy of manners, *The Witty Fair One,* 1628, was published in 1633. A comedy of manners, *The Ball,* 1632, published in 1639 by a strange error as the joint work of Chapman and Shirley, provoked the following comment from Herbert: "In the play of *The Ball* . . . there were divers personated so naturally, both of lords and others of the court, that I took it ill, and would have forbidden the play, but that Biston [Beeston, manager of the company] promiste many things that I found faulte withall should be left out and that he would not suffer it to be done by the poett any more, who deserves to be punisht." Sir Henry certainly was a stricter censor than any of his predecessors. This appears in another note of his a year later: "The comedy called *The Yonge Admiral,* being free from oaths, prophaness, or obseanes, hath given mee much delight and satisfaction in the readinge, and may serve for a patterne to other poets. . . . When Mr Sherley hath read this approbation I know it will encourage him to pursue this beneficial and cleenly way of poetry." This play was acted at Court, November 19, 1633, and, according to Herbert, "likt by the K. and Queen." It was followed at Court a few months later, February, 1634, by *The Gamester,* "made by Sherley," Herbert notes, "out of a plot of the King's . . . and well likte. The King said it was the best play he had seen for seven years."

As a Court favorite Shirley naturally took its side in the pros-

ecution of Prynne for his alleged libellous attack on Queen Henrietta. His comedy, *The Bird in a Cage*, was published in 1633
with an ironical dedication to Prynne, then undergoing a sentence of life imprisonment. It was fitting that Shirley, an inmate
of Gray's Inn, should be chosen to write the text of the magnificent masque, *The Triumph of Peace*, which the four Inns
of Court presented to the King and Queen in February 1634 as
a proof of their loyalty. This was the most sumptuous and extravagant show ever seen in England; Inigo Jones devised the
scenery, and Lawes, Milton's friend, composed in part the music.
Shirley's text was published in three separate editions in this
year, a proof of his success and popularity.

In May, 1636, after an outbreak of plague in London, the theatres were closed, except for a brief period in the following
winter, until October, 1637. Shirley left London for Dublin
where the great Earl of Strafford was holding almost regal court.
In Dublin Shirley attached himself to Ogilby's theatre, for which
he revised old plays, wrote prologues, and composed several new
plays.

On his return from Ireland in the spring of 1640 Shirley
was invited by the King's Company to take over the post of playwright-in-chief which had been left vacant by the death of
Massinger. For this company he wrote some five or six plays,
including his fine tragedy, *The Cardinal*, 1641. With one exception, *The Doubtful Heir*, they were produced only at Blackfriars; that play was also staged at the Globe. For this performance Shirley wrote an amusing, if rather supercilious, prologue
asking the "grave understanders," *i.e.*, the groundlings, to excuse
the absence of "target-fighting, bawdry and ballads" in his play,
which was not meant for their "vast stage." Throughout his
career Shirley had been writing for the small and select audiences of the private theatres. His last play, *The Court Secret*,
was "never acted but prepared for the scene at Black-Friers."

With the closing of the theatres Shirley's occupation was
gone. He served in some capacity in the King's army under that
patron of letters, the Duke of Newcastle. With the overthrow of
the King's cause he returned to London, where he resumed for
a time his old vocation as schoolmaster. Yet he had not lost inter-

est in the stage. He penned the *Address to the Reader* prefixed to the 1647 Folio of Beaumont and Fletcher, congratulating the purchaser that "in this tragical age" he yet had liberty to read, if not to see, "these inimitable plays." He was allowed to present a masque, *Cupid and Death,* to the Portuguese Ambassador, 1653; and six years later a dramatic exhibition, *The Contention of Ajax and Ulysses,* was "nobly represented by young gentlemen of quality at a private entertainment."

It is pleasant to know that Shirley's last years were not overcast by poverty. His will, drawn in July, 1666, shows him leaving handsome bequests to five children and the remainder of his estate to his "loving wife," Frances. Mrs. Shirley, however, did not live to enjoy this bequest. The great fire of London, which broke out in September of that year, drove the Shirleys from their house into the parish of St. Giles in the Felds, "where, being in a manner overcome with affrightments, disconsolations and other miseries . . . they both died within the compass of a natural day: whereupon their bodies were buried in one grave."

Shirley belongs in the main to the school of Fletcher, and about a third of his plays are classed as tragi-comedies. They are that, however, with a difference; Shirley's genius ran rather towards comedy than tragedy, and it is not always easy to distinguish his so-called tragi-comedies from his romantic comedies, or these, in turn, from his comedies of manners.

The Young Admiral approaches nearly Shirley's typical tragi-comedy. There is but one action, based in tragi-comic fashion on the clash between love and honor, honor standing here for love of country. While Vittorio, the young admiral, wins victory for his country abroad, a lascivious prince plots against him at home to win the favor of Vittorio's mistress. Driven into exile, Vittorio and his lady fall into the hands of the enemy, and he is offered the choice of fighting for them against his country or seeing his beloved put to death. Love wins the day, but he is checked with a message that an attack on his country will bring about the instant death of his father, a prisoner of the wicked prince. As if this were not enough, Vittorio is led to doubt the virtue of his lady and implores the hostile King to order her death and his. At last, however, the daughter of this King, in love with the wicked prince, contrives a stratagem that brings about peace, clears the honor of Vittorio's lady, and wins the prince for herself. There is no death in the play; yet various characters come near it, as the opposing Kings of Naples and Sicily are given to shouting, like Alice's Queen of Hearts, "Off with his head."

The charming play of *The Royal Master* is, perhaps, the best example of Shirley's art in the blending of romantic comedy and tragi-comedy. The central theme of the plot is the pretty story told by Boccaccio of the love of Lisa for King Pedro of Sicily. It is a tale that has attracted others since Shirley; George Eliot retold it in a sentimental Victorian poem, *How Lisa Loved the King*, and Musset dramatized it in his pleasant comedy, *Carmosine*. Both these authors keep closer to the simple structure of the tale than Shirley, who embeds it in an elaborate plot of court intrigue. Not only that, but he makes considerable changes in the story; Shirley's King is a widower, so that it is possible for the deluded girl not only to love but to dream of wedding him. Shirley invents a new character, the Duke of Florence, a suitor for the King's sister, who turns from her to court the girl, re-baptized Domitilla, in the play. The angry princess threatens Domitilla's life, but is appeased when she learns that the girl cares not for the Duke, but loves the King. The dénouement, less gentle and chivalric than in Boccaccio, is dramatically most effective. Learning of the girl's infatuation, the King proceeds to cure her by proposing in the plainest terms to make her his mistress. In shocked revulsion she turns from him to accept the hand of a young noble who has sprung to her defense. The court intrigue in which this tale is set revolves about the figure of Montalto, the King's favorite, a true Machiavellian. His plot, which involves the honor of the princess and even the life of the Duke, gives a tragi-comic tone to an otherwise purely romantic play. Exposed at the end, he is let off in conventional fashion with the light sentence of banishment.

The especial charm of the play lies in the character of Domitilla; young, innocent, and high-spirited, it seems to her no miracle that the King should stoop to court her—girls of lower station, she knows, have become the brides of kings. Her passion for her royal master is but the day-dream of an innocent child, quickly conceived and easily dispelled. The whole action is cast in Shirley's most graceful and courtly verse.

The Witty Fair One, an entertaining comedy of manners, is a clever amalgam of Middletonian intrigue and Jonsonian humours, but it has something of Shirley's own. This is the character of Penelope, the witty fair one, the first of Shirley's girls who, by a combination of wit and virtue, succeed in converting their would-be seducers into suitors for their hands in honest marriage. The trick that Penelope plays on Mr. Fowler recalls that which Fletcher's Mary played on Monsieur Thomas. She admits him, flushed with hope of conquest, to her bedside in a darkened room; but where Mary triumphs by presenting to Tom a blackamoor sleeping in her bed, Penelope lures Fowler on to a further exhibition of his licentiousness only to expose him to open shame. Fletcher's device is a part of his unabashed delight in farcical fun; Shirley's carries something of a moral with it. That Penelope later accepts him as a husband when he "wakes to virtue" is not precisely in accord with Victorian standards, but passes very well in Elizabethan comedy.

In *Hyde Park,* 1632, a play acted at the opening of that pleasure ground to the London public, the witty fair one reappears, this time in a double role. The witty part is played by Mistress Carol, a direct descendant of the scornful lady of the Beaumont-Fletcher comedy. Her humour is to mock her lover, on whom she plays trick after trick till at last, fearing to lose him, she consents to marry him at once. The other role is that of the modest Julietta. Exposed to the wanton pursuit of a young lord, she succeeds in converting him, not by any trick, but by a straightforward appeal to his honor. More interesting than the complicated plot of this play is the realistic background: the sports in Hyde Park, foot-races and horse-races while the spectators lay bets, the gentlemen in gold pieces, the ladies in silk stockings and perfumed gloves. When Pepys saw the first performance of a revival of this play, horses were actually brought upon the stage. This was of course impossible in the small private theatre where *Hyde Park* was produced, but the animation of the dialogue is such that we almost see the horses.

The Lady of Pleasure, 1635, is Shirley's most fully developed comedy of manners. Two distinct actions are neatly joined together to bring out his main purpose. This was apparently to draw a contrast between extravagance and liberality, between licentiousness and innocent gayety. These opposing moods are represented by Lady Bornwell, the wife of a country gentleman, and Celestina, a young, rich, and lovely London widow. Lady Bornwell has come to town to indulge a reckless extravagance in complete disregard of her husband's wishes and of his purse. She gathers a crowd of pretended fashionables about her, stoops to a low intrigue with one of them, and is moved to repentance and reform only when her eyes are opened to her husband's impending ruin and to her own shame. Celestina, on the other hand, uses her wealth to draw together a better society; she has a keen eye to expose the impostors whom Lady Bornwell's jealousy sets on to abuse her. Her character portrait of the unnamed Lord reveals her ideal—which of course is Shirley's—of true nobility; she tests his constancy to the memory of his dead wife, and when for a moment he wavers and seeks her for his mistress, she recalls him to virtue by an appeal to his ancestral honor. Along with this serious theme goes a group of scenes exploiting various humours, among them a lad fresh from Oxford, plunged into the dissipation of the town by the folly of his aunt, Lady Bornwell. These add, of course, to the gayety of the performance and keep it from becoming a serious and sentimental sermon.

Shirley himself thought well of this play: he calls it in his dedicatory epistle "one that may challenge a place in the first form of the author's compositions." This was, perhaps, because of its moral purpose, in which it approaches the comedy of Jonson, though the tone is lighter and the atmosphere is more like that of Fletcher. But Shirley lacked Jonson's mastery of construction, and there are several defects in the conduct of the action. There seems no need for Lady Bornwell to employ a bawd to promote her intrigue; the business of witchcraft and deviltry which she devises to lure Kickshaw to her arms is quite unnecessary; and Shirley's easy condonation of her adultery is unparalleled in earlier Elizabethan drama. The characterization of Celestina, Shirley's conception of a lady moving unstained in a dissolute society, is not always consistent. The volte-face of the Lord, when he entreats her favor in a high-flown speech, is not motivated, but merely invented to give Celestina an opportunity to show her wit in a clever parody, and her honor in recalling him to his own. In spite of these faults, more noticeable in the study than on the stage, *The Lady of Pleasure* is a graceful, swift-moving, and highly entertaining comedy.

The Gamester is a more realistic comedy of manners; but its main action, a domestic drama, is diversified by a romantic subplot and some scenes of farcical comedy. It is, in fact, a brilliant piece of stage-craft which not only won the applause of the King, but held the stage in various adaptations well into the nineteenth century. The action is swift and lively, and there is a vivid background in the drinking and gambling scenes.

As a professional playwright Shirley was, of course, called on from time to time to furnish his company with a tragedy, and he was craftsman enough to turn out occasionally a good acting piece of this genre. Some half dozen of his plays may be classed as tragedies; one or two, like *The Duke's Mistress*, hover on the brink between tragedy and tragi-comedy. There are, however, two that deserve attention as characteristic specimens of tragedy in the last days of Elizabethan drama.

The first of these is *The Traitor*, 1631. This is in a sense a historical drama since it relates the betrayal and murder of the first Duke of Florence by his kinsman and favorite, Lorenzo, or Lorenzino, de Medici. Shirley found this tale in the *Heptameron*. The story there tells how the Duke, madly in love with his favorite's sister, forced him on pain of death to play the pander. Rather than sacrifice the honor of his sister, however, the favorite with the aid of a bravo murdered the Duke at a rendezvous where he expected to meet the lady, and then escaped to Venice. The simple story of the source, however, did not satisfy Shirley's taste for elaborate intrigue. He proceeded to involve it in a complex plot built up of incidents from earlier plays, notably *The Maid's Tragedy*. In Shirley's play the lady whom the Duke pursues is the sister, not of his favorite, but of a gallant nobleman, Schiarra. In an effective scene she actually converts the wicked Duke. Later, however, he relapses and under the influence of Lorenzo once more attempts to win her. The situation has by this time become more critical; her brother has killed a gentleman who broke his engagement with the lady to wed another; arrested and threatened with death unless he will prostitute his sister, he feigns consent and kills her to save her honor. Her body is laid on a bed in Lorenzo's house where the Duke, thinking to enjoy her, discovers to his horror that he is embracing a corpse. Here he is surprised and killed by Lorenzo, who himself falls soon after in a combat in which he and Schiarra kill each other.

So brief a summary, while it brings out the complexity of Shirley's plot, quite fails to do justice to the play. The central figure, Lorenzo, the traitor, is a vividly drawn character. A master of dissimulation he persuades both the Duke and Schiarra that he is their devoted friend; it is not until the very end that Schiarra learns the truth and turns upon him.

The Traitor is an effective stage-play, but it falls short of tragic height and power. In his effort to elaborate and diversify the action, Shirley has spent so much time on the story of the sister's broken engagement and her brother's revenge that it obscures the main theme, the treasonous designs of Lorenzo. More important still, there is no development in the character of his protagonist: Lorenzo is introduced at the beginning as a traitor, and he remains such till the end. Shirley could hardly be expected to penetrate the character of the historic Lorenzino, but he might have made the motives of his action somewhat clearer. There is, in truth, no special reason why he should whet on the Duke in his pursuit of a virtuous lady unless he expected her brother to revenge her. But Shirley cannot allow any one but the protagonist to kill the Duke; nor can he, true to the tragic convention, allow the murderer to escape. In short Shirley gives us instead of the tragedy of a strangely blended character only a clever presentation of a villain in action.

The Cardinal, 1641, is in some ways a better play than *The Traitor*. Shirley, at any rate, thought so; "the best of my flock," he calls it in his dedication. There is no known source; it is said to be reminiscent of *The Duchess of Malfi*; but it is as superior to Webster's play in craftsmanship as it falls below it in tragic intensity. It seems possible that Shirley took over from Webster two leading characters, the distressed Duchess and the wicked Cardinal. About these two he wove a play which combines old and new elements, the old theme of revenge and the new complications of tragi-comedy. A threefold thread of revenge is woven into the structure of this play: the revenge of Colombo on the bridegroom, who has supplanted him with the Duchess; the revenge of the Duchess on the murderer of her husband; and the Cardinal's revenge on the Duchess herself, this last complicated by the fact that his revenge brings about his own death. There is a stronger concentration of interest in this play than in *The Traitor*; no side issue disturbs the central action, the contest between the love and craft of the Duchess and the dominating power of her opponent. The two minor figures who take part in this action recall somewhat two of the characters in Webster's play: the ruthless Colombo corresponds to Duke Ferdinand, the bitter Hernando who champions the Duchess, to Bosola. This, of course, is not to say that Shirley's people come to life as Webster's do: they are, after all, creatures of the theatre. But what superb theatre!

Here in the last year of Elizabethan drama is a tragedy that in breathless speed of action, thrilling situations, and crashing catastrophe can hold its own with any but the greatest masterpieces of that age. What it lacks, and the lack is an indication of Shirley's weakness, is a tragic hero. Sympathetic as the Duchess is, she cannot rise to the height of her sister in Webster's tragedy. Nor can the play be taken as the tragedy of the Cardinal; until almost the end he is a figure in the background never definitely characterized. His hideous purpose of revenge by rape and poison comes as a surprise and shock. In this respect, and in this alone, the absence of a central tragic figure like Lorenzo, does the play fall below *The Traitor*. Yet that so gentle a genius as Shirley's should have been twice capable of such near-great tragedies gives him no mean place among Elizabethan tragic poets.

Scholar, poet, gentleman, and Court favorite, Shirley occupies a peculiar position among Elizabethan playwrights. Like the old god Janus, he faces both ways, looking back upon the past glories of Elizabethan drama, and forward to the brilliance of Restoration comedy. He commanded all the resources of earlier drama and exploited them to the full; yet it would be wrong to call him a mere imitator. He is a student in the diverse schools of Jonson and of Fletcher, but he knows how to combine and assimilate what he draws from them to his own ends. His best work, his comedy of manners, is a union of Jonson's realistic observation and Fletcher's light-hearted gayety. It is in these plays that he anticipates the work of Restoration dramatists, but with a difference that is characteristic both of his audience and of his own temperament. Shirley wrote almost exclusively for the private theatres frequented by the courtiers, and there is as great difference between the gay, pleasure-loving Court of Charles I and the licentious and cynical society that surrounded the throne and imitated the manners of his son, as there is between the comedies of Shirley and those of Etherege and Dryden. This is especially evident in Shirley's favorite character, the witty fair one, the Caroline girl, frank, outspoken, fond of male society, but pure at heart, and capable not only of resisting temptation but of converting the tempter. There is something essentially feminine in Shirley's genius, easy, graceful, mildly satiric, and implicitly rather than emphatically moral. This appears too in the quality of his verse. Shirley is a true poet, but he never rises to the dramatic intensity of Webster or the poignancy of Ford. On the other hand, compared with Davenant and the courtiers who wrote for the stage in his day, Shirley is still the poet-playwright. And he is always the skilled dramatic artist, aptly selecting, combining, and elaborating his material into effective stage-plays.

Massinger and Shirley continued until the closing of the theatres the old tradition of the professional playwright supplying plays to established companies. This tradition, however, was broken in the last period of Elizabethan drama by the appearance on the scene of a group of amateurs who wrote primarily for the entertainment of the Court. Their competition was bitterly resented by the older professionals, more particularly when, as sometimes happened, these newcomers paid the actors to perform their plays, spent lavishly on costumes, and borrowed scenery from Court productions to enhance the public performance. These performances were given as a rule in the private theatres, and the professional playwrights for these houses found themselves obliged more or less to adapt their own work to the demand of the courtly audience that filled them. Few plays by these courtly amateurs have any interest except for special students; a brief mention of some of the most prominent will be sufficient.

Lodowick Carlell, a courtier and groom of the chamber, entertained the Court with a tragi-comedy, *The Deserving Favorite*, published in 1629 as "lately acted before the King's Majestie and since publickly at the Black-friers." His last play, *The Passionate Lovers*, a ten-act romance founded on a story told the author by King Charles, was performed at Whitehall and later at Blackfriars. A younger Cavalier, Thomas Killigrew, brought up as a page at Court, took part in private theatricals, turned playwright, and in 1635–36 furnished the Queen's Company with three romantic plays: *The Prisoners*, *Claricilla*, and *The Princess*. "Natural easy Suckling" is better known as a poet than as a dramatist, but he too joined the mob of gentlemen that invaded the stage. His first play, *Aglaura*, performed at Blackfriars, was so bloody a tragedy that for a later Court performance Sir John transformed it into a comedy, bringing the dead, all the main characters, to life and pairing the lovers off in happy marriage. It cost Suckling, gossip said, £300 or £400 to produce it, and its publication in folio form, a slender page of type between broad margins, roused the wrath of the hard-working Brome, who compared it to a baby lying in the great bed of Ware.

Cavalier courtiers were not the only amateurs of drama. Shirley has an amusing thrust in *The Witty Fair One* at the many Oxford and Cambridge scholars who come to London "like market-women with dossers full of lamentable tragedies and ridiculous comedies." The most successful of these scholars was William Cartwright, "the most florid and seraphical preacher of the university." His tragi-comedy, *The Royal Slave*, was performed by students of Christ Church before the King and Queen during their visit to Oxford in 1636. It so delighted their Majesties that by special request it was repeated at Court by professional actors. Another Oxford preacher and poet, Jasper Mayne, entertained the Court with a comedy, *The City Match,* which was later passed on to the King's Men for performance at Blackfriars.

One man serves as a link between these courtly amateurs and the professional playwrights. This is William Davenant, 1606–1668, the son of John, an Oxford tavern keeper, "a lover of plays and play makers, especially of Shakespeare who frequented his house on his journeys between Warwickshire and London." John, who died in 1622, left directions that William, then a youth of sixteen, should be apprenticed in London. William, however, had other views; he went to London indeed, but managed to secure a post as page in the household of Lodowick Stuart, Duke of Lennox, a cousin of King James. This is the beginning of Davenant's connection with the Court, one that continued and grew firmer throughout his long and active life. His first play, *The Cruel Brother,* was produced at Blackfriars in 1627. It seems to have been anything but a success, for his second attempt, *Albovine, King of the Lombards,* was rejected by the actors, and Davenant was forced to appeal to the public in print. The quarto appeared in 1629, heralded by a group of commendatory verses. In the meantime Davenant took part as a volunteer in two disastrous expeditions launched by Buckingham against France. Shortly after his return in 1629 he managed to get another play, *The Just Italian,* a tragi-comedy, produced at Blackfriars with only a doubtful success.

A long illness, caused by sexual indulgence and unskilful treatment, left Davenant with a disfigured nose which was to prove a source of malicious jests for the rest of his life. He was befriended at this time by Endymion Porter, a favorite of King Charles and a generous patron of the arts. This friendship stood Davenant in good stead, for the first play written after his recovery, *The Wits,* 1634, was so severely censored by the Master of the Revels that the poet used Porter's influence to appeal directly to the King. An amusing note in Herbert's office-book tells how King Charles went over the manuscript with him, pronounced "faith" and "slight," which Herbert had deleted as oaths, to be harmless "asseverations" and sent back the copy cor rected by the royal hand. It was produced at Blackfriars and later at Court, where Herbert notes grudgingly that it was "well likt."

A tragi-comedy, *Love and Honour,* played at Blackfriars and at Court by the King's Men in 1634, is the first of Davenant's plays to reflect the high-flown romanticism fashionable at the Court and to introduce him to the attention of the Queen. At her command he composed a masque, *The Temple of Love,* 1635, presented at Whitehall by the Queen and her ladies. In the published text Davenant, gracefully yielding precedence to Inigo Jones (cf. p. 131) who designed the setting, calls himself "her Majesty's Servant," a title he was to make good in later years by harder work than the composition of masques. A second masque, *The Triumph of the Prince D'Amour,* presented at the Middle Temple in 1636, was honored by the attendance of the Queen and her ladies.

News from Plymouth, a lively realistic comedy, was produced by the King's Men in their summer theatre, the Globe, in 1635, the only play by Davenant acted, so far as we know, in one of the old public theatres. *The Platonic Lovers,* a romantic comedy, followed in 1636 at Blackfriars. By this time Davenant had definitely established himself as poet and playwright, and after Jonson's death in 1637 he was granted a pension of £100 a year and generally recognized as poet laureate. His *Unfortunate Lovers,* a tragedy of blood relieved by a strain of sentiment, obtained a marked success; it was acted at Blackfriars, 1638, and twice before the Court. It was promptly revived at the Restoration and became a stock piece in the repertoire of the Duke's Company.

In 1639 he received permission to build a new theatre, and though the permission was later withdrawn, he was recompensed in 1640 by his appointment to be manager of the company at the Cockpit. In the same year he composed the last of the splendid Court Masques, *Salmacida Spolia,* in which both Charles and the Queen took part.

The outbreak of the Civil War put an end to Davenant's dramatic activity. He joined the King's army, was knighted at the siege of Gloucester, and took an active part in running supplies across the Channel. After the ruin of the royal cause and the execution of the King, Davenant joined the group of exiles about the Queen in Paris and divided his time between political intrigue and the composition of his long romantic epic, *Gondibert*. In 1650 he was appointed Governor of Maryland in place of Lord Baltimore, "who doth visibly adhere to the rebels in England." He set sail, but got no farther than the Channel when he was captured and confined in an English prison. Released, in 1652, by the intervention of a friend high in favor with Cromwell, he began to look about him for means of livelihood. His first step was to marry a French wife, apparently a lady of some means; his next, in defiance of the law against plays and players, was to organize a company to build a theatre. The project failed, of course, but the undaunted poet evaded the law by offering an "Entertainment . . . by Declamations and Musick . . . after the manner of the Ancients" at Rutland House. Even a government spy who attended the first performance, May 23, 1656, could report nothing objectionable, and Davenant was encouraged to proceed. He next put on what he called an "opera," *The Siege of Rhodes*, with music by Henry Lawes, and movable scenes. This was so successful that Davenant shifted his activity to his old theatre, the Cockpit, where in quick succession he produced *The Cruelty of the Spaniards in Peru* and *The History of Sir Francis Drake*, topics quite agreeable to Cromwell's government, at that time engaged in war with Spain. Growing bolder he now presented the second part of *The Siege of Rhodes*, 1659, a full-dress play, though still disguised under the name of opera. Rigorous Puritans grew alarmed, and a committee was ordered to take action against "plays—and things of the like nature called Opera." But the tide of Puritan rule was fast ebbing, and with the return of Charles II Davenant was free to take up his old profession of play-maker and theatrical manager.

His friend, Tom Killigrew, became the manager of the newly organized King's Company; Davenant presided over the Duke's Company playing in the old private theatre of Salisbury Court. His repertoire consisted largely of Elizabethan plays, Shakespeare's and others, sometimes acted in their original form, sometimes with unfortunate alterations. His own contribution consisted mainly in adaptations of old plays and in a couple of arrangements from the French. He died in 1668 and was buried in state in Westminster Abbey. His widow collected and published his works in a grand folio volume in 1673.

Three plays of Davenant's brief career, 1634-39, as a successful playwright in the last years of Elizabethan drama deserve some consideration. The first of these, *The Wits*, is a gay farce-comedy developing an action suggested, perhaps, by the title of Fletcher's comedy, *Wit without Money*. Two oldish country gentlemen come to town with the strange idea of living by their wits, especially at the expense of women. So far from succeeding they are tricked into all sorts of ridiculous situations, locked up in chests, and arrested by the city watch, through the superior wit-power of a man-about-town, the younger brother of one of the visitors. The complicated intrigue resembles that of a Middleton rather than of a Fletcher play, and some amusing city-watch scenes hark back to earlier realistic comedy. At the Court performance King Charles, Herbert says, disliked the plot and the characters. This is not surprising, since the plot is a mere assemblage of farcical incidents and the characters little better than a pack of fools and knaves. The younger brother, the main-spring of action, is a prototype of the Restoration rake, particularly in his behavior to his sweetheart. It is not surprising that this play carried over into the Restoration theatre. It had the unusual run of eight days when it was revived in 1661, and held the stage well into the eighteenth century. In fact *The Wits* anticipates certain features of Restoration comedy in its lively dialogue ranging from witty epigram to coarse abuse and in its exaltation of city knavery over the foolish simplicity of the country.

The Platonic Lovers is a very different play. In form it is a romantic comedy dealing with an action in an imaginary Sicilian Court. Essentially it is a comedy of manners, mildly satirizing the fashion of Platonic love in vogue at the Court of Charles I. Davenant was too much of the courtier to risk the Queen's displeasure by open ridicule of the fashion that she patronized; on the other hand he was too sensible an Englishman to accept the notion of "a love abstracted from all corporal gross impressions," contented with "contemplations and ideas of the mind."

Two young Dukes are in love, each with the other's sister. Theander and Eurithea are "lovers of a pure celestial kind, such as some style Platonical"; Phylamont and Ariola, on the other hand, "affect for natural ends." A group of courtiers wishing to secure an heir to the throne by a normal union between Theander and Eurithea summon to Court a learned doctor to promote their design. He quite disclaims the ancestry of the fashionable doctrine:

> I still beseech you not to wrong
> My good old friend, Plato, with this Court calumny;
> They father on him a fantastic love
> He never knew, poor gentleman.

and administers a love-potion which rouses in Theander desires that startle him and dismay his mistress. In the meantime Ariola, converted by her brother's "holy lectures," flatly refuses to marry Phylamont. A further complication caused by the intrigue of a villain is solved by the good doctor, and the play closes with a double marriage, and the line

> There are Platonic lovers, though but few.

In strong contrast to the frank realism of *The Wits*, the atmosphere of *The Platonic Lovers* is idealized and fantastic. A comic under-plot is subdued to proper proportions, and the dialogue is restrained and polished. Both sides of the argument are gracefully presented, and while earthly love triumphs, the Platonic lovers remain charming, if rather fantastic characters.

Love and Honor is the most important of Davenant's plays. It is a link between Fletcherian tragi-comedy and the Restoration heroic play, perhaps the first Elizabethan drama to anticipate distinctly certain features of the later genre. On the surface it appears only one of the many imitations of Fletcher's tragi-comedy; it is marked by his romanticism, suspense, surprise, and happy solution of a tragic situation. Yet it is something more than this. Like the heroic play it involves the characters in a tumult of war and dynastic struggles; the action turns on a contest between love and honor, and the characters are exalted to superhuman heights of virtue and of wickedness. All it needs to make it a perfect forerunner of the heroic play is the substitution of rhyme for blank verse, and the excision of the comic underplot.

Briefly the complicated plot runs as follows: In a war between Milan and Savoy the Princess Evandra of Milan, along with her champion, Leonell, is captured by the young soldier, Prospero. His friend, Alvaro, Prince of Savoy, threatens him with death since

> A cholerick bear or hungry panther would
> Have us'd her with more soft remorse.

To save Evandra from the rage of Alvaro's father, who has vowed to kill any member of the house of Milan who falls into his hands, Prospero conceals her in a cave. The cruel Duke threatens death in turn to Prospero and to his son unless the lady is delivered. Evandra, hearing of this, determines to save her generous enemies by giving herself up, but she is forestalled by her friend Melora, Leonell's sister, who has joined her in the cave. Eventually both ladies appear before the Duke, each insisting she is the princess. To solve the riddle in the simplest way the Duke orders them both to be executed next morning. Alvaro, Prospero, and Leonell, all three vowed lovers of the Princess, resolve to attend the "dismal tragedy" and then "swell up our sad and injur'd hearts untill they break." The tragedy is, of course, averted. An ambassador from Milan reveals himself as the Duke's brother, whose supposed murder by the Milan prince had caused the Duke's vow. Leonell turns out to be the Prince of Parma and weds Evandra; Alvaro contents himself with Melora; and Prospero, for whom no fitting mate is provided, goes off to the wars.

In strong contrast to the high-flown sentiment of this action, the sub-plot dealing with the wooing and wedding of a rich and decrepit old widow is couched in coarse, at times almost brutal, language. This did not hinder the success of the play, which was performed at Court as well as at Blackfriars. It was revived with great splendor early in the Restoration, when King Charles gave Betterton, who played Alvaro, his Coronation suit, Prince James gave his to Harris, and the Earl of Oxford, in love with the lady who played Evandra, costumed Prince Leonell. Pepys broke a vow of abstinence to attend the first performance and came again two days later, pronouncing it "a very good play." The revival, we are told, "produced the company great gain and estimation from the town," a sufficient proof of its anticipation in late Elizabethan days of Restoration taste.

Davenant's drama is interesting because of its historical significance rather than for its intrinsic merit. It bridges, as did the author's life, the gap between the Elizabethan and the Restoration age. He was a versatile practising playwright who even under the restrictions of Puritan prohibition was able to offer the public a taste of dramatic entertainment. Yet with the exception of *The Siege of Rhodes,* which belongs rather to Restoration than to Elizabethan drama, there is no single play of his that deserves inclusion in a dramatic anthology. He is a clever rather than a gifted playwright. He has a sense of construction that, after his first failures, permits him to tell an interesting story in swiftly moving dramatic form. He was no poet; for the poetry of earlier drama he substitutes a witty utterance that finds expression in epigrams and fantastic similes; and he is by long odds a cleaner playwright than the cynical gentlemen who wrote Restoration comedy.

No account of Elizabethan drama would be complete without mention of a form of dramatic art which began at Court and came to have a not inconsiderable influence on the regular drama. This form is the Masque, or, to speak more precisely, the Court Masque.

Introduced into England by the pleasure-loving Henry VIII, the Masque was at first rather an aristocratic form of social entertainment than a dramatic genre. Essentially it was little more than a dance performed by lords and ladies, masked and costumed as strangers, shepherds, or characters from classical mythology. After completing their formal dance the masquers were wont to separate and invite members of the audience to join with them in the customary dances of the day, the so-called "revels." This innovation on the old-fashioned "disguising" promptly established itself, no doubt because of the opportunity it afforded for amorous discourse and caresses. "Sweetheart," says Shakespeare's Henry VIII, disguised as a shepherd, to Anne Boleyn, whom he has chosen for his partner in the mixed dance,

> I were unmannerly to take you out
> And not to kiss you.

After the mixed dance the masquers removed their vizards and mingled with the audience or, as in later and more elaborate forms of the entertainment, withdrew into a pageant of some kind, a ship, a castle, or some other device which had ushered them into the Court.

There was in the Masque from the beginning the dramatic element of impersonation. Like actors on the stage the masquers pretended to be other than what they really were; King Henry was a shepherd; Queen Anne an Ethiopian beauty. Furthermore as the Masque developed, it grew into an action of some kind; the dance became a symbolic representation of something else, a marriage, a profession of loyalty, a contest between rival divinities. A contest is easily understood, but other forms of symbolic representation were so elaborate as quite to bewilder the audience. This difficulty was met by the introduction of a speaker to act as interpreter of the show. As early as 1517 we find Cornish, Master of the Chapel Royal, disguised as a stranger, speaking a prologue to show "the effect and intent" of *The Garden of Esperance.* So early did speech enter the Masque, and in this instance we note also the presence among the courtly dancers of the professional entertainer, a fact of considerable significance in its evolution.

It was a natural consequence of the growth of the drama proper during the reign of Elizabeth that dramatic elements should develop until they tended to overshadow, though never to obliterate, the essential features of the Masque: the masked dance and the revels. *Proteus and the Adamantine Rock,* presented to the Queen in 1595 by the gentlemen of Gray's Inn, elaborates a definite theme, the glory of Elizabeth, by means of a contest between Proteus, *i.e.,* inconstancy, and the Prince of Purpoole, representing the loyal devotion of the Inn.

Elizabeth was fond of entertainment and always ready to dance; yet she was not inclined to spend money on such entertainments; she preferred to be honored with masques presented to her by loyal subjects. Matters changed with vengeance on the accession of the Stuarts. James delighted in the allegorical and classical elements of the Masque; his wife was passionately devoted to dressing up and dancing; and neither of them shared Elizabeth's desire to economize. As a result the Court Masque under the Stuarts developed into an elaborate and expensive show with music by the best composers, scenery static and movable devised by such architects as Inigo Jones, and texts by the most distinguished poets and playwrights of the day, with one notable exception—Shakespeare was never called on to furnish a masque at Court. Among other playwrights Jonson, Marston, Chapman, Beaumont, Middleton, Shirley, and Davenant all wrote masques for Court performance during the reigns of James and Charles. Of these Jonson was by far the most prolific, writing over twenty masques proper in addition to various other masquelike entertainments. Jonson, too, above all other masque-writers, was successful in preserving the dramatic character of the Masque. When he lost his post at Court after his quarrel with Jones, the Masque rapidly degenerated into a mere spectacle where elaborate scenery and gorgeous costumes blotted out the dramatic element. Jonson's special contribution to the Masque was his elaboration of the anti-masque, the comic dance contrasting with the formal dances of the main masquers, into an essential feature of the performance. He introduced speaking characters into the anti-masque and developed it until it became in his latest works a lively bit of satiric comedy deftly inserted into a splendid show. It is certain that many of Jonson's anti-masques were performed by professional actors; lords and ladies could go through the elaborate movements of the formal dance; they were quite incapable of acting Jonsonian comedy.

It was not long before the influence of this Court Masque made itself felt in the regular drama. Reports of these magnificent shows spread like wildfire and provoked a keen desire to see them among citizens who had no access to the Court. Later Elizabethan comedies contain many a jest at the price citizens, particularly citizens' wives, were willing to pay for admission to a Court Masque. Strenuous measures were taken to prevent the entry of unauthorized persons, but these were not always successful. The performance of Beaumont's *Masque of Gray's Inn and the Inner Temple* had to be postponed because Whitehall was so packed with an intruding mob that it could not be cleared for the show. This, of course, was an unusual instance; the pleasure-loving public debarred as a rule from Court naturally turned to the theatre, where for the small price of admission they might see something resembling the famous masques. Playwrights responded to the public demand by introducing into their work sometimes the same comic dances which professional actors had performed at Court. The morris dance of country folk in *The Two Noble Kinsmen* is taken over directly from Beaumont's *Masque*; the dance of satyrs at the sheep-shearing in *The Winter's Tale* was performed by members of the company who had danced before the King in Jonson's *Masque of Oberon*.

Playwrights, however, went further than this and wove into the texture of their work such formal masques as appear in *Antonio's Revenge, The Maid's Tragedy*, and *Women Beware Women*. Unable to present in the narrow confines of the theatre the scenery and startling transformations of the Court Masque, the actors strained every effort to please their audience with music, gorgeous costumes, and the quaint devices which play such a part in *The Tempest*. Towards the end of the era, in fact, there is an evident attempt by the professionals to equip the stage with scenery. *Microcosmus, A Moral Masque* was produced at Salisbury Court with a full setting of scenes; the scenery devised by Jones for *The Royal Slave* at Oxford was loaned by the University to the King's Company for a performance at Hampton Court. In 1639 the license obtained by Davenant for the theatre that he never built authorized him to "exercise scenes" as well as action and music. His *Siege of Rhodes* was equipped with five changes of scenes, "eleven foot in height and about fifteen in depth" painted in "prospective."

It cannot be said that the influence of the Court Masque on later Elizabethan drama was a power for good. The playwrights might protest against it; yet they were to some extent forced to comply with the public taste. Fletcher invented an ingenious combination of drama and masque in *Four Plays in One*. This takes the form of a masque presented at a royal wedding composed of four separate shows. The first three are one-act playlets; the last a formal masque: *The Triumph of Time*, with music, grotesque dancing, and spectacular transformations. Nothing else in Elizabethan drama shows such a complete assimilation of the characteristic features of the Masque; it must have strained to the utmost the resources of any theatre. Naturally playwrights preferred to introduce less costly and troublesome features; to use a masque in comedy by way of the solution of a tangled intrigue, in tragedy as a contrast to the bloody catastrophe. In general the influence of the Masque on the regular drama tended to distract attention from the speakers and the action and to concentrate it upon such non-essentials as music, dancing, and spectacle. Only at times was a master playwright able to use the innovations with such dramatic effect as Ford in the last act of *The Broken Heart*. The supreme achievement of this kind is Shakespeare's; the formal masque in *The Tempest*, celebrating a royal betrothal, harmonizes perfectly with the theme of the play: the healing of old feuds by forgiveness, reconciliation, and perfect union.

* * * * * * *

The story of Elizabethan drama has been told in the foregoing pages. A backward glance at its rise and fall may serve to sum up what has been said; a brief estimate of its present value may recommend it to the modern reader.

Elizabethan drama was essentially a native growth. It sprang from the liturgy of the Church, passed from the sacred Latin of the services into the universally intelligible English, and shook off Church control in the guild cycles and the Morals. It was profoundly influenced by the humanism of the Renaissance; its form was strengthened, its speech at once enriched and purified. Yet it never succumbed, as did the drama in Italy and France, to a slavish subservience to classic models. It absorbed the poetic outburst of the sixteenth century and broke into a sudden flower of passionate beauty unmatched elsewhere in English literature. At its height it was the supreme expression of the hopes and fears, the limitations and aspirations of a newly awakened and united nation. When it ceased to be so, when the rift between the people and the government developed and deepened, the drama lost its hold upon the nation and sank till it became the plaything of the Court. And that meant its swift end, for drama above all other forms of art demands and needs popular support.

Elizabethan drama was written for the stage, not for the study. It was not till a comparatively late period that it became generally accessible to the reading public, as in the Jonson Folio of 1616 and the Shakespeare of 1623. With the closing of the theatres the publication of plays increased; people would still read if they could no longer see the plays in action. That is essentially our case today. With the exception of a group of Shakespeare's plays and an occasional academic revival of a play by one of his contemporaries, the Elizabethan drama has lost its natural home upon the stage. It still remains, however, an open field to the reader, one of the richest and most varied in the wide domain of English literature.

Some knowledge of the conditions under which Elizabethan plays were written and produced is necessary to a complete appreciation of their value by a reader. Such knowledge, it is hoped, has been given in the preceding pages of this book. There are, of course, some who have an ingrained dislike to the reading of plays as compared to fiction, and, no doubt, a play meant for representation presents certain difficulties to the reader. Yet with patience and good will these difficulties may be overcome. In fact the practice of contemporary playwrights in publishing their works seems to show a public ready to accept in printed form what it cannot see in action. If readers knew the treasure buried in what is for most of them an unexplored field, they might well turn from the ephemeral products of the day to find entertainment, delight, and profit in what Elizabethan drama has still to offer. And the best work of Elizabethan playwrights is easily accessible today in admirable anthologies and handy editions of single plays.

In the first place Elizabethan drama meets what is, perhaps, the first demand of the average reader, an interesting story. *Tales from Shakespeare* has been a household book for generations, and while Shakespeare is the best story-teller of his time, he is not the only one. Elizabethan drama offers tales of love, of war, and adventure, of open and of secret murder, of bloody revenge, and of Christian forgiveness. They are often simple stories such as might easily be grasped by the naïve audiences of the early theatres; there are no puzzling complications in such a play as Greene's *Friar Bacon*. Yet a simple tale may embody a profound lesson, as does Marlowe's *Dr. Faustus*. As the drama grows in strength, it becomes more varied and complex; there is a sheer intellectual delight in following the skilfully woven intrigue of such a play as *The Alchemist*. The Elizabethan was a laughter-loving age, and its drama offers all varieties of the comic from the horse-play of *Gammer Gurton's Needle* to the rollicking farce of Fletcher's comedies and the ridiculous paradoxes of Brome's *Antipodes*. High-strung and emotional, the Elizabethans moved rapidly from laughter to tears; there are sad tales enough in the repertoire of their drama, from the madness of Hieronimo to the sufferings of the Duchess of Malfi and the tragic consequences of a fatal dowry.

There is another characteristic of Elizabethan drama more important than this gift of story-telling. The best stories are not simply narratives of action, but those about men and women, people credibly enough portrayed to convince us of their reality. And most Elizabethan playwrights seem to have this happy gift of character creation. It is an old saying that Shakespeare's men and women seem much more alive than those that we see about our streets, and Shakespeare's magic is shared, though in a less degree, by many of his fellows. Even so careless an artist as Dekker possesses the magic touch which makes Simon Eyre or Bellafront and her father come to life before our eyes. If the proper study of mankind is man, if there is pleasure and profit to be found in exploring the various shades of human nature, there is no richer field for the student than the almost infinite variety of characters, grave and gay, sober and reckless, pathetic and tragic, which once played their parts upon a vanished stage and are still ready to reappear at the call of a sympathetic imagination.

The present vogue of the historical novel seems to show an awakened interest among readers in the re-creation of the past. Now drama, as Shakespeare tells us, holds the mirror up to nature. All drama does so more or less, but Elizabethan drama excels in its full and varied reflection of the most fascinating age in the history of the English-speaking people. It mirrors the vigorous Elizabethan patriotism in its chronicle plays, the sheer joy of life in its early comedies, the bitter disillusion that set in as the great age slowly faded. The Elizabethan playwrights were primarily interested in the life of their own day, and their drama presents this life in vivid and often in minute detail: in the new habit, for instance, of "drinking" tobacco, in the modern fashion of the private ball, in the London prentices with their call of "What d'ye lack?" and their readiness to rush out like a swarm of wasps at the cry of "clubs." It reveals the rise to power of the merchant class that was later to control the destiny of England, and it pictures, perhaps not always fairly, the strict discipline of the Puritans who finally made an end of the old drama. The lover of Elizabethan plays may travel back in imagination to London town, wander from the Court at Whitehall along the Strand to Cheapside and the Tower, stopping at the Mermaid tavern for a glass of sack. Or he may take a pair of oars at Blackfriars, shoot the dangerous arches of London Bridge and drop down to Greenwich, where Drake's *Golden Hind* lies at anchor. Either tour by land or water may be made, perhaps with more pleasure, certainly with more safety, than would have been possible in the good old days.

Some such re-creation of past life may be found in the best of English fiction. What cannot be found in any novel is that which is the peculiar glory of Elizabethan drama, its poetry. The Elizabethan age was the most musical in English history, and this music poured into the language of the drama. It is not only the frequent songs that give this poetic value to the Elizabethan drama. The whole tenor of the diction is poetic; the very prose has a rhythmic value which raises it above the common speech of men. All the romance of the Elizabethan age, its awareness of new words, its love of adventure, its worship of beauty, finds fit expression in the poetry of Elizabethan drama.

The appeal of poetry unfortunately is limited; there are many who are tone-deaf as others are color-blind. In that period of English life and letters least appreciative of imaginative poetry, the eighteenth century, the poetic value of Elizabethan drama seems to have been almost completely ignored. Shakespeare, to be sure, was still highly praised, but rather for other qualities than his poetic diction. Actor-managers and editors alike deliberately toned down his language and at times inserted into his text prosaic matter that stuck out against the original like a patch of dull brick upon a marble wall. It was only with the advent of the Romantic age and the appearance of such poets and poetic critics as Coleridge and Charles Lamb that the doors leading to the poetic treasure of the old drama were again unlocked. Whatever fault may be found with Romantic criticism, there can be no doubt that it fostered an appreciation and, indeed, a love of pure poetry. Since then there has been a steady advance both in understanding and in appreciation of Elizabethan dramatic poetry. Recent experiments by contemporary playwrights seem to show the need the artist feels for restoring to the stage-play something of the value lost when poetry in the drama gave place to prose and prosaic verse.

The appeal of poetry may be limited but it is poignant. A truth expressed, a sentiment revealed in poetic form finds readier reception and truer appreciation than its paraphrase in prose. To the lovers of poetry, to those who are willing to discard the vulgar prejudice against all but the baldest statement of fact, Elizabethan drama makes this direct and powerful appeal. It is from beginning to end a poetic drama, opening with the crashing chords of Marlowe, dying away in the melancholy music of Ford and the gentle melodies of Shirley. Here is one of the most beautiful and splendid creations of English poetic genius. We need only say of it as a voice from heaven once said to St. Augustine: *"Tolle, lege"*—take up and read.

SELECTIVE BIBLIOGRAPHY

THE following bibliography lists only in part those publications to which the authors are indebted; it is intended rather to assist readers by indicating major source materials and by giving suggestions for supplementary examination. Only books are cited; a few have been chosen because they are provocative. The first section includes books of reference on the English drama as a whole, and more specifically on Elizabethan drama, as well as anthologies. Thereafter works recommended are grouped under chapter designations and the names of dramatists. In each case the texts of the playwrights discussed are put first, followed by biographical and critical studies. Of the latter some of the best are contained in the editions of the various dramatists mentioned. Full titles have in some cases been shortened.

GENERAL

a. ENGLISH DRAMA

Archer, W., *The Old Drama and the New*, Boston, 1923.
Bridges-Adams, W., *The Irresistible Theatre*, Cleveland, 1957.
Downer, A. S., *The British Drama*, New York, 1950.
Eaton, W. P., *The Drama in English*, New York, 1930.
Miles, B., *The British Theatre*, London, 1948.
Thorndike, A. H., *Tragedy*, Boston, 1908.
 English Comedy, New York, 1929.
Trewin, J. C., *The English Theatre*, London, 1948.

b. ELIZABETHAN DRAMA

Boas, F. S., *An Introduction to Tudor Drama*, Oxford, 1933.
An Introduction to Stuart Drama, London, 1946.
Brooke, C. F. T., *The Tudor Drama*, Boston, 1911.
Doran, M., *Endeavors of Art*, Madison, 1954.
Eliot, T. S., *Essays on Elizabethan Drama*, New York, 1956.
Ellis-Fermor, U. M., *The Jacobean Drama*, New York, 1936.
Harrison, G. B., *Elizabethan Plays and Players*, Ann Arbor, 1956.
The Story of Elizabethan Drama, New York, 1924.
Mackenzie, A. M., *The Playgoer's Handbook to the English Renaissance Drama*, London, 1927.
Nicoll, A., *The Elizabethans*, New York, 1957.
Schelling, F. E., *Elizabethan Drama*, 2 vols., Boston, 1908.
Swinburne, A. C., *The Age of Shakespeare*, New York, 1908.
Wilson, F. P., *Elizabethan and Jacobean*, Oxford, 1945.

c. ANTHOLOGIES

Adams, J. Q., *Chief Pre-Shakespearean Dramas*, Boston, 1924.
Baskervill, C. R., Heltzel, V. B., and Nethercot, A. H., *Elizabethan and Stuart Plays*, New York, 1934.
Brooke, C. F. T., and Paradise, N. B., *English Drama, 1580-1642*, Boston, 1933.
Manly, J. M., *Specimens of the Pre-Shakespearean Drama*, 2 vols., Boston, 1897.
Parks, E. W., and Beatty, R. C., *The English Drama, 900-1642*, New York, 1935.
Schelling, F. E., and Black, M. W., *Typical Elizabethan Plays*, New York, 1949.
Schweikert, H. C., *Early English Plays, 900-1600*, New York, 1928.
Spencer, H., *Elizabethan Plays*, Boston, 1933.
Walley, H., and Wilson, J. H., *Early Seventeenth Century Plays, 1600-1642*, New York, 1930.

CHAPTERS I and II

a. TEXTS

Child, C. G., *The Second Shepherd's Play, Everyman, and Other Early Plays*, Boston, 1910.

Cunliffe, J. W., *Early English Classical Tragedies*, Oxford, 1912.

Deimling, H., *The Chester Plays*, 2 vols., London, 1893-1916.

Duckworth, G., *The Complete Roman Drama*, 2 vols., New York, 1942.

England, G., and Pollard, A. W., *The Townley Plays*, London, 1897.

Halliwell Phillipps, J. O., *Ludus Coventriae*, London, 1841.

Milligan, B. A., *John Heywood's Works and Miscellaneous Short Poems*, Urbana, 1946.

Pollard, A. W., *English Miracle Plays, Moralities, and Interludes*, Oxford, 1904.

Purvis, J. S., *The York Cycle of Mystery Plays*, New York, 1957.

Smith, L. T., *The York Plays*, London, 1885.

b. HISTORICAL

Bolwell, R. W., *The Life and Works of John Heywood*, New York, 1921.

Chambers, E. K., *The English Folk Play*, Oxford, 1933.
  The Medieval Stage, 2 vols., Oxford, 1903.

de la Bere, R., *John Heywood, Entertainer*, New York, 1937.

Craig, H., *English Religious Drama of the Middle Ages*, Oxford, 1955.

Farnham, W., *The Medieval Heritage of Elizabethan Tragedy*, Berkeley, 1936.

Gayley, C. M., *Plays of Our Forefathers*, New York, 1907.

Mackenzie, W. R., *The English Moralities*, Boston, 1914.

Owst, G. R., *Literature and Pulpit in Medieval England*, Cambridge, 1933.

Reed, A. W., *Early Tudor Drama*, London, 1926.

Rossiter, A. P., *English Drama from Early Times to the Elizabethans*, London, 1950.

Solter, F. M., *Medieval Drama in Chester*, Toronto, 1955.

Spencer, M. L., *Corpus Christi Pageants in England*, New York, 1911.

Young, K., *The Drama of the Medieval Church*, 2 vols., Oxford, 1933.

CHAPTER III

Adams, J. C., *The Globe Playhouse*, Cambridge (Mass.), 1942.

Adams, J. Q., *Shakespearean Playhouses*, Boston, 1917.

Baldwin, T. W., *The Organization and Personnel of the Shakespearean Company*, Princeton, 1927.

Bentley, G. E., *The Jacobean and Caroline Stage*, 5 vols., incomplete, Oxford, 1941-1956.

Bradbrook, M. C., *Elizabethan Stage Conditions*, Cambridge, 1932.

Chambers, E. K., *The Elizabethan Stage*, 4 vols., Oxford, 1923.

Harbage, A., *As They Liked It*, New York, 1947.
  Shakespeare's Audience, New York, 1941.

Hodges, C. W., *The Globe Restored*, London, 1953.

Lawrence, W. J., *The Physical Conditions of the Elizabethan Public Playhouse*, Cambridge (Mass.), 1927.

Murray, J. T., *English Dramatic Companies*, 1558-1642, 2 vols., London, 1910.

Nicoll, A., *The English Theatre*, New York, 1936.

Nungezer, E., *A Dictionary of Actors*, New Haven, 1929.

Reynolds, G. R., *The Staging of Elizabethan Plays at the Red Bull Theater, 1605-1625*, New York, 1940.

Smith, I., *Shakespeare's Globe Playhouse*, New York, 1956.

Thorndike, A. H., *Shakespeare's Theatre*, New York, 1916.

CHAPTER IV

a. Texts

Lyly. R. W. Bond, *The Complete Works of John Lyly*, 3 vols., Oxford, 1902.

Peele. A. H. Bullen, *The Works of George Peele*, 2 vols., London, 1888.

Greene. J. C. Collins, *The Plays and Poems of Robert Greene*, 2 vols., Oxford, 1905.

Kyd. F. S. Boas, *The Works of Thomas Kyd*, Oxford, 1901.

Marlowe. R. H. Case (gen. ed.), *The Works and Life of Christopher Marlowe*, 6 vols., London, 1930-1933.
  C. F. T. Brooke, *The Works of Christopher Marlowe*, Oxford, 1910.

b. Biographical, Critical

Lyly. A. Feuillerat, *John Lyly*, Cambridge, 1910.

Peele. P. H. Cheffaud, *George Peele*, Paris, 1913.
    D. H. Horne, *The Life and Minor Works of George Peele*, Vol. I, New Haven, 1952.
Kyd. F. Carrère, *Le Théâtre de Thomas Kyd*, Toulouse, 1951.
Marlowe. J. Bakeless, *The Tragical History of Christopher Marlowe*, 2 vols., Cambridge (Mass.), 1942.
    F. S. Boas, *Christopher Marlowe*, Oxford, 1940.
    U. M. Ellis-Fermor, *Christopher Marlowe*, London, 1927.
    P. Henderson, *Christopher Marlowe*, London, 1952.
    P. H. Kocher, *Christopher Marlowe*, Chapel Hill, 1946.
    H. Levin, *The Overreacher*, Cambridge (Mass.), 1952.
    M. Poirier, *Christopher Marlowe*, London, 1951.

CHAPTER V

a. TEXTS

Chapman. T. M. Parrott, *The Tragedies of George Chapman*, New York, 1910.
    The Comedies of George Chapman, New York, 1913.
Dekker. F. T. Bowers, *The Dramatic Works of Thomas Dekker*, 2 vols., incomplete, Cambridge, 1953-1955.
    R. H. Shepherd, *The Dramatic Works of Thomas Dekker*, 4 vols., London, 1873.
    E. Rhys, *The Best Plays of Dekker* (Mermaid Series), London, 1887.
Heywood. R. H. Shepherd, *The Dramatic Works of Thomas Heywood*, 6 vols., London, 1874.
    A. W. Verity, *The Best Plays of Heywood* (Mermaid Series), London 1888.

b. BIOGRAPHICAL, CRITICAL

Henslowe. W. W. Greg, *Henslowe's Diary*, 2 vols., London, 1904-1908.
    The Henslowe Papers, London, 1907.
Chapman. J. Jacquot, *George Chapman*, Paris, 1951.
    E. Rees, *The Tragedies of George Chapman*, Cambridge (Mass.), 1955.

Dekker. K. L. Gregg, *Thomas Dekker*, Seattle, 1924.
  M. L. Hunt, *Thomas Dekker*, New York, 1911.
Heywood. F. S. Boas, *Thomas Heywood*, London, 1950.
  A. M. Clark, *Thomas Heywood*, Oxford, 1931.
  O. Cromwell, *Thomas Heywood*, New Haven, 1928.

CHAPTER VI

a. TEXTS

Jonson. C. H. Herford and P. Simpson, *Ben Jonson*, 8 vols., Oxford, 1925-1947.
  B. Nicholson and C. H. Herford, *The Best Plays of Ben Jonson* (Mermaid Series), 3 vols., London, 1893-1894.

b. BIOGRAPHICAL, CRITICAL

Jonson. C. R. Baskervill, *English Elements in Jonson's Early Comedies*, Austin, 1911.
  H. W. Baum, *The Satiric and Didactic in Ben Jonson's Comedy*, Chapel Hill, 1947.
  G. E. Bentley, *Shakespeare and Jonson*, 2 vols., Chicago, 1945.
  M. Castelain, *Ben Jonson*, Paris, 1907.
  M. Chute, *Ben Jonson of Westminster*, New York, 1953.
  E. C. Dunn, *Ben Jonson's Art*, Northampton, 1925.
  J. J. Enck, *Jonson and the Comic Truth*, Madison, 1957.
  M. Kerr, *Influence of Ben Jonson on English Comedy, 1598-1642*, New York, 1912.
  L. C. Knights, *Drama and Society in the Age of Jonson*, London, 1937.
  R. G. Noyes, *Ben Jonson on the English Stage, 1660-1776*, Cambridge (Mass.), 1935.
  J. Palmer, *Ben Jonson*, London, 1934.
  F. L. Townsend, *Apologie for Bartholomew Fayre: The Art of Jonson's Comedies*, New York, 1947.
  E. Woodbridge, *Studies in Ben Jonson's Comedies*, New Haven, 1898.

CHAPTER VII

a. TEXTS

Marston. A. H. Bullen, *The Works of John Marston*, 3 vols., London, 1887.
H. H. Wood, *The Plays of John Marston*, 3 vols., London, 1934-1939.
Middleton. A. H. Bullen, *The Works of Thomas Middleton*, 8 vols., London, 1885-1886.
A. C. Swinburne and H. Ellis, *The Best Plays of Thomas Middleton* (Mermaid Series), 2 vols., London, 1887-1890.
Brome. R. H. Shepherd, *The Dramatic Works of Richard Brome*, 3 vols., 1873.

b. BIOGRAPHICAL, CRITICAL

Marston. A. J. Axelrad, *Un Malcontent Elizabéthain: John Marston*, Paris, 1956.
Middleton. W. D. Dunkel, *The Dramatic Technique of Thomas Middleton*, Chicago, 1925.
S. Schoenbaum, *Middleton's Tragedies*, New York, 1955.
Brome. C. E. Andrews, *Richard Brome*, New Haven, 1913.

CHAPTER VIII

a. TEXTS

Beaumont and Fletcher. A. Dyce, *The Works of Beaumont and Fletcher*, 11 vols., London, 1843-1846.
Various editors, *The Works of Francis Beaumont and John Fletcher*, Variorum ed., 4 vols., incomplete, London, 1904-1912.
J. S. Strachey, *The Best Plays of Beaumont and Fletcher* (Mermaid Series), 2 vols., London, 1904.
W. P. Frijlinck, *The Tragedy of Sir John Van Olden Barnavelt*, Amsterdam, 1922.

b. BIOGRAPHICAL, CRITICAL

Beaumont and Fletcher. M. Chelli, *Étude sur la collaboration de Massinger avec Fletcher et son groupe*, Paris, 1936.

C. M. Gayley, *Beaumont the Dramatist*, New York, 1914.
O. L. Hatcher, *John Fletcher*, Chicago, 1905.
E. H. C. Oliphant, *The Plays of Beaumont and Fletcher*, New Haven, 1927.
F. H. Ristine, *English Tragicomedy*, New York, 1910.
A. C. Sprague, *Beaumont and Fletcher on the Restoration Stage*, Cambridge (Mass.), 1926.
L. B. Wallis, *Fletcher, Beaumont & Company*, New York, 1947.

CHAPTER IX

a. TEXTS

Tourneur. A. Nicoll, *The Works of Cyril Tourneur*, London, 1930.
    J. A. Symonds, *Webster and Tourneur* (Mermaid Series), London, 1888.
Webster. F. L. Lucas, *The Complete Works of John Webster*, 4 vols., Boston, 1928.
Ford. W. Gifford and A. Dyce, rev. A. H. Bullen, *The Works of John Ford*, 3 vols., London, 1895.
    H. Ellis, *The Best Plays of John Ford* (Mermaid Series), London, 1888.

b. BIOGRAPHICAL, CRITICAL

Webster. T. Bogard, *The Tragic Satire of John Webster*, Berkeley, 1955.
    R. Brooke, *John Webster and the Elizabethan Drama*, New York, 1916.
    C. Leech, *John Webster*, Philadelphia, 1925.
Ford. R. Davril, *Le Drame de John Ford*, Paris, 1954.
    C. Leech, *John Ford and the Drama of His Time*, Fairlawn, 1957.
    H. J. Oliver, *The Problem of John Ford*, Carlton (Victoria), 1955.
    G. F. Sensabaugh, *The Tragic Muse of John Ford*, Stanford, 1944.
    M. J. Sergeaunt, *John Ford*, Oxford, 1935.

CHAPTER X

a. Texts

Massinger. W. Gifford, *The Plays of Philip Massinger,* 4 vols., London, 1813.

    A. Symons, *The Best Plays of Massinger* (Mermaid Series), 2 vols., London, 1887-1889.

Shirley. W. Gifford and A. Dyce, *Dramatic Works and Poems of James Shirley,* 6 vols., London, 1833.

    E. Gosse, *The Best Plays of Shirley* (Mermaid Series), London, 1888.

Davenant. J. Maidment and W. H. Logan, *The Dramatic Works of William D'Avenant,* 5 vols., London, 1872-1874.

b. Biographical, Critical

Massinger. R. H. Ball, *The Amazing Career of Sir Giles Overreach,* Princeton, 1939.

    M. Chelli, *Le Drame de Massinger,* Lyon, 1923.

    A. H. Cruickshank, *Philip Massinger,* Oxford, 1920.

Shirley. R. S. Forsythe, *The Relation of Shirley's Plays to the Elizabethan Drama,* New York, 1914.

    A. H. Nason, *James Shirley,* New York, 1915.

    H. T. Parlin, *Shirley's Comedies of London Life,* Austin, 1914.

Davenant. A. Harbage, *Cavalier Drama,* New York, 1936.

    Sir William Davenant, Philadelphia, 1935.

    A. H. Nethercot, *Sir William Davenant,* Chicago, 1939.

    E. Welsford, *The Court Masque,* Cambridge, 1927.

INDEX

Abraham and Isaac (Brome), 8, 15
Adelphi, 97
Aethiopica, 41
Aglaura, 279
Albovine, King of the Lombards, 280
Alchemist, The, 129, 141–2, 149, 150, 175, 180, 292
All Fools, 97–8, 105
All is True. See *Henry VIII*
All's Lost by Lust, 165
Alleyn, Edward, 50, 61, 81, 83, 85, 93, 94, 127
Alphonsus, King of Aragon, 70, 71
Amadis of France, 41
Anatomy of Melancholy, The, 242
Antipodes, The, 173, 174, 177–8, 180, 292
Antonio and Mellida, 154–5, 210
Antonio's Revenge, 155, 210–11, 220, 289
Antony and Cleopatra, 262
Anything for a Quiet Life, 160, 164–5, 224
Apology for Actors, 75, 115, 223
Appius and Virginia, 29, 30–1
Appius and Virginia (Webster and Heywood), 224, 234
Apuleius, 41
Arcadia, 193, 242, 243, 244, 257
Arden of Feversham, 29, 75, 121
Ariosto, Lodovico, 43
Aristophanes, 144, 169
Aristotle, 28, 85, 86
Armin, Robert, 51, 61
Arraignment of London, The, 214
Arraignment of Paris, The, 67
As You Like It, 61, 66–7, 72, 74, 81, 150
Ascension, The (York), 12
Astrophel and Stella, 239, 242, 243, 244–5
Atheist's Tragedy, The, 213, 218–22

Bacon, Francis, 38
Bale, John, 20, 21, 29
Ball, The, 269
Bartholomew Fair, 129, 142–3, 150, 171, 172, 175
Bashful Lover, The, 256
Battle of Alcazar, The, 67
Bear-garden, 94
Beaumont, Francis, 50, 73, 98, 112, 116, 124, 182–8, 190–5, 196, 198, 202, 203, 238, 241, 248, 250, 254, 273, 288, 289
Beauty in a Trance, 240
Beeston, Christopher, 269
Beeston's Boys, 173
Beggar's Bush, 179
Beggar's Opera, The, 174

Bel Savage, The, inn, 47
Believe as you List, 263–4
Bell, The, inn, 47
Bellman of London, The, 214
Betterton, Thomas, 256, 286
Beverly, plays at, 13, 16
Bird in a Cage, The, 270
Black Book, The, 159
Blackfriars, theatre, 49, 51, 54, 97, 98, 99, 103, 128, 129, 130, 140, 172, 208, 213, 223, 225, 240, 244, 260, 270, 279, 280, 281, 285
Blind Beggar of Alexandria, The, 96
Bloody Brother, The, 198
Blount, Edward, 64
Blurt, Master Constable, 159
Boar's Head, The, inn, 47
Boccaccio, Giovanni, 38, 272
Bondman, The, 255, 256–7
Bonduca, 195
Brazen Age, The, 118
Bristow Merchant, The, 240
Broken Heart, The, 240, 242–4, 246, 247, 248, 251, 290
Brome, Alexander, 173
Brome, Richard, 123, 171–81, 253, 292
Brooke, Arthur, 229, 230
Browning, Robert, 249
Buckingham, George Villiers, Duke of, 207
Buffeting of Christ, The (Wakefield), 9, 11
Building of the Ark, The (York), 12
Bunyan, John, 17, 166
Burbage, Cuthbert, 49
Burbage, James, 47, 49, 50, 54
Burbage, Richard, 49, 50, 51, 54, 61, 127, 196, 223, 225
Burton, Robert, 242
Bussy D'Ambois, 36, 52, 101–2, 103, 104, 212
Byron. See *The Conspiracy and Tragedy of Charles Duke of Byron*

Caesar's Fall, 95, 110, 159
Calisto and Melibea, 42, 44
Cambises, 28, 29, 30, 74, 117
Campaspe, 65, 66
Captives, The, 115, 123
Cardinal, The, 210, 270, 276–7
Carlell, Lodowick, 279
Carmosine, 272
Cartwright, William, 279
Case Is Altered, The, 132–3
Castle of Perseverance, The, 17–18, 19, 46
Catiline, 129, 146, 147–8

Celestina, 42
Cervantes Saavedra, Miguel de, 167, 187, 204, 206
Chabot. See The Tragedy of Chabot Admiral of France
Challenge for Beauty, A, 119
Chances, The, 206
Changeling, The, 160, 168, 236-7, 238
Chapman, George, 36, 50, 52, 79, 80, 96-106, 110, 114, 189, 212, 228, 269, 288
Character of Robert Earle of Salesburye, The, 213-14
Characters, 224
Chaste Maid in Cheapside, A, 159, 163-4, 238
Chaucer, Geoffrey, 11, 12, 41, 45
Chester Cycle, 10, 14
Children of the Chapel, 51, 54, 67, 78, 97, 98, 99, 103, 128, 129, 137, 154, 159, 186, 203, 225
Children of Paul's, 49, 51, 54, 64, 99, 101, 109, 137, 154, 159, 186, 210, 223
Children of the Queen's Revels, 154
Children of Windsor, 51
Christmas Comes but Once a Year, 222
Cicero, 148
City Madam, The, 260-1
City Match, The, 280
City Wit, The, 173, 174-5
Claricilla, 279
Clytemnestra, 1
Cockpit, The. See The Phoenix
Coleridge, Samuel Taylor, 294
Common Conditions, 42
Conquest of the Indies, The, 95
Conspiracy and Tragedy of Charles Duke of Byron, The, 103-4, 106, 154
Contention of Ajax and Ulysses, The, 271
Cornélie, 75
Court Beggar, The, 173
Court Secret, The, 270
Coventry, plays at, 13
Coxcomb, The, 194-5
Creation and the Fall of Lucifer (York), 12
Creation to the Fifth Day, The (York), 12
Cross Keys, The, inn, 47
Crucifixion, The (York), 12
Cruel Brother, The, 280
Cruelty of a Stepmother, The, 29
Cruelty of the Spaniards in Peru, The, 282
Cupid and Death, 271
Cupid's Revenge, 193
Cure for a Cuckold, A, 224, 233-4
Curtain, The, theatre, 49
Cymbeline, 74
Cynthia's Revels, 128, 136, 137, 225

Daborne, Robert, 214, 255
Damoiselle, The, 173

Davenant, Sir William, 50, 253, 280-6, 288, 289
David and Bethsabe, 67, 69
De Guiana, 100
De vera nobilitate, 23
Debauchee, The, 174
Dekker, Thomas, 50, 95, 99, 106-15, 121, 128, 137, 138, 149, 156, 159, 168, 170, 171, 172, 176, 177, 184, 214, 222, 223, 224, 225, 228, 240, 241, 255, 292
Derby's Men, Earl of, 50
Deserving Favorite, The, 279
Devil Is an Ass, The, 129, 143
Devil's Law-Case, The, 224, 233, 235
Diary (Henslowe), 83, 93, 94, 95, 97, 106, 127, 153, 159, 222, 223
Dickens, Charles, 150
Dido, Queen of Carthage, 78
Discoveries, 131
Dr. Faustus, 14, 71, 72, 83-5, 88-9, 90, 91, 102, 292
Don Quixote, 187
Donne, John, 152, 154
Doomsday (York), 12
Double Marriage, The, 198
Doubtful Heir, The, 270
Drayton, Michael, 80, 95, 222
Drummond of Hawthornden, William, 130, 132, 137, 146
Dryden, John, 140, 184, 204, 278
Dublin, theatre, 270
Duchess of Malfi, The, 211, 223, 228-32, 233, 246, 276, 292
Duke of Milan, The, 255, 262-3
Duke's Mistress, The, 275
Dutch Courtezan, The, 156-7, 158

Eastward Ho, 99-100, 110, 129, 138, 154, 158, 260
Edward I, 67, 69
Edward II, 88-9, 91, 92
Edward IV, 117
Elder Brother, The, 208
Elegies (Ovid), 78
Eliot, George, 272
Endimion, 65, 66
English Moor, The, 173
English Traveller, The, 115, 122
Entertainment . . . by Declamations and Musick, 282
Epicoene, 129, 140, 141, 175, 191
Etherege, Sir George, 278
Euphues, 64
Euripides, 252
Every Man In His Humour, 44, 127, 129, 132, 133-5, 145, 149, 150, 171
Every Man Out of His Humour, 128, 134, 135-6, 137, 139, 154, 225
Everyman, 18, 19
Exemplary Novels, 204, 206

Faerie Queene, The, 69, 217
Fair Maid of the Inn, The, 224

Fair Maid of the West, The, 120–1, 124
Fair Penitent, The, 266
Fair Quarrel, A, 160, 166–7, 171
Fairy Knight, The, 240
Faithful Shepherdess, The, 146, 189–90
False One, The, 196, 198
Family of Love, The, 159, 162
Fancies, Chaste and Noble, The, 241, 248–9, 251
Farquhar, George, 206
Fatal Dowry, The, 201, 255, 265–7, 292
Father Hubbard's Tale, 159
Father's Own Son. See *Monsieur Thomas*
Fault in Friendship, A, 172
Female Patriot, The, 256
Ferrex and Porrex. See *Gorboduc*
Field, Nathan, 52, 102, 201–2, 255, 265, 267
Fig for Momus, A, 152
First Part of Fortunatus, The, 106
First Shepherds Play (Wakefield), 11
Five New Plays, 173
Fletcher, Giles, 184
Fletcher, John, 50, 73, 98, 105, 112, 119, 146, 159, 160, 164, 174, 182–5, 187–209, 233, 234, 238, 241, 248, 250, 252, 253, 255, 256, 257, 261, 267, 268, 271, 273, 274, 278, 283, 284, 290, 292
Fletcher, Phineas, 184
Force of Blood, The, 167
Ford, John, 112, 113, 125, 172. 223, 224, 238–52, 253, 268, 269, 278, 290, 294
Fortune, The, theatre, 48, 49, 50, 52, 94, 156, 253
Fortune by Land and Sea, 120
Four P's, The, 24–6, 33
Four Plays in One, 201, 290
Four Prentices of London, The, 116–17
Fox, The. See *Volpone*
Friar Bacon and Friar Bungay, 22, 71–2, 73, 292
Fulgens and Lucres, 23–4, 46
Funeral Poem upon the Death of . . . Sir Francis Vere, A, 213, 218–19

Galathea, 65–6, 67
Game at Chess, A, 144, 160, 168–70, 180, 197, 205, 263
Gamester, The, 269, 275
Gammer Gurton's Needle, 32–3, 292
Garden of Esperance, The, 287
Garnier, Robert, 75
Garrick, David, 205, 207
Gascoigne, George, 43–4
Gentle Craft, The. See *The Shoemaker's Holiday*
Gentleman Usher, The, 98–9, 105, 190
Gismonde of Salerne, 38, 42
Globe, The, theatre, 48, 49, 51, 53, 94, 128, 137, 155, 172, 195, 213, 223, 225, 253, 270, 281

God's Revenge Against Murder, 236
Goethe, Johann Wolfgang von, 84
Golden Age, The, 118
Golden Ass, The, 41
Golden Mean, The, 239
Gondibert, 282
Gorboduc, 37–8, 74, 91
Gosson, Stephen, 41
Great Duke of Florence, The, 256, 261
Greene, Robert, 22, 43, 69–74, 107, 109, 116, 119, 152, 174, 267, 292
Grief on the Death of Prince Henry, A, 214
Guarini, Giovanni Battista, 146
Guilpin, Edward, 153
Guise, 224
Gull's Hornbook, The, 112
Gulliver's Travels, 178

Hall, Joseph, 153
Hamlet, 28, 36, 40, 51, 75, 88, 102, 137, 190, 210, 220
Hamlet (Kyd), 75, 93, 210
Harris, Henry, 286
Hart, Charles, 102
Hathway, Richard, 95
Heautontimoroumenos, 97
Hegge Plays. See *Ludus Coventriae*
Heliodorus, 41
Henry IV, 173
Henry V, 52, 90
Henry VI, 89
Henry VIII, 15, 185, 287
Henslowe, Philip, 49, 50, 58, 76, 83, 93–6, 97, 106, 107, 108, 110, 114, 115, 121, 127, 128, 133, 153, 159, 214, 222, 235, 255
Heptameron, 275
Heywood, John, 24–6, 32, 34
Heywood, Thomas, 50, 75, 115–25, 127, 149, 158, 165, 173, 184, 199, 214, 223, 224, 233, 234
History of Sir Francis Drake, The, 282
Histriomastix, 137, 154
Hogarth, William, 99
Holinshed, Raphael, 88, 121
Holy War, The, 17
Homer, 96, 105
Honest Man's Revenge, The. See *The Atheist's Tragedy*
Honest Whore, The, 110–11, 156, 159, 292
Honor Triumphant, 239
Hope, The, theatre, 49, 50, 94, 142
Horace, 265
Horestes, 29–30, 74
How Lisa Loved the King, 272
Hughes, Thomas, 38–9
Humourous Day's Mirth, An, 96–7
Humourous Lieutenant, The, 198, 199–200
Hyde Park, 273

If It be not Good, the Devil is in It, 112
If You Know not Me, You Know Nobody, 117
Incendium, 1
Iron Age, The, 118–19
Island Princess, The, 198
Isle of Dogs, The, 127

Jack Drum's Entertainment, 155
James IV, 72–3, 109, 190
Jephthah, 107
Jew of Malta, The, 85–7, 88, 91
John John, Tib, and Sir John, 24, 26
Jones, Inigo, 124, 128, 131, 132, 146, 270, 281, 288, 289
Jonson, Ben, 28, 33, 44, 50, 66, 76, 93, 96, 97, 99, 100, 105, 106, 107, 109, 110, 114, 125, 126–51, 152, 153, 154, 156, 158, 159, 160, 163, 170, 171, 172, 175, 179, 180, 184, 186, 189, 199, 202, 203, 211, 225, 227, 235, 236, 241, 248, 249, 250, 253, 254, 259, 264, 267, 269, 273, 274, 278, 281, 288, 289, 291, 292
Jonson, Ben, Jr., 172
Jonsonus Virbius, 126
Jovial Crew, The, 173, 174, 178–9, 180
Judgment (Wakefield), 22
Julius Caesar, 147, 185, 234
Just Italian, The, 280

Keep the Widow Waking, 113, 224, 240
Kemp, Will, 51, 61, 127
Killigrew, Thomas, 279, 282
King and No King, A, 174, 192–3, 246
King and Subject, The, 256
King John (Bale), 21, 29
King John (Shakespeare), 88
King Lear, 32, 61, 232
King Leir, 68
King's Men, The, 50, 102, 105, 115, 129, 130, 140, 143, 155, 159, 160, 164, 165, 166, 172, 173, 177, 185, 188, 190, 192, 195, 196, 197, 200, 201, 202, 203, 205, 207, 213, 223, 225, 240, 244, 255, 256, 261, 270, 280, 281, 289
King's Revels Company, 173
Knack to Know a Knave, A, 261
Knight of Malta, The, 201–2, 255
Knight of the Burning Bush, The, 42
Knight of the Burning Pestle, The, 43, 116, 124, 144, 176, 186–7, 192
Kyd, Thomas, 34, 38, 39, 63, 74–7, 79, 85, 91, 101, 210, 216, 251

Lady Elizabeth's Men, 115, 129, 142, 159, 160, 167, 240, 255
Lady Jane. See *Sir Thomas Wyatt*
Lady of Pleasure, The, 274
Lady's Trial, The, 241, 249, 250, 251
Lamb, Charles, 174, 292, 294

Late Lancashire Witches, The, 122–3, 173
Laugh and Lie Down, 213
Lawes, Henry, 270, 282
Leicester's Men, Earl of, 47, 48, 50
Line of Life, A, 239–40
Little French Lawyer, The, 208
Little Gipsy, The, 167
Livy, 171
Lodge, Thomas, 70, 152
Looking-Glass for London and England, A, 70–1
Lord Admiral's Men, 50, 76, 85, 93, 94, 95, 96, 106, 107, 159, 210
Lord Chamberlain's Men, 50, 51, 93, 109, 121, 127, 128, 135, 137, 210
Lord Hunsdon's Men, 50
Lord Strange's Men, 50, 76
Love and Honour, 281, 284–6
Love Tricks, 269
Lover's Melancholy, The, 240, 241–2, 249, 250
Love's Labour's Lost, 61, 66
Love's Metamorphosis, 67
Love's Mistress, 123–4
Love's Sacrifice, 240, 244–6, 247, 251
Lovesick Court, The, 173, 174
Lovesick Maid, The, 172
Lowin, John, 223
Loyal Subject, The, 119, 198, 199
Ludus Accidiae (York), 16
Ludus Coventriae, 10, 13, 45
Lusty Juventus, 20, 22
Lyly, John, 34, 43, 51, 61, 63, 64–7, 68, 69, 70, 72, 73, 74, 98, 108, 136

Macbeth, 28, 31, 36, 86, 88, 165, 211, 264
Machiavelli, Niccolo, 77, 85, 86, 196, 212, 264, 272
Mad Couple Well Match'd, A, 173, 176
Mad Lover, The, 198
Mad World, My Masters, A, 159, 162–3, 170
Magi, The (Wakefield), 11
Magi, The (York), 12
Magnetic Lady, The, 131, 145
Maid of Honor, The, 255, 257–9, 268
Maidenhead Well Lost, A, 119
Maid's Tragedy, The, 193–4, 275, 289
Malcontent, The, 155–6, 157, 158, 216, 223, 225
Malory, Sir Thomas, 41
Mamillia, 70
Mankind, 18–19, 46, 47
Marlowe, Christopher, 38, 39, 50, 61, 63, 69, 70, 71, 74, 75, 78–92, 101, 104, 147, 210, 228, 250, 251, 292, 294
Marston, John, 52, 99, 100, 110, 137, 138, 153–8, 159, 210–12, 216, 218, 225, 232, 247, 251, 288
Masque of Blackness, The, 129
Masque of Gray's Inn and the Inner Temple, 184, 185, 289

Masque of Oberon, 289
Masque of the Middle Temple and Lincoln's Inn, The, 100
Massacre at Paris, The, 89
Massey, Charles, 95
Massinger, Philip, 50, 112, 161, 166, 185, 196-8, 200, 207-8, 228, 254-68, 270, 278
Match Me in London, 112
May Day, 98
May Lord, 146
Mayne, Jasper, 280
Mayor of Queenborough, The, 160, 166
Measure for Measure, 190, 233
Medwall, Henry, 23-4
Memorial to . . . Sir Thomas Overbury, A, 239
Merchant of Venice, The, 134, 150, 185
Meres, Francis, 68, 80
Merry Jests of George Peele, The, 68
Michaelmas Term, 159, 162
Microcosmus, 289
Microcynicon, 159
Midas, 65
Middleton, Thomas, 50, 99, 110, 112, 123, 125, 153, 158-71, 174, 175, 180, 201, 222, 223, 224, 236-8, 253, 254, 259, 263, 283, 288
Midsummer Night's Dream, A, 61, 67
Milton, John, 170, 270
Misfortunes of Arthur, The, 34, 38-9
Monsieur D'Olive, 98, 105
Monsieur Thomas, 207, 273
Monumental Column, A, 223
Monuments of Honor, 222
More Dissemblers Besides Women, 159, 164
Morte D'Arthur, 41
Mostellaria, 141
Much Ado About Nothing, 61, 66
Munday, Anthony, 95, 107, 133, 222
Murderous Michael, 29
Musset, Alfred de, 272

N. Town Plays. See *Ludus Coventriae*
Nashe, Thomas, 78, 79, 80, 127, 152, 159
Nature of the Four Elements, The, 19, 22
New Academy, The, 173
New Inn, The, 131, 144-5, 172
New Way to Pay Old Debts, A, 161, 256, 259-60, 268
Newington Butts, theatre, 49
News from Plymouth, 281
No Wit, No Help Like a Woman's, 159, 164
Noah (Wakefield), 11, 14
Noah and the Flood (York), 12
Nobleman, The, 213
Northern Lass, The, 171, 172, 173, 174, 176, 180
Northward Ho, 110, 223, 224
Norton, Thomas, 37

Norwich, plays at, 14
Novella, The, 173, 174

Ode to Himself, 131, 172
Ogilby, John, 270
Old Fortunatus, 106, 107-8
Old Law, The, 160, 166, 215
Old Wives' Tale, The, 43, 67-8, **69**
Orlando Furioso, 71, 116
Othello, 67, 87, 121, 125, 229, 245, 262, 264
Overbury, Sir Thomas, 224, 239
Ovid, 78, 265

Page of Plymouth, 107
Painter, William, 41, 228, 229, 257, 258
Palace of Pleasure, The, 41, 228, 229, 257
Palladis Tamia, 80
Palsgrave's Men, The, 240
Pardoner and the Friar, The, 24
Parasitaster, 156
Parliament of Love, The, 255
Passionate Lovers, The, 279
Pastor Fido, Il, 146
Pater Noster (Beverly), 16
Pater Noster (York), 16
Peele, George, 67-9, 74, 80, 91, 157
Penelope's Web, 174
Pepys, Samuel, 47, 85, 102, 140, 147, 174, 189, 256, 273, 286
Perkin Warbeck, 241, 248, 251
Pernet qui va au vin, 26
Phaeton, 95
Philaster, 125, 184, 190-1, 192
Phoenix, The, 159, 160-1
Phoenix, The (Cockpit), theatre, 49, 113, 124, 173, 241, 269, 281, 282
Pickeryng, John, 30
Piers Plowman, 16
Pilgrim, The, 198
Plato, 15, 245, 283, 284
Platonic Lovers, The, 281, 283-4
Plautus, 31, 43, 123, 141, 164
Play of Love, The, 24
Play of the Weather, The, 24
Plays Confuted, 41
Plutarch, 31
Plutus, 144
Poetaster, 109, 128, 137-8, 139, 140, 149, 150, 156, 158
Porter, Henry, 152
Prince Charles's Men, 160, 240
Prince Henry's Men, 50, 159
Princess, The, 279
Prisoners, The, 279
Processus Prophetarum, 11
Proteus and the Adamantine Rock, 287
Prudentius, 15
Prynne, William, 270
Psychomachia, 15, 17
Puritan, The, 159

Queen, The, 241, 247–8
Queen and the Concubine, The, 173, 174
Queen Anne's Men, 50, 223, 224
Queen Henrietta's Men, 115, 124, 140, 173, 176, 187, 256, 269, 279
Queen of Corinth, The, 201
Queen's Exchange, The, 173, 174
Queen's Masque, The. See Love's Mistress
Queen's Revels. See Children of the Chapel
Quem Quaeritis, 4–5, 11

Racine, Jean, 252
Ralph Roister Doister, 32
Randal, Earl of Chester, 159
Rankins, William, 95
Rape of Lucrece, The, 117, 234
Rare Triumphs of Love and Fortune, The, 42
Rastell, John, 19, 24, 42
Red Bull, The, theatre, 49, 119, 183, 223, 253, 255
Renegado, The, 255
Respublica, 20
Revenge of Bussy, The, 102–3
Revenger's Tragedy, The, 102, 213, 215–18, 219, 221, 222, 244
Richard Crookback, 128
Richard III, 51, 88, 90
Rivals, The, 175
Roaring Girl, The, 112, 159
Roman Actor, The, 264–5
Roman de la Rose, 16
Romeo and Juliet, 36, 42, 58, 110, 154, 229–30
Rose, The, theatre, 49, 50, 96
Rowe, Nicholas, 266
Rowley, Samuel, 95
Rowley, William, 112–13, 120, 160, 164, 165–8, 201, 223, 224, 233, 236, 237, 240
Royal King and the Loyal Subject, The, 119
Royal Master, The, 272–3
Royal Slave, The, 279, 289
Rudens, 123
Rule a Wife and Have a Wife, 204–5, 206

Sackville, Thomas, 37, 38
Sad Shepherd, The, 131, 146
St. Augustine, 294
St. Paul's Cathedral. See Children of Paul's
Salisbury Court, theatre, 49, 173
Sallust, 148
Salmacida Spolia, 281
Salmacis and Hermaphroditus, 184
Sapho and Phao, 65
Satiromastix, 109, 137, 138–9
Scornful Lady, The, 194, 203, 273
Second Maiden's Tragedy, The, 262

Second Shepherds Play (Wakefield), 11, 14
Secunda Pastorum. See Second Shepherds Play (Wakefield)
Sejanus, 105–6, 128, 129, 139, 146, 147, 211, 235, 264
Seneca, 34, 35–7, 38, 39, 40, 74, 75, 76, 81, 84, 101, 102, 104, 148, 216, 221, 222, 232
Shadow of Night, The, 96
Shakespeare, William, 10, 14, 22, 27, 28, 30, 31, 33, 34, 37, 40, 42, 43, 44, 49, 50, 51, 52, 55, 57, 64, 66, 68, 72, 73, 74, 75, 76, 77, 79, 81, 86, 87, 88, 89, 90, 91, 92, 93, 94, 95, 98, 100, 106, 107, 115, 116, 126, 127, 128, 132, 133, 134, 147, 148, 149, 150, 154, 165, 173, 177, 185, 186, 188, 191, 194, 210, 211, 216, 228, 229, 230, 232, 233, 234, 236, 238, 239, 245, 250, 252, 254, 259, 262, 280, 282, 287, 288, 290, 291, 292, 293, 294
Shelley, Percy Bysshe, 252
Shepheardes Calendar, The, 41
Shirley, James, 104, 180, 183, 208, 210, 248, 253, 254, 268–78, 288, 294
Shoemaker's Holiday, The, 108–9, 111, 171, 292
Sidney, Sir Philip, 36, 42, 43, 193, 239, 242, 243, 245
Siege of Rhodes, The, 282, 286, 289
Silent Woman, The. See Epicoene
Silver Age, The, 118
Sir Clyomon and Clamydes, 42, 116
Sir Francis Drake. See The History of Sir Francis Drake
Sir John Van Olden Barnavelt, 197–8
Sir Thomas More, 20
Sir Thomas Overbury's Ghost, 239
Sir Thomas Wyatt, 222, 224
Soliman and Perseda, 75
Solitary Knight, The, 42
Sophonisba, 52, 211–12
Spanish Curate, The, 208
Spanish Gipsy, The, 160, 167–8, 179, 201
Spanish Tragedy, The, 36, 58, 71, 74, 75–7, 102, 127, 128, 187, 210, 292
Sparagus Garden, The, 173, 175–6
Spencer, Gabriel, 127
Spenser, Edmund, 41, 44, 69, 91, 184, 216, 217
Staple of News, The, 130, 144, 253
Stevenson, William, 32–3, 34
Suckling, Sir John, 279
Summoning of Everyman, The. See Everyman
Sun's Darling, The, 113, 240, 241
Supposes, The, 43–4
Suppositi, I, 43
Surrey, Henry Howard, Earl of, 38
Swan, The, theatre, 49, 127
Swift, Jonathan, 178

Tacitus, 171
Tale of a Tub. A, 131, 132, 146
Tales from Shakespeare, 292
Tamburlaine, 58, 70, 71, 78, 81–3, 84, 85, 88, 89, 90, 92, 101
Tamer Tamed, The. See *The Woman's Prize*
Taming of a Shrew, The, 44
Taming of the Shrew, The, 44, 188
Tancred and Gismunda, 38
Tempest, The, 55, 58, 289, 290
Temple of Love, The, 281
Ten Arches of Triumph, 223
Terence, 2, 31, 33, 43, 97
Theatre, The, 48, 49, 93
Theocritus, 189
Thierry and Theodoret, 198
Thyestes, 40
Time Poets, The, 249
Timon of Athens, 210
'Tis Pity She's a Whore, 240, 246–7, 250, 251
Titus Andronicus, 76
Titus Andronicus (lost), 68
Tourneur, Cyril, 212–22, 223, 232, 238
Towneley Cycle. See Wakefield Cycle
Tragedy of Chabot Admiral of France, The, 104–5
Traitor, The, 275–6, 277
Transformed Metamorphosis, The, 213, 216
Trick to Catch the Old One, A, 159, 161, 162, 174, 259
Triumph of Honor, The, 201
Triumph of Love, The, 201
Triumph of Peace, The, 270
Triumph of the Prince D'Amour, The, 281
Triumph of Time, The, 290
Troilus and Cressida (lost), 107
Troublesome Reign of King John, The, 68
Twelfth Night, 61, 72, 74, 191, 239
Two Angry Women of Abingdon, The, 152
Two Noble Kinsmen, The, 174, 185, 289

Udall, Nicholas, 32, 33, 34
Uncle Tom's Cabin, 75–6
Unfortunate Lovers, The, 281

Valentinian, 195–6, 197, 199
Valerius Maximus, 266

Very Woman, A, 201
Viper and Her Brood, The, 159
Virgil, 38, 171, 189
Virgin Martyr, The, 112, 255
Volpone, 129, 139–40, 150, 162, 184, 259

Wakefield Cycle, 9, 11, 14
War of the Theatres, 109, 128, 137, 139
Warning for Fair Women, A, 29, 121
Watson, Thomas, 79
Webster, John, 96, 99, 110, 113, 125, 155, 159, 160, 165, 198, 211, 214, 222–36, 238, 240, 244, 246, 253, 276, 277, 278
Wedding, The, 269
Weeding of Covent Garden, The, 173, 175
Westward Ho, 99, 110, 223, 224
Wever, R., 20
What You Will, 155
White Devil, The, 223, 225–8, 231, 232, 233
Whitefriars, theatre, 49, 102, 129
Widow, The, 160, 164
Widow's Tears, The, 98
Wife, The, 239
Wife for a Month, A, 198, 199
Wild-Goose Chase, The, 205–6
Wilmot, Robert, 38
Winter's Tale, The, 59, 289
Wise Woman of Hogsden, The, 123
Wit without Money, 203–4, 283
Witch, The, 159, 160, 165
Witch of Edmonton, The, 112–13, 240, 241
Wits, The, 280, 283, 284
Witty and Witless, 24
Witty Fair One, The, 269, 273, 279
Woman Hater, The, 186
Woman Killed with Kindness, A, 29, 121–2, 125
Woman's Prize, The, 188–9, 205
Women Beware Women, 160, 168, 236, 237–8, 244, 289
Women Pleased, 198
Worcester's Men, Earl of, 50
Workes of Benjamin Jonson, The, 130
World Tossed at Tennis, The, 160
Wyclif, John, 16

York Cycle, 10, 11, 12, 13
Young Admiral, The, 269, 271–2
Your Five Gallants, 159, 162